P9-AON-273

Lithuania

the Bradt Travel Guide

Gordon McLachlan

edition
5

914.79
MAC

www.bradtguides.com

Bradt Travel Guides Ltd, UK
The Globe Pequot Press Inc, USA

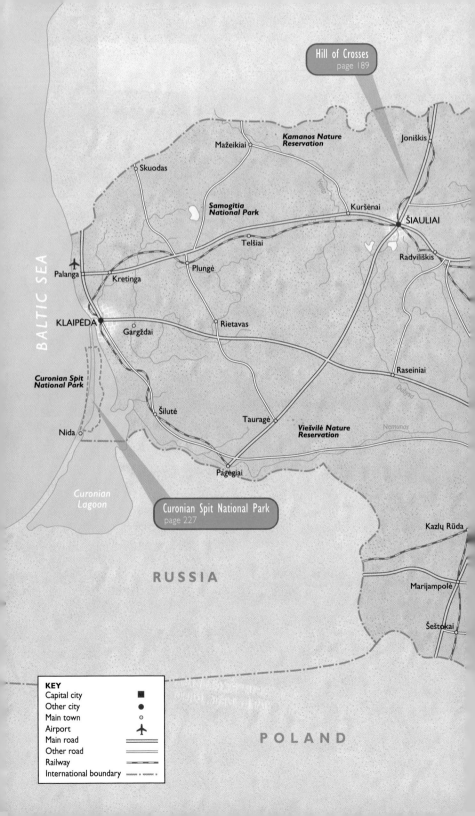

Hill of Crosses
page 189

Joniškis

Mažeikiai

*Kamanos Nature
Reservation*

Skuodas

*Samogitia
National Park*

Kuršėnai

ŠIAULIAI

Telšiai

Radviliškis

Palanga

Plungė

Kretinga

KLAIPĖDA

Gargždai

Rietavas

Raseiniai

*Curonian Spit
National Park*

Šilutė

Tauragė

Nida

*Viešvilė Nature
Reservation*

Nemunas

Pagegiai

Curonian Spit National Park
page 227

*Curonian
Lagoon*

Kazlų Rūda

RUSSIA

Marijampolė

Šeštokai

BALTIC SEA

Venta

Dubysa

KEY
Capital city   ■
Other city   ●
Main town   ○
Airport   ✈
Main road
Other road
Railway
International boundary

POLAND

N

Bradt

LATVIA

Biržai

Pasvalys

Rokiškis

Zarasai

Turmantas

Visaginas

PANEVĖŽYS

Rubikiai

Anykščiai

Utena

Aukštaitija
National Park

LITHUANIA

Ukmergė

Molėtai

Ignalina

Kėdainiai

Jonava

Kaišiadorys

KAUNAS

VILNIUS

Vilnius
page 90

Trakai Historical
National Park

Trakai

BELARUS

Žuvintas
Nature
Reservation

ALYTUS

Šalčininkai

Varėna

Dzūkija
National Park

Čepkeliai
Nature Reservation

Trakai Island Castle
page 114

Druskininkai

Kaunas Old Town
page 149

0 ———— 30km
0 ———— 20 miles

Lithuania
Don't
miss...

Vilnius
A view over the Old Town
(GMcL) page 90

Hill of Crosses
Near Šiauliai
(GMcL) page 189

Trakai Island Castle
(JS) page 114

Kaunas Old Town
Beside Nemunas River
(WB/TIPS) page 149

Curonian Spit
Dead dunes, near Pervalka
(GMcL) page 227

above **Karaite houses, Trakai** (GMcL) page 114

below left **Living Archeology Days Festival, Kernavė** (GMcL) page 116

below right **Replica sailing craft on Lake Galvė, Trakai** (GMcL) page 113

AUTHOR

Gordon McLachlan was born in Edinburgh. Following graduation from Edinburgh University, he worked for several years on the sales side of publishing, then assumed a full-time writing career in 1987. His many published books include guides to Germany, Berlin, Poland and Edinburgh, and it was his long professional association with the southern Baltic region which inspired him to add Lithuania to this list. His special interests include music, photography, art and architecture, reading, hiking and gastronomy.

ACKNOWLEDGEMENTS

The author would like to thank the following people for their help: Aušrinė Oželienė, Rūta Draugšienė and family, Maria Lenn. Thanks also to my project manager Emma Thomson, Sally Brock for typesetting and Alan Whitaker for cartography.

PUBLISHER'S FOREWORD

Hilary Bradt

The first Bradt travel guide was written in 1974 by George and Hilary Bradt on a river barge floating down a tributary of the Amazon. In the 1980s and '90s the focus shifted away from hiking to broader-based guides covering new destinations – usually the first to be published about these places. In the 21st century Bradt continues to publish such ground-breaking guides, as well as others to established holiday destinations, incorporating in-depth information on culture and natural history with the nuts and bolts of where to stay and what to see.

Bradt authors support responsible travel, and provide advice not only on minimum impact but also on how to give something back through local charities. In this way a true synergy is achieved between the traveller and local communities.

* * *

Watching the popularity of the Baltic states grow with the three Bradt guides that introduced them to the holiday market has been wonderfully rewarding. Each country has its own personality which is brought out by the interests and enthusiasms of the different authors. Gordon McLachlan's particular interest is architecture, and his educated observations on the buildings you'll come across – from formal palaces to rustic wooden churches – will certainly enrich your visit.

Fifth edition March 2008   First published 1995

Bradt Travel Guides Ltd, 23 High Street, Chalfont St Peter, Bucks SL9 9QE, England.
www.bradtguides.com
Published in the USA by The Globe Pequot Press Inc, 246 Goose Lane,
PO Box 480, Guilford, Connecticut 06475-0480

Text copyright © 2008 Gordon McLachlan
Maps copyright © 2008 Bradt Travel Guides Ltd
Illustrations copyright © 2008 Individual photographers and artists
Editorial Project Manager: Emma Thomson

ISBN-10: 1 84162 228 1   ISBN-13: 978 1 84162 228 6
British Library Cataloguing in Publication Data
A catalogue record for this book is available from the British Library

Photographs Gordon McLachlan (GMcL), Jon Smith (JS), Wojtek Buss/TIPS (WB/TIPS), !hotimagery!/Alamy (hi/Alamy)
Front cover Boat near Trakai Island Castle (hi/Alamy)
Back cover Church of Saints Peter and Paul, Vilnius (GMcL); Icon of the Madonna of Mercy, Gates of Dawn, Vilnius (GMcL)
Title page Woodcarving, Witches Hill (GMcL); Folklore group (GMcL); Church of St Anne, Vilnius (GMcL)
Illustrations Carole Vincer   **Maps** Alan Whitaker, Steve Munns (colour map)
Typeset from the author's disc by Wakewing
Printed and bound in Italy by LEGO Spa-Lavis (TN)

Contents

Introduction

In the years 1990 and 1991, the attention of the world's media was often fixed on Lithuania, or Lietuva, as it is known by its own citizens. Before then Lithuania was the largest and southernmost of the three Baltic republics of the USSR and, like its neighbours, it had been annexed illegally in 1940 by the Soviets. However, in 1990–91 Lithuania staged a peaceful revolution which threw off the shackles of Soviet rule and re-established its independence. It was the first of the republics to break free from the Soviet Union, and its example acted as an inspiration to others, with the result that the last of the world's great empires quickly collapsed.

Media attention has long ago moved elsewhere, save for a period of attention in 2004, when Lithuania was one of ten countries simultaneously admitted to membership of the European Union. Although this cherished political goal was achieved far more quickly than had been anticipated even a few years previously, other changes are proceeding far less rapidly. For the forseeable future Lithuania will be a nation of genuinely striking contrasts, one where new businesses using the very latest in global technology co-exist with hangovers from Soviet times, as well as traditions, such as subsistence farming, with a centuries-old pedigree.

Although almost invariably bracketed with Latvia and Estonia, Lithuania is very different from its two northern neighbours; in particular, much of its history stands in total contrast to theirs. While they lived under permanent foreign subjugation from the time they were conquered by German crusaders in the 13th century – and while other Baltic peoples failed to survive the Middle Ages at all, becoming exterminated or assimilated by their colonisers – Lithuania established itself as a powerful independent state in its own right. Not only did it finally emerge victorious after 150 years of almost continuous warfare with the crusaders, it had itself by then embarked on an ambitious programme of foreign expansion, annexing the principalities of Ruthenia by a skilful mixture of warfare and diplomacy, and eventually stretching all the way from the Baltic to the Black Sea, and to within striking distance of Moscow.

The royal union with neighbouring Poland in 1386 was a key event in Lithuanian history, one which led immediately to the end of its status as Europe's last pagan country, and soon afterwards to the irrevocable decline of the Teutonic Knights, the crusading order which had been a perpetual threat to both countries. In 1569 the two nations formally merged into a Commonwealth, and thus became the largest – and, at times, the most powerful – empire in Europe. While Poles tend to look back on this era as a golden age, Lithuanians do so with conflicting emotions, largely because Lithuanian language and culture became ever more marginalised as the Polish tongue and Polish ways assumed precedence. Moreover, the huge joint state became too unwieldy for its own good, and between 1772 and 1795 was gradually wiped off the map altogether. Not until 1918 did either country regain its independence. It is by no more than an accident of history that the borders of the modern Lithuanian state closely resemble those of the 13th century, when the nation first emerged.

In Vilnius, the country has a likeable and suitably cosmopolitan capital, one which preserves the multi-cultural flavour of the old Polish-Lithuanian Commonwealth better than any other city which once lay within its borders. It has a beautiful Old Town which has been placed on UNESCO's highly prestigious World Heritage List, one whose manifold attractions include one of the finest array of Baroque monuments anywhere in Europe. Kaunas, the second city, is another obvious highlight. Not the least of its fascinations is that it looks and feels so very different from Vilnius. Indeed, within Europe it is only in Scotland – where Edinburgh and Glasgow form a similarly contrasting pair – that two such dramatically contrasted principal cities exist in close proximity.

The best of the country's scenery, which can all too glibly be dismissed as a landscape of rivers, lakes, forests and low hills, can be seen in the five national parks. Two of these lie on the well-established tourist trail: Trakai Historical National Park, which includes the country's most spectacular castle, and is an easy excursion from Vilnius; and the Curonian Spit National Park, a truly astonishing natural wonder whose present appearance is due to sometimes unwitting human interventions. Of the other parks, Dzūkija features some extraordinary old villages of wooden farms; Samogitia incorporates Žemaičiu Kalvarija, a major place of pilgrimage; while Aukštaitija includes the country's most extensive lake district.

Other obvious Lithuanian highlights are Kernavė, the original capital and most important archaeological site; the Hill of Crosses outside Šiauliai, a poignant reminder of the centrality of the Christian faith in the national struggles of the last two centuries; the animated Baltic beach resort of Palanga, whose spanking new upmarket hotels charge what are, by Western standards, bargain prices; and the constrastingly restful spa of Druskininkai in the far south of the country.

The relatively small size of Lithuania, coupled with a decent transport infrastructure, mean that it is possible to see the main attractions in the course of a fortnight's holiday. However, a full exploration of all the places covered in this book requires a good two months at the very least.

Lithuania is also, for the most part, a safe, inexpensive, friendly and hospitable country, and one where the use of English is on the increase. The main cities are well endowed with a choice of hotels, restaurants and cafés which meet Western standards in every respect. While the same cannot be said for small towns and the countryside, a step back into the past is an essential part of the Lithuanian travel experience.

Part One

GENERAL INFORMATION

Area 65,300 km^2

Population 3.37 million (85% ethnic Lithuanian)

Head of state The President, directly elected for a five-year term

Government Parliamentary democracy, with general elections every four years

Capital city Vilnius

Currency Litas

Language Lithuanian

Alphabet Latin

Religion Predominantly Roman Catholic

Weights and measures Metric

Electricity 220 volts, 50Hz

National anthem Tautinė giesmė by Vincas Kudirka

National bird Stork

National flower Rue (Rūta)

National emblem Vytis, a mounted knight

National flag Yellow–green–red (horizontal stripes)

National holidays (resulting in general shutdown) 1 January (New Year's Day), 16 February (Independence Day – the anniversary of the declaration of independence in 1918), 11 March (Restoration of Independence Day – the anniversary of the declaration of independence in 1990), variable dates in March/April (Easter Sunday and Monday), First Sunday in May (Mothering Sunday), 6 July (Day of Statehood – anniversary of the coronation of King Mindaugas), 23 August (Black Ribbon Day – the anniversary of the signing of the Nazi–Soviet Pact), 1 November (All Saints' Day), 25 and 26 December (Christmas).

Commemorative holidays (not resulting in shutdown) 13 January (Defenders of Freedom Day – commemorating the demonstrators who were killed by Soviet troops in 1991), 14 June (Day of Mourning and Hope – the anniversary of the first mass deportations of Lithuanian citizens to Siberia in 1941), 15 August (Feast of the Assumption), 8 September (Day of the Nation – commemorates the birth of the Virgin Mary, Patroness of Lithuania, and the planned coronation in 1430 of Vytautas the Great), 25 October (Constitution Day).

I

The Country

GEOGRAPHY

Lithuania has an area of 65,300km² and 3.37 million inhabitants, and is thereby the largest and most populous of the three Baltic states. Although usually considered to be a small country, it occupies a far larger land area than either Denmark or Switzerland, and actually exceeds the combined total of Belgium and the Netherlands. The Republic of Ireland is the European country which most closely resembles it in size and population density, being marginally larger in both area and number of inhabitants.

According to the calculations of the French National Geographical Institute, Lithuania lies in the exact centre of Europe. This is a matter of some considerable pride in Lithuania itself, where it is seldom mentioned that the premises on which the calculations were based are controversial, and that there are alternative candidates for the honour.

At its widest, Lithuania stretches 373km from east to west and 276km from north to south. It has a total of 1,747km of land borders, which are with Belarus, Latvia, the Kaliningrad *oblast* of Russia and Poland. Additionally, it has 99km of coast on the Baltic Sea, consisting of a continuous stretch of fine sandy beach backed by dunes, which are in turn sheltered by pine forests. Pieces of amber, a fossilised tree resin dating back millions of years, are washed up along the coast and this has been an important mineral resource for two millennia. Almost exactly half of the coastline forms part of the country's most impressive natural feature, the Curonian Spit, a narrow strip of land separating the sea from the shallow Curonian Lagoon. The lagoon shoreline is spectacular, preserving as it does two large areas of littoral dunes, one of which is still moving. Like the spit, the lagoon is divided between Lithuania (which has 613km² out of its total area of 1,610km², as well as its sole outlet to the sea) and the Kaliningrad *oblast*.

Otherwise, the Lithuanian landscape is for the most part a characteristic mixture of low-lying plains, which came into existence during the last Ice Age, and hilly uplands formed by glacial drift. The latter do not reach any great heights; indeed, the highest point in the country, the Juozapinės Hill near Medininkai, is a mere 294m. Huge isolated boulders of rock are another legacy of glacial drift, and can be found in various locations in northern Lithuania.

About 28% of the country is forested, a total which has increased in the last 50 years, though this still goes only a small way towards compensating for the heavy deforestation of centuries past, when woods were felled in order that more land could be given over to agricultural use. Just over 3% of the country is marshland, a figure which fell by half, through the implementation of drainage schemes, in the course of the 20th century.

Lakes are recurrent features of the Lithuanian landscape. There are around 3,000 in all, accounting for 2% of the total 'land' area. The man-made Kaunas Sea, which was created as part of a hydro-electric project, is now the country's

3

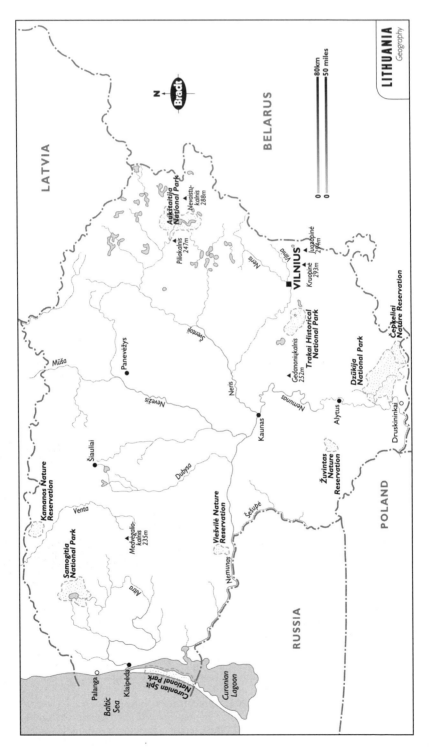

LITHUANIA
Geography

LATVIA

BELARUS

RUSSIA

POLAND

Baltic
Sea

Curonian
Lagoon

Palanga
Klaipėda
Curonian Spit
National Park

Samogitia
National Park

Kamanos Nature
Reservation

Medvėgalio-
kalnis
235m

Šiauliai

Viešvilė Nature
Reservation

Panevėžys

Piliakalnis
247m

Aukštaitija
National Park

Neviašų-
kalnis
288m

Kaunas

Trakai Historical
National Park

Gediminaukalnis
252m

VILNIUS

Kruopinė
293m

Jugožapinė
294m

Dzūkija
National Park

Alytus

Druskininkai

Čepkeliai
Nature Reservation

Žuvintas
Nature
Reservation

Mūša
Venta
Nevėžis
Dubysa
Jūra
Nemunas
Šešupė
Neris
Šventoji
Neris
Vilnia
Nemunas

N

Bradt

0   80km
0   50 miles

4

largest stretch of inland water. Of the natural lakes, Drūkšiai has the biggest area, while Tauragnas is the deepest. Both of these lie in the northeast of the country, where the main concentration of lakes is to be found.

Lithuania's most important river is the Nemunas (or Niemen), which rises in Belarus and disgorges itself into the Curonian Lagoon. Of its total length of 937km, 475km lie within Lithuania, and it follows a stately and at times serpentine course through the southern part of the country, before turning westwards to pursue a direct route towards its mouth. The Neris is Lithuania's second river, with 235km of its 510km lying within the country. Vilnius, the national capital, stands on its banks, while Kaunas, the second city, is situated at the point where the Neris converges with the Nemunas. Most of the other main rivers are also Nemunas tributaries, and tend to be similarly slow-moving. The country has an abundant supply of short streams, many of which have very fresh and pure water.

About a third of Lithuania's population (which has fallen, largely as a result of emigration, by around 350,000 in the past few years) lives in the three major cities of Vilnius (548,000), Kaunas (358,000) and the port of Klaipėda (185,000), which is located by the Curonian Lagoon's outlet to the Baltic. Only two other cities, Šiauliai (128,000) and Panevėžys (114,000), have more than 100,000 inhabitants. The rest of the population is very scattered indeed, living in a host of medium-sized and small towns, villages and hamlets dotted all over the country.

REGIONAL DIVISIONS Lithuania is traditionally divided into two main areas – Aukštaitija (the Highlands) and Samogitia or Žemaitija (the Lowlands) – though the actual difference in altitude between the two is marginal. Dzūkija (which lies between the Nemunas and Neris) and Suvalkija (which lies west and south of the Nemunas) were originally considered to belong to Aukštaitija, but are now usually given the status of separate geographic and ethnographic entities in their own right. Suvalkija is now very truncated, much of its territory (including virtually all the places of scenic and historic interest) having become part of Poland after World War I, though this retains a significant Lithuanian minority population to this day. The term 'Lithuania Minor' is commonly used in connection with the coastal area, most of which did not become part of Lithuania until 1923, as well as the territory further to the south and southeast, which historically had a sizeable Lithuanian population but never officially formed part of the country.

Although these divisions are of very long standing, they are all of imprecise definition. For example, the term Aukštaitija is often used nowadays in connection with the northeast of the country only, though strictly speaking it certainly includes Vilnius and, more debatably, Kaunas, which for a time was the seat of the Bishop of Samogitia.

The main administrative unit of modern Lithuania is the county (*apskritis*). There are ten of these, each of which is named after its capital – Vilnius, Alytus, Marijampolė, Kaunas, Utena, Panevėžys, Šiauliai, Telšiai, Tauragė and Klaipėda. Alytus County corresponds roughly to Dzūkija, Marijampolė County to the surviving portion of Suvalkija, but others are purely artificial; Šiauliai County, for instance, straddles the historic division between Aukštaitija and Samogitia. A region (*rajonas*) is an administrative sub-division of a county.

NATURAL HISTORY

FLORA The make-up of Lithuania's woodland has changed a great deal in the course of the centuries. The only old forests which have survived are those which have sandy soil, which was unsuitable for conversion into farmland. Some fine surviving examples can be seen in Dzūkija, the most heavily forested part of the country, but even there most of the trees are no older than middle-aged. Despite the significance of oaks in the pagan worship which survived into medieval times, they now make up just 1.4% of the country's stock of trees. However, a number of ancient examples survive, some of which have been classified as Monuments of Nature. The oldest, which may date back as much as 1,500 years, is in the village of Stelmužė in Aukštaitija.

Nowadays, around 40% of Lithuania's trees are pines. These include both indigenous and imported species, with the latter being prominent along the Baltic coast, particularly on the Curonian Spit. Birches and spruces are the two other most common trees, and together they make up a similar percentage of the woodland to the pines. Aspens, alders, ashes, elms and lindens are among the other species of trees which can regularly be seen.

The pine forests are notable for their thick undergrowth of lichen, of which around 400 different varieties exist in Lithuania. Wild berries and mushrooms (both edible and poisonous) also grow in abundance, and the picking of these ranks among the country's most popular outdoor pastimes.

About 17% of Lithuania is covered by grassland, but only a small portion of this is natural uncultivated meadow. In spring and summer, this is carpeted with wild flowers, of which there are around 2,000 different species.

MAMMALS Arctic fauna appeared in Lithuania after the last Ice Age. Most of these animals died out as the climate became warmer, though some still survive, including the blue hare. Taiga species became prevalent as the amount of woodland increased. Many of the country's most characteristic forest animals – notably the European bison, the brown bear and the beaver – were, however, subsequently hunted to total or virtual extinction, though the first and last of these have since been re-introduced to the wild.

Currently 63 land mammals and five aquatic mammals live in Lithuania. The large mammals most likely to be encountered are red and roe deer, elk and wild boar. Carnivores such as the wolf, fox, pine marten, polecat, raccoon, lynx and wild cat tend to live deep in the forests and are thus rarely seen. There are, however, plenty of small rodents, such as field mice, dormice and squirrels, as well as brown hare and mountain hare. Otters are found in many rivers, while seals and porpoises live in the coastal waters of the Baltic.

BIRDS About 300 different species of bird can be found in Lithuania, of which 210 nest there, with 55 of these living permanently in the country. The white stork has been adopted as the national bird, and according to tradition it never nests at the home of an evil man. Virtually every rural farm seems to have one during the nesting season, which lasts from April to August, when the storks migrate to Africa for the winter. Black storks are much less numerous, but still fairly common nevertheless.

There are colonies of cormorants and grey herons on the Curonian Spit. Other aquatic birds include swans, gulls, lapwings, grebes and bitterns. The four nature reservations are important breeding grounds, notably for cranes, capercaillies, black grouse, marsh harriers and plovers. Woodpeckers are a recurrent sight (and sound) of Lithuania's forests, where chaffinches, tits and thrushes are also found in abundance. Among Lithuania's 16 birds of prey are falcons, harriers, hawks, buzzards, owls and eagle-owls. Members of the starling family, and hooded crows, are a common sight in towns.

OTHER WILDLIFE Lithuania's rivers and streams are very rich in fish. Some 25 different varieties of carp account for about 40% of the freshwater fish stock,

Lithuania has five national parks. All of these are, relatively speaking, quite large, and incorporate villages, hamlets and farmsteads, and in some cases small towns as well. Strictly controlled zones of special scientific interest typically account for only a very small percentage of the area of the national parks, and these are the only places where any limitations are made on public access. In the regional chapters of this book, detailed information on the geography, flora, fauna and ethnography of each national park (with the exception of Trakai, which has the special designation of a Historical National Park, and is primarily of interest for its monuments rather than its natural history) precedes the description of the main places to visit.

Four small wilderness areas, all of which incorporate marshland where large numbers of birds nest, have been declared nature reservations. These are much more difficult of access than the national parks, and there are usually (at least in theory) stringent restrictions on public entry, particularly during the breeding season. In addition to the national parks and nature reservations, there are around 30 regional parks dotted all over the country. Most of these are of secondary interest to foreign visitors, though the more important are described in the text.

NATIONAL PARKS
Aukštaitija (see pages 167–71)
Curonian Spit (see pages 227–37)
Dzūkija (see pages 124–30)
Samogitia (see pages 194–200)
Trakai (see pages 110–15)

NATURE RESERVATIONS
Čepkeliai (see pages 129)
Kamanos (see page 190)
Viešvilė (see page 161)
Žuvintas (see pages 119–20)

with salmon, trout, tench, bream, eel, pike and pike-perch being among the other species. Herring, cod, ling and sprats are among the many varieties of Baltic fish, while both saltwater and freshwater fish inhabit the Curonian Lagoon.

The climate is not favourable for reptiles, and only seven species live in Lithuania: sand and wood lizards, smooth and ringed snakes, adders, marsh tortoises and slow-worms. On the other hand, amphibians such as newts, frogs and toads are quite common. The insect life includes such hazardous species as mosquitoes, which proliferate in summer around the coast and lakes, and ticks, which are found *en masse* at the edge of woods and in long grass. There are also hundreds of types of butterfly.

ENVIRONMENTAL ISSUES

During the Soviet years, Lithuania was transformed from an agricultural to an industrial society, with no regard for environmental considerations. Air and water pollution levels were consequently often quite high, though the damage to the landscape and historic buildings was less marked than in many other countries of the communist bloc.

Conservation has been an important political issue ever since the rise of the *Sajūdis* movement in the late 1980s. Many measures have been enacted, including the closure of much of the heavy industry base, a cleaning-up of the Baltic shore and coastal waters, a reduction in the use of chemical fertilisers, extensive

The Country ENVIRONMENTAL ISSUES | —

restoration works on many key architectural monuments, and an increase in the number of national parks from one to five.

Despite this progress, many old problems remain. The worst environmental black spot, the Ignalina nuclear power plant at Visaginas, continues to function, and, while the first of its two reactors shut down at the end of 2004, the other is due to remain in action until 2009, and following exhaustive checks by Western engineers, is now reckoned to be disaster-proof. It is due to be replaced by a brand new nuclear plant on Lithuanian soil which will cover the whole of the Baltic states and be operational around 2015.

Although plenty of people choose to swim in the Baltic, some experts believe that it is still too polluted for safety. There is, moreover, still a long way to go before the Curonian Lagoon will be clean enough for bathing – notwithstanding the fact that it remains an important fishing ground. Throughout the country, the national parks included, unsightly overhead power cables continue to disfigure the landscape.

The shaking-off of the Soviet yoke has also brought new environmental problems in its wake. Not the least of these is the vast increase in the ownership of private cars, which has had a damaging effect on the air quality of all the cities, especially Vilnius, where traffic congestion has become acute during the morning and evening rush hours. The discovery of offshore oil deposits has also been a mixed blessing, with the construction of a new terminal at Būtingė drawing protests about possible environmental dangers from Latvia, on whose border it lies.

ECONOMY

Lithuania has the largest and most diverse economy of the Baltic states, one which, like the others, has undergone a radical structural overhaul during the past two decades. The first steps away from central planning towards a market economy were actually taken during the very end of the Soviet era, though the privatisation drive only really began in earnest following the international recognition of Lithuanian independence in 1991.

During the following five years, the agricultural, retail and housing sectors were largely returned to private ownership, and the rapid growth of small and medium-sized enterprises – which now number over 150,000 – was facilitated. At the same time, many loss-making concerns which found themselves cut off from previously captive markets were allowed to go out of business. This inevitably resulted in high unemployment, particularly in the heavy industrial sector. A second, and still ongoing phase of privatisation was begun in 1996, with the sale of assets in some of the larger state-run enterprises, the aim being to attract both internal and foreign investment. To date, by far the largest deal has been the purchase of a 60% stake in Lithuanian Telecommunications by the Swedish-Finnish consortium Amber Teleholdings in 1998; this consisted of a downpayment of US$510m plus the promise of a further US$221m investment over the following two years.

The foundations of the present banking system, on the Western model of a central bank (the Bank of Lithuania) and various clearing banks, were actually established in 1988. For the first few years after independence, the private banking sector boomed, and regulatory controls were unable to keep pace with this growth. This led to a banking crisis in 1995, when the Bank of Lithuania was forced to suspend the commercial operators of the country's two largest banks on grounds of malpractice, and both subsequently collapsed. Since then, far stricter regulations have been introduced, including international standards of auditing and a limitation of risk. Lithuania currently has ten commercial banks. Of these, comfortably the largest in terms of assets is Vilniaus, in which the Swedish Skandinaviska Enskilda Banken has a substantial stake. Next in line are the Lithuanian Savings Bank (which actually has a slightly larger share capital than Vilniaus) and the Lithuanian Agricultural Bank; these were the last two commercial banks to remain in state hands. The Lithuanian Stock Exchange, the first in the Baltic states, was founded with French help in 1993, and remains by far the largest in the region.

Lithuania's inter-war currency, the Litas, was re-introduced in the same year, and pegged at the rate of 4 to the US$. This link, the last one in Europe to survive, was retained until 2002, when it was replaced by a similar one to the euro. Under the re-instated currency, inflation was initially high, running at 189% in 1993, but it dropped to 45% the following year and declined steadily thereafter. From 1999 - and especially in 2002-3 - there were regularly extended periods of deflation. However, inflation duly returned, climbing to 4.5% in 2006. This was a major factor in the narrow failure to meet the entry criteria for the euro by the target date of 2007.

Just over half the total land area of Lithuania is cultivated, but the agricultural sector has been shrinking steadily, to the extent that it now employs less than 11% of the workforce, and contributes no more than 5% of the country's GDP. The Soviet policy of collectivisation – which had anyway not touched some of the smaller farms, particularly in Drūkija – was reversed in 1989, and a restitution programme begun two years later. As a result, there are now some 200,000 family farms supplemented by 350,000 smallholdings which are mostly used purely to supply private needs. Rather more than half Lithuania's abundant forests remain in state hands, and are regarded as being among the country's most valued natural resources. Timber and timber products together account for over 5% of all exports.

Industry employs a fraction under 30% of the labour force. Among the Soviet-era industries, oil refining and distribution remain of key importance. The refinery at Mažeikiai has an annual capacity of 12 million tonnes, and is now able to import oil via the new terminal at Būtingė on the outskirts of Palanga, rather than from Russia. Other major industries are food processing, textiles and clothing, chemicals, and the production of machinery, radio, TV and telecommunications equipment. In all, just over half of all goods produced in the country are sold abroad.

Lithuania has achieved commendable annual growth rates in recent years, running as high as 10.3% in 2003, and around 7.5% in each subsequent year. It has been aided in its development by a sound transport infrastructure: the ice-free Baltic port of Klaipėda, four international airports (Vilnius, Kaunas, Šiauliai and Palanga) and a motorway system that is the best in the former Soviet Union. The under-utilised rail network, which suffers from having a different gauge from that used in the West, is the only obvious weak link.

Other significant economic indicators are also promising. Almost 60% of the workforce is now employed in the service sector. Unemployment has fallen steadily from 17.4% in 2001 to 5.6% in 2006. Lithuania has moved from almost total dependence on the Soviet Union to a situation where the EU was the largest trading partner for several years before the country gained admission, and now accounts for around 63% of both exports and imports. Foreign investment is readily attracted by the prospects for growth and the low employment costs. However, the last point also needs to be seen as a major problem. The total per capita share of GDP is only 24157Lt, with average monthly earnings of 1826Lt, and there can be little doubt that – despite the burgeoning number of glitzy shops, bars and restaurants – a sizeable part of the Lithuanian population faces a daily struggle to make ends meet. Nor is it only subsistence farmers and the ranks of the unemployed (numbering 79,500 in 2006) who are affected. Many salaried professionals need to work for a month to earn what their Western counterparts make in a couple of days. For precisely this reason, EU accession – generally seen as a major success – has also resulted in heavy emigration and concern about a 'brain drain'. Although there has been significant immigration over the same period, it has not filled the void.

Grand Duke Gediminas

2

History

ANCIENT HISTORY OF THE BALTS

The territory that is now Lithuania was first settled around 10,000BC, when migrants arrived from the south and southwest. These Stone Age people camped on the shores of the many lakes and river banks, and survived by hunting and fishing with bows, arrows and spears. Some 7,000 years later they were joined by Finno-Ugric tribes, who were likewise hunters and fishermen. Around 2,000BC there was a far more extensive and significant new wave of immigration by Indo-Europeans. Exactly what their origins were remains a matter of dispute: they may have come from central or southeastern Europe, or from the area around the Caspian Sea in Asia. The new settlers supplemented the traditional methods of survival by cultivating crops and rearing animals. They mingled with and assimilated those existing tribes who did not subsequently move northwards, thereby forming the race which subsequently came to be known as the Balts.

During the Bronze Age, which lasted from roughly the 16th century to the 6th century BC, the population steadily increased, and it became necessary to build fortified farms on hills or mounds as a protection against attackers. Although the Iron Age began in the 5th century BC, it was not until the 1st century AD that the making of iron objects such as axes, knives, scissors, scythes, sickles and needles became widespread in the Baltic. By this time, the local tribes had established profitable trade routes with the outside world, including the Roman Empire, in which the amber they collected from the sea became a key component. The first written information about the Balts comes from Pliny the Elder, who wrote in the 1st century AD about the journey of a merchant to the Baltic Sea to obtain amber for the decoration of Rome's amphitheatre. In the 2nd century AD, the historian Tacitus and the geographer Ptolemy also mentioned the Baltic peoples in their writings, though their information was scanty and based on hearsay.

EARLY MEDIEVAL PERIOD

During the later stages of the first millennium, the Balts began to form various distinctive regional groupings. On the territory of what subsequently became Lithuania there lived several different tribes. Initially, the name Lithuanian was used only in conjunction with those based in the southeast. They subsequently formed a tribal union with their neighbours to the north and west, the Aukštaitijans (or Highlanders). Further west lived the Samogitians (or Lowlanders). The Curonians (or Kurs) lived along the coast, mainly in what is now Latvia; the Semigallians (or Zemgalians) further to the east, to the north of the Samogitians. At the fringes were two tribes about whom little is known: the Selonians in the northeast, and the Scalvians in the lower valley of the River Nemunas. What is now the far southwest of Lithuania and the northeast of Poland was home to the Jatzvingians (or Yotvingians), while the Prussians (or Pruzzi) were the westernmost Balts, living between two great rivers, the Nemunas and Vistula.

The Balts remained firmly tribal for several centuries after the peoples to the west and north had organised themselves into nations. Most of the population lived off the land, and long experience had made them capable peasant farmers, typically organised into hamlets of several farmsteads. They cultivated cereals and vegetables on a two- or three-year field rotation system, bred cattle and horses, fished in the rivers, lakes and sea, and were also adept at exploiting the natural resources of the forest. Tribute was paid in cash and kind to the local members of the mounted warrior class (who subsequently became known as *boyars*).

At a time when the rest of Europe had adopted one or other form of Christianity, the Balts remained resolutely pagan. In 997 the first attempt to convert them was made by the Czech missionary bishop St Adalbert, but he and his companions were murdered by Prussians as a punishment for having slept in a sacred grove. Lithuania's name is mentioned for the first time in the *Quedlinburg Annals* of 1009 in connection with a mission led by St Boniface which likewise ended in the martyrdom of all the participants.

Attacks on the Balts from Scandinavia, which had begun in the 9th century, became increasingly frequent in the 11th and 12th centuries, with the desire to spread Christianity used as a pretext. This policy was taken up and developed by the Germans, who had set up a number of trading bases along the Baltic coast. A bishopric was established at Riga in 1201, and the following year a quasi-monastic military order, the Brothers of the Knighthood of Christ in Livonia (commonly known as the Sword Brothers because of the emblem on their white tunics), was founded to spread the Gospel by force. Although small in number and regarded even within Church circles as a highly disreputable body – one whose track record included the massacre of converts and repeated refusals to adhere to rulings of their own bishop and papal envoys – the brotherhood quickly subdued most of the Latvian and Estonian tribes.

In 1225 a Polish duke, Conrad of Mazovia, invited another group of German warrior monks, the Knights of the Teutonic Order (also known as the Knights of the Cross because of the black cross emblazoned on their white tunics) to come and subdue the Western Balts who were prone to invading his duchy. He granted them the county of Chełmno on the River Vistula as a fief, with the promise that they could keep any territory conquered from the heathen. In contrast to their Livonian counterparts, the Teutonic Knights initially enjoyed an unblemished reputation. Founded as a hospitaller community in Palestine in 1190, they were experienced crusaders, renowned for their strict military and monastic discipline, who set about their new task with relish, initially against the Prussians and Jatzvingians.

CREATION OF THE LITHUANIAN STATE

Under the prevailing circumstances of the 13th century, it is remarkable enough that the Lithuanian tribes avoided the fate of their Latvian and Estonian counterparts, who remained under foreign subjugation for centuries, or of the Prussians and Jatzvingians, who underwent a mixture of extermination and assimilation at the hands of the Teutonic Knights. What is truly extraordinary is that the Lithuanians not only managed to preserve their independence by transforming themselves into an effective nation, but that they also metamorphosed into one of the great predatory powers of Europe – and did so despite being engaged almost constantly, throughout the better part of two centuries, in defending their homeland from attack in wars which inflicted huge casualties and were a constant drain on resources.

In 1236 the Sword Brothers, having secured the territory of Livonia (which consisted of much of modern-day Latvia and Estonia), turned their attentions southwards and invaded eastern Samogitia. Near Šiauliai, they were trapped in the marshes by the army of Duke Vykintas of Samogitia, and annihilated in the ensuing battle. Only a minority of the Brothers survived, and were thereafter re-organised into a Livonian branch of the Teutonic Knights.

Paradoxically, this only made the German threat all the greater, and it became imperative for the Lithuanian tribes to unite if they were to stand any chance of retaining control of their lands. By the early 1240s, they had duly been moulded into a nation by Duke Mindaugas. Little is known of the early life of this ruthless operator, who seems to have begun his career as one of about a score of great noblemen, but gradually eliminated or established precedence over his rivals. Mindaugas put the country on a war footing, with every able-bodied man liable for conscription. His mounted warriors were equipped with chain mail, swords and short spears (often captured from defeated foes), his infantry with pikes, axes and crossbows. He began a policy of expanding to the east, capturing some of the sparsely populated western territories of the early Russian state, Kievan Rus, which had collapsed as a result of the Mongol Tatar invasion. Although he fought the German crusaders, he was prepared to come to terms with them, and around 1251 accepted Christianity, an act which led to him being recognised two years later by the papacy as a king and therefore of equal rank to all the other monarchs of Europe. As it turned out, he was the only king Lithuania has ever had, his successors preferring the title of Grand Duke.

In reality, Mindaugas's conversion was little more than an opportunistic façade, as he continued to practise paganism in private. None the less, it was one of a number of policies which antagonised Duke Treniota of Samogitia, a province which remained militantly heathen. In 1263 Mindaugas and his sons were assassinated by followers of Treniota, who replaced him as ruler only to suffer a similar fate two years later. Lithuania reverted to being a pagan country, and over the next few decades underwent a process of internal consolidation.

WARS WITH THE TEUTONIC KNIGHTS

The threat from the west grew much greater after 1283, when the Teutonic Knights completed their conquest of Prussia, and made the Lithuanian campaign their main priority. By this time, the Order had moved away from its original objective of converting heathens. It had already established a powerful independent state which controlled a substantial part of the Baltic lands, along with their highly profitable trade links. Lithuania was now the only obstacle barring it from linking up its two territories, thereby gaining hegemony over the entire region. With the Crusades in the Holy Land seeming to be less rewarding after the fall of Acre to the Saracens in 1291, the Lithuanians became the substitute infidel against whom Christian warriors from all over Europe were encouraged to fight.

However, they were to prove far more formidable foes than those the Teutonic Knights had previously encountered. Grand Duke Gediminas, who reigned from 1316–41, established a dynasty which was to rule Lithuania for more than a quarter of a millennium. He continued the policy of expansion to the east by a combination of military campaigns and dynastic marriages, profiting from the weakness of Kievan Rus and the ever-increasing threat posed by the Mongol Tatars, which led many of the Ruthenian principalities to choose

Lithuania's protection as the lesser of two evils. He placed several of his brothers and sons in control of these territories, even if this entailed their conversion to Orthodoxy.

At the same time, in order to raise Lithuania's economic and cultural standards, and to undermine the moral claims of the Teutonic Knights, he encouraged settlers – whether tradesmen, craftsmen, peasants or priests – from all over Europe, promoting the country as an open and tolerant society. The story of his foundation of Vilnius at the site where he dreamt of a howling iron wolf belongs to the realm of legend, though he did make the city the permanent capital of the Grand Duchy.

In 1345 Gediminas's son and successor Jaunutis was overthrown by his brothers Algirdas, the Prince of Vitebsk, and Kęstutis, the Duke of Trakai. Algirdas assumed the title of Grand Duke and took charge of Lithuania's eastward expansion. His victory over the Mongol Tatars at the Battle of Sinye Vody (Blue Water) in 1363 gained the provinces of Kiev and Podolia, and in so doing he established control over most of present-day Ukraine. Not content with this, he pushed eastwards in the direction of Moscow, but never managed to capture the city.

Meanwhile, the threat from the Teutonic Knights grew ever more frequent. During Algirdas's reign they launched no fewer than 70 attacks from Prussia and 30 from Livonia. Under Winrich von Kniprode, who became Grand Master in 1351, the Knights reached the height of their international prestige and influence, and their fortress headquarters at Marienburg in Prussia (now the Polish town of Malbork) was transformed into the greatest castle of the European Middle Ages, with a brilliant courtly life – one wholly at odds with the original austere ideals of the Order – to match. Nevertheless, Duke Kęstutis, who was entrusted with the defence of the Lithuanian homeland, held out stubbornly, and launched many counter-attacks of his own.

The situation changed when Algirdas's son Jogaila became Grand Duke on his father's death in 1377. He wished to make peace with the Knights, and considered undergoing baptism with a view to converting the ethnic part of Lithuania to Christianity, a move which seemed overdue, given that around two-thirds of the inhabitants of the Grand Duchy were Orthodox Christians. In 1381 he signed a treaty with Kniprode which was secretly directed against his uncle. When Kęstutis heard about this, he seized Vilnius and deposed Jogaila, assuming the title of Grand Duke for himself. The following year he began an offensive against the Teutonic Knights, but had to withdraw in order to quell a rebellion in one of the Russian provinces, leaving his son Vytautas in control of Lithuania.

While Kęstutis was away, Jogaila staged a successful coup in Vilnius, and his Teutonic allies took control of Samogitia and Kęstutis's ancestral seat of Trakai. Vytautas fled to Gardinas (now Grodno in Belarus), where he met up with his father. Their army marched on Trakai, where they were offered a safe passage to conduct negotiations. Instead, they were arrested, and Kęstutis died soon afterwards. He was almost certainly murdered, although it was claimed he committed suicide. Vytautas, however, managed to escape. Winrich died the same year, and Jogaila fell out with his successor, believing that the latter harboured designs of partitioning Lithuania between himself and Vytautas.

ROYAL UNION WITH POLAND

Matters took another twist when the death of Louis of Anjou led to the throne of Poland passing to his young daughter Jadwiga. Seeking a more suitable husband for her than her long-term betrothed, Wilhelm von Habsburg, the Polish nobility decided Jogaila would make the best choice, and his acceptance of the offer was confirmed by the Treaty of Krèva of 1385. The following year, Jogaila was baptised and married in the Polish capital of Cracow (Kraków), and was thereafter known as King Władysław II Jagiełło.

This event had many profound consequences. As part of the marriage agreement, Lithuania was required to adopt Christianity, and mass baptisms were undertaken in 1387, with Polish priests dispatched to minister to the country. As a result, Polish and Latin soon came to be the accepted written languages of Lithuania, and Polish also became the spoken language of the upper classes, as they strove to gain an equal footing with their more privileged Polish counterparts.

Like Lithuania, Poland was a multi-national and multi-cultural state. Moreover, it was resentful of the Teutonic Knights, who were in control of a great deal of territory the Poles regarded as rightfully their own, depriving them of direct access to the sea. In any case, the peaceful conversion of Lithuania had deprived the Knights of their very *raison d'être*. Their continued presence on the Baltic showed that they were in reality an imperial power in disguise.

Despite their common interests, Poland and Lithuania did not immediately become a super-state. As Jogaila was obliged to have his main base in Cracow, he was too far away from Vilnius to remain in effective control, and in 1392 came to an agreement with Vytautas, whereby the latter was recognised as Lithuania's Grand Duke. Conrad von Jungingen, who became Grand Master of the Teutonic Knights the following year, skilfully played the cousins off against one another, even forcing Vytautas to renounce his interest in Samogitia, which was still largely a pagan province, in 1398. He also encouraged Vytautas' dreams of expansion eastwards to the lands of the Golden Horde, but this was brought to an abrupt end by Vytautas's defeat at the Battle of Vorskla in 1399.

The Samogitians, who had not been party to the agreement between Vytautas and Conrad, proved almost impossible to control, and were not subdued until 1406. In 1409 they rebelled again, and this time Vytautas and Władysław decided to support them, so precipitating a major showdown with the hot-headed Ulrich von Jungingen, who had succeeded his late brother as the Knights' Grand Master. A combined army of 150,000 men was raised, supplemented by Czech, Hungarian and Vlach mercenaries. Although the Knights could muster a force of just 80,000, they were none the less confident of victory when the armies met at Grunwald in East Prussia in 1410. Known in Lithuania as the Battle of Žalgiris, the day-long conflict ended in a crushing victory for the Polish–Lithuanian alliance. Among the Teutonic Knights' 18,000 fatalities were its entire high command, and its 185-year Baltic crusade was brought decisively to an end. Had the victors not remained behind to bury their own dead, rather than pursue those Knights who retreated to the safety of Marienburg, they might have brought down the Teutonic state itself. Instead, it survived in a weakened form for more than a century.

FULL UNION WITH POLAND

Under Vytautas, who subsequently gained the sobriquet 'the Great', Lithuania reached its largest extent. The resolution of the long-standing dispute over the ownership of Samogitia, which lost its status as the last outpost of paganism in Europe when Christianity was finally introduced in 1413, gave the Grand Duchy a toe-hold on the Baltic coast at Palanga. At its southern extremity, it held 150km of shoreline on the Black Sea, between the mouths of the Dnieper and Dnester. To the east, its borders fell just over 100km short of Moscow.

When Vytautas died without issue in 1430, there was a period of internecine struggle. This was finally resolved when Kazimierz Jagiellończyk (Casimir Jagiellon), the younger son of Władysław by his second wife, became King of Poland in 1447, seven years into his reign as Lithuania's Grand Duke. Thereafter, the two titles were always conferred on the same monarch, who ruled the countries in personal union. The dominant role of Poland in the partnership is illustrated by the fact that Kazimierz was the last Grand Duke who was able to speak the Lithuanian language.

Lithuania played only a minor role in the Thirteen Years' War of 1454–66, in which the Teutonic state's German settlers combined with Poland in another landmark defeat for the Knights, whose territory was partitioned. The western section, including their Vistula heartlands, was re-named Royal Prussia and made a dependency of the Polish crown, and the Order was forced to re-locate to new headquarters at Königsberg.

Not long after the German *Drang nach Osten* ('drive to the east') was finally brought to an end, a new and dangerous enemy for both Poland and Lithuania was arising in the other direction. The Grand Dukes of Muscovy set themselves up as protectors and 'liberators' of the Orthodox principalities of Ruthenia – even those which showed a marked reluctance to accept such assistance – and in so doing set out to establish a successor to the old empire of Kievan Rus. In 1500 the Muscovite army began its westwards push, initiating a policy which, it could be argued, was pursued relentlessly from then until the 1980s. In 1512 the long-standing Lithuanian city of Smolensk became the first important place they captured.

The reigns of the last two monarchs of the Gediminian line, Zygmunt the Old (1506–48) and Zygmunt August (1548–72) saw the introduction of Renaissance ideas into Poland and Lithuania, thanks in large part to the Italian connections forged as a result of the former's marriage to Bona Sforza. Then in its early years, the Lutheran Reformation also made an impact. An early convert was Zygmunt's nephew Albrecht von Hohenzollern, the last Grand Master of the Teutonic Knights, who in 1525 secularised the Order's remaining Prussian holdings into a duchy (thereafter known as Ducal Prussia or East Prussia) under the Polish crown. The Reformed (Calvinist) version of Protestantism gained many strong supporters among the Lithuanian nobility, most notably the powerful Radvila (Radziwiłł) clan.

These developments made the wars with Muscovy into defining clashes between the West and the East and between the forces of enlightenment and tyranny. This was particularly true following the accession of Ivan the Terrible, the epitome of the brutal despot, who assumed the title of Tsar (derived from Caesar) in accordance with his imperialistic ambitions. In 1558 he launched an attack on Livonia, the last remaining German outpost on the Baltic. Poland–Lithuania and Sweden both intervened, and shared in the territorial partition which followed the departure of the Livonian Order in 1562; Poland–Lithuania also acted as protector of the new Duchy of Courland founded by the Knights' last Master.

The same year, Ivan the Terrible's troops burned down Vitebsk and Orsha, and the following year captured the trading city of Polotsk, which had been under Lithuanian control for the previous three centuries. In 1564 the Russian progress was halted as a result of the decisive defeat at the Battle of Ūla by the much smaller army of the Grand Hetman of Lithuania, Mikalojus Radvila 'the Red'. However, the Lithuanians were unable to recapture the territories that had already been lost. Lacking an heir, Zygmunt August spent his final years trying to forge an alliance strong enough to counter the threat from the east.

POLISH–LITHUANIAN COMMONWEALTH

A combined Polish–Lithuanian state, which had first been mooted in 1501, finally came into being as a result of the Union of Lublin of 1569. This created a Commonwealth (often known by its Polish name of *Rzeczpospolita*) consisting of the two main countries plus the dependencies of Royal Prussia and Livonia.

Although Poland and Lithuania retained their own laws, administration, treasury and army, a common currency was introduced and neither was allowed to conclude a foreign treaty without the consent of the other. The parliament (*Sejm*) was to be convened every two years. Warsaw, which lay midway between the old capitals of Cracow and Vilnius, became its main seat, and soon afterwards the new official capital of Poland, and effectively of the whole Commonwealth. Because of Poland's senior role in the new partnership, the stage was set for the Polonisation of Lithuania to spread beyond the higher echelons of society to which it had hitherto been confined.

Although the new state was a republic, the combined office of King of Poland and Grand Duke of Lithuania was retained but made an elected one, decided by a mounted assembly of the entire nobility, encompassing everyone from great magnates to the holders of tiny impoverished estates. This enfranchised about 10% of the total population – a figure far in advance of that of any other European country at the time. However, it also strengthened the feudalistic social system embodied in the land reforms dating from 1557, and had unfavourable long-term consequences, impeding capitalist development and the emergence of a significant bourgeoisie. The monarch's status was little more than that of a managerial servant of the nobility, who retained the right to depose him should he fall from favour.

Membership of the Roman Catholic Church was a prerequisite for candidates for the monarchy, but otherwise the religious freedom which already existed in the Commonwealth was underpinned by the Compact of Warsaw of 1573. However, the hugely successful Counter-Reformation left only a few Protestant strongholds. A large section of the aristocracy was re-converted, while others who had made the switch from Orthodoxy to Calvinism were persuaded to change allegiance one more time. Vilnius was a leading centre of the Counter-Reformation movement, largely as a result of the efforts of the Jesuits who arrived there in 1569, establishing a university, Lithuania's first, ten years later. The position of the Orthodox Church, once dominant in the eastern parts of the Commonwealth, was further weakened by the schism leading to the foundation in 1596 of the Uniate (or Greek Catholic) Church, which retained Orthodox practices and ritual while accepting the authority of the Pope.

In 1573 Henri Valois became the first elected head of the Commonwealth, but on the death of his brother five months later he returned to France, where he assumed the throne. It was not until 1576 that his replacement, the Transylvanian prince Stefan Bathory, was chosen. His ten-year reign was the most successful in the history of the Commonwealth. Having conducted thorough military reforms, he launched a campaign against the Russians in which some of the territories which had previously been lost were recaptured. A peace treaty was signed in 1582, and the threat from the east thereafter abated, not to revive until the middle of the following century.

VASA DYNASTY AND AFTER

The foreign policy of the next three elected monarchs, all members of the Swedish Vasa (Waza) dynasty, was far less fortunate. Zygmunt III, who succeeded Bathory in 1587, was a Catholic bigot who came into conflict with the almost exclusively Protestant population of his native land, whose throne he gained in 1593. He was deposed by the Swedes in 1604, but ruled the Commonwealth for a further 28 years, in the process obtaining for it a new and increasingly powerful enemy. He had more success in his wars with Muscovy, which had been plunged into turmoil following Boris Godunov's usurpation of the throne and his subsequent replacement by two impersonators of the murdered heir Dmitri. Following the recapture of Smolensk in 1611, the Commonwealth army occupied Moscow itself. However, it was driven out the following year, leaving Zygmunt's ambition to become Tsar unfulfilled.

Under his son and successor, Władysław IV, part of Livonia was lost to Sweden. The Commonwealth did, however, manage to avoid the worst of the calamitous series of Europe-wide conflicts known as the Thirty Years' War (1618–48), from which Sweden emerged as the continent's leading military power.

The reign of Władysław's brother, Jan Kazimierz, saw the fortunes of Poland–Lithuania start to plummet. In 1648, the year of his election, Bohdan Chmielnicki led a Cossack revolt whose goal was the establishment of an independent Ukrainian state. The rebels allied themselves with the Russians, who occupied the eastern part of the Commonwealth in 1654. Vilnius was one of the many places which was devastated, and afterwards lost half its population to the plague.

The Russians' success inspired the Swedes to launch an invasion of their own the following year, using as a pretext Jan Kazimierz's claims on the Swedish throne. Jonušas Radvila, the Grand Hetman of Lithuania, saw this as an opportunity to dissolve the union with Poland, which his family, as Calvinists, had always opposed. By the Treaty of Kėdainiai, which was signed by Radvila, many of Lithuania's leading noblemen and the Swedish chief of staff, the Commonwealth was replaced by a new union with Sweden. However, the agreement was never ratified, and the Swedes proceeded to overrun Poland. Following a heroic fight-back, the war ended in stalemate in 1660 with the Treaty of Oliwa.

This offered some relief in the concurrent war with the Russians, which dragged on for a further seven years, during which Vilnius suffered a long period of occupation. The Commonwealth's economy was left devastated by the cumulative effects of repelling the two invaders, and a quarter of the population had perished. For the general mass of its people – as opposed to the few fabulously wealthy magnate dynasties who increasingly dominated its affairs – the standard of living was probably lower than it had been two centuries before.

A further significant development during this period had been the first use in 1652 of the *liberum veto*, whereby a single vote against a measure in the Sejm was enough to defeat it. The principle behind this was that the nobility governed the Commonwealth as a collective conscience in a wholly disinterested manner, and thus would be expected to act unanimously. The first time someone objected to a measure, there was some debate as to whether his veto was sufficient to override the will of the majority. Once it had been established that it was, the practice became widespread in the protection of petty interests. Worse still, it was later discovered that a single dissenter was constitutionally empowered to dissolve the Sejm itself, and in the process repeal all the legislation it had passed. Thus the Commonwealth soon found itself careering down the slippery slope towards ungovernability.

Before that happened, Poland had its greatest-ever triumphs on the international stage, playing the pivotal role in saving Western Europe from invasion by the Ottoman Turks. Thanks in large part to his victory at the Battle of Chocim in 1673, Poland's Grand Hetman, Jan Sobieski, won the Commonwealth's monarchical election the following year. In 1683 he inspired the successful defence of Vienna, but the fact that the Lithuanians pointedly refused to send troops to help him until the Turks were in retreat was an indication of the Commonwealth's increasingly fragile state.

Moreover, Sobieski's adventures abroad led to a neglect of domestic affairs and an increasingly anarchic use of the *liberum veto*. They also enabled Austria, a future enemy, to recover as an imperial power, and facilitated the inexorable rise of the predatory military state of Brandenburg–Prussia. The latter had come into being in 1657 as a result of the union of the Hohenzollern family's heartlands around Berlin with Ducal Prussia, which was wrested from the last vestiges of Polish suzerainty.

DECLINE AND PARTITION

Known as Augustus the Strong in part because of his physical prowess (he could break a horseshoe with his hands), and in part because he sired over 300 children, Sobieski's successor, the Saxon Elector August Wettin, was in fact a weak ruler who was unable to shake off his debts to the Russians who had supported his election in 1697. In 1701 a fellow Elector of the Holy Roman Empire of Germany, Friedrich III of Brandenburg–Prussia, openly defied him by having himself crowned at Königsberg, his pretext being the wholly spurious claim that Ducal Prussia had the right to royal status. Thereafter known simply as Prussia, the newly elevated kingdom set out to dominate the Baltic in a manner the Teutonic Knights never came close to achieving.

Augustus also mismanaged his dealings with the Swedes, against whom he launched a war for control of Livonia. This conflict showed up the calamitous decline in the Commonwealth's military standing, and the victorious Swedes deposed Augustus in 1704, securing the election of their favoured candidate, Stanisław Leszczyński, in his place. Augustus was reinstated in 1710, courtesy of Tsar Peter the Great, who effectively reduced the Commonwealth to a client state in the process, thereafter treating the once-great empire as a buffer against the powers of Western Europe.

With the 'Silent Sejm' of 1717, effective parliamentary life came to an end, and the Commonwealth was left virtually defenceless, being allowed an army of just 24,000 men (of whom a quarter were based in Lithuania), at a time when its counterparts in Russia and Austria numbered 300,000 and 150,000 men respectively. When Leszczyński won the election to succeed Augustus in 1733, the Russians intervened almost immediately to have him replaced by the deceased ruler's only legitimate son. Although less debauched than his father, he proved to be an even more inept custodian of the Commonwealth's interests.

Following the death of the younger August Wettin in 1763, the Russians once again interfered with the election, this time to ensure the victory of Stanisław August Poniatowski, the former lover of their empress, Catherine the Great. However, Poniatowski refused to act as a puppet ruler, and instead initiated a programme of reforms. A revolt against Russia's persistent meddling in the Commonwealth's internal affairs left the Russians with a dilemma. Doing nothing would have allowed the independence movement to gather momentum; a heavy-handed crackdown risked the intervention of foreign rivals.

As a compromise, they supported a Prussian plan for a partition of the Commonwealth. This had originally been devised as a means of curbing Russia's designs on the Ottoman Empire, at a time when Austria was preparing to come

2

to the latter's aid. By a treaty of 1772, the Commonwealth lost around 30% of its territory. The eastern sectors of White Ruthenia – which had been part of Lithuania for centuries – were ceded to Russia, while the Prussians took over most of Royal Prussia and the Austrians all of southern Poland, including Red Ruthenia.

Shocked by these losses, the Sejm stepped up the reform process. Among the measures taken were the partial emancipation of serfs and the abolition of the *liberum veto*. In 1791 the Commonwealth was given the first codified constitution in Europe since classical antiquity and the second in the modern world, following the example of the United States. This was too much for the Russians, who invaded the country the following year, having bought off the Prussians with the promise of control of Danzig (Gdańsk), the mercantile metropolis of the Baltic which, although a city-state, paid allegiance to the Polish crown. Despite a tenacious resistance led by the Polish–Lithuanian nobleman Tadeusz Kościuszko, erstwhile hero of the American Wars of Independence, the Russians emerged victorious. By the second partition of 1793, the constitution was annulled and the Russians annexed the remainder of Ruthenia, while the Prussians took parts of central Poland in addition to Danzig.

Kościuszko launched an insurrection in 1794, and achieved a stunning victory over the Russian army at the Battle of Racławice with a militia largely made up of scythe-wielding peasants. The Lithuanian army forces of Jokubas Jasinskis took control of several major cities, including Vilnius and Kaunas. However, these proved to be no more than temporary triumphs which were soon crushed by the sheer force of Russia's military might. By the third partition of 1795, the remaining parts of Poland and Lithuania were divided up among Russia, Prussia and Austria, thereby wiping both these historic nations off the map altogether. Nearly all of Lithuania was annexed by Russia, the only exception being Užnemunė, the territory west of the Nemunas, which was allocated to Prussia.

LITHUANIA UNDER THE TSARS

Revolutionary France was the country to which Polish and Lithuanian patriots looked in their struggles to regain independence, with hopes crystallising around Napoleon Bonaparte, who assumed power in 1799. French victories over Prussia and Russia led, in 1807, to the Treaty of Tilsit, agreed by Napoleon and Tsar Alexander I. This created the Duchy of Warsaw, a buffer state made up of territories, including Užnemunė, which the Prussians had taken from the Commonwealth, but patriotic hopes of a Duchy of Lithuania along similar lines were not fulfilled.

Hopes were revived in 1812 when the French marched on Russia. In June of that year, Alexander arrived in Vilnius just as Napoleon began the tricky operation of crossing the Nemunas and Neris at Kaunas, which he made into a French garrison and storage centre. As the Tsar retreated, Napoleon occupied the Lithuanian capital, remaining there for 19 days. Although lukewarm about the idea of re-establishing Lithuanian independence, he allowed the formation of a provisional government backed up by five cavalry and four infantry regiments. Following his retreat from Moscow and then defeat at the Battle of Berezina in November, Napoleon returned to Vilnius with the demoralised remnant of his army but scarcely paused in his retreat. The city was recaptured by the Russians a few days later, and Lithuanian hopes of independence were crushed.

At the Congress of Vienna of 1814–15, set up to organise post-Napoleonic Europe, the Duchy of Warsaw was renamed the Congress Kingdom of Poland

and placed under the dominion of the Tsar. This meant that the entire territory of the former Grand Duchy of Lithuania now lay within the Russian Empire, where it would remain for exactly a century.

Lithuania's first significant revolt against Tsarist rule took place in 1831, the rising having spread from Poland, where it had begun late the previous year. Although the rebels took over much of the countryside, they failed to capture either Vilnius or Kaunas. The authorities soon re-established control, and then implemented a series of repressive measures. Noblemen who had supported the uprising had their estates confiscated. Many monasteries were forced to close, and plenty of churches were taken from the Catholics and thereafter used for Orthodox worship. Vilnius University was shut down, leaving Lithuania without a high-level educational institution. In many schools, the Lithuanian language was replaced by Russian. These events led many to abandon nationalist aspirations, and the first wave of emigration, principally to North America, began soon after.

In 1863 there was another rebellion, which was crushed by the forces of the Russian governor-general, Count Mikhail Muravyov, who earned the nickname 'The Hangman' for ordering the public execution of over 100 participants, including the two most prominent Lithuanian leaders, the army captain Zigmantas Sierakauskas and the priest Antanas Mackevičius. As a result of the failure of the revolt, the Congress Kingdom lost any vestiges of autonomy, becoming yet another Russian province. The repressive measures introduced after the 1831 revolt were stepped up. Ethnic Russians were settled in Lithuania, and new Orthodox churches built for them. Bans or restrictions were placed on the building and repair of Catholic churches, and religious processions were forbidden. In schools, the use of Lithuanian was allowed only at the elementary level; all lessons in high schools were in Russian. The use of the Cyrillic alphabet was made compulsory, even in books written in the Lithuanian language.

In order to circumvent this, Lithuanian books were printed in the Latin alphabet in nearby East Prussia and then smuggled over the border. The Bishop of Samogitia, Motiejus Valančius, played an important role in this illicit trade, and was himself a prolific writer and dedicated educationalist who fought hard to keep the national language and culture alive. He was also active in establishing temperance societies, which antagonised the authorities by causing a huge drop in the lucrative tax revenues which came from the sale of alcohol.

Another important development in the history of the nationalist movement was the foundation in 1883 of the first Lithuanian-language newspaper, *Aušra* ('Dawn'), by a group of intellectuals led by Jonas Basanavičius, a doctor, historian and ethnologist. This folded after 4 years, but found a worthy successor in *Varpas* ('Bell'), edited by Vincas Kudirka, author of the words of Lithuania's national anthem.

It was not until Russia's 1904–05 war with Japan, which ended in crushing defeat for the Russians, that the shakiness of the Tsarist Empire began to become apparent. In the same year as the defeat a congress of 2,000 Lithuanians met in Vilnius and called for autonomy within the empire. The decade also saw a renaissance in Lithuania's cultural life, thanks in large part to the annual art exhibitions organised by the composer-painter Mikalojus Konstantinas Čiurlionis and his associates.

RESURRECTION OF LITHUANIA

World War I smashed the great empires which had dominated continental Europe for the previous century and as a result a host of new and revived states came into

2

being. The chain of events leading to Lithuania's resurrection began in August 1915, when the Germans captured the powerful chain of fortresses around Kaunas. They went on to occupy Vilnius the following month, leaving the Russians pinned back in the far northeast of the ethnic part of Lithuania. In March 1916 a Lithuanian conference in Switzerland decided to seek the restoration of the country's independence, and in September 1917 the German occupying forces allowed a congress to be summoned in Vilnius. Chaired by Antanas Smetona, this formally demanded the setting-up of a Lithuanian state with Vilnius as its capital, and elected a council to oversee the task. On February 16 1918, independence was declared.

Kaiser Wilhelm II of Germany gave his official seal of approval the following month, though it was not until November 9 that a Lithuanian government was formally set up. However, this failed to gain international recognition, and its delegation was refused admission to the Paris Peace Conference which was established to determine the future map of Europe.

Józef Piłsudski, the military strongman who assumed leadership of the revived Polish state which was established virtually simultaneously, was the scion of an impoverished Lithuanian noble family which had long before been thoroughly Polonised. He was opposed to Lithuanian independence, preferring instead to try to re-create the old Commonwealth in a new guise. Only this, he believed, would be strong enough to be a bulwark against the threat from Soviet Russia, which had come into being following the 1917 Revolution. Its stated mission to spread communism to the West posed a major challenge to the new European order and was one that small states on its borders were ill-equipped to resist.

The Peace Conference proved largely impotent in settling the disputes involving Russia, Poland and Lithuania, and the issues of national boundaries were determined in a series of local wars over the following two years. In December 1918 the Bolsheviks invaded Lithuania and established a provisional government, but were driven out again the following year by the new Lithuanian army. In July 1920 a treaty was signed, whereby the Soviets recognised the independence of Lithuania.

However, Lithuania was still involved in an armed conflict with Poland, which in turn was at war with Russia. The latter was a see-saw struggle which eventually ended in victory for the Poles, who thereby inflicted on the Red Army the only outright defeat it ever suffered in the field. Poland was able to set its boundaries far to the east, encompassing large tracts of both White and Red Ruthenia. However, it failed to prevent the short-lived Ukrainian Republic from falling into Bolshevik hands, and thus Piłsudski's hopes of creating a sufficiently powerful revival of the old Commonwealth were dashed.

A peace treaty between Poland and Lithuania was signed on October 7 1920, a few days before the end of the Polish–Soviet War. Just two days later, however, the forces of General Lucjan Żeligowski occupied the southeastern part of Lithuania, including Vilnius. He did this under the pretence of being an insurgent, but was actually acting with the full consent of Piłsudski, who was determined that Vilnius (or Wilno), which he regarded as his own home city, should be incorporated into Poland. Although no-one could dispute that it was the historic capital of Lithuania, only a tiny minority of the city's inhabitants spoke Lithuanian. At least 40% of the population was Jewish, there having been a steady flow of migrant Jews from other parts of the Russian Empire throughout the 19th century; most of the remainder, whatever their ethnic origin, were Polish-speaking.

In November Żeligowski's advance was halted, but Vilnius and the surrounding area remained in Polish hands, pending an international inquiry into the dispute. In 1922 the Conference of Ambassadors decided that the Poles had the right to continue occupying the territory. This prompted Lithuania to break off diplomatic ties with Poland, and the two countries remained at loggerheads throughout the inter-war period. Kaunas, Lithuania's second city, was chosen as the seat of government, but was designated a 'temporary' capital only, as a clear notice of intent to regain Vilnius at some future date. It was nevertheless made into something of a national showpiece through the implementation of a series of prestige projects, including the foundation of a new university.

INTER-WAR REPUBLIC

The Lithuanian republic was very different from the old Grand Duchy, being of comparable size to the two other Baltic states of Latvia and Estonia, which took their place on the political map of Europe for the very first time. Indeed, it fell well short of including all the lands which had been regarded as ethnically Lithuanian since the early Middle Ages.

The first elections were held in 1920 and resulted in the Christian Democrats winning an absolute majority of the seats in the constituent Seimas, as the parliament was known. This passed laws on land reform, brought in a new currency called the Litas, and drafted a liberal-minded constitution, which guaranteed citizens a range of rights and freedoms and provided for elections to the Seimas every three years. The Seimas elected the president, who in turn appointed the prime minister. Following further elections, the Christian Democrats remained in power, and Aleksandras Stulginskis became president.

In 1923 an important territorial acquisition was made which provided some consolation for the loss of Vilnius. Memel, the easternmost city of pre-war Germany and an important Baltic port since the days of the Teutonic Knights, had been confiscated from Germany under the terms of the Treaty of Versailles and placed under the control of a French occupying force. With its long-term future uncertain, and tensions growing among the different nationalities who made up its population, the Lithuanian army seized the chance of protecting the interests of its own ethnic minority, and drove out the French, who showed little interest in protecting what was for them a dubious asset. Under the new name of Klaipėda, the city and its region were annexed to Lithuania.

The Christian Democrats were voted out of office in 1926, to be replaced by a Populist coalition government with Kazys Grinius as president. A few months later, this government was overthrown by a military coup which re-installed independence leader Antanas Smetona as president, with Augustinas Voldemaras appointed prime minister of a right-wing cabinet. Following the dissolution of the Seimas, a new constitution, which provided for greatly increased presidential powers, was introduced. The Communist Party was banned, and restrictions were placed on the activities of other left and centre groups. Voldemaras, who was sacked in 1929, attempted a coup of his own in 1936; as a result of its failure, he was sentenced to 12 years' hard labour, though this was commuted after a year.

In March 1939, Klaipėda and the surrounding area were invaded by Hitler and re-incorporated into Germany. In September 1939 the German invasion of Poland launched World War II a few days after the secret Molotov–Ribbentrop Nazi–Soviet Pact, which allocated the Baltic states to the Soviet sphere of influence. Poland was carved up by the Nazis and Soviets, with the Soviets taking over the eastern half of the country. The following month, under the terms of a Soviet–Lithuanian 'Mutual Assistance Agreement', Vilnius was restored to Lithuania as its capital, together with some of the surrounding territory, though

2

the boundaries were drawn somewhat short of what had historically been regarded as ethnic Lithuania. There was a heavy price to pay for this, with the Soviets being allowed to establish military bases on the republic's territory. This was in reality only the prelude to full annexation the following summer. In June 1940 the erstwhile dictator Smetona fled via Germany to the United States, where he died in a house fire, possibly assassinated by the KGB, four years later. Elections to a new Seimas were held in July; only communist-backed candidates were permitted to stand, and the new parliament duly applied for Lithuania's incorporation in the USSR. The nation formally lost its independence once again in August 1940.

TOTALITARIAN RULE

Lithuania was quickly adapted to the Soviet way of life. The Seimas became a Supreme Soviet, which appointed the Council of People's Commissars. All political parties other than the Communist Party were outlawed, and most cultural organisations were dissolved. Many industrial and commercial enterprises were nationalised. Drastic changes were made to the pattern of landholding. Estate owners whose predecessors had owned serfs had their properties confiscated; other landowners were only allowed to keep land they worked themselves; and the first state and collective farms were set up. A reign of terror was established, with mass deportations to Siberia.

In June 1941 the Nazis turned on their erstwhile ally and invaded the Soviet Union. Within a week they had occupied Lithuania, which was joined with Latvia, Estonia and Byelorussia (now Belarus) to form the new German province of Ostland. There then followed the most controversial period in Lithuanian history – one which still occasions much heated debate. In reaction to the depredations of the Soviets, some greeted the conquerors as liberators, though the Nazis failed to come anywhere near fulfilling the quota of Lithuanians they hoped to recruit to their army; they were also unable to raise a local SS unit. A shameful minority collaborated in the massacre of the Jews, gaining a reputation for brutality equal to that of the Nazis themselves. What had been one of Lithuania's most significant minority communities for over half a millennium was reduced to a tiny rump, with an estimated 200,000 people murdered, principally at Kaunas, Paneriai and Alytus. Many nationalist historians and commentators interpret the country's involvement in the Holocaust as a knee-jerk backlash against the Lithuanian Communist Party, an organisation in which Jews played a disproportionately dominant role, and which was widely blamed for the country's loss of independence and subsequent sufferings.

By 1944, the tide of the war had turned following the German defeats at Stalingrad and Kursk, and the Red Army was pushing westwards. Vilnius was recaptured in July, and when Klaipėda fell the following January, the Soviets were back in control of the whole of Lithuania. The country suffered huge destruction in the course of the war, with all its major cities left in ruins and several sizeable towns being almost totally destroyed.

Between 1945 and 1952 deportations to Siberia and other far-flung parts of the Soviet Union were carried out on a much larger scale than hitherto. Official statistics show that 120,000 people were involved, though the true figure may well have been more than twice that number. Ethnic Russians moved in the other direction to take their places, but this was done on a smaller scale than in Latvia and Estonia. Armed resistance continued throughout this period, largely in the countryside by the 'Forest Brothers', but gradually petered out when it became obvious that no worthwhile international support was forthcoming, and that Lithuania was irrevocably part of the Soviet Union for the foreseeable future (even though this was never formally recognised by the United States and other Western countries).

The rapid enforced collectivisation of the land led to a sharp downturn in agricultural production, which stayed below its pre-war levels until the late 1960s. It was accompanied, in accordance with communist ideology, with huge developments in the country's industrial base. This culminated in a vast prestige project, the building of the Ignalina nuclear power plant in a new town originally named in honour of Antanas Sniečkus, who served continuously as the head of Soviet Lithuania from its foundation until 1974.

Throughout the decades of communist rule cultural life in Lithuania, as everywhere else in the Soviet orbit, was subordinated to Party dictates and inevitably stagnated. Such opposition as there was came from the Roman Catholic Church, which maintained the loyalty of the majority of the population, despite the fact that many places of worship were confiscated and adapted for a wide range of secular uses. The Church's underground newspaper, *Chronicles of the Lithuanian Catholic Church*, kept the West informed about Soviet activities, including human rights abuses.

Genuine hopes for the restitution of Lithuanian independence lay dormant until the reformist Mikhail Gorbachev took over the leadership of the Soviet Union in 1985. As a result of his encouragement of greater openness, and loosening of the Communist Party's iron grip on all aspects of society, a group of Lithuanian intellectuals founded the *Sajūdis* movement in 1988. The same year saw some notable stirrings of popular protest, including a large demonstration in Vilnius on the anniversary of the Molotov–Ribbentrop Pact, and another against the construction of a third nuclear reactor at the Ignalina plant. Christmas was celebrated openly for the first time in the Soviet period.

The following summer saw Lithuanians join with Latvians and Estonians in forming a huge human chain stretching all the way from Vilnius to Tallinn in a peaceful protest marking the 50th anniversary of the Molotov–Ribbentrop Pact. In November 1989 the fall of the Berlin Wall ushered in the peaceful revolutions which toppled the communist governments of the Soviet Union's Eastern European satellite states. A month later, the Lithuanian Communist Party split away from its Soviet parent.

SECOND LITHUANIAN REPUBLIC

On March 4 1990 the first free elections of the Soviet era resulted in an overwhelming victory for the *Sajūdis*; on March 11 the restoration of Lithuania's independence was declared by the Supreme Council under the chairmanship of Vytautas Landsbergis, scion of a distinguished Lithuanian family and himself a well-known pianist and musicologist. Thus Lithuania became the first republic to break away from the Soviet Union. The Kremlin refused to recognise this, however, and began an economic blockade the following month.

Tensions mounted the following year. On January 13 Soviet troops opened fire on the peaceful demonstrators who had gathered outside the TV tower in Vilnius, killing 14 unarmed civilians. A Soviet attack on the border post at Medininkai on July 31 led to the deaths of seven Lithuanian guards. However, the failure of the Moscow coup against Gorbachev the following month resulted in Lithuania's independence being recognised by Western countries, with the Soviet Union soon following suit. On September 17 Lithuania, along with her Baltic neighbours, was admitted to the United Nations.

Thereafter, events progressed rapidly as the shackles of half a century of foreign domination were thrown off and the economy opened up to foreign investors and local entrepreneurs. A referendum in May rejected Landsbergis's plans for a strongly presidential system of government. Instead, a system based on the French model, with a division of powers between the president and the Seimas, was approved in another referendum held in October in tandem with new parliamentary elections. As a result of dissatisfaction about spiralling unemployment and living costs, these resulted in a landslide victory for the reformed communists, the Lithuanian Democratic Labour Party.

With his popularity at a low ebb because of persistent charges of authoritarianism, Landsbergis did not stand in the presidential election the following February, which was won with ease by Algirdas Brazauskas who, as General Secretary of the Communist Party, had been the de facto leader of Soviet Lithuania in its later years. In May 1992 Lithuania joined the Council of Europe, and in June the Litas was re-introduced as the national currency. The last Soviet soldiers departed for home at the end of August and a few days later Pope John Paul II paid an official visit.

In 1995 Lithuania took the first tentative steps towards joining the European Union. At the end of that year the country was rocked by a financial scandal in which the two largest banks went bust, with their chairmen arrested on charges of fraud. Prime Minister Adolfas Šleževičius was also implicated in the affair, and was forced out of office the following February.

Right-wing parties returned to power in the November 1996 elections to the Seimas, which saw Landsbergis make a comeback from the political wilderness as the new parliamentary chairman. In January 1998 the presidential election was won, after an extremely tight race, by an independent candidate, Valdas Adamkus, who had emigrated to the United States in 1944, latterly serving as a senior environmental officer in Chicago. He thereby became the first American to assume the leadership of a former communist country, though he was obliged to renounce his US citizenship prior to taking up office.

The 2000 elections were inconclusive, though Landsbergis's Conservatives lost badly. By putting on a united front, left-wing parties made significant gains, and subsequently merged into a new Social Democratic Party under the leadership of former president Algirdas Brazauskas. Although this became the largest parliamentary party, power was assumed by a minority coalition of centrist parties known as the New Policy bloc. However, clear policy differences between the two main partners, the Liberals and the Social Liberals, were evident from the outset, and the government lasted for a mere eight months. In July 2001, Brazauskas cemented his reputation as a great political survivor by becoming prime minister of a new coalition of Social Democrats and Social Liberals.

It was generally assumed that the highly respected Adamkus would have little difficulty in winning a second term. He had a big lead in the first round of the presidential ballot, but in the run-off in January 2003 suffered a shock defeat against Rolandas Paksas, a former stunt pilot with a populist agenda. Although Paksas duly assumed office, it soon became clear that his success had been bankrolled by a Russian businessman, and that his National Security Advisor had links to organised crime. Impeachment proceedings were initiated, and he was dismissed in April 2004 – in the midst of what was otherwise a triumphant period for the country, with its successive admission to NATO and the EU. Adamkus re-gained the presidency in June, following a narrow win in fresh elections from which Paksas was barred.

3

The People

ETHNIC GROUPS

Lithuania has been a multi-national and multi-cultural society since the Middle Ages, though its ethnic profile has changed many times in the course of the centuries. Nowadays, some 85% of its 3.37 million populace is classified as Lithuanian, which is to say that they are the direct descendants of the original Baltic tribes. The percentage is similar to that in 1923, when the country's population (in a smaller geographical area) numbered 2.15 million. This means, on the one hand, that present-day Lithuania is far more homogeneous than the other two Baltic states of Latvia and Estonia, where the locals are barely in the majority; but on the other that it has preserved its historic tradition as a melting-pot far better than neighbouring Poland, which lost virtually all its minorities as a result of World War II and its immediate aftermath.

The Poles are currently the largest minority group, numbering 6.3% of the populace. Most are concentrated in Vilnius and the southeast of the country, areas which were occupied by Poland in the inter-war period. This minority has itself a rather complex make-up. Some of its members, strangely enough, are the descendants of ethnic Lithuanian families who were Polonised during the long period of union with Poland, while others descend from Belarussians who underwent a similar process. Those who are ethnically as well as linguistically Polish include descendants of families resident in Lithuania since the days when the distinction between the two countries was blurred, as well as those who only settled there between the wars.

Relations between Poles and Lithuanians have been problematic since the bitter dispute over ownership of Vilnius immediately after World War I. There was another flashpoint in 1990 when the Polish minority in Lithuania was accused of undermining the fledgling state's independence by supporting the abortive Moscow coup, but matters have improved since the signing of a Friendship and Co-operation Treaty between the two countries in 1994.

At a fraction over 5%, the Russians are the other main minority, though their number has declined significantly since the collapse of communism, and continues to fall. They have a strong presence in both Vilnius and Klaipėda, and are in a large majority in the town of Visaginas, home of the notorious nuclear power plant. Russians have lived in the country since the 14th century, when large parts of their original state, Kievan Rus, were under Lithuanian rule. There were around 50,000 Russians living in the inter-war Lithuanian Republic, a figure which increased sevenfold in the Soviet era, with large numbers being settled in the country at the times when Lithuanians were being deported *en masse* to Siberia. Tensions exist between locals and the Russians, who are often viewed as unwanted leftovers from a regime of foreign occupation. However, because the Russian minority is too small to pose any sort of threat, relations are generally far more relaxed than in Latvia or Estonia.

By far the most important change in Lithuania's ethnic make-up in the past century has been the virtual elimination of the Jewish community, which had been a significant force in the country since the 14th century. In the 18th century, it is estimated, there were 250,000 Jews living in the Grand Duchy, though only around 15,000 in ethnic Lithuania. Due to internal migration within the Russian Empire, the latter figure had risen to 300,000 by the end of the 19th century, with Jews the largest single group in Vilnius, accounting for over 40% of its population. At over 7%, Jews were also comfortably the largest minority in the inter-war Lithuanian Republic (which of course excluded Vilnius), and were at the forefront of the country's commercial, legal and medical life. However, during the German occupation period of 1941–44 (by which time Vilnius had been re-incorporated into Lithuania) an estimated 90% of the Jewish inhabitants were massacred by the Nazis and their Lithuanian sympathisers. The actions of at least some of the latter were motivated, it would seem, by hatred of the Lithuanian Communist Party, which had played a collaborative role in the Soviet occupation of 1940–41 and had a large Jewish membership. Today only 0.3% of the population is Jewish.

The Germans are the other significant minority which has all but disappeared from Lithuania in recent times. There had been a German mercantile presence since the Middle Ages, and when Lithuania annexed the long-time German city of Memel (now Klaipėda) and the surrounding region in 1923, Germans became the country's largest minority after the Jews. However, as a result of defeat in World War II, virtually all the surviving German inhabitants either fled or were deported.

Apart from the Russians and Poles, only the Belarussians account for more than 1% of Lithuania's present-day population, albeit not by much; the Ukrainians have now slipped below that figure. Two other long-standing minorities – both of them originally invited by Vytautas the Great – are the Tatars and Karaites, though the Karaites' position is now precarious; their population is under 300 and still falling.

Post-communist Lithuania's tiny English-speaking community, which helps provide commercial expertise and a variety of professional services, can be seen as heirs to a tradition dating back to the early 17th century, when Scots settled in both Kėdainiai and Memel. They were joined in the latter city by English merchants, shipbuilders and factory-owners, whose colony became so large and prosperous that an Anglican church, which had been mooted since the late 18th century, was built in 1868.

RELIGION

PAGANISM Prior to 1387 Lithuania was a pagan country. Many different gods were worshipped, of whom the most senior was *Dievas*, a father-figure in the mode of Zeus or Jupiter, who ruled the universe from his kingdom in the sky. Next in order of precedence, and akin to Thor in Norse and Anglo-Saxon mythology, was *Perkūnas*, the god of thunder, lightning and the atmosphere. The stern but just eldest son of Dievas, he resided on top of a high mountain and rode around in a chariot. His sworn enemy was *Velnias*, otherwise known as *Pikuolis*, the ruler of the underworld and the god of magic. Other male deities included *Bangputys* (the god of the sea), *Žemėpatis* (the god of the land and protector of farms and animals), *Dimstipatis* (the guardian of homes) and *Patrimpas* (the protector of plants and fruits). Among the female deities, particular importance was attached to *Laima*, the winged goddess of fate who determined an individual's future fortune or misfortune at birth. Other goddesses were *Žemyna* (the earth-mother), *Veliona* (the guardian of the souls of the dead), *Gabija* (fire), *Milda* (love), *Aušrinė* (the morning star) and *Vakarinė* (the evening star).

A pagan place of worship was known as an *alkas*, and was usually situated on a hill close to a river or stream. Ceremonies were conducted by a *krivis* (priest). They were held in the open air, under the shade of a grove of trees, usually ancient oaks. Although there is no evidence that the trees themselves were ever worshipped, they were regarded as the sacred abode of the gods. Indeed, all of living nature was respected, with the grass-snake (*žaltys*) being the most venerated creature. Large stones served as altars, while shrines were usually quite simple round or oval buildings containing an effigy of a deity and an eternal sacred flame tended by virginal priestesses known as *vaidilutės*. Regular sacrifices were made to the different gods, though the practice of offering live humans stopped long before the end of the pagan era, to be substituted by wax models.

None the less, the Lithuanian pagan religion had no sense of the sanctity of human life. Suicides, including mass suicides, were considered honourable acts, and certainly far preferable to falling into the hands of a mortal enemy. Those who committed suicide, or for any other reason died before the time-span which had been allotted to them at birth, remained on earth as living dead for the remainder of the period. In any case, the dead could only depart from the world on one or two days each year, so some were always to be found on earth.

There was a strong belief in the after-life, and the dead were buried with food, drink and their household goods. Deceased rulers were given spectacular funerals: in 1382, just five years before the adoption of Christianity, the deposed Grand Duke Kęstutis was buried in the company of his horses, falcons and hounds. In a clear mirroring of the Roman Catholic belief in purgatory, the righteous ascended to heaven via Perkūnas's mountain, and the ease of ascent was dependent on just how well they had behaved when alive. The wicked were dispatched to the underworld, where they were given a suitable form of eternal punishment for the crimes they had committed.

Paganism continued to be practised in Lithuania long after the adoption of Christianity. Under the name of *Romuva*, it had a mini-revival in the inter-war independent Lithuanian republic, and has had another following the collapse of Soviet rule. In its modern form, the emphasis is on a love of nature, and there is no attempt to denigrate other religions.

CHRISTIANITY The Christian religion was first accepted by the future King Mindaugas in 1251, though this was little more than a sham which lasted no longer than a decade and did not lead to the conversion of any significant sector of the population. Not until 1387 did the ethnic part of the Grand Duchy of Lithuania adopt Christianity, acceptance of the Roman Catholic faith having been made a precondition of the dynastic union with Poland. Because of its uncertain political status, Samogitia was not converted until 1413, making it the last place in Europe to abandon paganism.

In the 16th century, the Reformation had a strong impact, not least because it made the common tongue of the Lithuanian people into a written language for the first time. Many leading noble families, notably the Radvilas, adopted the radical Calvinist form of the faith. However, Protestantism remained a minority religion, and its advances were put firmly into reverse by the end of the century as a result of the success of the Jesuit-led Counter-Reformation.

Despite the promotion of Russian Orthodoxy during the long period of Tsarist rule, the Catholic Church never lost its hold on the populace. If anything, it gained in strength by becoming a focus for nationalist aspirations, and several of its bishops and priests played key roles in the political and cultural struggles of the time.

A more serious threat to the Church's authority came during the Soviet era, when atheism became the official religion. Around a third of all Catholic priests were deported to Siberia. All monasteries and convents were dissolved and many parish churches were confiscated and turned into warehouses, sports halls and art galleries. The Church of St Casimir in Vilnius suffered the ultimate indignity of being made into a Museum of Atheism. Although a few churches were kept open, people who chose to worship openly put their careers at risk.

However, these acts of repression only served to strengthen the identification of the Church with the nationalist cause, and people flocked back to services when churches started to be handed back to believers at the very end of the Soviet period. Huge numbers of Lithuanians underwent adult baptism, or made a religious renewal of marriage vows previously taken in wedding palaces.

Currently, nearly three-quarters of Lithuanians are members or adherents of the Roman Catholic Church. Around a third of the population attends services at least once a month, while a similar percentage goes irregularly, usually to celebrate the main religious festivals. As there is still a relative shortage of church buildings, this means that Sunday morning masses are usually very crowded. None the less, it is noticeable that Catholicism in Lithuania is far more staid and less passionate than in neighbouring Poland. Significantly, it is the country's Polish minority which ranks as the most devout section of the population.

There are Catholic archbishops in Vilnius and Kaunas, and whoever has been longer in office normally serves as the primate. Five further bishops are responsible for other dioceses. There are three seminaries (in Vilnius, Kaunas and Telšiai) for the training of priests. The main places of pilgrimage are the Gates of Dawn in Vilnius and the small town of Žemaičių Kalvarija. Lithuania's patron saint is St Casimir (1458–84), the son of Kazimierz Jagiellończyk (Casimir Jagiellon), King of Poland and Grand Duke of Lithuania, and his wife Elisabeth von Habsburg. Canonised in 1603, his mortal remains rest in a magnificent chapel in Vilnius Cathedral, with his feast day celebrated on March 4.

The Russian Orthodox Church is the second largest religious group, claiming the support of around 4% of the population. Most of these are ethnic Russians, though Lithuania's Russian minority also contains a high number of atheists and agnostics. Two splinter groups from Orthodoxy are also active: the Uniates (or Greek Catholics), who recognise the authority of the Pope; and the Old Believers, who broke away because of opposition to various reforms.

Just under 1% of the populace is Protestant, with many of these being regular worshippers. The Lutheran Church has some strong pockets of support in the Klaipėda region, and has 45 congregations scattered throughout the country, whereas the Reformed Church has only nine. As in all the former communist states of Eastern Europe, missionaries (principally from the United States) from a variety of evangelical sects are currently active in Lithuania.

LANGUAGE

Lithuanian is an Indo-European language. Within Lithuania itself, it is popularly believed to have its roots in Sanskrit, the long-dead language of the epics of ancient India, and this is regarded as a matter of great national pride. However scholars of linguistics see the connection rather differently. In common with all the 140 or so known Indo-European tongues, Lithuanian ultimately derives from a vanished parent language from which Sanskrit provides the most complete surviving systems of nouns, verbs and consonants. Lithuanian likewise preserves much of the sound system of the parent language; indeed, its vowel sounds are believed to be even closer to the original than those of Sanskrit, and the same is true of its basic vocabulary, though its verbal system has undergone significant modification. No other living Indo-European language preserves so much of its archaic character – not even Latvian, the only one to which Lithuanian bears much resemblance, though the two have developed separately since the 7th century or earlier.

It was not until the 16th century that Lithuanian became a written language, and it was first used for official purposes as recently as 1918, when the Lithuanian Republic was established. The administration and diplomacy of the medieval Grand Duchy was originally conducted in old Slavonic and Latin, with Polish gradually taking over following the royal union, and becoming totally dominant after the establishment of the Commonwealth in 1569. Russian was forced on the Lithuanians in the 19th century, with publications in their own language officially banned for four decades following the failure of the 1863 rebellion. In the Soviet era, the learning of Russian was made compulsory, and many institutions operated mainly or even exclusively in Russian. The premier status of Lithuanian in the country was only restored in 1989, when a requirement was placed on the staff of public bodies to acquire proficiency in the language.

There are several different Lithuanian dialects, with that of Western Aukštaitija (otherwise known as Suvalkija) having been adopted as the language's standard form. The grammar is quite complicated. Verbs have four tenses, while nouns are divided into two genders and have seven different cases, each with a different ending. There are 32 letters in the Lithuanian alphabet and the combination ch is also featured separately in alphabetical lists (see *Appendix 1*, page 238). Some 400,000 words are to be found in the national dictionary, which runs to 20 volumes.

Lithuanian surnames first began to emerge after the adoption of Christianity, but only became the norm among the common people in the 17th century. Some are derived from old nicknames or trade names, but most are adaptations of names imported from Western languages. A peculiarity of Lithuanian surnames is that they are adapted in order to make clear both a person's sex and the marital status of a woman. Thus a husband, wife and unmarried daughter all have slightly different forms of the same name. Most male surnames of Lithuanian origin end with one or other of the suffixes -as, -us or -ys. Married women take their husband's name, substituting -ienė for the original suffix. For single women, the father's suffix is replaced by a basic -tė suffix which in some circumstances is preceded by one or two other letters, for example ai, ū or y. Many artistic and professional women choose to use their maiden name only, while it is increasingly common to favour a double-barrelled surname made up of maiden and married names. A few feminists insist on using male surnames.

Most Lithuanian Christian names are derived from Western names, usually with classical roots: for example Marija (Mary or Maria), Petras (Peter), Andrius (Andrew). However, since the late 19th-century national revival, it has been popular to choose old Lithuanian names, for example of Grand Dukes for boys (Gediminas, Mindaugas, Vytautas) or of goddesses for girls (Aušrinė, Laima, Milda).

One practice which alternately amuses or annoys visitors is the habit of rendering virtually all foreign names into Lithuanian. In most cases, this merely involves adding appropriate suffixes in order to make clear an individual's sex and (in the case of women) marital status, though a Christian name will be translated if a direct Lithuanian equivalent exists. Where famous historical figures are concerned, the surname is usually adapted as well; thus, for example, William Shakespeare is known in Lithuania as Viljamas Šekspiras.

Words with English roots are gradually creeping into Lithuanian, thanks in large part to increasing use of computers and the internet. English was taught in schools even in the Soviet period, and is gradually supplanting Russian as the favoured second language. It is quite widely spoken in the cities, especially Vilnius, though very much less so in the countryside. Many people in Klaipėda and the surrounding area speak some German, partly for historical reasons and partly because of the large volume of tourists from Germany.

The Gates of Dawn

4

Culture

CUSTOMS AND FESTIVALS

Because of Lithuania's late conversion to Christianity, the intertwining of many pagan and Church festivals is clearly marked. Thus Shrovetide (*Užgavėnės*), the week of mirth and feasting immediately preceding the stringencies of the Lenten season, has mingled with an older festival marking the end of winter and the ushering-in of springtime. The event is particularly popular in Samogitia; it features a lot of dressing-up and wearing of wooden masks. There are several stock figures: *Morė*, an old maid dragged along on a cart; *Kanapinis*, a lean man, often in the guise of a gypsy; and *Lašininis*, a fat man who is usually a Jew. The climax is on Shrove Tuesday, when pancakes and hearty meat dishes are consumed.

Similarly, St John's Night (*Joninės*) on 23 June, with its bonfires, singing and dancing, is a continuation of the tradition of *Rasos*, the old summer solstice festival, held on the eve of Midsummer's Day. All Souls' Day (*Velinės*) on November 2, when Lithuanians congregate at cemeteries to light candles, is a re-working of *Ilgės*, a pagan autumn festival in honour of the dead. Even Christmas Eve (*Kūčios*), which in Lithuania is the climax of the Yuletide celebrations, has clear parallels with the old winter solstice festival, not least in the tradition of having a family meal in which places are set for absent members, and which features 12 courses – nowadays symbolising the apostles, rather than the months.

As is normal in Roman Catholic countries, Holy Week is the high point of the Church calendar. Palm Sunday celebrations are quite distinctive. In the Vilnius region, it is customary to carry bunches of dried flowers to worship; elsewhere, green twigs (normally juniper) are taken. Eggs play an important symbolic role on Easter Day. They are presented to children in the morning, and are invariably the first dish eaten at the main meal. Patterned Easter eggs have a tradition dating back to the Middle Ages. A design is put on with hot wax, after which the egg is dipped in dye, then placed in heated water or an oven, so that the wax can melt.

One specifically Lithuanian religious festival is that in honour of the native-born patron saint, St Casimir, on 4 March. A market is held in Vilnius, in which preserved flowers and grasses as well as handicrafts are on sale. In early July the Feast of the Visitation is marked by ten days of pilgrimages to Žemaičių Kalvarija.

Of the many secular festivals, the most spectacular is the World Lithuanian Song Festival, held every four or five years at the beginning of July (with the next one in 2009). The *Baltika* folklore festival, lasting for a week in mid-July, rotates among the Baltic capitals. There are also many similar annual events on a smaller scale, particularly in Vilnius and Kaunas.

FOLK MUSIC

The richest and most diverse part of Lithuania's cultural heritage is undoubtedly its folk music. To this day it remains true to its origins as a genuinely popular activity in which anyone can take part, and it retains its ability to appeal across the generations. All over Lithuania, even in the remotest villages, there are ethnographic ensembles specialising in performing local folk songs, dances or instrumental music (or any combination of the three). Most groups nowadays offer what might be described as 'sanitised' arrangements of traditional folk music, using for the accompaniments modified forms of the original instruments which tend to be more comfortable to play and are easier to keep in tune. However, there are also a few ensembles, sometimes consisting of people who have undertaken ethno-musicological research, favouring the 'pure' original forms and instruments.

FOLK SONGS A staggering total of 500,000 Lithuanian folk songs, including variants, has been collated. These include work songs, songs about love and family life, songs of lamentation, festive songs, songs of history and myth, songs of war, songs of protest and songs of emigration. Work songs are the most numerous, and tend to be associated with specific traditional activities, such as hay-making, harvesting, grinding grain, processing flax, spinning and weaving. The motifs of work and love are often intertwined, with industriousness seen as the greatest of all virtues. Motherhood is idealised, though the stock character of

FOLK INSTRUMENTS

Lithuanian folk music employs a number of instruments also encountered elsewhere, as well as those described below, which are distinctive to the country.

BIRBYNĖ A cow-bell is attached to the lower end of this wind instrument, which is made from maple or ash, has five or six finger-holes, and a mouthpiece at the upper end.

DAUDYTĖ This enormously long cylindrical shepherd's trumpet is powerful enough to be heard up to 10km away. The traditional way of making it was a time-consuming process involving shaping the outside from a large length of bark of alder, ash or spruce, cutting it into two longitudinal sections, which were then hollowed out and fastened together at the sides; afterwards, the surface was covered with tar and wrapped with linen yarn, then covered with birch bark soaked in hot water. It can play a nominal scale, though generally only two or three notes are used for accompanying sutartinės.

KANKLĖS This plucked stringed instrument, trapezoid in shape, derives from the medieval psaltery and is a close relation of the zither. It is used to accompany sutartinės and other songs. The body is traditionally made from a single hollowed-out piece of limewood, ash, aspen or oak, though it can also consist of several pieces of wood joined together. Its soundboard may be of spruce, fir, limewood, ash or aspen. The tuning pegs were once also always wooden, but now are usually iron. The number of strings – originally of gut, but now of iron, steel or copper – varies widely. There are four to seven in a normal-sized kanklės (five is the commonest number), seven to 12 in the enlarged version, with upwards of 20 in the modified form of the instrument. Soundholes are geometric in shape, and are usually circular. The player rests the kanklės on the knees, plucks the strings with the right hand, and damps them with the left.

the wicked mother-in-law is invoked in many songs. Lamentations (*raudos*) are sung not only at funerals, but at any time of parting, including weddings. There are songs for many different festivals, including Christmas, New Year, Shrovetide, Easter and Midsummer, though even those associated with Church feast-days seldom have much of a religious message or content. Songs with a historical, mythical or war theme also tend towards generalisations, eschewing reference to specific events and places.

Traditionally, Lithuanian folk songs were performed almost exclusively by women, with men confined to providing the instrumental accompaniment, when this exists. Singing is very much a group activity, and solos are very rare. The poetry of the songs does not usually rhyme, nor does it necessarily scan, with the result that the melody may vary somewhat from one verse to another. Some poems use imagery, the most popular motifs being the sun, moon and stars, followed by the plant and animal kingdoms.

Although Dzūkija is the region most strongly associated with folk songs, the most remarkable examples of the genre are the elaborate polyphonic songs known as *sutartinės*, which are unique to the northern part of Aukštaitija. These employ a melody with two similar yet distinct parts with duple rhythm and

KELMAS The indigenous Lithuanian drum is made from a hollowed-out tree stump with a covering of animal skin.

LUMZDELIS This shepherd's flute with a beak-shaped upper cusp is often played in pairs. It is made of bird-cherry, willow or aspen, has six to nine finger-holes, and produces a diatonic scale.

OŽRAGIS Originally used for herding livestock, this goat's horn has five finger-holes which together produce a major pentachord.

RAGAS First noted in a 12th-century source, this wooden trumpet is used for signalling purposes, as well as for magic and ritual functions, and to accompany *sutartinės*. It is made by hollowing out a piece of ash split along its length, then fastening the two parts together with birch bark, with a mouthpiece added to the upper end. As each instrument can produce only one note, five *ragai* are normally needed for an ensemble performance.

SKRABALAI These small wooden bells, of the type hung round the necks of farm animals, have evolved into percussion instruments. Made of ash or oak, they can be equipped with wooden or metal clappers and are held in the player's hand, or else are placed on poles and struck with sticks. The modified form consists of a set of 27 bells without clappers; these are tuned harmonically and attached on horizontal bars to a frame which can itself be attached to a *kelmas*.

SKUDUČIAI The Lithuanian version of the panpipes can be made from willow or linden bark collected in the spring, from hollow stems of plants cut in the autumn, or from ash, maple or alder. The bottom end of each pipe is plugged with a stopper; the upper end has two sickle-shaped cuts, the shallower of which is placed against the lower lip in performance. Each pipe is of a different size, ranging from 8cm to 20cm, and produces one note only; each player in a group takes between one and three pipes.

accented syncopation. They fall into three main categories: the contrapuntal form has two voices; the canonic form has three voices performing a continuous chain of two-part counterpart; while the antiphonal form is mainly used in association with dancing.

FOLK DANCES Some forms of Lithuanian folk dancing have instrumental accompaniment only, others also have singing. Dances are predominantly for women only, and solos are non-existent. Among the oldest are those performed in conjunction with *sutartinės*; they tend to feature simple movements such as walking in rows or in a circle, turning, gliding and stamping feet. Game dances (*rateliai*) have plots in which at least some of the participants act a role; many are concerned with work themes, some with specific festivals and celebrations, while others include imitations of the movements of animals and birds. Round dances, which do not include singing, sometimes form part of game dances, though they also exist in their own right. Usually they start with basic movements, then gradually become more complicated. Many folk groups also perform polkas, waltzes and quadrilles, all of which were introduced to Lithuania in the 19th century.

ART MUSIC

As far as can be ascertained, music played a fairly important role in the courtly life of the Grand Duchy of Lithuania. In the early 16th century, an orchestra of 80 is said to have performed at Trakai. At the same period, choir and music schools are known to have been in existence at both the Cathedral and the Church of SS John in Vilnius. The city's first organ is documented in 1551, while an organ-building workshop is mentioned in 1585. Throughout the 16th and 17th centuries, violin-makers worked in the city.

Stanisław Moniuszko (1819–72), the foremost 19th-century Polish composer after Chopin, lived for nearly two decades in Vilnius as organist of SS John. He is best-known for his operas, notably *Halka* and *The Haunted Manor*. These show a debt to Rossini and to French *opéra comique*, but make a greater use of the chorus and are given local colour by the inclusion of Polish dances, especially the polonaise. Moniuszko also published 267 songs, mostly simple strophic settings which often employ dance rhythms, as well as the cantatas *Phantoms* and *Crimean Sonnets*, both to texts by Adam Mickiewicz.

Leopold Godowsky (1870–1938), a Pole who was born just outside Vilnius, emigrated to the United States in 1891 and became one of the most admired pianists of his time, not least for his barnstorming performances of his own fiendishly difficult transcriptions of famous orchestral compositions. An even more celebrated émigré instrumental virtuoso was Jascha Heifetz (1901–87), who was born into Vilnius's large Jewish community but left for America as a teenage prodigy, becoming naturalised in the US in 1925. A dazzling globetrotting career ensued, and many critics consider him to have been the greatest violinist of the 20th century.

The first distinctively Lithuanian composer of note was Mikalojus Konstantinas Čiurlionis (1875–1911), who profited from his early training at the orchestral and choral school founded by Duke Mykolas Oginskis in Plungė. About half of Čiurlionis's approximately 300 surviving compositions are small-scale works for solo piano. His early pieces are melodic, with echoes of Chopin as well as other nationalist composers such as Smetana and Grieg. Later works are reminiscent of Debussy in their Impressionistic approach (though it has been proved that Čiurlionis was unfamiliar with the work of the French composer), while his final piano compositions adopt a serial technique anticipating Schoenberg and the Second Viennese School. Čiurlionis's most ambitious musical compositions are the tone poems for full orchestra *In the Forest* and *The Sea*, both of which show Wagnerian touches. He also wrote a string quartet and many folk song arrangements, but plans to write the first-ever Lithuanian opera and symphony were forestalled by his increasing preoccupation with painting and his early death. For more information, see the feature on pages 122–4 and *Fine Arts* on pages 40–1 below.

It fell to Mikas Petrauskas (1873–1937) to compose the first Lithuanian opera. This honour is usually bestowed on *Birutė*, but as this is really incidental music to a play, it more properly belongs to the slightly later *Eglė, Queen of the Grass Snakes*. Juozas Gruodis (1884–1948), founder of the Kaunas Conservatoire, was a key figure in the musical life of the inter-war republic. In his compositions, he aimed at a distinctively nationalist style, in which Romantic and Impressionist forms are given a folksong colouring.

Bronius Kutavičius (b1932) is perhaps the nearest there is to a successor to Čiurlionis. Indeed, his works, which typically have a strong spiritual dimension, include the large-scale organ piece *Ad Patres*, which draws its inspiration from Čiurlionis's *Funeral Symphony*, the first of his cycles of paintings with a musical title. Among Kutavičius' other compositions are *The Pantheistic Oratorio*, the opera *The Thrush*, and many works for chamber ensembles, often featuring unconventional combinations of instruments.

The works of Feliksas Bajoras (b1934) are notable for their polyphonic complexity, though the influence of folk music is often apparent. Bajoras has a particular penchant for the theatre and has written a great deal of incidental music for plays and films, as well as the opera *The Lamb of God*.

Osvaldas Balakauskas (b1937) is as well known as a political activist as a composer, having been a leading member of the *Sajūdis* movement. His work draws on an eclectic range of influences, ranging from classical composers via jazz to minimalism. He has written five symphonies, a *Requiem*, and many works for electronic instruments, including the ballet *Macbeth*.

Algirdas Martinaitis (b1950) is the leading representative of the younger generation of Lithuanian composers. His early works are Neo-Romantic, drawing heavily on literary sources for inspiration. The cantata *Cantus ad Futurum*, one of the five parts of *The Book of Living Nature*, is considered his finest essay in this vein. Latterly he has turned to spiritual subjects and in *St Francis' Hymn to the Sun* combines the traditions of church chanting with Lithuanian folk music.

Works by Lithuanian composers are regularly featured alongside more familiar classical composers in the concerts of the country's leading professional orchestras and choirs. Vilnius is home to the Opera Theatre, originally founded in Kaunas in 1920, as well as the Lithuanian National Symphony Orchestra, the Lithuanian State Symphony Orchestra, the Lithuanian Chamber Orchestra, the St Christopher Chamber Orchestra, the Vilnius and Čiurlionis string quartets and the choirs Jauna Muzika and Aidija. Other leading professional bodies include the Kaunas Chamber Orchestra and Kaunas State Choir, Klaipėda's Symphony Orchestra of Lithuania Minor, and Šiauliai's Polifonija choir.

Among solo instrumentalists, the cellist David Geringas (b1946), who won the International Tchaikovsky competition in 1970, has enjoyed a distinguished international career. Lithuania is one of the few countries still adhering to the old tradition whereby the relationship between conductors and orchestras is characterised by extreme longevity. The Lithuanian Chamber Orchestra, which was formed in 1960, is still in the hands of its founder, Saulius Sondeckis (b1928), while the former viola player Donatas Katkus (b1942) has directed the St Christopher Chamber Orchestra since its establishment in 1994. Juozas Domarkas (b1943) has been musical director of the Lithuanian National Symphony Orchestra since his appointment, while still a student, in 1964; while Gintaras Rinkevičius (b1960), who won prizes at several international conducting competitions, has been in charge of the Lithuanian State Symphony Orchestra since he founded it in 1988.

The best-known Lithuanian-born performer is undoubtedly Violeta Urmana (b1959), who in the latter half of the 1990s established herself as one of the most sought-after mezzo-sopranos by the great opera houses of the world, not least because her voice – which has the extraordinarily wide range of three octaves – is (most unusually) equally suitable for singing Verdi and Wagner. She has latterly turned her attention to dramatic soprano roles and to song recitals, repeating her earlier critical successes. In her home country, where she still appears regularly, she uses her original surname of Urmanavičiūtė as a prefix to the shortened version she has adopted for her international career.

Classical concerts in Lithuania are often attended by rituals redolent of a past age. It remains common for the performers and the music to be introduced by a formally attired announcer, while many members of the audience come equipped with bouquets of flowers to hand over to the soloist or conductor during the applause at the end.

FOLK ART

Lithuanian folk art is notable for its highly distinctive ornamental forms. Particularly remarkable is the way ancient pagan motifs – especially those associated with the sun and other celestial bodies – have survived down the centuries and been mingled with Christian symbols to create patterns which have no parallel anywhere else in art history. The folk art tradition is seen at its finest in sculpture, particularly in the graveyard iron crosses, wooden pillar crosses and wayside shrines, some of which have the dimensions of small chapels. All of these are found throughout the country, though are seen at their most elaborate in Samogitia, where they are also most numerous.

Wooden crosses are often situated outside farmsteads, and in such cases their size served as an indicator of the farmer's wealth or status. They are also present at road junctions and other prominent locations, and were often erected to commemorate some special occasion. Most crosses have a single bar, though in Aukštaitija and Dzūkija in particular it is not uncommon to find two, these usually having been erected at a time of disaster. Iron crosses almost invariably incorporate a sun, which is normally depicted as a circle surrounded by a six-pointed star. Many wooden crosses also feature a crucifix within a highly stylised representation of the sun. Half-moons, flowers, plants and various geometric shapes (particularly triangles, circles and squares) are also used in the decoration of many crosses.

Shrines and small chapels normally contain figurines of saints. The most popular subjects are Christ crucified and the Virgin Mary. Only slightly less ubiquitous are the characteristically Lithuanian representations of the Man of Sorrows (*Rūpintojėlis*), which are commonly found on shrines attached to trees. Developed from an earlier pagan subject, they feature a pensive Christ resting his chin on the palm of his right hand. A distinctive iconography is attached to the figure of St Isidore, which is commonly found on shrines placed on poles in the middle of fields. He is depicted as a farmer dressed in local garb who is sowing grain while an angel ploughs the land. (Sometimes these two roles are reversed.) St George, in his capacity as a dragon-slayer, is another favourite subject, and is commonly placed by the gate through which animals are driven to and from pasture.

The Hill of Crosses near Šiauliai is the most spectacular example of the continuing vibrancy of the folk art tradition. It is also the most genuine, in that the crosses which are still being added to the site on a daily basis are usually anonymous, and inspired by genuine religious piety. On the other hand, many other works which are often categorised as 'folk art' – including such well-known large-scale projects as the Witches' Hill in Juodkrantė and the Čiurlionis Road between Varėna and Druskininkai – are in reality the creations of named sculptors who are influenced by the folk tradition, and who have moved away from purely devotional images to ones inspired by Lithuanian history and myth.

Most other forms of Lithuanian folk art belong to the sphere of handicrafts. Wood is used to imaginative effect in the making of distaffs, which are often elaborately carved, using the same sorts of symbols as those found on crosses. 'Sculptures' made from flax or straw are also popular, the most intricate being the so-called 'wedding gardens' made in Aukštaitija. Home-made fabrics, generally of linen and with a mixture of colours and patterns, were the norm in Lithuanian households right up until the early 20th century.

COSTUME

Folk costumes are common sights in Lithuania, worn by the country's many ethnographic folklore ensembles, and by members of the general public for dances, religious processions and public festivals. What is now classified as traditional dress evolved in the early 19th century from much older traditions of special festive attire, which originally varied from village to village.

There are strong regional variations to folk costumes, at least for women. In Aukštaitija the preference is for light colours, especially white. Typically, aprons are checked or striped, with horizontal patterns in red cotton at the foot. Skirts are also usually checked, while married women wear a head-dress called a *nuometas*. In Suvalkija, on the other hand, bright colours are favoured. Aprons are particularly splendid, often featuring patterns of lilies, clovers or suns. Skirts have vertical stripes, while bodices are usually long and adorned with broad sashes. A contrast of colours is one of the hallmarks of the costume of Samogitia, in which the apron has vertical stripes and horizontal patterned bands, while the skirt is vertically striped. Wooden shoes (*klumpės*) are traditionally worn, while the head and shoulders are covered by a shawl. In the Klaipėda region dark colours predominate. Aprons have vertical stripes with a patterned band at the bottom, while skirts have vertical checks or stripes. Intricately patterned sashes and stoles are characteristic, as is the *delmonas*, a handbag fastened to a waistband. The Dzūkijan costume includes checked, striped or plain white aprons, wide sashes and checked skirts. Throughout Lithuania, a necklace is a common accessory to a folk costume, with those made from amber being particularly popular. Unmarried women generally wear ribbons and beads in their hair, or else have no headwear at all. Married women, however, invariably cover their hair with a head-dress, cap, hat or kerchief.

Men's clothing is subject to far fewer regional peculiarities. There are trousers for summer and winter, the former of white or checked cloth, the latter of grey or dark cloth. Those for festivals have a waistband, those for everyday wear a drawstring. Shirts are long-sleeved and made of linen or cloth. Straw hats are worn in summer, more substantial headwear at other times. Winter greatcoats are double-breasted and grey in colour with stripes on the pockets, cuffs and collar, and are girded with sashes worn around the waist.

FINE ARTS

The earliest monumental painting to survive in Lithuania is a late 14th-century mural of *The Crucifixion* in the crypt of Vilnius Cathedral. A number of medieval devotional paintings also survive, which were all executed under the influence of the Byzantine tradition, even as late as the 16th century, when the style was wholly archaic. Aristocratic portraits by (or executed under the influence of) Western artists first appeared in Lithuania in the 15th century, though these never progressed beyond being crude provincial examples of the genre.

Far superior in quality are the sculptures and frescos adorning the country's multitude of Baroque churches, though the best of these are by Italian masters. Particularly outstanding is the sumptuous stuccowork of SS Peter and Paul in Vilnius by Pietro Peretti and Giovanni Maria Galli. The most capable of the many Italian frescoists active in Lithuania was Michelangelo Palloni (1637–c1705), whose work can be seen at St Casimir's Chapel in Vilnius Cathedral and Pažaislis Monastery in the outskirts of Kaunas.

Paradoxically, a recognisably Lithuanian fine arts tradition only emerged after the country lost its independence. A School of Drawing and Painting was founded as an adjunct to Vilnius University in 1797; this merged in 1805 with the School of Architecture founded four years earlier and the slightly later Schools of Sculpture and Engraving to form the Vilnius School of Art.

The first head, who is in consequence considered the founder of modern Lithuanian art, was Franciszek Smuglewicz, otherwise known as Pranciškus Smuglevičius (1745–1807). He was born in Warsaw of mixed Polish–Lithuanian ancestry, and lived for 21 years in Rome, where he became an admired practitioner of the Neo-Classical style. A specialist in grandiose altar-pieces and history paintings, Smuglewicz also made many naturalistic landscape drawings during the decade he spent in Vilnius, bequeathing a valuable documentary record of the city's buildings.

He was succeeded by his protégé Jonas Rustemas (1762–1835), who ran the School of Art until its closure by the Russian authorities in 1835. A man with a colourful background – he was born in Constantinople to parents of Armenian origin – Rustemas was a versatile artist whose choice of subject ranged from formal Neo-Classical portraits via Romantic landscapes to Biedermeier genre scenes. He also designed a set of satirical playing cards which enjoyed great popularity.

Leading alumni of the School, adept at both landscape painting and portraiture, were Valentinas Vankavičius (1799–1842) and Kanutas Ruseckas (1800–60). Ruseckas was also involved in the creation of *The Vilnius Album*, an ambitious publishing project funded by a retired doctor, Jonas Kazimieras Vilčinskis. Other artists who contributed drawings for the album's engravings were Mykolas Kulieša (1800–63), Albertas Žametas-Žemaitis (1819–76) and Mykolas Elviras Andriolis (1836–93). The last-named also illustrated books by Adam Mickiewicz, and painted historical and religious scenes.

Following the relaxation of censorship by the Russian authorities in 1904, a remarkable group of local painters and sculptors began organising regular exhibitions of Lithuanian art. The composer Mikalojus Konstantinas Čiurlionis (1875–1911) was a leading member of this circle, and devoted increasing amounts of his time to painting. Although active in this field for just seven years, he worked rapidly, often creating five or six pictures in a single day, among them many unforgettably haunting Symbolist images inspired by such diverse interests as music, cosmology and Lithuanian mythology: see the feature on pages 122–3 for more details.

Whereas Čiurlionis died sadly young, two of his closest associates went on to enjoy long careers which spanned the entire period of the revived Lithuanian state plus the early decades of Soviet rule. Antanas Žmuidzinavičius (1876–1966), nowadays best known as the founder of the Devil Museum in Kaunas, was a painter of landscapes at home and abroad, as well as portraits and genre scenes. The sculptor Petras Rimša (1881–1961) worked in a variety of idioms, including Realism and Art Nouveau. He also made an extensive study of traditional woodcarving, and was particularly accomplished as a portrait medallist.

More obviously influenced by Čiurlionis's example were Petras Kalpokas (1880–1945), whose paintings marry Symbolist and Art Nouveau touches, and Kazys Šimonis (1887–1978), who began as a Symbolist but who later in his long life turned successively to Expressionism and Constructivism.

Standing somewhat apart is Mstislavas Dobužinskis (1875–1957), who is more commonly known by the Russian form of his name, Mstislav Dobuzhinsky. He had a globetrotting career as a scenographer, designing sets for more than 40 operas and plays for many of the great stages of the world - in London, Paris, Rome, Naples and New York, among others. In the early decades of the 20th century he also travelled widely in Lithuania itself, making numerous drawings and paintings of the country, especially its architecture.

The Jewish sculptor Jacques Lipchitz (1891–1973) had by far the most internationally successful career of any of the country's artists, though it is only courtesy of his Druskininkai birthplace that he can in any way be considered a Lithuanian. He emigrated to Paris long before Lithuania regained its independence, and the rest of his life was divided between France and America. His early works derive from the Cubists, but his reputation is largely based on the highly individualistic transparent openwork sculptures he began producing in the 1920s.

The grand old man of 20th-century Lithuanian art was Antanas Gudaitis (1904–89), who spent several years among the Paris avant-garde before returning home in 1933, becoming a founder member of the Union of Lithuanian Artists two years later. From 1944 until 1985 he was a professor at the State Art Institute, teaching nearly all of the country's young painters. Gudaitis's own works, which include landscapes, still lifes, portraits and figurative scenes, are marked by lyricism and strong colours. They show a debt to a wide variety of artistic influences, such as Expressionism, Abstraction and Art Deco.

Following Lithuania's loss of independence, several artists chose to go into exile in the United States. Vytautas Jonynas (1907–98) executed stained glass windows and large-scale sculptural works for several churches. Vytautas Kašuba (1915–97) likewise undertook ecclesiastical commissions, and also made classically inspired relief portraits, medallions, and humorous hollowed-out carvings. Jurgis Mačiūnas (1931–78), who anglicised his name to George Maciunas, was the founder of *Fluxus*, a somewhat jokey experimental movement of the 1960s which reacted against both abstract and traditional art. Another prominent exile was Antanas Mončys (1921–93), who settled in France, where he produced an output of strikingly tactile sculptures, which he encouraged viewers to handle.

Samuel Bak (b1933) was a precocious child artist, and many of the drawings he made while living in the Vilnius ghetto still survive in the collections of the city's Jewish Museum. He escaped from Lithuania in 1945, and has led a peripatetic life, residing in Germany, Israel, France, Italy, Switzerland and (currently) the United States. For a time, he painted in an abstract style, but is best known for representational paintings which show a clear debt to Surrealism, with the important difference that their underlying inspiration is memory rather than dreams. The lost world of Eastern European Jewry is a recurrent theme in these works.

Despite the influential role of the essentially non-political art of Gudaitis, Lithuania's indigenous artistic scene – and sculpture in particular – suffered throughout the communist years by the sterile dictates of the officially sponsored Socialist Realism. The best-known practitioner of the style was Gediminas Jakubonis (b1927), who made a statue of Lenin for Moscow's Ill'ich Square and, at the very end of the Soviet era, the monument to Adam Mickiewicz in Vilnius. There was one major dissident artist, the Franciscan mystic Vilius Orvydas (1952––92), whose highly idiosyncratic sculptural creations are largely concentrated in the garden he laid out on his family's farm of Gargždelė near Salantai.

Independence has brought in its wake a welcome revival of the visual arts and there are now artists working in all kinds of different styles, some of which (Surrealism for example) are quite new to the country. Sculptors have benefited from the many public commissions for monuments honouring past heroes. Towards the end of his life, Kašuba returned to Lithuania to design the statue to Grand Duke Gediminas in Vilnius.

Antanas Kmieliauskas (b1932) offers an updated version of the Italian Renaissance style in his sculptures and the fresco cycle for Vilnius University's bookshop, while Petras Repšys (b1940) presents a minutely detailed evocation of history and myth in his frescos for the same institution's Centre for Lithuanian Studies. Kęstutis Kasparavičius (b1955) has gained an international reputation for his whimsical illustrations for children's books. The sculptor Gintaras Karosas (b1968) has a preference for the grand manner, having created several spectacular conceptual works for the Open-Air Museum of the Centre of Europe, which he himself founded.

ARCHITECTURE

Lithuania's turbulent history has taken a huge toll on the country's architectural heritage, not least on buildings dating from before the 17th century. Early fortresses were of wood, and had understandably short life-spans. The technique of building in brick was imported from Kievan Rus, and three of the most important 14th-century castles – Trakai, Vilnius and Kaunas – still survive, though the first is largely a modern rebuild, while only fragments remain of the other two. In all three, water (whether a lake or a river) was an essential part of the defensive system.

Because of the late arrival of Christianity, there are no churches from earlier than the Gothic period, with the oldest being St Nicholas in Vilnius, which actually pre-dates the Christianisation of the country, having been built for the use of German merchants and artisans. Its Gothic brickwork style was adopted for all the churches built in the wake of the mass conversion of the nation in 1387, and for more than a century and a half afterwards. Of the Cathedral which was immediately constructed in Vilnius on the site of the main pagan temple, only the crypt remains. Thus the Vytautas Church in Kaunas is probably the oldest surviving intact church post-dating the adoption of Christianity. It was joined in the course of the 15th century by several other churches in the same city, the largest and most notable being that which is now the Cathedral. Also from this era are the churches in Trakai and Merkinė, and SS John in Vilnius, though all of these subsequently underwent considerable modification.

Traditional wooden buildings are a common sight in Lithuania: they can even be found within the centres of many large towns and cities, though the finest and most characteristic examples are mostly in rural communities. The style of these buildings has changed very little in centuries, though very few which still survive date back more than 300 years, and the vast majority are much younger than this.

When farmsteads are grouped in villages, the dwelling house normally faces the street. Behind it is an enclosed yard containing a number of structures, the most common being a well, a barn and one or two granaries. If there is only a single granary it is normally divided internally. Larger farms (which are particularly prevalent in Samogitia) may also have stables, kennels, a cow shed, a pigsty, a hen-house, a smoke-house and a bath-house. There is invariably a communal version of the last-named, usually located at the edge of the village beside a lake or a stream. Wooden farmsteads have a variety of different types of roofs, the oldest usually being hipped, the more recent saddled; these may be covered with thatch, shingles or tiles. Well-preserved agricultural villages and hamlets, whose architecture varies somewhat by region, can be found in the national parks of Dzūkija, Aukštaitija and Samogitia. Many fine redundant farmsteads can also be seen in the country's open-air museums, notably Rumšiškės, Telšiai and Kleboniškiai, where there is the bonus of being able to see some of the interiors.

The tradition of folk architecture in wood is also responsible for many fine churches, which were invariably designed and built by local craftsmen rather than professional architects. These are plainer than in many other countries of Central and Eastern Europe, usually having unadorned exterior walls and a ground-plan consisting of a rectangular nave with or without aisles and a projecting apse; the belfry is normally detached, and may double as a gateway to the churchyard. Some churches, however, adopt features from Baroque stone architecture, such as twin towers and façade pediments, while others have more complicated ground-plans. Even if the exterior is simple, the interior is almost always richly and colourfully decorated with altars and other furnishings. The most notable surviving wooden churches nearly all date from the 18th century, and include those at Stelmužė, Beržoras, Palūšė, Plateliai, Prieniai, Smilgiai, Seda and Alsėdžiai.

By far the finest achievement of Lithuanian Gothic is the ensemble of the Bernardine Friary in Vilnius, which was built in the highly decorative final phase of the style in the late 15th century and early 16th century. Particularly outstanding is the fabulously ornate façade of the Church of St Anne, a dazzling exercise in patterned brickwork. The Perkūnas House in Kaunas is a rare surviving example of a secular building in a similar manner.

Italian architects working at the court of Zygmunt the Old introduced the Renaissance to Lithuania in the early 16th century. Although the royal palace they built in Vilnius has not survived, its appearance is well documented, and it is currently in the process of being reconstructed. Otherwise, the city's only major Renaissance legacy is the Church of St Michael, begun towards the end of the century to serve as a mausoleum for the Sapieha family. Surviving examples of Renaissance architecture are similarly thin on the ground elsewhere in the country. Two early 17th-century buildings which are nominally in the style, the Bernardine Friaries in Kretinga and Tytuvėnai, both retain archaic Gothic features, whereas the contemporaneous Cathedral in Šiauliai already has Baroque touches. Early Protestant churches, with their emphasis on clarity and simplicity of design, adopt a much purer approach. In Kėdainiai, there is a fascinating early 17th-century pairing of a small Lutheran Church and a much larger and grander Reformed Church which comes close to being Mannerist in style. The Protestant branch of the Radvila family, who controlled Kėdainiai, also built a Renaissance castle in their other main seat of Biržai. Likewise from the early 17th century is Vilnius University's Great Courtyard, the country's sole example of full-blown Mannerism.

By this time, the Baroque, the architectural style which was to become most characteristic of Lithuania, was already firmly established, having been introduced, ironically enough, by the Catholic branch of the Radvilas, who sponsored the building of the Jesuit Church at Nesvyžius (now Nesvizh in Belarus) in the 1580s. This was based on the design of the Order's mother church, Il Gesù in Rome, and was built by the Italian Giovanni Maria Bernardoni. The same architect may also have provided the plans for the first of what was to become a host of Baroque monasteries in Vilnius, the Jesuit St Casimir. This was built in the first decade of the 17th century by a local man, Jan Prochowitz, and differs from its Roman model in having twin façade towers, a favourite motif in Lithuanian architecture. Another Italian, Constantino Tencalla (c1590–1646), was responsible for two other important examples of early Baroque in the capital – the towerless Carmelite Convent of St Teresa and the domed Chapel of St Casimir in the Cathedral.

The High Baroque style was imported, again from Rome, immediately after the conclusion of the mid-17th-century wars with Sweden and Russia. Thanks to the patronage of the Pacas (Pac) family, two spectacular projects – the Camaldolese Monastery at Pažaislis in the outskirts of Kaunas, and the Church of SS Peter and Paul in Vilnius – were inaugurated. Both feature a twin-towered church with a massive central dome, and an overall unity of architecture and decoration (with frescos predominating in the former, stuccowork sculptures in the latter). The Pacs additionally commissioned a splendid mansion for themselves in Vilnius. Pietro Putini, one of the architects of Pažaislis, also designed the Trinitarian Convent at Trinapolis, a suburb of Vilnius, which adopts the extreme curvaceous forms pioneered in Rome by Francesco Borromini. Around the same time, the Sapieha family sponsored another monastery for the same order in the inner suburb of Antakalnis, and this was built in tandem with their own estate mansion alongside. One other High Baroque building worthy of special note is the cathedral in Varniai.

During the last and most ornate phase of Baroque in the 18th century, the main influences on Lithuanian architecture came from Central Europe rather than Italy. The Dominican Priory in Liškiava is a fine early example of this tendency, which was at its most pronounced in mid-century Vilnius. There, an outstanding architect of Silesian origin, Jan Krzysztof Glaubitz (c1700–67), carried out major transformations of a number of existing buildings, including the Church of SS John, the Benedictine Convent of St Catherine, the Missionaries' Monastery, the Orthodox Monastery of the Holy Spirit and the Basilian Monastery of the Holy Trinity, to which he added a magnificent entrance gateway.

Vilnius's main secular building of the period is the university observatory. Later ecclesiastical projects in the city include the Calvary Church and the remodelling of the Dominican Church of the Holy Spirit, whose interiors are richly decorated in a more or less Rococo manner. Important late Baroque churches elsewhere in Lithuania are the Bernardine Friary, now the Cathedral, in Telšiai, and the Church of the Visitation in Žemaičių Kalvarija, which shows a transition to the emerging Neo-Classical style. The remodelled Town Hall in Kaunas, with its soaring tower, is a masterly example of the secular architecture of the time.

Full-blooded Neo-Classicism was introduced quite early from revolutionary France. Indeed, Lithuania soon produced an outstanding practitioner of the style in Laurynas Gucevičius, otherwise known as Wawrzyniec Guciewicz (1753–98), who studied in Paris as well as Vilnius and Rome. Before his untimely death, he carried out a radical remodelling of Vilnius Cathedral and designed a splendid new Town Hall for the capital. The Neo-Classical style continued to flourish in Vilnius until well into the 19th century, when the leading architect was Karol Podczaszyński (1790–1860), whose finest work is the Reformed Church.

Many Neo-Classical manor-houses were built for aristocratic landowners in the Lithuanian countryside during the Tsarist period, though in the later years of the 19th century tastes became somewhat more eclectic, and buildings were erected in a variety of Historicist styles. Orthodox churches were constructed all over the country, partly to cater for Russian immigrants and partly in an unsuccessful attempt to wean Lithuanians away from Catholicism. These were all built in a very traditional manner, and there are no especially distinguished examples.

In the two decades prior to World War I, an increasing sense of national awareness led to the building of bloated Neo-Gothic brick churches in many towns, including Anykščiai, Salantai and Palanga, though these cannot really be said to have much in common with their medieval predecessors, on which they were supposedly modelled. Neo-Baroque churches were also built during this period, and these are generally more successful at imitating the appearance of their models.

The restoration of Lithuanian independence in 1918 led to attempts to forge a distinctive national architectural style, especially in the 'temporary' capital of Kaunas, where many prestige projects were initiated. Because the new state lacked financial resources, these stressed functionality, but also aimed to be pleasing to the eye. The dominant architect of the period was Mykolas Songaila (1874–1941), the head of the Department of Architecture at Kaunas University, who designed highly aesthetic banks for several Lithuanian towns.

During the communist period, housing was the main architectural preoccupation, and all the cities of Lithuania became ringed with vast high-rise suburbs. Fortunately, the country is noticeably lacking in any of the huge and ugly public showpiece buildings of the Stalinist era which disfigure so many places which were in the Soviet sphere. The one big prestige project of the era, the rebuilding of the ruined Island Castle in Trakai, was a surprising choice to say the least, given that its nationalistic and feudalistic connotations stood so squarely at odds with the prevailing ideology. Since independence, the restoration and adaptation of old buildings have been the main priorities, rather than any brand new projects.

LITERATURE

Lithuania's earliest literature dates back to the 15th century, and is in the form of manuscript chronicles which recount ancient legends and pagan mythology, as well as the lives, loves and wars of the Grand Dukes. Although their purpose was to provide a written definition of Lithuania's statehood, and thereby preserve the memory of the past, the chronicles were not written in Lithuanian – which was, after all, the language of only a minority of the inhabitants of the sprawling Grand Duchy – but rather in the old Slavonic language of Kievan Rus.

The emergence of Lithuanian as a written language began in the mid-16th century. Ironically, this happened not in Lithuania itself, but in the Duchy of Prussia, which was founded in 1525 as the successor state to that of the Teutonic Knights. Nominally subject to the Polish crown, Prussia had a substantial Lithuanian community but was ruled and dominated by Germans. From the outset Prussia was a bastion of the Protestant faith, one of whose key tenets was the use of the vernacular in worship. The foundation of Königsberg University in 1542 provided a stimulus for an increase in the output of printed texts, and in 1547 a Lithuanian version of the Protestant Catechism by Martinas Mažvydas (1510–63) was published, to be followed two years later by a hymn book compiled by the same author. Jonas Bretkunas (1535–1602) made the first translation of the Bible into Lithuanian, but this remained in manuscript only, kept at Königsberg University Library.

As the vanguard of the Counter-Reformation, it was the Jesuits of Vilnius who were responsible for the first Lithuanian books published in Lithuania itself, beginning in 1595 with a translation of the Roman Catholic Catechism from Polish by Mikalojus Daukša (1527–1613). Back in Prussia, the first Lithuanian grammar, the *Grammatica Lituanica*, was published in 1653 by Danielius Kleinas (1609–66), the pastor of Tilsit.

Remarkably, the first major poem in Lithuanian, the four-part epic *The Seasons* by Kristijonas Donelaitis (1714–80), is a masterpiece of international standing which remains to this day the greatest piece of literature ever written in the language. A Lutheran clergyman, Donelaitis spent most of his career in the obscure Prussian village of Tolminkiemis. His poem, written in strict classical hexameters, vividly describes the work, recreations, beliefs, superstitions, festivals and (not least) eating habits of the Lithuanian peasants who made up his congregation, using the changing seasons of the natural world as a backdrop. The many didactic passages clearly originated as sermons, and it seems that the epic was never intended for publication. It survived by pure chance, and was not published until 1818, in an abridged German translation which won the admiration of Goethe.

One of the greatest poets of European Romanticism, Adam Mickiewicz (1798–1855) is claimed as one of their own by the Lithuanians (who know him as Adomas Mickevičius), though he wrote solely in Polish and was born in what is now Belarus. Despite living after its demise, Mickiewicz was the poet *par excellence* of the Polish–Lithuanian Commonwealth, considering himself to be a Lithuanian at a time when this was far from incompatible with an acceptance of the primacy of Polish language and culture. His masterpiece, *Pan Tadeusz*, is considered Poland's national epic, although it begins with a florid invocation to Lithuania, is sub-titled *The Last Foray in Lithuania*, and has as its subject the false hopes Napoleon inspired among the Lithuanian gentry. Both of his works in a Byronic vein, *Grażyna* and *Konrad Wallenrod*, use the backdrop of medieval Lithuania's wars with the Teutonic Knights.

The struggle to keep the Lithuanian language alive during the period of Tsarist rule was begun by Simonas Daukantas (1793–1860), who made the first systematic study of the nation's ethnography, customs and beliefs in *The Character of Ancient Lithuanian*s. He also formulated rules for Lithuanian grammar, compiled dictionaries and collected folklore. The other key figures in the movement were two Catholic priests, both of whom subsequently became bishops. Motiejus Valančius (1801–75), whose prolific output includes both serious spiritual works and popular didactic tales such as *Palangos Juzė*, also played an important role in combating the Tsarist ban on the printing of books in the Latin alphabet in 1863, which meant that Lithuanian texts had to be published in Prussia and then smuggled into the country. His career is described in more detail in the feature on page 202. Antanas Baranauskas (1834–1902) wrote the lyric epic *The Anykščiai Grove* (sometimes called *The Forest of Anykščiai*) – which is both a haunting description of nature and a lament for Lithuania's plight – while still a seminary student, and he then went on to compose many popular patriotic songs and hymns.

As founder of *Aušra*, the first Lithuanian-language newspaper, Jonas Basanavičius (1851–1927) is considered the father-figure of the nationalist movement whose activities paved the way for the regaining of independence. Both Basanavičius and Vincas Kudirka (1858–99), founder of the magazine *Varpas*, were practising doctors who had to fit their literary activities into their spare time. Among Kudirka's slender poetic output is the song which subsequently became Lithuania's national anthem. Kudirka also wrote satirical short stories, notably *Recollections of a Lithuanian Bridge*, in which a bridge takes on a persona and narrates the events which take place on it. Lithuania's finest woman writer, Julija Beniuševičiūtė-Žymantienė (1845–1921), known as Žemaitė, was another prominent nationalist.

The great poet of the Lithuanian national revival was Jonas Mačiulis (1862–1932), a Catholic priest who adopted the pseudonym of Maironis. His works include the collection *Voices of Spring*, which glorifies the Lithuanian countryside; he also wrote ballads, satires and a trilogy of verse dramas about medieval Grand Dukes – *The Death of Kęstutis*, *Vytautas with the Crusaders* and *Vytautas the Great*.

When the ban on Lithuanian texts was lifted in 1904, the national literature quickly became much more diversified. Among the leading authors of the period were Vilius Storasta (1868–1957), known as Vydūnas, a Symbolist dramatist; Juozas Tumas (1869–1933), known as Vaižgantas, a Neo-Romantic who was also an influential literary critic; and Jonas Biliūnas (1879–1907) and Antanas Žukauskas (1882–1957), known as Vienuolis, both short story writers in the Realist tradition.

Vincas Krėvė (1882–1954) wrote historical dramas and published a collection of legends of his native Dainava land prior to a disastrous spell as foreign minister immediately after the Soviet occupation in 1940 in which he unwittingly found himself cast in the role of a stooge. He escaped to America, where he wrote a Biblical epic, *The Sons of Heaven and Earth*. The Impressionist Ignas Šeinius (1889–1959), who pursued a dual literary and diplomatic career, is principally remembered for the satirical novel *The Rejuvenation of Siegfried Immerselbe*. Published in 1934 (though not translated into English until 1965), this provided a remarkably astute critique of Nazism long before the world at large had grasped its true nature. Vincas Mykolaitis-Putinas (1893–1967) was a defrocked priest whose trilogy *In the Shadow of Altars* is loosely based on his own life story. His other novels include *The Crisis*, which is dedicated to independent Lithuania, and *The Rebels*, about the unsuccessful 1863 rebellion. Balys Sruoga (1896–1947) began his literary career as a Symbolist, but is best-known for his concentration-camp memoirs, *The Forest of the Gods*, which present a very different approach from the Jewish emphasis characteristic of most Holocaust literature.

Having been born in Lithuania and possessing mixed Polish–Lithuanian parentage, the winner of the 1980 Nobel Prize for Literature, Czesław Miłosz (1911–2004), deserves to be mentioned, though he wrote in Polish and went into exile in 1951, adopting American nationality in 1970. He was primarily a poet, but also wrote two novels, one of which, *The Issa Valley*, is set in rural Lithuania. Among his many trenchant works of non-fiction are *Native Realm*, an unconventional autobiography of his early life, which includes a stimulating analysis of the Polish–Lithuanian dichotomy, and *The Captive Mind*, a study of the corruption of intellectuals by totalitarian governments, which concludes with a chapter on the Soviet occupation of the Baltic states.

Literature stagnated even more than most other forms of creative activity in Lithuania during the Soviet period, but has revived well. That said, the only contemporary writer in the Lithuanian language to have gained any sort of international reputation is the poet Tomas Venclova (b1937), who has spent much of his life in the United States, teaching Slavonic languages and literatures at Yale University. *Vilnius Review* (formerly *Vilnius*), the English-language magazine of the Lithuanian Writers' Union, offers a chance to sample contemporary Lithuanian poetry and prose, and often features translated excerpts from some of the country's greatest literary classics. The best place to obtain a copy is in the Littera or Pilies bookshops in Vilnius (see page 88).

5

Practical Information

WHEN AND WHERE TO GO

CLIMATE AND SEASONS Lithuania has a temperate climate, which is kept relatively mild for its northerly location by the influence of an arm of the Gulf Stream. In the more easterly regions of the country, the climate takes on continental characteristics, and is usually several degrees colder than in the coastal areas – except at the height of summer, when it is marginally warmer.

Winters are long. Typically, the first frosts arrive in the Dzūkija region towards the end of September, and in Vilnius two or three weeks later. However, it is far from unknown for them to arrive in the capital before the beginning of October, though it is generally not until the end of that month that they reach the coast. November usually sees the first snowfalls and thereafter large parts of the country are under a more-or-less permanent cover of snow until March. Average temperatures during the winter months are several degrees below freezing (–5°C/23°F is a normal figure for January), though it is only during the harshest spells of weather, which do not occur every year, that they plummet to lows of –40°C/–40°F.

Spring is a contrastingly short season. Indeed, in some years it is virtually non-existent; winter woollies might still be necessary until well into May, when an abrupt change in temperature means that these can immediately be discarded in favour of light summer wear. A more typical pattern, however, is for the entire month of April to be an unpredictable and ever-changing mix of cold and mild days.

Summer usually lasts from mid-May until late August and, with the twin benefits of (usually) warm weather and long days, it is the obvious time to visit Lithuania. There are over 18 hours of daylight in June; in July, the warmest month, temperatures average around 17°C/62°F on the coast, 18°C/64°F in Vilnius, but can reach highs of around 35°C/95°F. Except during the hottest spells, summer evenings can be cool, while showers or more persistent periods of rain are also to be expected, making it advisable to carry a raincoat or umbrella at all times.

As nearly all Lithuanians take their main annual vacation at the height of the summer, causing severe congestion in the most popular holiday areas, it is well worth considering the autumn as an alternative time to visit. This is by far the most beautiful season, with much of the countryside – and the ample parkland in cities such as Vilnius and Kaunas – a wonderful blaze of colour throughout September and October. The downsides are the progressive shortening of the days, and the noticeable drop in temperature which is evident long before the first frosts start to appear.

HIGHLIGHTS

Vilnius, and in particular its magnificent Old Town, is at the top of most people's places to visit, and rightly so. Its legacy of historic monuments surpasses that of the whole of the rest of the country, and it also offers by far the best choice of live entertainment, shopping and places to eat and drink. There are enough diversions to keep even the most demanding visitor occupied for a week or more.

A visit to Kaunas, the second city, is an essential supplement, not least because it is so strikingly different from the capital. In addition to another very pretty Old Town, it has several quirky visitor attractions and a group of museums rivalling those of Vilnius. Lithuania's other cities are far less obviously tourist magnets, though Klaipėda has a certain enigmatic appeal while Šiauliai's name has become indelibly associated with the nearby Hill of Crosses, one of the country's strangest, most moving and most famous sites.

Just as Vilnius is Lithuania's outstanding cultural draw, so is the Curonian Spit National Park, with its awesome moving and stabilised sand dunes, its undisputed scenic highlight. Of the country's other national parks, the only one that sees many foreign visitors is Trakai, which differs from the others in having as its primary function the preservation of the monumental heritage of the eponymous town, rather than the landscape. Not the least of the attractions of the remaining national parks – Dzūkija, Aukštaitija and Samogitia – is that they are well off the beaten tourist track. In addition to much beautiful scenery, they all feature well-preserved villages where traditional rural lifestyles are still the norm. Kernavė, the country's only cultural reservation, is likely to attract an increasing numbers of visitors, now that it has gained admission to the UNESCO World Heritage list.

The noisy, animated Baltic beach resort of Palanga is the favourite holiday destination of the Lithuanians themselves, and no visit to the country is quite complete without seeing it during the crowded summer season. There are also a few quieter alternatives for a seaside break, notably Nida and Juodkrantė, which both lie within the Curonian Spit National Park. For a really relaxing holiday, however, the place to go is the spa of Druskininkai located in the far south of the country, on one of the most majestic stages of the River Nemunas.

If visiting in high summer, the short cruise on the Nemunas from Druskininkai, and the various boat trips available from Nida, should on no account be missed. One other transport facility worth making a special detour to travel on is the narrow-gauge railway from Panevėžys to Anykščiai. Many other rewarding yet seldom-visited places are to be found all over the country, and are described in each of the following chapters.

TOUR OPERATORS

UK

Baltics and Beyond 1 Amy St, Bingley, W Yorks BD16 4NE; ☎ 0845 094 2125; e info@balticsandbeyond.com; www.balticsandbeyond.com

Baltic Holidays 40 Princess St, Manchester M1 6DE; ☎ 0845 070 5711; e info@balticholidays.com; www.balticholidays.com. Until recently this was the only UK travel company to deal solely with the Baltic states, but it now covers adjacent countries as well.

Regent Holidays 15 John St, Bristol BS1 2HR; ☎ 0845 877 3317; e regent@regent-holidays.co.uk; www.regent-holidays.co.uk, www.holidays-in-baltic.co.uk. In addition to making flight & hotel bookings, the UK's pioneering Baltic specialist offers short breaks in Vilnius, various guided tours of Lithuania & the other Baltic states, & tailor-made itineraries for independent travellers.

Specialised Tours 4 Copthorne Bank, Copthorne, Crawley, West Sussex RH10 3QX; ☎ 01342 712785; f 01342 717042; e info@specialisedtours.com; www.specialisedtours.com. Offers package tours to Vilnius & other destinations in the Baltic states.

USA

Union Tours 245 Fifth Avenue, New York, NY 10016; ☎ 212 683 9500; f 212 683 9511. This company has specialised in travel to the Baltic region since 1931.

Vytis Tours 40–24 235th Street, Douglaston, New York 11363; ☎ 718 423 6161; e tours@ vytistours.com; www.vytistours.com. A dependable firm with over a quarter of a century's experience in travel to Lithuania.

RED TAPE

A valid passport should be carried at all times. Huge progress has been made towards relaxing visa requirements since the fall of the USSR. Currently, citizens of the following countries do **not** need a visa to enter Lithuania: all EU member states, plus Andorra, Argentina, Armenia, Australia, Brazil, Brunei, Canada, Chile, Costa Rica, Croatia, El Salvador, Guatemala, Holy See, Honduras, Hong Kong, Iceland, Israel, Japan, Liechtenstein, Macao, Malaysia, Mexico, Monaco, New Zealand, Nicaragua, Norway, Panama, Paraguay, San Marino, Singapore, South Korea, Switzerland, USA, Uruguay, Venezuela.

Nationals of all other countries should acquire a valid visa from a Lithuanian embassy (see below) prior to entering the country. Except for citizens of EU states, all foreign nationals, whether or not they require a visa, need to apply for a residence or work permit if planning an uninterrupted stay of more than 90 days. If travelling onwards from Lithuania to Belarus or Russia (including the Kaliningrad *oblast*), the relevant visa(s) must be obtained beforehand.

Travellers needing Lithuanian visas who return to Lithuania from Kaliningrad or Belarus should ensure that they have a double-entry Lithuanian visa.

Note that visa requirements are subject to change and the latest situation should be checked carefully before departure as they can be influenced by various factors, such as a deterioration in diplomatic relations with another country. Details can always be found on the website of the Lithuanian Ministry of Foreign Affairs: www.urm.lt.

LITHUANIAN EMBASSIES Lithuania maintains the foreign embassies listed below; note that some serve more than one country. The telephone and fax numbers give firstly the country code if calling from abroad (which needs, of course, to be preceded by the international access number used by the country from which the call is made), followed after a space by the city code if required (which, if calling within the country itself, usually needs to be preceded by the relevant access number, normally 0).

Belarus Zacharova 68, 220029 Minsk; ☎ +375 17 2852 448; f +375 17 2853 337; e amb.by@urm.lt; www.by.mfa.lt

Canada 130 Albert St, Suite 204, Ottawa, Ontario K1P 5G4; ☎ +1 613 567 5458; f +1 613 567 5315; e amb.ca@urm.lt; lithuanianembassy.ca

Estonia Uus tn. 15, Tallinn, EE0100; ☎ +372 616 4991; f +372 641 2013; e amb.ee@urm.lt, www.ee.mfa.lt

Finland Rauhankatu 13a, 00170 Helsinki; ☎ +358 9 684 4880; f +358 9 6844 8820; e amb.fi@urm.lt; www.fi.mfa.lt

France 22 Bd de Courcelles, 75017 Paris; ☎ +33 140 545050; f +33 140 545075; e chancellerie@ amb.lituanie.lt; www.fr.mfa.lt

Germany Charitestrasse 9, 10117 Berlin; ☎ +49 30 8906810; f +49 30 89068115; e info@botschaft-litauen.de; www.de.mfa.lt

Ireland 90 Merrion Rd, Ballsbridge, Dublin 4; ☎ +353 1 6688292; f +353 1 6781025; e amb.ie@urm.lt; www. ie.mfa.lt

Israel 8 Shaul Hameleh Bd, Tel Aviv 64733; ☎ +972 3 6958 685; f +972 3 6958 691; e amb.il@urm.lt; www.il.mfa.lt. Also serves South Africa & Cyprus.

Latvia Rupniecibos iela 24, LV-1010 Riga; ☎ +371 2 321519; f +371 2 321589; e lt@apollo.lv; www.lv.mfa.lt

Poland al Ujazdowskie 14, 00-478 Warsaw; ☎ +48 22 625 3368; f +48 22 625 3440; e amb.pl@urm.lt; www.lietuva.pl

Russia 10 Borisoglebskij per, 121069 Moscow; ☎ +7 095 785 8605/705 8625; f +7 095 7858600; e amb.ru@urm.lt; www.ru.mfa.lt. There are also consultates in the following locations: Proletarskaja 133, Kaliningrad; ☎ +7 401 295 7688; f +7 011 295 6838;

e kons.kalinigradas@urm.lt; www.consulate-kaliningrad.mfa.lt; Ryleyeva 37, 191123 St Petersburg; ☎ +7 812 327 0230; f 7 812 327 2615; e st.peterburgas@peterstar.lt; www.consulate-stpetersburg.mfa.lt
Ukraine 21 Buslivska, 010901 Kiev; ☎ +380 44 2540920; f +380 44 2540928; e amb.ua@urm.lt; www.ua.mfa.lt.
UK 84 Gloucester Pl, London W1U 6AU; ☎ +44 20 7486 6401/2; f +44 20 7486 6403; e amb.uk@urm.lt; www.uk.mfa.lt

USA 4590 MacArthur Bd NW, Suite 200, Washington, DC 20007-4226; ☎ +1 202 231 5860; f +1 202 328 0466; e amb.us@urm.lt; www.ltembassyus.org. Also serves Mexico. There are consulates in the following locations: 211 E Ontario, Suite 1500, Chicago, IL 60611; ☎ +1 312 397 0382; f +1 312 397 0385; e kons.cikaga@urm.lt; www.konsulatas.org; 420 Fifth Av, New York, NY 10018; ☎ +1 212 354 7840; f +1 212 354 7849; e kons.niujorkas@urm.lt; www.consny.org

There are Lithuanian embassies or diplomatic missions in many other countries. Full details of these are published on the web at www.urm.lt.

FOREIGN EMBASSIES IN LITHUANIA These are listed in the Vilnius chapter, see page 87.

CUSTOMS REGULATIONS If a visit to Lithuania forms part of a journey within the EU, it is (with few exceptions) possible to import or export goods for personal use without incurring excise duties (eg: 90 litres of wine or 110 litres of beer, but note that cigarettes are limited to 200). With non-EU countries, the maximum amount of tobacco that can be imported duty-free is 250g (200 cigarettes, 100 cigarillos or 50 cigars), while the alcohol limits are one litre of spirits or two litres of wine or beer. The importation of firearms, ammunition, explosives, drugs and pornography is strictly forbidden.

The main restriction on exports concerns works of art which are more than 50 years old. In order to obtain permission, it is necessary to take the work in question, along with two photographs of it, to the Committee of Cultural Heritage, Šnipiškių 3, Vilnius, ☎ 5) 2724005 or 2724113, who will determine its value and the duty payable. There are also regulations covering the export of amber, though pieces worth under 1,000Lt can be exported duty-free. It is necessary to complete a customs declaration form at the border if taking in or out of Lithuania cash in any currencies with a value in excess of €10,000.

GETTING THERE

✈ **BY AIR** The most convenient way to reach Lithuania from almost any other country in the world is by air. Vilnius is the arrival point for the overwhelming majority of flights, though there are small international airports at Kaunas and Palanga.

The operator with the widest choice of routes is Lithuanian Airlines (*www.flylal.com*), which flies once or twice daily from many major European airports, including London Gatwick. Its fares, which were once higher than most competitors and seemingly geared towards Lithuanians (with return flights from Vilnius costing far less than those in the opposite direction), have become more reasonable. Indeed, it even anticipated competition from budget carriers by introducing bargain one-way fares.

The challenge was duly taken up by Ryanair (*UK* ☎ *0871 246 0000; www.ryanair.com*), which now offers daily flights to Kaunas from London Stansted, and others from Glasgow Prestwick (replacing that from Liverpool), Dublin and Shannon. Ryanair has a much larger base at Rīga, which is only a bus ride of a couple of hours from the northern Lithuanian cities of Šiauliai and Panevėžys;

there are flights from London Stansted, Bristol, East Midlands, Liverpool, Glasgow Prestwick, Dublin and Shannon. In the past BA (*UK* ✎ *0870 850 9850; www.britishairways.com*) has flown to both Vilnius and Rīga, but is not currently serving either of these airports.

The Latvian carrier Air Baltic (*www.airbaltic.com*) offers an ever-growing number of flights to Vilnius from various European cities, including daily from London Gatwick. Its parent company SAS (*UK* ✎ *0870 607 27727; www.scandanavian.net*) has a wide range of options for travellers from the British Isles, with flights on a once- or twice-daily basis from London Heathrow, Manchester, Edinburgh, Glasgow and Dublin via Copenhagen or Stockholm. They also fly daily from Copenhagen to Palanga.

Other possibilities, which are often circuitous but not necessarily more expensive, are to fly with Austrian Air (*UK* ✎ *0870 124 2625; www.aua.com*) via Vienna; with Czech Airlines (*UK* ✎ *0870 444 3747; www.czechairlines.com*) via Prague; with Finnair (*UK* ✎ *0870 241 4411; www.finnair.com*) via Helsinki; with LOT (*UK* ✎ *0845 601 0949; www.lot.com*) via Warsaw; or with Lufthansa (*UK* ✎ *0870 8377 747; www.lufthansa.com*) via Frankfurt.

There are no direct flights to Lithuania from North America, but Lufthansa (via Frankfurt), SAS and Finnair all offer attractive deals from a variety of cities which involve one change only. They also offer the advantage of serving the other Baltic capitals.

For fully up-to-date information on services, as well as lower fares than the airlines are likely to offer if approached directly, it is best to contact a travel agent specialising in the Baltic countries (see overleaf). Alternatively, search and booking facilities are available on several online sites, including www.cheapflights.co.uk (in US: www.cheapflights.com), www.ebookers.com, www.expedia.co.uk (in US: expedia.com), www.lastminute.com and www.opodo.co.uk.

BY TRAIN Lithuania is not covered by Eurail or Inter-Rail passes, and travelling there by train from Western Europe is likely to cost at least as much as a flight, which is only worth doing if stopovers are made *en route*. The principal means of access by rail used to be the Berlin–Warsaw–Vilnius–St Petersburg express, whose route included a short stretch within Belarus which necessitated the purchase of an extortionately priced transit visa in both directions. However, this service does not currently operate. Instead, there is one train between Warsaw and the Lithuanian frontier town of Šeštokai, from where there are direct connections to and from Vilnius via Kaunas. There is currently only one direct daily train in each direction linking Lithuania and Latvia. The website www.litrail.lt gives all services in English.

BY BUS It is a straightforward matter to reach Lithuania by bus from Estonia or Latvia. The same is also true of Poland, even if the most frequent and convenient means of doing so is directly from Warsaw, rather than, as was once the case, from the towns near the Lithuanian border in the far northeast of the country.

On the other hand, the journey from Western Europe is a gruelling one which can take up to two full days and nights – as is the case from the UK – and it is doubtful if any savings really outweigh the discomfort and inconvenience which must be endured. Plenty of Lithuanians seem undeterred, however: services to and from Germany are sometimes booked out weeks in advance. The operator with the widest choice of routes is the umbrella organization known as Eurolines (*www.eurolines.co.uk*), which offers daily services from London Victoria to Warsaw, from where there are connecting services (after a wait of 3–4 hours) to Vilnius. A direct service from London, with connections to and from Dublin, is run thrice weekly by the Latvian company Ecolines (*www.ecolines.lv or ecolines.lt*), which also serves many other European destinations.

⚓ BY FERRY Klaipėda, Lithuania's only commercial maritime harbour, is linked by ferries to several German and Swedish ports. For information, see page 219.

✚ HEALTH AND SAFETY

MEDICAL CARE AND PRECAUTIONS Lithuanian standards of medical care still lag behind those of the West, though the gap is narrowing. The only hospital in the country (or in any of the Baltic states) which offers a Western-style service is the Baltic–American Clinic in Vilnius (see page 86), which is expensive but does accept insurance policies. Otherwise, embassies should be able to recommend English-speaking doctors, but in the case of serious illness it may be better, if possible, to return home. However, rich Lithuanians do not generally see any need to seek their medical treatment outside the country.

There are few obvious health hazards in Lithuania, other than those encountered anywhere else in Europe. However, it is advisable to be up to date with tetanus/diphtheria, polio and hepatitis A vaccinations. For longer trips or for those working in special circumstances then hepatitis B (in hospitals or with children) and/or rabies vaccine (with animals or for those who are more than 24 hours from medical help) would be wise. Ideally both the hepatitis B and rabies course entails three doses of vaccine which can be taken over a minimum of 21 days if time is short.

If you are planning on visiting deep-forested areas outside the capital during the summer months you should consult your doctor or travel clinic tick-borne encephalitis. The vaccine is issued on a named-patient basis in the UK and is sometimes hard to come by. Whether or not you are vaccinated before travel, you should do everything you can to protect yourself against ticks. Use tick repellents, wear long sleeved clothing, a hat and tuck trousers into boots. At the end of the day it is important to check yourself for ticks, or better still get someone else to do it for you as they are small and easy to miss. For those travelling with children, in particular check their hair as ticks have a habit of falling off tree branches – about head height for some! Ticks should ideally be removed as soon as possible as leaving ticks on the body increases the chance of infection. They should be removed with special tick tweezers that can be bought in good travel shops. Failing that you can use your finger nails by grasping the tick as close to your body as possible and pull steadily and firmly away at right angles to your skin. The tick will then come away complete as long as you do not jerk or twist. If possible douse the wound with alcohol (any spirit will do) or iodine. Irritants (eg: Olbas oil) or lit cigarettes are to be discouraged since they can cause the ticks to regurgitate and therefore increase the risk of disease. It is best to get a travelling companion to check you for ticks and if you are travelling with small children remember to check their heads, and particularly behind the ears. An area of spreading redness around the bite site, or a rash or fever coming on a few days or more after the bite, should stimulate a trip to the doctor.

As is always the case when travelling, it is advisable to carry a basic medical kit containing scissors, bandages, antiseptic creams, aspirin and the like. In summer, it is a good idea to supplement this with insect repellent; mosquitoes can be a particular nuisance, as can ticks (which may also be a health hazard) in forest areas.

Bathing in the Baltic Sea carries a slight health risk because of the presence of chemicals and untreated sewage, though this deters very few Lithuanians. Tap water is supposedly safe to drink throughout the country, but is best avoided, particularly in Vilnius, where it often takes on an alarming brownish tinge; moreover, the low cost of mineral water and other soft drinks makes drinking tap water a totally false economy. As Lithuanian food is generally very wholesome, few visitors contract stomach bugs.

There are reasonably well-stocked pharmacies in every town of any size, and in the major cities many have long opening hours, with one staying open round the clock. Quick-service opticians have started to appear in recent years, so it is now possible to get replacement glasses within a couple of hours. None the less, it is advisable to bring a spare pair.

TRAVEL CLINICS AND HEALTH INFORMATION A full list of current travel clinic websites worldwide is available from the International Society of Travel Medicine on www.istm.org. For other journey preparation information, consult www.tripprep.com. Information about various medications may be found on www.emedicine.com.

CRIME Lithuania is generally considered a safe place to visit. Visitors from American cities in particular often comment on how little visible crime, or even threat of crime, there is; even in Vilnius or Kaunas there seems no need to be on constant guard against the threat of pickpockets. Muggings of foreign tourists are rare enough to be treated as front-page news by national newspapers, and are also likely to make television bulletins. However, it is advisable to take the usual precautions, such as avoiding dimly lit city streets at night, or bars frequented by prostitutes and gangsters, and not flaunting valuables in crowded environments such as rush-hour trolleybuses and open-air markets.

A couple of riders also need to be added. Firstly, there is a racist undercurrent at the fringes of Lithuanian society, which needs be understood as a by-product of half a century of Russian oppression and closure to other outside influences. The Russian minority is the main target of this hatred, which is usually carried out by skinhead gangs, though there have also been occasional violent and irrational attacks on others who stand out from the crowd for any reason at all, such as having a different colour of skin.

Secondly, as is the case throughout the entire former Soviet bloc, there is a great deal of organised crime (ranging from drug trafficking via protection rackets to the buying-up of old state-run companies for a song by threatening other would-be investors with violence) perpetrated by mafia-style organisations of various nationalities. Thankfully, most foreign visitors never come into contact with any of these unsavoury characters, though anyone who is travelling by car (particularly a Western car) should beware that the theft of vehicles, and of vehicle parts, is a regular and lucrative activity for many mafia gangs.

GETTING AROUND

BY TRAIN The network of Lithuanian Railways (*www.litrail.lt*) is quite extensive, but badly needs a large amount of investment, which will probably have to be found abroad. Cutbacks implemented in recent years have meant that passenger services have been withdrawn from many lines. This is apparently a permanent arrangement in some cases, but in others the possibility of reinstatement has been left open. Although there are no longer any scheduled services on the Panevėžys–Anykščiai line, the only survivor of the once dense network of narrow-gauge railways (some of which are still shown on many maps), it is being preserved as a tourist attraction. Panevėžys, Lithuania's fifth city, is now served by just four passenger trains per day, while Alytus, the country's next largest town, has been removed from the network altogether. There are other unexpected gaps in the system. Palanga, which has an international airport, not to mention a huge flow of summertime visitors, is not served by trains; while there is no cross-country route parallel to the A1 between Kaunas and Klaipėda. In fact the rail link between these last two cities is twice as long in mileage terms, and currently has no direct services. However, the rail line between Vilnius and Klaipėda, while still much more circuitous than the road, is served by two daytime expresses in each direction which offer a quicker means than any bus of getting to some of the places *en route*, including Šiauliai.

The frequency of service on most lines is lower than might be expected, and has actually decreased over the past few years. Apart from a few express services which have soft couches which can be converted into beds, seating is generally on hard wooden benches. Even the express trains are very slow by Western standards, though at least they are inexpensive and, as a general rule, quite punctual. In the chapters which follow, the accounts of all the main towns include details of the frequency of their train connections, as per the 2007–08 national timetable.

🚌 BY BUS Buses form the mainstay of Lithuania's public transport system. Despite heavy cutbacks in the immediate aftermath of the fall of the Soviet Union and the subsequent mushrooming of car ownership, they still cover most of the country, with a few notable exceptions, such as the eastern part of the Dzūkija National Park (which is, however, served by trains). The frequency of service varies very widely, from one or more per hour on the most popular inter-city routes to just two or three per day in rural areas. As with the trains, details of bus services are included in the descriptions of the main towns, though it should be borne in mind that some of these are subject to seasonal variations, while others can change (either upwards or downwards) at the weekend – and sometimes on individual weekdays as well.

Comfortable modern coaches ply the cross-country express routes linking Vilnius and Kaunas with Klaipėda and Palanga, though these alternate with older and far less salubrious vehicles of the type which provide the overwhelming majority of services elsewhere. In the most thinly populated rural areas, ancient boneshaker buses remain in operation. The afore-mentioned express buses really are quite fast, their route being dual carriageway all the way, as is the route of the Vilnius–Panevėžys buses. However, many other routes are painfully slow, involving detours into every village along the road. For example, from Klaipėda it takes about as long to get to Telšiai by a normal bus as it does to reach Kaunas, which is three times further away, by an express.

The minibuses and microbuses which link some towns and ply the streets of the main cities are not for the faint-hearted, as passengers are crammed in with little concern for comfort or safety. For more information about municipal transport, see the travel sections in the accounts of the main cities.

🚗 BY CAR A car is of little use for visiting Lithuania's cities, where vehicle ownership is now at such levels that motorists face the same familiar problems as elsewhere in Europe, in particular a shortage of parking places in the city centres and traffic jams during the morning and evening rush hours. In both Vilnius and Kaunas, trolleybuses can pose problems for drivers unused to sharing the road with such vehicles, which are capable of swinging quite far out from the roadside. Although it now seems to be on the decline, an established menace, particularly in Vilnius, is the alarming number of young and not so young boy (and girl) racers, who labour under the delusion that macho driving habits – such as accelerating so fast that the tyres screech, ignoring traffic lights and cutting up other road users – are signs of maturity.

Outside the cities, on the other hand, a car can be invaluable for seeing places which are inaccessible or time-consuming to reach by public transport. The secondary roads are being improved all the time, though it is always necessary to keep a sharp lookout for pot-holes. It is also still quite common for asphalt to peter out without warning, giving way to gravel or a dirt track.

Driving with any alcohol whatsoever in the bloodstream is strictly forbidden. Speed limits, unless signs indicate otherwise, are 50km/h (31mph) in urban areas, 90km/h (56mph) on secondary roads, and 130km per hour (81mph) on highways, reduced to 110km/h (69mph) between October and March, except for the busy Vilnius–Kaunas section of the A1, where the limit is 100km/h (62mph) all year round. These are rigidly enforced by traffic police armed with radar guns, who hide away at the side of roads and are empowered to stop motorists for any reason they choose, and to enforce on-the-spot fines for transgressions.

A driving licence and the vehicle registration document should be carried at all times, along with a letter of permission to drive the vehicle from the owner, if this is not the same person as the driver. A passport or international driving licence needs to be carried as well if the holder's photograph does not feature on the driving licence (as is the case with some issued in the UK).

Taking a car into Lithuania has three main drawbacks: the long overland journey that is usually necessary to get there, the tiresome delays that can be encountered at border crossing points (though those with Poland and Latvia are now far less problematic, now that all three countries are in the EU), and the risk of damage or theft by mafia groups. In most circumstances, hiring a car in Lithuania is a far more attractive option, though it is also a very expensive one when compared with the cost of public transport; rates are upwards of 200Lt per day for an unlimited mileage deal. Purchasing fuel should no longer be a problem, though it makes sense to fill up the tank before going into remote areas, where pumps are scarce.

BY BIKE As a largely flat landscape punctuated by low hills, Lithuania is an ideal country for cycling. However, with the notable exception of the major cities, which have all introduced bike lanes, it lags a long way behind Scandinavia, Germany and the Netherlands in making any sort of special provision for cyclists. Nor are there any formal arrangements for taking bikes on public transport, though bus drivers will usually allow them to be stored alongside other baggage in the bowels of the vehicle, and they can be carried on trains if an extra ticket is purchased.

ELECTRICITY

Lithuanian electricity works on the standard continental system (220V and round two-pin plugs).

$ MONEY

CURRENCY In 1993 Lithuania re-introduced its pre-war currency, the *Litas* (abbreviated throughout this book as Lt), which is divided into 100 *centas*. This has been the only legal tender within the country ever since. It comes in notes of 10, 20, 50, 100, 200 and 500Lt, while there are coins of 1, 2, 5, 10, 20 and 50 centas and 1, 2 and 5Lt.

On the re-introduction of the currency, the exchange rate was fixed at 4Lt to US$1, and remained pegged at that level until 2002, when it was replaced by a similar fixed link, that of 3.4528Lt to €1. This is scheduled to remain in place until Lithuania formally joins the single European currency; the initial target date of 2007 having been missed, entry is now unlikely until after the end of the decade. Although it was potentially risky, the policy of a fixed exchange has been largely successful, achieving currency stability without creating any unwelcome side-effects, such as high unemployment.

CHANGING MONEY Lithuanian currency may now be ordered from British banks, and is also available at London Gatwick. Vilnius, where most visitors arrive, has several 24-hour currency exchanges, including one at the airport and another beside the bus and railway stations. Indeed, changing money is hardly likely to be a problem in the cities and other major tourist destinations, all of which are well- equipped with banks and currency exchanges.

Some of the latter are private operations, often within shops, and change banknotes only (the euro and the US$ are always accepted; rates for other currencies which are taken are invariably displayed on a board). This means that it is worth carrying a small supply of foreign cash, particularly if spending a lot of time in rural areas, where chances for exchanging currency are obviously limited.

However, there is no longer any need to run the risks entailed in carrying around large wads of hard currency. Banks and exchange offices, which are bank subsidiaries, can be found in even small provincial towns, and can be counted on to cash travellers' cheques and give advances on credit cards. The Lietuvos Taupomasis Bankas (Lithuanian Savings Bank) is particularly widespread and reliable, while the little circular booths of Bankas Snoras, which have become a familiar sight all over the country, are usually the easiest to locate. Note that the Thomas Cook cheques with the MasterCard logo are the ones with which Lithuanian banks are most familiar, and are therefore the best ones to carry. British visitors should beware the very real possibility of being heavily short-changed by a cashier confusing (in all innocence) the UK£ with the US$.

The use of credit cards, particularly Visa and MasterCard examples, has become very widespread in Lithuania during the past few years and it is well worth carrying at least one or both of these. In addition to obtaining cash advances at banks, they can also be used in the many Automatic Teller Machines (ATMs). These are sometimes located within banks, post offices or shops, but many are on the street, offering another 24-hour banking facility. They generally offer instructions in five languages, including English. Credit cards are also accepted in a large percentage of the country's hotels, as well as by many restaurants and shops. A credit card is pretty well mandatory for hiring a car, as most rental companies, and in particular the international ones, insist payment is made that way.

Do not, under any circumstances, change money with street hustlers, who are only out to rip off the unwary. The black market, which once offered several times the official rate of exchange, was killed stone dead by currency stabilisation. Thus it is impossible for anyone to offer a more favourable rate than that available from a bank or a properly accredited exchange.

COSTS It is likely that a major expense in visiting Lithuania will be the cost of getting there. Once inside the country, it becomes harder to generalise, as it is easy enough to travel very cheaply, yet also feasible to knock up large expenses. However, most goods and services, as a rule, cost considerably less than they do in the West, sometimes only a fraction as much, and are noticeably cheaper than in the other two Baltic states.

A charge is almost invariably made for entry to museums and monuments – even Holocaust memorial sites, which certainly ought to be free. However, the fees are, without exception, minimal: usually 5Lt or less.

The fare for a journey all the way across the country (for example from Vilnius to Klaipėda) by bus or train is no more than 40Lt, while a medium-length trip, such as Vilnius to Marcinkonys in the Dzūkija National Park, or to Ignalina, gateway to the Aukštaitija National Park, costs around 7Lt. In some (though by no means all) of the best restaurants in Vilnius a three-course meal with drink will leave change from 50Lt, while in smaller towns it can be difficult to make the bill rise much above 25Lt, even by ordering all the extras, such as coffee and liqueurs. In total contrast, car hire rates are similar to those in the West.

Accommodation presents a mixed picture. The new generation of ultra-modern hotels (which already occupy the predominant market position in Vilnius) are aimed squarely at Western business visitors; they offer Western facilities and charge Western prices. Their single rooms are particularly expensive, usually costing upwards of three-quarters of the price two people pay for a double. Starting rates of 250Lt are common, and in Vilnius they are usually considerably more than that. Yet accommodation need not be expensive, even in the capital and other large cities, where bed and breakfast in private houses makes an enticing alternative to comparably priced rooms in rundown hotels. In some towns and villages, the only accommodation available is in cheap rooms. Indeed, if visiting, say, the Aukštaitija or Samogitia National Parks, it is all but impossible (unless hiring a car) to incur travel expenses in excess of 100Lt a day, and easy enough to spend half that or less.

 ## ACCOMMODATION

HOTELS The number and quality of hotels in Lithuania have grown enormously in recent years, though most of the newcomers are concentrated in a handful of locations, with Palanga and Vilnius leading the way. Those in the cities are mostly geared to business visitors, and concentrate on providing facilities such as faxes, photocopiers and a car rental service, as well as all possible creature comforts in the bedrooms. Some are in brand new buildings, while others are refurbishments of historic houses and grand hotels of the pre-Soviet years. The new generation of luxury hotels on the Baltic coast are predominantly in the modern designer style and aimed at well-heeled German and Scandinavian tourists. Although comparable in price to the business-class hotels in the cities, they usually offer better value for money. Instead of just a bedroom with bathroom attached, they have suites of two or three rooms, and/or fully self-contained apartments with kitchen.

Western companies have taken over and refurbished some of Lithuania's stock of Soviet-era hotels, including a few of the huge tower blocks which disfigure every city centre. However, other such establishments still survive in a time-warped state. Typically, their rooms are spartan in appearance, containing a single bed or beds with wooden boards on two or three of the sides plus a dressing table with an ancient television set. There is nearly always a small bathroom attached, equipped with toilet, washbasin and a showerhead which discharges its water through a hole in the floor. Some of these hotels have been allowed to go to seed, and sheets with holes, stained furniture, worn carpets and leaky plumbing are to be expected. Others try to be a bit more salubrious, while a few have begun a slow programme of renovations, and are thus able to offer a choice of 'Western' and 'Soviet' rooms, though the former are often overpriced, costing two or three times as much as the latter, and not much less than a room in a far more attractive post-independence hotel. The iniquitous two- or three-tier pricing system, whereby Western guests were charged considerably more than Lithuanians and citizens of the former Soviet Union, continued in many establishments for several years after the fall of communism, but has now died out. In the last few years, the Lithuanian State Department of Tourism has introduced an official starring system for hotels. Beware that stars are awarded for the range of services provided, rather than quality. The general effect of this is that stars are awarded more generously than they are in most Western countries.

Breakfast is normally included in the price of a room. Occasionally, however, it is an optional extra, while it is not served at all in some of the cheaper places. As a rule, bedrooms always have en suite facilities, even if only very basic ones, except in the most primitive hotels in rural areas. In the case of apartments (and many of the suites) this covers a minimum of four people (and sometimes even more). Note that in the cities many hotels in the upper and middle ranges offer all sorts of discounts on the standard rates. Special weekend deals are ubiquitous, as are online promotions – which means that it is always worth checking the website. In the holiday resorts, particularly those at the seaside, rates can go drastically upwards and downwards according to demand.

OTHER ACCOMMODATION A good alternative to a budget hotel, though not necessarily a cheaper one, is private bed and breakfast accommodation. This is readily available (usually with host, but sometimes without) in Vilnius, Kaunas, Klaipėda, Palanga and the villages of the Curonian Spit. Many farmhouses also offer this facility, often very cheaply indeed, and some serve full meals as well, giving a good opportunity to sample real Lithuanian home cooking. The snag is not one of accessibility (they are often in villages served by public transport), but finding them in the first place. However, tourist offices should be able to provide information about those in their area, while many are listed in the widely available Lithuanian Tourism Board publication, *Countryside Holidays*.

The resthouse or holiday home (*poilsio namai*) is a ubiquitous feature of the country's main resorts, particularly on the Baltic. In Soviet times, these were often reserved for the use of members of particular organisations such as trade unions, but are now open to the general public. Some are very basic and still somewhat institutional, but the best are indistinguishable from good-quality hotels. Sanatoria, which are found in the spa towns of Druskininkai and Birštonas, are another accommodation option, but are primarily interested in long-stay guests seeking a cure for a particular medical problem. As yet, the Lithuanian Youth Hostel Association has only a handful of hostels, and thus has only associated-member status of the IYHF.

Lithuanian campsites are very different from those in Western Europe. Although they do have ground on which tents can be pitched for a nominal fee, most of their accommodation is in wooden chalets. Often these are divided into separately rented upper and lower apartments, though it may be possible to rent just a room in a large chalet, and share its communal kitchen and bathroom. Chalets are very cheap, particularly if travelling in a family or a group, but the campsites themselves are more often than not in obscure rural locations and therefore only a realistic option if travelling by car.

✖ EATING AND DRINKING

Lithuanian cuisine is based on traditional countryside fare, in which home-produced or fresh market ingredients predominate. It is generally both healthy and tasty, though it will not please those accustomed to strongly spiced food.

As is so often the case, the best place to enjoy genuine traditional fare is in a household, especially when a festival is being celebrated. However, home-style cooking can be sampled all over the country in restaurants and cafés. Vilnius has some fine restaurants specialising in Lithuanian dishes, and these seem to be managing to hold their own against strong competition from the many foreign cuisines introduced since the fall of communism. For basic local fare at rock-bottom prices, look out for a canteen (*valgykla*). This once-ubiquitous institution is now an endangered species and eating in one can be rather a lottery. Some serve delicious, freshly prepared food, others are truly awful. Lunch is the main meal of the day for most Lithuanians, and is a moveable feast, with some adopting the favoured Western lunchtime hours (roughly 12.00–14.00), while others remain loyal to the Russian preference for mid-afternoon.

FOOD For many Lithuanians, breakfast consists of nothing fancier than a platter of bread (*duona*) with butter (*sviestas*), cheese (*sūris*), curd cheese (*varškė*) and sausages (*dešrelės*), and some basic salad ingredients, such as lettuce (*salotos*), cabbage (*kopūstai*), tomatoes (*pomidorai*) and cucumbers (*agurkai*). Pancakes (variously known as *blynai*, *blyneliai* or *lietiniai*) make a good hot breakfast dish, but are equally popular at other times of the day. The most common savoury fillings are cheese, curd cheese and mushrooms (*grybai*).

Main meals usually begin with an hors d'oeuvre, such as salad (*mišrainė*), herring (*silkė*), smoked sausage (*skilandis*) or yellow split peas with pork crackling (*žirniai su spirgais*). Another popular appetiser, traditionally eaten with beer, is crunchy fried bread (*kepta duona*), which is rubbed with raw garlic and salted. Black caviar (*juodi ikrai*) is fairly expensive, but red caviar (*raudoni ikrai*) is often quite reasonably priced, and makes a wonderful pancake filling. *Koldūnai*, the Lithuanian version of ravioli, is either fried as a starter or side dish, or else boiled and served in a bouillon (*sultinys*).

The cold, creamed beetroot soup *šaltibarščiai* is arguably the most distinctive creation of the Lithuanian kitchen, and is very refreshing on a hot day, for all its lurid pink colour. It usually contains cold eggs (*kiaušiniai*), and is served with a side dish of hot boiled potatoes (*bulvės*). There is also a Lithuanian version of borscht (*lietuviški barščiai*), the Russian hot beetroot soup; this sometimes contains mushrooms and can be accompanied by rissoles (*kotletai*).

Many potato dishes are substantial enough to be main courses in their own right. Lithuania's national dish is *cepelinai*, a grated potato dumpling whose name literally means 'Zeppelin', in honour of its cylindrical shape. It is usually stuffed with meat and served in a sauce made with bacon and onions, though mushrooms or cheese can be substituted in order to make it suitable for vegetarians, who are fairly well (but by no means outstandingly) catered for in Lithuanian restaurants and cafés. *Bulviniai blynai* are pancakes made with potatoes and flour, usually served with sour cream (*grietinė*); *bulviniai vėdarai* are potato 'sausages', while *kugelis* is a potato pudding which can also include carrots (*morkos*). Other dishes are *balandėliai*, stuffed cabbage leaves, and *virtiniai*, small curd dumplings stuffed with meat, cheese or mushrooms.

The word *kepsnys*, which means fillet, figures regularly on Lithuanian menus, and is used in connection with all types of meat, of which pork (*kiauliena*) is the most popular. Virtually every part of the pig is eaten, including the foot (*koja*) and the ear (*ausis*), though the most common pork dish is *karbonadas*, a breaded cutlet similar to a Wiener schnitzel. Beef (*jautiena*) and chicken (*vištiena*) are also standard menu items. All meat dishes are normally accompanied by a selection of both hot and cold vegetables.

There is an abundant supply of fish from the Baltic Sea and Curonian Lagoon, and in this region it is smoked in a traditional manner and sold at wayside stalls as a very superior form of fast food. Lithuania's many rivers are also well-stocked with fish. Cod (*menkė*), plaice (*plekšnė*), pike-perch (*sterkas*), salmon (*lašiša*), trout (*upėtakis*), carp (*karpis*) and eel (*ungurys*) are among the fish most commonly found on restaurant menus, while sturgeon (*eršketas*) is the most expensive and prestigious.

Typical desserts are fruit compote (*kompotas*), honey cake (*medauninkas*), pastries (*pyragaičiai*) and ice-cream (*ledai*), while *kisielius* is a fruit pudding which is especially popular at Christmas.

DRINKS Milk (*pienas*) is widely consumed both hot and cold. The traditional Lithuanian method of preparing coffee (*kava*) and chocolate (*šokoladas*) is over a hot sand pit, but this is increasingly giving way to espresso machines. Tea (*arbata*) is usually served black (*juodoji*) or with lemon (*su citrina*), and it is quite common for it to arrive with sugar already added. Soft drinks include juice (*sultys*) and mineral water (*mineralinis vanduo*). Lithuania's most distinctive beverage is *gira*, a fermented rye-based summertime refreshener (which is either non-alcoholic or with a very low alcohol content, usually of about 1%).

Each of Lithuania's cities has its own brewery: these are *Vilniaus Tauras* (Vilnius), *Ragutis* and *Kauno Alus* (Kaunas), *Švyturys* (Klaipėda), *Gubernija* (Šiauliai) and *Kalnapilis* (Panevėžys). Other major breweries are *Utenos* (Utena) and *Biržai* in the town of the same name. Vilnius, Kaunas and Klaipėda all now have new-generation home-brew taverns, while some other restaurants have their own special house brand which is made under licence by one of the larger breweries. Lithuanian beer (*alus*) is of high quality, and is generally both stronger and sweeter than in Western European countries. Several brews have an alcohol content of over 8%, with 6.5% being quite normal. The dark *porteris*, which is produced by several different breweries, is particularly fine, and is similar in style to the now rarely produced English porter ale.

Although Lithuania is too far north to be able to produce wine (*vynas*), a number of well-regarded sparkling vintages are made from imported grapes by *Alita*, a company which also makes several fruit-based wines. Among many locally produced spirits are several types of vodka (*degtinė*), of which *Kvietinė* is considered the best. The honey-based mead (*midus*) has enjoyed something of a revival in recent years; most varieties are quite mild, but the medicinal balsam (*balzamas*) version is 50% proof. Other liqueurs with a high alcohol content are *Dainava* and *Palanga*, which are both made from mixed berries; the golden-coloured, herb-based *Medžiotojų*; and the brownish *Starka*, which includes the leaves of fruit trees among its ingredients.

MEDIA AND COMMUNICATIONS

TIME Lithuania uses the 24-hour clock, not the am/pm system favoured in the UK and USA. Although it spent several years in the Central European time zone (GMT+1) in a calculated gesture of solidarity with the standardisation obsessions of the EU, it has now moved back to the Eastern European time zone (GMT+2), where it logically belongs.

POST The Lithuanian postal system (*www.post.lt*) works quite efficiently. Airmail letters and postcards to and from the UK and other parts of Europe can take as little as two days, though four or five days is the average; a week to ten days is the norm for North American destinations. Current airmail rates for postcards and letters up to 20g are 2.15Lt to EU countries, 2.45Lt elsewhere in the world; these rise to 2.45Lt and 2.90Lt respectively for priority items.

TELEPHONES Telephone codes for dialling within Lithuania are given throughout the book. If calling locally, they should be omitted altogether; if calling another part of the country, they must be dialled in full and preceded by the national access number 8. When calling Lithuania from abroad, dial the international access code (usually 00), then the country code (370), then the local code (for example 5 for Vilnius, 37 for Kaunas, 46 for Klaipėda), then the subscriber's number.

Public telephones can be used for direct dialling to any number in the world. They operate only with chip phonecards, which cost 9Lt, 13Lt, 16Lt or 30Lt, and can be purchased from post offices or newspaper kiosks. Calls to the UK and the US currently cost 1.39Lt per minute from 06.00 to 20.00, 0.99Lt per minute at other times.

Lithuania has three mobile phone operators – Omnitel, Bitė and TELE2 – which all offer prepaid SIM cards allowing calls within the country at local rates. Calling a Lithuanian mobile, whether from another mobile or a fixed line, involves dialling a total of nine digits, the first of which is always 8.

Useful phone numbers

Fire	➲ 01
Police	➲ 02
Ambulance	➲ 03
Directory enquiries	➲ 118
International calls via English-speaking operator	➲ 1573
International collect (reverse charge) calls via English-speaking operator	➲ 1591

OTHER COMMUNICATIONS SERVICES Many Lithuanian businesses and organisations can be contacted by fax, and both outgoing and incoming fax services are available from post offices and many hotels. The use of the internet, particularly for email, is now as ubiquitous in Lithuania's business world as it is in the USA or UK. Cybercafés can be found in the main cities. See the list of general websites in *Appendix 2* (pages 247–8).

NEWSPAPERS AND MAGAZINES Certain foreign newspapers, including *The Financial Times* and *The International Herald Tribune*, are readily obtainable in the larger Lithuanian towns, though not in rural areas, while a larger selection of titles can be found in Vilnius. Events in all three Baltic states are covered in *The Baltic Times* (*www.baltictimes.com*), an English-language weekly published in Rīga, and in *Baltische Rundschau* (*www.baltische-rundschau.info*), a German-language monthly published in Vilnius. Likewise published in Vilnius is *Lithuanian Weekly*, which concentrates on Lithuania.

Lithuanian Airlines' in-flight magazine, *Lithuania In The World* (*www.liw.lt*), is also put on general sale, and is worth reading for its wide range of glossy features about all aspects of the country. The *In Your Pocket* (*www.inyourpocket.com*) listings magazines to Vilnius, Kaunas and Klaipėda have acquired the status of mandatory purchases for visitors to these cities. The guides to these cities now have competition from the free *Exploring* series (*www.exploring.eu*), which suffer from unidiomatic English but have useful listings and descriptive information, if little in the way of reviews.

TV AND RADIO Hotel rooms, except in the cheapest establishments, invariably have a television set. Modern business-class hotels generally offer a range of satellite and/or cable channels, including many in English. The local stations only broadcast a few English-language programmes: the state-owned LTV-1 shows an evening news bulletin from the BBC, while the commercial Tele 3 and Baltic TV both offer CNN news. Soundtracks on English-language films are only variably audible behind the spoken Lithuanian translation, which is normally delivered by a single actor. Big sporting events, especially basketball and football, are regularly featured on the network, though commercial breaks often overrun, with the result that crucial incidents can be missed.

The BBC World Service can be heard by tuning in to 100.1FM, while Voice of America is on 105.6FM. English-language programmes are also broadcast on the popular music station M1, which can be found at 106.2FM.

OTHER PRACTICALITIES

ADDRESSES Most Lithuanian addresses are written as one word only, as it is customary to omit words such as *gatvė* (street), *kelias* (road), *alėja* (avenue) or *prospektas* (boulevard) which officially form the latter part of the designation. However, *aikštė* (square) is not normally omitted.When there are two numbers in the address, the first signifies the number on the street, the second the number of the apartment or office within that building.

BUSINESS AND OPENING HOURS Offices tend to work from 08.00–17.00 Monday–Friday; banks often close an hour earlier, though some stay open as late as 19.00. Shops keep variable hours, but those selling food are generally open from 07.00 until late in the evening. Restaurants tend to be open continuously from midday (if not before) until around midnight. Museum hours, which are listed throughout the following chapters (but are prone to minor changes, such as opening or closing an hour earlier or later), are not generous. Most museums are only open five or six hours a day, and closed on Mondays (and often at least one other day as well). However, many historic churches are kept open throughout the day; those that are not can usually be seen (unless closed for restoration) in the early part of the morning and in the late afternoon or early evening.

ETIQUETTE Lithuanians tend to favour the formal handshake, even when meeting friends; very few greet one another with a kiss. If giving flowers as a present, make sure the bunch contains an odd number of blooms, as even numbers are associated with mournful occasions. When entering a house it is customary to remove outdoor footwear once over the threshold.

MAPS Good quality maps of Lithuania and its cities are widely available in bookshops and tourist offices. Those published in Latvia by Jāņa Sēta and in Vilnius by Briedis are usually the best and most reliable.

NUISANCES The most persistent nuisances are those which have arisen as a result of the recent massive increase in car ownership, which has not only spawned a great deal of incompetent and boorish driving, but also a mania for owning hyper-sensitive car alarms, which go off at the slightest provocation (such as someone walking nearby or the owner opening the door) and have become a round-the-clock irritant in the major cities. Non-smokers should note that smoking is still a widespread habit, despite the ban introduced in 2007, which extended that already in force on public transport to all entertainment venues, including restaurants, bars and cafés. Paradoxically, urban bus stops and the platforms of bus and railway stations are among the worst places for smoke pollution, as smokers take the opportunity to inhale as much nicotine as possible before boarding. Aggressive beggars (usually young males) frequent popular tourist areas, notably the heart of Vilnius's Old Town.

PUBLIC TOILETS Whenever possible, use toilets in restaurants or cafés, as public conveniences are usually filthy, and in rural areas are often no more than a wooden shack with a hole in the ground. The letter M (for *moterų*) or an upward pointing triangle signify a female toilet; the letter V (for *vyrų*) or a downward pointing triangle a male toilet. A point to note when travelling by rail is that large sections of track (clearly identified on maps posted in the carriages) are designated as clean areas. As the train approaches one of these, the toilets are locked by the on-board crew, and are kept inaccessible until the end of that particular stretch.

SOUVENIRS Amber (*gintaras*) and amber objects are the most popular Lithuanian souvenirs, though the raw material is nowadays usually imported from neighbouring Kaliningrad. Unfortunately, amber is often faked and it is therefore best to buy any such items from a reputable dealer rather than from street traders, who do not necessarily sell the genuine article. Locally made handicrafts such as woodcarvings, wickerwork, ceramics, glassware and linen are good and inexpensive mementoes of a visit.

SPORTS Basketball is Lithuania's national sport, far surpassing football in popularity both as a participatory and spectator activity. The country's obsession with the game has its roots in the gold medal victory at the 1936 Olympic Games of the US team, which was captained by Frank Lubin, the son of Lithuanian immigrants to California. The Lithuanian team won the bronze medal at the 1992, 1996 and 2000 Olympiads. In the semi-finals of the last of these they narrowly missed scoring a last-minute basket which would have inflicted an improbable defeat on the US 'dream team'. Having triumphed at the 2003 European championships, the Lithuanians went to the 2004 Olympics with high hopes of becoming gold medallists. Yet, despite an unexpectedly poor showing by the Americans, they failed to win a medal of any colour. Many top Lithuanians now ply their trade in the NBA, though the country's top clubs – led by Zalgiris Kaunas, the 1998 European club champions – are able to lure Americans in the other direction. Track and field athletics and cycling are the other sports at which Lithuanians have enjoyed international success in recent years.

TIPPING Many Lithuanians do not tip at all, though most will round up restaurant or taxi bills to the next Lt. Some establishments add on a small service charge, usually 5% or so, though this seldom goes directly to the waiting staff. If service has been particularly attentive, a tip is certainly in order, though it should not be more than 10% of the bill.

TOURIST INFORMATION Tourist offices are now to be found throughout Lithuania, and their addresses and opening times are given in the chapters which follow. Most maps and leaflets have to be paid for.

European bison

Part Two

THE GUIDE

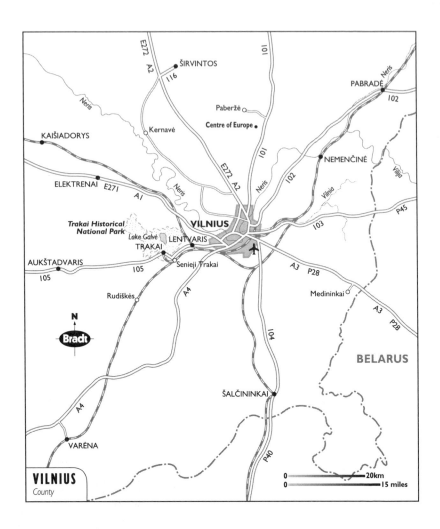

ŠIRVINTOS

E272
A2
116

Neris

101

PABRADĖ
Neris
102

KAIŠIADORYS

Kernavė

Paberžė

Centre of Europe

ELEKTRENAI E271 A1

Neris

E272
A2

101

Neris

102

NEMENČINĖ

Vilija

Vilnia

P45

Trakai Historical
National Park

Lake Galvė LENTVARIS

TRAKAI

VILNIUS

103

AUKŠTADVARIS

105

105

Senieji Trakai

A4

A3 P28

Rudiškės

Medininkai

A3
P28

N

Bradt

BELARUS

104

ŠALČININKAI

A4

VARĖNA

P40

0   20km
0   15 miles

VILNIUS
County

6

Vilnius County

That the name of Lithuania's largest city and national capital exists in several slightly differing versions – Vilnius to the Lithuanians, Wilno to the Poles, Vilna to the Jews and Russians – is a reflection of its eventful history as a melting-pot in which different ethnic groups have competed with one another for predominance. By the vagaries of fate, it is the only one of the many traditionally multi-national and multi-cultural cities of the old Polish–Lithuanian Commonwealth which has preserved a mixed profile right down to the present day. Despite its key role in modern Lithuania, little more than a bare majority of its inhabitants are ethnic Lithuanians; the Russian and Polish minorities are both substantial, while there is also a significant number of Belarussians, and smaller representations of a host of other nationalities.

The diversity of the city's make-up is given a very visible expression in the Old Town, whose outstanding quality has gained it a coveted place on UNESCO's World Heritage List – one of only three places in Lithuania to be so honoured. Although its Jewish quarter is now a sad shadow of its former self, the Old Town is otherwise substantially intact, with the domes of the Orthodox churches competing for attention with the towers of their far more numerous Catholic counterparts. Most of the latter were established by mendicant or missionary orders, and all but a few were either built or totally reconstructed in the Baroque era. Vilnius boasts one of the greatest assemblages of Baroque monuments outside Rome, having developed over nearly two centuries a distinctively indigenous interpretation of the style.

The re-establishment of Lithuania's independence in 1991 meant that Vilnius regained its role as capital of a sovereign state after a gap of well over four centuries. This development has inevitably led to huge changes. By no means all of these are welcome, but there have been many undoubted benefits, not least the ever-increasing numbers of recommendable hotels, restaurants, bars and cafés which have helped make the city a favourite holiday destination, especially for members of the (predominantly North American) Lithuanian diaspora.

Vilnius's location in the far southeast of Lithuania means that it is not ideally placed for day-trips into the countryside. However, its administrative county does have a few attractive destinations, notably the outstanding medieval town of Trakai, which probably preceded it as the nation's capital.

VILNIUS

The city of Vilnius has a population of around 548,000, which is well spread out over a municipal area liberally endowed with areas of greenery; indeed, only about a third of the municipal area is built up. There are two distinct parts to the city centre. The Old Town, which is very large by the standards of its time, lies at the confluence of the Vilnia with the Neris, west of the former and south of

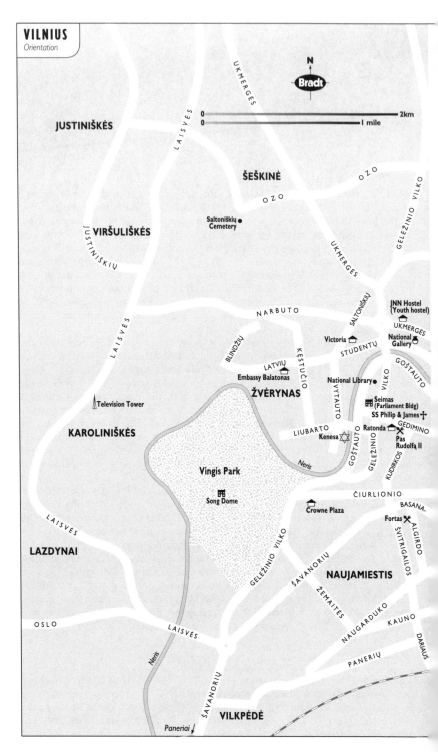

Calvary Church, Verkiai Park & Green Lakes

✝✝ Trinapolis Convent & Verkiai Park

ŽIRMŪNAI

KALVARIJŲ

ŽVALGŲ

VERKIŲ

KAREIVIŲ

ANTAKALNIO

OZO

ŽIRMŪNŲ

Neris

ANTAKALNIS

ŽALGIRIO

KALVARIJŲ

MINTIES

ŠNIPIŠKĖS

RINKTINĖS

TUSKULĖNŲ

✕ Marceliukės Klėtis

✝ Our Lord Jesus

ŽIRMŪNŲ

ANTAKALNIO

SAPIEGOS

● Antakalnis Cemetery

Calvary Market

Reval Lietuva

🏠 Naujasis Vilnius

Ecotel

ŠNIPIŠKIŲ

UPĖS

Planetarium ●

🏠 Holiday Inn

St Raphael ✝

🏠 Kalvarija

ŠEIMYNIŠKIŲ

🏛 Šarūnas

🏋 Žalgiris Stadium

✝ SS Peter & Paul

ŽVEJŲ

ŽYGIMANTŲ

ARSENALO

Congress

VRUBLEVESKIO

OLANDŲ

BATORO

VILNIAUS

🏰 Higher Castle Hill Park

✝ Cathedral of SS Stanislaus & Ladislaus

FILARETŲ

🏠 Filaretai Hostel

UŽUPIS

Genocide Museum

ŠVENTARAGIO

🏛 Vilnius University

PILIES

MAIRONIO

Vilnia

UŽUPIO

Čagino ✕

🏠 Magdė

VIČIAUS

✕ Čingischanas

SENAMIESTIS

DIDŽIOJI

🏠 Bernardine Cemetery
Jaunujų Turistu Centras ●

PAUPYS

ZARASŲ

MARKUČIAI

MINDAUGO

✕ Rytai

SUBAČIAUS

RASŲ

SUBAČIAUS

🏠 Pushkin Memorial Museum

ŠOPENO

PELESOS

GELEŽINKELIO

RASŲ

SUKILĖLIŲ

Bus station 🚌

see page 76

LIEPKALNIO

Railway station

PELESOS

● Rasos Cemetery

RASOS

GARDINO

GIRENO

↓ Airport

the latter. It is now joined seamlessly to the west by the New Town, which grew up in the 19th century. Although the Old Town contains the lion's share of the city's sights, many others, including some of the most important, are scattered all over the inner and outer suburbs.

HISTORY According to legend, Vilnius was founded in 1323 by Grand Duke Gediminas, progenitor of the Gediminian dynasty which ruled Lithuania, latterly in union with Poland, for over 250 years. The story goes that, after a successful day's hunting, Gediminas decided to pitch camp for the night at the point where the Vilnia flows into the Neris, rather than return to his castle in Trakai. On falling asleep, he had a strange dream of a huge iron wolf on the hill above, which howled with the ferocity of a pack of a hundred wolves. The pagan high priest Lizdeika interpreted this dream as a message from the gods instructing Gediminas to build a city on the hill where he had seen the iron wolf in his dream. This city would grow so great that its fame would reverberate around the world with the force of the howls of a hundred wolves.

The truth of the matter is that there was a settlement beside the Neris–Vilnia confluence at least as far back as the 1st century AD. Moreover, a wooden castle was built atop what is now known as Gediminas Hill in the 11th century. Vilnius (which takes its name from the river) was certainly a well-established town by Gediminas's time, though his role in its history is none the less an important one since it was in one of his letters of 1323 that it is documented for the first time, and it was probably he who raised it to the status of Lithuania's permanent capital.

Under Gediminas and his successors Vilnius occupied a small, tightly packed site protected by a fortification system which included three castles. Between 1365 and 1402 it was attacked by the Teutonic Knights on seven separate occasions, but despite inflicting considerable damage they never managed to capture it. In 1387, the year after the royal union with Poland, Vilnius was granted municipal rights, though it was only after the decisive defeat of the Teutonic Knights at the Battle of Žalgiris in 1410 that it was able to expand southwards from the confines of the original site.

Between 1503 and 1522, in response to a threat of invasion by the Tatars, the whole city was enclosed within a 2.4km-long wall. With the advent of more peaceful times, Vilnius flourished as a city of merchants and craftsmen, becoming one of the great book-printing centres of Europe. The year 1569 was one of crucial significance, as the Union of Lublin, which created the Polish–Lithuanian Commonwealth, had the inevitable consequence of Vilnius (like Cracow) losing its roles as a royal residence and administrative capital, as Warsaw, thanks to its central location, became the hub of the huge unified state.

However, 1569 also saw the arrival of the Jesuits in Vilnius, and as a result the city played a leading role in the Counter-Reformation, which saw the Roman

Catholic Church recover most of the ground it had lost in Lithuania. The school founded by the Jesuits in 1570 was raised to university status in 1579, and quickly established itself as one of the great academic institutions of Europe.

It was also the Jesuits who were responsible for introducing the new Baroque style of architecture, and this soon came to dominate the face of Vilnius's Old Town. Many of Vilnius's early Baroque buildings were destroyed in the mid-17th-century wars with the Swedes and Russians, during which the city lost half its population, principally as a result of the plague of 1657–58. None the less, it recovered well, and was embellished with a host of new aristocratic palaces, churches and monastic buildings. Initially, these were inspired by the Roman High Baroque style, but in the 18th century a distinctive local style, derived from German and Central European models, was developed.

With the Third Partition of the Commonwealth in 1795, Vilnius, along with most of the rest of Lithuania, became part of the Tsarist Empire. Paradoxically, this led to it regaining its role as a capital, as it was chosen as the seat of a large administrative province. Nevertheless, there were patriotic hopes for a revival of Lithuanian independence, with the French dictator Napoleon Bonaparte, who captured Vilnius in June 1812, seen as the potential saviour. During the 19 days he spent in the city, he showed himself to be no more than a lukewarm supporter, though he did authorise the formation of a provisional government supported by an army. A dispirited Napoleon returned to the city in December of the same year in retreat from the Russians, but stayed for only a couple of hours before continuing to flee. The Russians recaptured Vilnius soon after, ending its hopes of re-establishing itself as capital of an independent Lithuania within the foreseeable future.

Throughout the failed rebellion of 1831, the authorities remained in control of Vilnius, but in the repressive measures introduced in its aftermath the city was made to suffer heavily. Its university, the most venerable in the Russian Empire, was closed down; the religious houses were dissolved, and several churches were transferred to Orthodox congregations. The next unsuccessful revolt, in 1863, resulted in the public executions of the ringleaders.

However, the 19th century also saw Vilnius develop as a major industrial centre, and it expanded greatly in size, with the construction of the New Town and suburban areas. Its population grew from 18,000 to 138,000, an increase which was in part due to an influx of Jews from elsewhere in Russia. Indeed, a census taken towards the end of the century made Jews the biggest ethnic group within the city, accounting for over 40% of the population. Poles were the next largest, at around 30%, with Russians numbering 20%, and Lithuanians little more than 2%. Language seems to have been the determining characteristic in these figures, whose significance is still much disputed: it is likely that many of the Poles (perhaps even the overwhelming majority) were ethnic Lithuanians whose (often distant) ancestors had adopted the Polish tongue.

Despite the paucity of Lithuanian speakers in Vilnius, the city became the focal point of the national awakening which gathered momentum in the early years of the 20th century. The so-called Great Seimas, a gathering of 2,000 Lithuanians, met there in 1905 and demanded autonomy within the empire. Although nothing came of this, the city's long-dormant dream to become a national capital was revived once more as a result of World War I, which saw the Russians abandoning Vilnius to the advancing German army in September 1915.

A census by the occupying forces the following year produced a somewhat different result from that of the Russians a couple of decades earlier. The percentage of Jewish residents was virtually unchanged, but Poles were now said to number a fraction over 50% of the population. Despite these findings, the

Germans allowed a Lithuanian congress to meet in the city in September 1917. This made the formal demand for Vilnius to be made capital of a Lithuanian state, and independence was duly declared in 1918.

However, the city found itself a major bone of contention in the conflicts following World War I which saw Soviet Russia and the newly resurrected nations of Lithuania and Poland tussle with one another for territory. In July 1920 the Soviets recognised Lithuania's right to Vilnius, and the Poles apparently followed suit by the Treaty of Suwałki of October 7. Two days later, however, ostensibly rebel troops commanded by General Lucian Żeligowski, a Polonised Lithuanian, captured Vilnius and the surrounding area. In this action, they were secretly supported by the Polish leader, Marshal Józef Piłsudski, another ethnic Lithuanian, who was determined that the city where he had grown up would become an integral part of Poland.

Following two years of somewhat half-hearted international mediation, the dispute over Vilnius was resolved in Poland's favour largely by default, there being no readily enforceable alternative to leaving it in the hands of the occupying power. From a purely objective standpoint there is no doubt that the Poles had a strong claim on the city, though for Vilnius itself the result was certainly not fortuitous, as it was reduced to a provincial role within Poland, while Kaunas was developed as the showpiece Lithuanian capital in its stead.

Following the carve-up of Poland between Nazi Germany and the Soviet Union at the beginning of World War II, the Soviets restored Vilnius to Lithuania in October 1939 as its capital in return for the right to establish military bases there, a move which paved the way for the annexation of the country the following June. The Nazi occupation of 1941–44 led to the elimination of almost all of Vilnius's large Jewish community, many of whom were murdered in the Paneriai Forest in the outskirts. When the war ended with the Soviets back in control, the city's population had fallen to 110,000, a reduction of around 100,000 on what it had been in 1939. Over the following decade, a large percentage of the local Polish population was deported to Poland. They were replaced by Russians and migrant Lithuanians, and the city's population grew steadily, with most of the newcomers housed in high-rise suburbs constructed according to Soviet principles.

For Vilnius, the Soviet decades did at least offer the compensation of its re-establishment as a national capital, albeit one under foreign occupation. It was therefore inevitable that it was in the vanguard of the successful drive towards independence, and the scene of the most dramatic flashpoint in the largely peaceful struggle – the storming of the television tower by Soviet tanks in January 1991, which resulted in the martyrdom of 14 citizens.

Now the proud capital of an independent nation-state once again, Vilnius is gradually modernising and transforming itself in the hope and belief that this role will never again be lost. Poland formally renounced any claim to the city in the Friendship and Co-operation Treaty of 1994, though it declined Lithuania's request to apologise for having annexed it in 1920.

GETTING THERE AND AROUND
By air

The **airport** (*Rodūnios 2;* ☎ *5 273 9305; www.vilnius-airport.lt*) which can be reached by bus 1 or 2, is situated 5km south of the stations. In the arrivals hall in the older front building are a 24-hour currency exchange, a tourist information office, and the booths of several car hire companies. The airline ticket offices are all in the departure hall to the rear. Beware that the range and number of services is subject to quite extensive change.

✈ **Aeroflot** ☎ 5 232 9300; www.aeroflot.com. Also at Pylimo 8-2; ☎/f 5 212 4189. 5 flights per week to Moscow in a code-share arrangement with Lithuanian Airlines.

✈ **Air Baltic** ☎ 5 235 6000; f 5 235 6001; www.airbaltic.com. Flies daily to Vilnius from London Gatwick. Also flies to Rīga & Tallinn 3 times a day Mon–Fri, to Helsinki twice a day Mon–Fri, 6 per week to Dublin & Brussels, 4 per week to Oslo, Berlin, Hamburg, Munich & Milan, 3 to Düsseldorf, Rome & Zurich, 2 to Malaga, 1 to Barcelona.

✈ **Austrian Airlines** Basanavičiaus 11-1; ☎ 5 279 1416; f 5 279 1417; www.austrianairlines.lt. Daily flights to Vienna.

✈ **Czech Airlines** Valančiaus 4-9; ☎ 5 215 1503; f 5 215 1504; e csavilnius@czechairlines.lt; www.czech-airlines.com. 2 flights daily to Prague.

✈ **Estonian Airlines** ☎ 5 273 9022; f 5 273 9016; e vilnius@estonian-air.ee; www.estonian-air.com. 1 or 2 flights daily to Tallinn.

✈ **Finnair** ☎ 5 261 9339; f 5 233 6824; www.finnair.com. 1 or 2 flights per day to Helsinki.

✈ **Lithuanian Airlines** ☎ 5 252 5555; f 5 252 5540. Also at Konstitucijos 12; ☎ 5 275 2585; f 5 272 4852; e info@flylal.com; www.flylal.com. Flies daily to Vilnius from London Gatwick. Also flies twice daily to Amsterdam, daily to Helsinki & Frankfurt, 6 per week to Brussels & Kiev, 5 to Tallinn, 3 to Dublin, Paris & Milan, 2 to Istanbul, 1 to Hanover.

✈ **LOT** ☎ 5 273 9020; f 5 273 9019; e lotvno@lot.com; www.lot.com. 1 or 2 daily flights to Warsaw.

✈ **Lufthansa** ☎ 5 230 6031; f 5 232 9292; www.lufthansa.com. 1 or 2 daily flights to Frankfurt. SAS ☎ 5 235 6000; f 5 235 6001; f sas.vilnius@sas.dk; www.sas.lt. 3 daily flights to Copenhagen (with connections onwards to London & other British cities); 1 or 2 daily to Stockholm.

By bus The bus station (*Sodų 22;* ☎ *5 216 2977*) is located just south of the Old Town, and has a comprehensive network of services to other Lithuanian towns. These include at least a couple of buses an hour throughout most of the day to Kaunas. One or more buses per hour run to Panevėžys, while over 30 per day go to Trakai, often *en route* to another destination. Other approximate daily frequencies include 12 to Utena via Molėtai, 12 to Šiauliai, ten to Klaipėda, five to Druskininkai and, in season, 12 expresses to Palanga. In addition, a daily bus runs to Nida from June to August. Among the daily international services are seven to Minsk, five to Rīga, two to Tallinn, two to Kaliningrad, four to Warsaw, one to Białystok via Suwałki and one to Gdańsk; there are also four per week to Moscow. For destinations in Western Europe, it is normally necessary to change at Warsaw. However, there are also connections to the routes passing through Kaunas (see page 142) as well as a direct weekly service to a range of German cities. There is a left luggage room in the terminal building.

By train The railway station (*Geležinkelio 16;* ☎ *5 233 0088*) is a grand old building with a refurbished interior diagonally opposite the bus station. There are 12 trains daily to Kaunas, including two expresses which are far faster than any bus. Among the other daily domestic services are eight (six at weekends) to Trakai, six to Ignalina, four to Šiauliai, four to Varėna, of which three continue to Marcinkonys, two to Klaipėda via Telšiai, Plungė and Kretinga, and three direct to Šeštokai. There are also a number of daily international services: four to Kaliningrad, three to Moscow, one or two to St Petersburg, three to Minsk and one to Warsaw. There are new coin-operated left luggage lockers in the station basement, which can only be reached by the stairway in front of the building.

By city trolleybus and bus Networks of trolleybuses and buses cover virtually the whole city, though no services actually penetrate the Old Town, other than just within its eastern and northern perimeters, along Maironio and Radvilaitės. Tickets, which are now valid on both modes of transport, can be bought in advance from kiosks (currently 1.10Lt) or, with rare exceptions, from the driver (1.40Lt). A few bus routes which run beyond the city boundaries have slightly

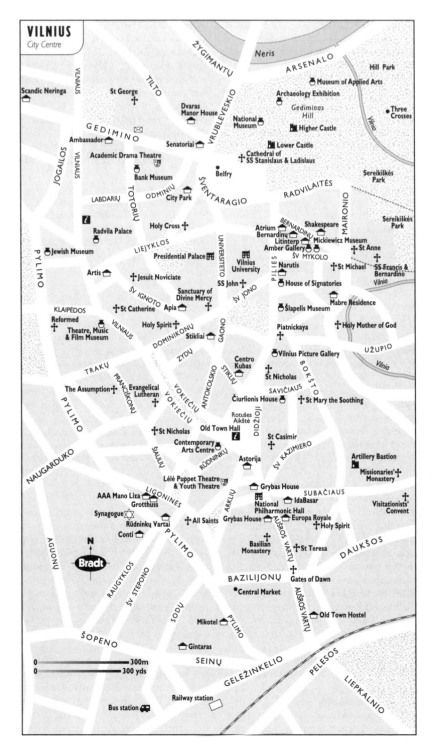

VILNIUS
City Centre

ŽYGIMANTŲ

Neris

ARSENALO

Hill Park

VILNIAUS

Scandic Neringa

St George ✝

TILTO

VRUBLEVSKIO

Dvaras Manor House

Museum of Applied Arts

Archaeology Exhibition

Gediminas Hill

Vilnia

Three Crosses

GEDIMINO ✉

National Museum

Higher Castle

Ambassador

VILNIAUS

Senatorial

Lower Castle

JOGAILOS

Academic Drama Theatre

Bank Museum

Belfry

Cathedral of SS Stanislaus & Ladislaus

Sereikiškės Park

LABDARIŲ

TOTORIŲ

ODMINIŲ

ŠVENTARAGIO

RADVILAITĖS

MAIRONIO

City Park

Sereikiškės Park

PYLIMO

ℹ

Radvila Palace

Holy Cross ✝

Atrium

Bernardinų

BERNARDINŲ

Shakespeare

SV MYKOLO

St Anne ✝

Jewish Museum

LIEJYKLOS

Presidential Palace

UNIVERSITETO

Litinterp

Amber Gallery

Mickiewicz Museum

Artis

Jesuit Noviciate

Vilnius University

Narutis

St Michael ✝

SS Francis & Bernardino

KLAIPĖDOS

ŠV IGNOTO

Sanctuary of Divine Mercy

SS John ✝

PILIES

House of Signatories

Vilnia

St Catherine

Apia

ŠV JONO

Mabre Residence

Reformed Theatre, Music & Film Museum

VILNIAUS

Holy Spirit ✝

DOMINIKONŲ

Stikliai

GAONO

Šlapelis Museum

Piatnickaya ✝

Holy Mother of God ✝

UŽUPIO

TRAKŲ

ŽYDŲ

Vilnius Picture Gallery

Vilnia

The Assumption ✝

PRANCIŠKONŲ

Evangelical Lutheran

VOKIEČIŲ

ANTOKOLSKIO

STIKLIŲ

Centro Kubas

St Nicholas ✝

SAVIČIAUS

Čiurlionis House

St Mary the Soothing ✝

PYLIMO

ŠIAULŲ

VOKIEČIŲ

Rotušes Aikštė

Old Town Hall ℹ

DIDŽIOJI

St Casimir ✝

St Nicholas ✝

Contemporary Arts Centre

NAUGARDUKO

RŪDNINKŲ

Astorija

ŠV KAZIMIERO

Artillery Bastion

Missionaries' ✝ Monastery

Lėlė Puppet Theatre & Youth Theatre

Grybas House

SUBAČIAUS

AAA Mano Liza

LIGONINĖS

ARKLIŲ

National Philharmonic Hall

IdaBasar

Visitationists' Convent ✝

Grotthuss

Synagogue

Rūdninkų Vartai

All Saints ✝

Grybas House

AUŠROS VARTŲ

Europa Royale

Holy Spirit ✝

AGUONŲ

Conti

N

Bradt

RAUGYKLOS

ŠV STEPONO

PYLIMO

Basilian Monastery

St Teresa ✝

DAUKŠOS

BAZILIJONŲ

Gates of Dawn ✝

SODŲ

Central Market

AUŠROS VARTŲ

0   300m

0   300 yds

Mikotel

PYLIMO

Old Town Hostel

SEINŲ

Gintaras

ŠOPENO

GELEŽINKELIO

PELESOS

LIEPKALNIO

Railway station

Bus station

higher tariffs, with tickets sold by an on-board conductor. Otherwise, tickets – whether bought in advance or from the driver – must be punched in one of the machines positioned throughout the bus or trolleybus. Usually these are primitive devices which make different patterns of holes, though a few buses are now equipped with computerised machines which print out the date and time that the ticket has been validated.

For visiting all but the far-flung parts of the city, the trolleybuses cover most needs, though they are prone to be uncomfortably crowded throughout much of the day, and it is often necessary to jostle with other passengers in order to be able to alight and disembark. Particularly useful services are trolleybus 2, which travels from the railway station down the western side of the Old Town, the eastern part of Gedimino, then along the south bank of the Nevis to Antakalnis; and trolleybus 5, which likewise begins and ends at the station and goes down the western side of the Old Town, before continuing northwards over the Green Bridge and past the Calvary Market *en route* to Žirmėnai.

Bus 1 links the train station with the airport, while the more frequent bus 2 goes to the airport from the northern inner suburb of Šeškinė via the Green Bridge and the New Town. These and many other bus routes are duplicated by minibuses, which can be flagged down anywhere. Their destination and the fare (which is normally either 2Lt or 3Lt and paid directly to the driver) are displayed prominently on the windscreen.

By taxi Taxis are always worth considering, particularly if travelling as a family or in a group, as they are much more comfortable than the alternatives and are also very inexpensive by Western standards. They are often necessary for getting to the airport, as buses are only starting to run at the time it is necessary to check-in for some early flights. Outrageous rip-offs of tourists by taxi drivers, once commonplace, are now largely a thing of the past, though cars without meters or which do not display the name of a company should still be avoided. Ordering a taxi by telephone from one of the companies listed below, rather than picking one up at a rank, is a sure-fire way of avoiding any difficulties. Rates consist of a fixed charge of around 2Lt plus upwards of 1.50Lt per kilometre travelled; the latter figure is invariably increased at night, sometimes to as much as 2.50Lt.

🚗 **Ekipažas** ☎ 5 239 5540
🚗 **Kabrioletas** ☎ 5 239 5539
🚗 **Martono** ☎ 5 213 2332
🚗 **Vilniaus Taksi** ☎ 5 261 6161

Car hire

🚗 **Autorenta** Rodūnios 8-102; ☎ 687 77258; f 5 233 1612; e info@carrent.lt; www.carrent.lt
🚗 **Avis** Laisvės 3; ☎ 5 230 6820; f 5 230 6821; e avis@avis.lt; www.avis.lt. Also at the airport, ☎/f 5 232 9316; e apo@avis.lt
🚗 **Budget** At the airport; ☎ 5 230 6708; f 5 230 6709; e budget@budget.lt; www.budget.lt
🚗 **Europcar** Stuokos-Gucevičiaus 9-1; ☎ 5 212 0207/2739; f 5 212 0439; e city@europcar.lt;

www.europcar.lt. Also at the airport, ☎/f 5 216 3442.
🚗 **Hertz** Kalvarijų 14; ☎ 5 272 6940; f 5 272 6970; e hertz@hertz.lt; www.hertz.lt. Also at the airport, ☎/f 5 232 9301; e airport@hertz.lt
🚗 **Litinterp** Bernardinų 7-2; ☎ 5 212 3850; f 5 212 3559; e vilnius@litinterp.com; www.litinterp.com
🚗 **Sixt** At the airport; ☎ 5 239 5636; f 5 239 5635; e rent@sixt.lt; www.sixt.lt

INFORMATION AND MAPS Originally a Belgian-German venture, the English-language magazine *Vilnius In Your Pocket*, which is available from kiosks, newsagents and tourist offices, is a well-nigh essential acquisition, having attained near-legendary status among travellers. Published five times annually, it contains comprehensive reviews of hotels, restaurants, cafés and bars; information and dates of forthcoming events and entertainment; and a host of useful listings covering professional services, shopping, transport, communications and many other subjects. Not the least of its attractions is its quirky and irreverent style, though in recent editions the reviews increasingly seem to be striving too hard to be relentlessly witty. The text of the guide can also be accessed from its website at www.inyourpocket.com. *Explore Vilnius*, a widely distributed free publication which concentrates on facts rather than opinions, is the only real competitor. Another highly recommendable purchase is the 1:25,000 map of the city, with an enlargement of the Old and New Towns and A–Z street listings, by the Latvian publisher Jāṇa Sēta.

TOURIST OFFICES

Municipal Tourist Office Vilniaus 22; ℡ 5 262 9660; f 5 262 8169; e tic@vilnius.lt; www.vilnius-tourism.lt. ⊕all year 09.00–18.00 Mon–Fri, Jun–Sep also 10.00–16.00 Sat–Sun. In addition to selling the usual range of maps & brochures, the office keeps piles of free information leaflets about various aspects of the city & posts up current public transport timetables.

Municipal Tourist Office Didžioji 31; ℡ 5 262 6470; f 5 262 0762; e turizm.info@vilnius.lt. Located inside the Old Town Hall, this is another branch of the above, & has the same opening times. Other branches can be found in the railway station & at the airport.

TRAVEL AGENCIES

Active Holidays Rodūnios 8–102; ℡/f 5 698 24795; e vilnius@activeholidays.lt; www.activeholidays.lt
Baltic Travel Service Subačiaus 2; ℡ 5 212 0220; f 5 212 2196; e lcc@bts.lt; www.bts.lt
Lithuanian Holidays Šeimyniškių 1a; ℡ 5 263 6064; f 5 272 6864; e travel@lithuanianholidays.lt; www.lithuanianholidays.lt

Lithuanian Tours Šeimyniškių 12; ℡ 5 272 4154; f 5 272 1815; e contact@lithuaniantours.com; www.lithuaniantours.com

 WHERE TO STAY There is a wide choice of accommodation in Vilnius, ranging from dorm beds in hostels to super-luxury hotels. Prices are similarly variable, and are usually a fairly reliable indicator of the quality of any particular establishment.

Hotels Vilnius's stock of hotels has mushroomed since independence, and is likely to continue to expand for some years yet. The city now has plenty of highly recommendable upmarket establishments, including many which offer the bonus of an atmospheric Old Town location. However, it is very noticeable that the majority of these are geared primarily towards the business traveller. Promotional leaflets tend to emphasise the provision of conference rooms, computers with email access, fax machines, photocopiers and the like. Room rates in such hotels, although usually lower than they were a few years ago, are still often comparable with those in cities of similar size in the West. There remains something of a shortage of good medium-range and (especially) budget accommodation in the city; some very dubious customers can almost invariably be found in the cheaper hotels. Prices in these categories of accommodation tend to be at least 50% higher than they would be anywhere else in Lithuania. Receptionists in the better hotels usually speak adequate English; the same cannot be said for the middle and lower end of the market, though there is often a member of staff who can speak basic English or German.

All sorts of discounts on standard rates are available in many of the upper-range hotels. Special weekend packages, involving a stay of at least two nights, are commonplace. Direct online booking often brings a discount of around 10%, while reduced rate promotions during quiet periods are regularly featured on individual hotel websites. Travel agents may also be able to make bookings at prices lower than those a 'walk in' guest would have to pay.

Exclusive All the hotels listed in this section are the recipients of an official five-star rating from the Lithuanian State Department of Tourism.

🏠 **Astorija** Didžioji 35/2; ☎ 5 212 0110; 📠 5 212 1762; 📧 sales.vilnius@radissonsas.com; www.vilnius.radissonsas.com. This grand early 20th-century hotel in the heart of the Old Town has been refurbished by the Radisson SAS chain, & has a Business Service Centre prominent among its facilities. The hotel rooms & reception area are adorned with agricultural tools, with a model windmill in the lounge area. All rooms have hair dryer, trouser press, telephone, cable TV, safe & hot drinks machine. Prices include either a 'grab & run' or a full buffet b/fast. The brasserie has an international menu & is among the best restaurants in the city. $$$$$

🏠 **Le Meridien Villon** A2 highway; ☎ 5 273 9700; 📠 5 273 9730; 📧 info@lemeridien.lt; www.lemeridien.lt. A huge motel & conference centre, located 19km from the centre of Vilnius, beside the main dual carriageway to Panevėžys & Rīga. It lays on free shuttle buses to the city, & offers the services of a full holiday complex, including tennis courts, a fitness club, swimming pool, 3 saunas & a restaurant, Le Paysage, specialising in Gallic-influenced cuisine. $$$$$

🏠 **Narutis** Pilies 24; ☎ 5 212 2894; 📠 5 262 2882; 📧 info@narutis.com; www.narutis.com. This hotel on the Old Town's main artery occupies an originally Gothic mansion which was remodelled in Neo-Classical style. The bedrooms are tastefully furnished, & some have 19th-century murals. Other facilities

include a lounge in the glass-covered courtyard, a sauna, fitness room, a café & a cellar restaurant. $$$$$

🏠 **Stikliai** Gaono 7; ☎ 5 264 9595; 📠 5 212 3870; 📧 sales@stikliaihotel.lt; www.stikliaihotel.lt. A member of the Relais & Chateaux group, this hotel prides itself on being the most exclusive in the Baltic states, numbering foreign royalty & other dignitaries among its clients. Occupying a 17th-century building in a quiet Old Town backstreet, it is exquisitely furnished throughout. All bedrooms are soundproofed & air-conditioned, & have satellite TV & telephone. Other facilities include a sauna, swimming pool & fitness room. The hotel restaurant serves pricey French cuisine; close by are a couple of less formal & expensive eateries run by the same management (see page 85). $$$$$

🏠 **Crowne Plaza** Čiurlionio 84; ☎ 5 274 3400; 📠 5 274 3411; 📧 reservation@cpvilnius.com; www.cpvilnius.com. This huge tower block is a longish walk from the Old Town, though it profits from a pleasantly leafy location at the edge of Vingis Park. All the bedrooms are equipped to state-of-the-art business & conference standards. In the basement are a swimming pool, sauna & gym. Fine views over the city can be enjoyed from the 16th floor Horizon bar, while the restaurant, The Seasons, presents an international menu, including a choice of vegetarian dishes. $$$$

Luxury The hotels in this section have all been allocated a four-star rating.

🏠 **Mabre Residence** Maironio 13; ☎ 5 212 2087/2195; 📠 5 212 2240; 📧 mabre@mabre.lt; www.mabre.lt. Occupies the grand Neo-Classical courtyard buildings of a former Russian Orthodox monastery in the quiet eastern part of the Old Town. All rooms have satellite TV, telephone & minibar. Public facilities include a sauna, small pool & the Steakhouse Hazienda cellar restaurant, the city's leading steak specialist. $$$$, suites & apts $$$$$

🏠 **Shakespeare** Bernardinų 8/8; ☎ 5 266 5885; 📠 5 266 5886; 📧 info@shakespeare.lt; www.shakespeare.lt. This English-style country hotel on an Old Town back street adopts a literary theme, with most of the rooms named after famous writers & containing reading material linked to each. Many offer imposing views of

nearby landmarks, such as the Church of St Anne; all have safes, internet connections & underfloor bathroom heating, while the more expensive have AC. The Sonetas restaurant is one of the classiest & most expensive in Vilnius. $$$$$

🏠 **Artis** Liejykos 11/23; ☎ 5 266 0363/0366; 📠 5 266 0377; 📧 artis@centrumhotels.com; www.centrumhotels.com. The latest addition to Vilnius's Centrum group of hotels occupies a refurbished Old Town mansion, complete with swimming pool & gymn. It also has a fine restaurant. $$$$–$$$$$

🏠 **Atrium** Pilies 10; ☎ 5 210 7773; 📠 5 210 7770; 📧 hotel@atrim.lt; www.atrium.lt. Situated in a peaceful courtyard in the very heart of the Old Town, this boasts large & well-appointed bedrooms. It has an Argentinian restaurant, El Gaucho, which naturally specialises in steaks. The nightclub, Latin Heat, continues the South American theme. $$$$–$$$$$

⌂ **CityPark** Stuokos-Gucevičiaus 3; ☎ 5 212 3515; f 5 210 7460; e citypark@citypark.lt; www.citypark.lt. Architectural controversy surrounded the unabashedly modern extension to the original hotel located in a refurbished building with a central courtyard diagonally opposite the Cathedral. All rooms have telephone, satellite TV & minibar; facilities include an express laundry, sauna & swimming pool. There is also the rare facility of its own underground car park. Fine Italian cuisine is served in the hotel restaurant, Rossini. $$$$–$$$$$

⌂ **Congress** Vilniaus 2/15; ☎ 5 269 1919; f 5 251 4280; e info@congress.lt; www.congress.lt. Housed in a fine old building overlooking the Neris, this used to be a budget hotel, but it has been totally refurbished to business-class standards & given a new name. The facilities include a restaurant, sauna & fitness room. $$$$–$$$$$

⌂ **Conti** Raugyklos 7/2; ☎ 5 251 4111; f 5 251 4100; e info@contihotel.lt; www.contihotel.lt. The opening of this hotel in 2003 marked the beginning of the regeneration of the rundown area to the rear of the synagogue. It incorporates a host of modern design features including full disabled access, a welcoming lobby with waterfall, & well-appointed bedrooms with en suite facilities & internet access. Lithuanian & international dishes are served in the restaurant, Žiemos Sodas, while the kitchens are equipped to allow Jewish groups to prepare kosher food. $$$$–$$$$$

⌂ **Europa Royale** Aušros Vartų 6; ☎ 5 266 0770; f 5 261 2000; e reservation@europaroyale.com, www.europaroyale.com. A stylish modern hotel in a renovated Historicist building. Bedrooms have satellite TV, AC, minibar & heated bathroom tiles. $$$$–$$$$$

⌂ **Grotthuss** Ligoninės 7; ☎ 5 266 0322; f 5 266 0323; e info@grotthushotel.com; www.grotthushotel.com. New hotel with cellar restaurant in one of the most peaceful parts of the Old Town. All rooms offer internet access, a safe & a minibar. The restaurant, La Pergola, serves a range of international cuisine. $$$$–$$$$$

⌂ **Holiday Inn** Šeimyniškių 1; ☎ 5 210 3000; f 5 210 3001; e holiday-inn@ibc.lt; www.holidayinnvilnius.lt. Surprisingly, it took until 2002 for this well-known chain to open a hotel in Vilnius, its first venture into the Baltic states. The

location, immediately east of the new business district, suggests that it is aiming squarely at a commercial clientele. $$$$–$$$$$

⌂ **Naujasis Vilnius** Konstitucijos 14; ☎ 5 273 9595; f 5 273 9500; e office@vilniushotel.eu; www.hotelnv.lt. The smaller of the 2 giant hotel blocks on the north side of the Neris, the former Turistas is now a member of the Best Western group, having been made over by a Swiss joint venture company into a business-class hotel with the usual support services. $$$$, apts $$$$$

⌂ **Reval Lietuva** Konstitucijos 20; ☎ 5 272 6272; f 5 272 6270; e lietuva.sales@revalhotels.com; www.revalhotels.com. The former Intourist hotel is much the largest & most prominent in the city & is heavily used by organised tour groups. In 2000 it was acquired by the Reval chain, which has eliminated all Soviet features in a radical Scandinavian-style facelift. The even-numbered rooms offer grandstand views over the Old Town, as does the bar on the 22nd floor. $$$$, suites & apts $$$$$

⌂ **Scandic Neringa** Gedimino 23; ☎ 5 268 1910; f 5 261 4160; e neringa@scandic-hotels.com; www.scandic-hotels.com. This communist-era hotel on the main commercial street has been given a Swedish-style makeover by the Scandic chain, & is equipped with a gym, sauna, small pool, library & business centre. The restaurant, however, still preserves some outrageous Soviet décor in the form of murals depicting the fisherfolk of Neringa: it serves excellent, reasonably priced Lithuanian & international dishes. Once the home base of the internationally renowned Ganelin jazz trio, it continues to feature live music in the evenings. $$$$, suites $$$$$

⌂ **Embassy Balatonas** Latvių 38; ☎ 5 272 2250; f 5 272 2134; e info@embassyhotel.lt; www.embassyhotel.lt. This recently renovated hotel occupies a gleaming white historic villa set amid the wooden houses in the heart of the Žvėrynas district. Facilities include a sauna, swimming pool & a small café which serves full meals. $$$$

⌂ **IdaBasar** Subačiaus 1; ☎ 5 262 2909; f 5 2262 7834; e hotel@idabasar.lt; www.idabasar.lt. The guesthouse of this German joint-venture is an offshoot of the restaurant on the opposite side of the courtyard. All rooms have satellite TV & minibar; the apts also have a kitchen. $$$$

⌂ **Šarūnas** Raitininkų 4; ☎ 5 272 3666/3888; f 5 724355; e info@hotelsarunas.lt; www.hotelsarunas.lt. This modern business hotel near the Žalgiris stadium is owned by Šarūnas Marčiulionis, erstwhile player with the Sacramento Kings of America's National Basketball

Association. Sportsgear & trainers worn by leading stars of the NBA decorate the informal Rooney's Bar, which serves Lithuanian & American dishes, while the formal restaurant has an international menu & features live jazz on Fri evenings. A fitness room with weightlifting equipment supplements the obligatory sauna. $$$$

🏠 **AAA Mano Liza** Ligoninės 5; ✆ 5 212 2225; f 5 212 2608; e hotel@aaa.lt; www.hotelinvilnius.lt. A small guesthouse in the quiet southwestern part of the Old Town, which will arrange pick-up from the airport. All 8 rooms are equipped with satellite TV. The restaurant offers a nicely varied international menu. $$$–$$$$

🏠 **Dvaras Manor House** Tilto 3; ✆ 5 210 7370; f 5 261 8783; e hotel@dvaras.lt; www.dvaras.lt. A very select hotel, luxuriantly furnished in a traditional style. It has just 8 bedrooms, all of which have AC, minibar & internet access. There is a similarly classy restaurant, which serves international fare & has a notable wine list. $$$–$$$$

🏠 **Ratonda** Gedimino 52/1; ✆ 5 212 0670; f 5 212 0669; e ratonda@centrumhotels.com; www.centrumhotels.com. An offshoot of the Centrum mentioned below, this attracts tourists as well as business travellers. It is in fact located just off Gedimino & so is unaffected by traffic noise. $$$–$$$$

Mid-range These hotels are of two- or three-star standard.

🏠 **Europa City** Jasinskio 14; ✆ 5 251 4477; f 5 251 4476; e vilnius@europacity.lt; www.europacity.lt. Although a sister hotel to Europa Imperial, this newcomer is much larger & less exclusive. $$$, apts $$$$

🏠 **Ambassador** Gedimino 12; ✆ 5 261 5450; f 5 212 1716; e info@ambassador.lt; www.ambassador.lt. Handily located on the main business street, this hotel has been partially modernised, though the bedrooms still have many of the unmistakeable hallmarks of the Soviet era. $$$

🏠 **Apia** Šv Ignoto 12; ✆ 5 212 3426; f 5 212 3618; e apia@apia.lt; www.apia.lt. A 12-room guesthouse in an Old Town tenement. $$$

🏠 **Centro Kubas** Stiklių 3; ✆ 5 266 0860; f 5 266 0863; e hotel@centrokubas.lt; www.centrokubas.lt. A designer-style hotel decked out with old agricultural tools & with an adjoining linen shop. There are only 14 rooms, spread across 4 floors linked by a glass lift. It also has a fine cellar restaurant. $$$

🏠 **Centrum Uniquestay** Vytenio 9/24; ✆ 5 268 3462; f 5 213 2760; e hotel@centrum.lt; www.uniquestay.com. Located in the eponymous business centre in the western part of the New Town, this plush hotel was completely rebuilt in 2003, & is popular with business visitors (every room has its own computer with internet access, & the hotel has fax & photocopying facilities). It is also well frequented by tourists. $$$

🏠 **Grybas House** Aušros Vartų 3a; ✆ 5 261 9695, 264 7474; f 5 212 2416; e info@grybashouse.com; www.grybashouse.com. A delightful small hotel (there are only 9 rooms) in a refurbished Baroque house set in a quiet courtyard at the northern end of the Old Town. The décor includes sculptures from the Congo & the former pier in Palanga. Primarily geared to

tourists, it offers full travel agency services. All rooms have telephone, satellite TV, minibar, water filters & heated floors. There is a fine basement restaurant, with live classical music on Wed evenings. $$$

🏠 **Panorama** Sodų 14; ✆ 5 273 8011; f 5 216 3789; e reservation@hotelpanorama.lt; www.hotelpanorama.lt. What was for long Vilnius' most notorious hotel, a large Soviet-era block opposite the stations, was firstly given a new name, then a complete renovation. It is now popular with tour groups, & remains a convenient place to spend the night if arriving late or departing early. $$$

🏠 **Reval Inn** Ukmergės 363; ✆ 5 238 8000; f 5 238 8555; e vilnius@revalinn.com; www.revalinn.com. This box-like hotel at the far northern edge of the city was built to plug what was perceived to be a gap in the market – an establishment offering fully modern business-class standards at reasonable prices. $$$

🏠 **Rūdninkų Vartai** Rūdninkų 15/46; ✆ 5 261 3916; f 5 212 0507; e rudninkai@cityhotels.lt; www.cityhotels.lt. Named after the western gateway to the Old Town which formerly occupied the spot, the hotel is built round a courtyard which in summer serves as an open-air extension to its Belgian speciality restaurant, Paradis Belge 32. All rooms have satellite TV & telephone; some also have a minibar or refrigerator. A sauna & fitness room are the other main facilities. $$$

🏠 **Senatoriai** Tilto 2; ✆ 5 212 6491/7056; f 5 212 6372; e info@senatoriai.lt; www.senatoriai.lt. This small low-rise hotel profits from an excellent location, being discreetly tucked away down a side street immediately to the rear of Gedimino, just a stone's throw from the cathedral. $$$

🏠 **Adelita** Rodūnios 8; ✆ 5 232 9304; f 5 213 6463; e hotel.adelita@takas.lt; www.adelita.lt.

Occupying the same building as the budget Skrydis hotel at the airport, this is under different management & is fully renovated, with a fitness room, sauna & café among the facilities. $$-$$$
🏠 **Ecotel** Slucko 8; ☎ 5 210 2700; f 5 210 2707; e hotel@ecotel.lt; www.ecotel.lt. Another example of

a hotel aiming at a combination of modernity & economy. It occupies a former shoe factory between the new business district & the Žalgiris stadium. Among its quirky features are special rooms for allergy sufferers & extra-long beds for tall people. $$

Budget hotels and guesthouses These establishments have either one or two stars, or else have no official categorisation.

🏠 **Victoria** Saltoniškių 56; ☎ 5 272 4013; f 5 272 4320; e hotel@victoria.lt; www.victoria.lt. A choice of unrenovated & renovated rooms is on offer at this Swedish joint-venture hotel in the northeast of the Žvėrynas district. All rooms have satellite TV & telephone, & a Scandinavian b/fast buffet is included in the price. $$-$$$
🏠 **Bernardinų** Bernardinų 5; ☎ 5 261 5134; f 5 260 8410; e guesthouse@avevita.lt/guesthouse; www.avevita.lt/guesthouse. This new 11-room guesthouse on a quiet Old Town alley provides competition to the long-established Litinterp (see below) next door. Parking is available in the inner courtyard. $$

🏠 **Skrydis** Rodūnios 8; ☎ 5 232 9099; f 5 230 6498; e hotel@vno.lt; www.vilnius-airport.lt. Renovations at the airport hotel are proceeding at a leisurely pace, & many rooms are still of the Soviet era. It is certainly worth considering for at least sgl-night stays if arriving late or departing early. $$
🏠 **Jeruzalė** Kalvarijų 209; ☎ 5 271 4040; f 5 276 2627; e jeruzale@takas.lt; www.jeruzalehotel.com. Budget hotel in the northern residential district of the same name, a short distance south of the Calvary Church. The bedrooms are all en-suite, & a sauna & swimming pool are on the premises. It can be reached by buses 26, 35, 36 or 50. $-$$

Hostels

🏠 **JNN Hostel** Konstitucijos 25; ☎/f 5 272 2270; e jnn@lvjc.lt; www.jnn.lt. A short distance west of the new business district, this is a superior hostel in which all rooms have private facilities. 2 swimming pools, a sauna, solarium & massage facilities are also on the premises. $$
🏠 **IYHF Filaretai Hostel** Filarų 17; ☎ 5 215 4627; f 5 212 0149; e info@filaretaihostel.lt; www.filaretaihostel.lt. Much the larger of the 2 IYHF-affiliated hostels, situated at the northeastern edge of the Užupis district, & reached by bus 34. $

🏠 **IYHF Old Town Hostel** Aušros Vartų 20-10; ☎ 5 262 5357; f 5 268 5967; e oldtownhostel@lithuanianhostels.org; www.lithuanianhostels.org. Despite its name, this 23-bed hostel actually lies just beyond the southern edge of the Old Town, & is signposted from the railway station. $
🏠 **Jaunujų Turistų Centras** Polocko 7; ☎ 5 261 3576; f 5 262 7742; e vjtc@delfi.lt; www.vjtc.lt. The Young Tourists' Centre is in the eastern part of Užupis, & has a dozen rooms, each accommodating 3 or 4 people. $

Bed and breakfast

🏠 **Litinterp** Bernardinų 7/2; ☎ 5 212 3850; f 5 212 3559; e vilnius@litinterp.com; www.litinterp.com. ⊕08.30–17.30 Mon–Fri, 09.00–15.30 Sat. In addition to its own small, immaculately maintained guesthouse on the premises,

this offers rooms in private houses in central Vilnius & Trakai, & also has some apts for rent. Advance bookings for Kaunas, Klaipėda, Palanga & Nida can be made, & car hire, interpretation & translation services are also available. $$

✖ **WHERE TO EAT AND DRINK** In a welcome change from the Soviet years, Vilnius now has a huge range of restaurants, cafés, bars and pubs to choose from. Many of the leading cuisines of the world are represented, though this development thankfully has not (as it has in other capital cities of former communist countries) resulted in any diminution in the number or quality of establishments specialising in traditional local dishes. As is the case throughout Lithuania, some places are difficult to categorise, with many bars and cafés offering a full restaurant-type menu. The main concentrations of places to eat and drink are in the Old and New Towns, though there are a few restaurants further afield which well warrant the detour. Casualty rates have increased markedly since the turn of the millennium: many of the best-known eateries of the early post-communist years have now closed down, so it is likely that some on this list will follow.

For further recommendations, particularly for formal dining, see also Hotels above.

Restaurants

✗ **Čagino** Basanavičiaus 11. A small, intimate restaurant, mostly at basement level, serving old-style Russian cuisine. In the evenings, there is live Russian music, for which a small surcharge is made.

✗ **Čili** Didžioji 5 & Gedimino 23. These are the 2 most convenient branches of a well-regarded local pizza chain that has gradually spread all over the city, & to other Lithuanian towns. They also serve pasta, plus a few Tex-Mex dishes.

✗ **Čili Kaimas** Vokiečių 8. This inordinately popular venture aims to evoke a country atmosphere, not only in its menu but also in the amazing décor of its warren of rooms arranged around a glass-covered central courtyard.

✗ **Čingischanas** Basanavičiaus 8. This offers a rare opportunity to sample the spicy cuisine of the former Soviet republic of Kazakhstan. Fixed priced menus, which are not common in Lithuania, are available.

✗ **Csárda** Šv Mykolo 4/1. Fiery Magyar cuisines & Hungarian wines are served up in an intimate, elegantly furnished dining room & the small courtyard outside.

✗ **Da Antonio** Vilniaus 23. A traditional trattoria serving delicious pizzas made in a wood-fired oven, as well as a range of pasta dishes & other classic Italian fare. There is an offshoot (albeit with an electric oven) at Pilies 20.

✗ **Fortas** Algirdo 17. This New Town restaurant offers an eclectic menu of Lithuanian dishes, pizzas & Tex-Mex fare in a bar-type setting.

✗ **Divino** Didžioji 19. Small trattoria serving the main staples of the Italian kitchen, with outside seating on the square in summer.

✗ **Forto Dvaras** Pilies 16. Housed in a network of cellars, this presents examples of traditional home-style cooking from different regions of Lithuania, including many dishes which are rarely found on restaurant menus.

✗ **Freskos** Didžioji 31. Decorated with theatre costumes & posters as well as the frescos which give it its name, this occupies the rear part of the Old Town Hall. The international-style cuisine is prepared with a Gallic sense of flair, & while relatively expensive is good value none the less, the best bargains being the set lunches & help-yourself salad bar.

✗ **Gusto Blyninė** Aušros Vartų 6. Speciality pancake place, with a huge choice of both sweet & savoury varieties.

✗ **IdaBasar** Subačiaus 3. The cavernous cellar & the hearty portions successfully invoke the culinary tradition of the German joint-owners. There are some imaginative dishes on the menu, while among the beers on tap is the celebrated Jever, Germany's bitterest brew.

✗ **Konfucijus** Vilniaus 12. Offers both Chinese & Indonesian dishes, with bargain menus at lunchtime.

✗ **La Provence** Vokiečių 24. Advertising itself as '100% pure gourmet', this relatively pricey restaurant sandwiched between the 2 constituent parts of Žemaičių Smuklė serves Provençal & other Mediterranean cuisine.

✗ **Les Amis** Savičiaus 7. Pleasant, very modestly priced little French restaurant with back garden.

✗ **Lokys** Stiklių 8. Occupying a warren of brick Gothic cellars in one of the quietest parts of the Old Town, 'The Bear' is a stalwart of the Vilnius restaurant scene, & the only one which functions much as it did in the communist era. Game dishes, particularly elk & wild boar, are its main specialities, though it has a fine all-round menu in which salads & desserts also feature strongly.

✗ **Mano Gura** Vilniaus 22/1. Although not exclusively vegetarian, this offers healthy eating with an appropriately minimalist backdrop.

✗ **Marceliukės Klėtis** Tuskulėnų 35. A traditional family-orientated hostelry just northeast of the Calvary Market, whose rustic exterior is totally at odds with the surrounding high-rise apt blocks. Its amazing cluttered décor includes an old wooden bicycle suspended from the ceiling. Most of the staple dishes of the Lithuanian kitchen are featured on the menu, & professional folk groups perform most evenings.

✗ **Markus ir Ko** Žydų 4a, entrance from Antokolskio 9. Primarily a steakhouse offering a wide choice of succulent cuts, though there are plenty of other options, including salads & sweets, as well as a long drinks list. There is live piano music (usually jazz) most evenings.

✗ **Medininkai** Aušros Vartų 8. After a period of closure, this restaurant in a former monastery has reopened under the management of the adjoining

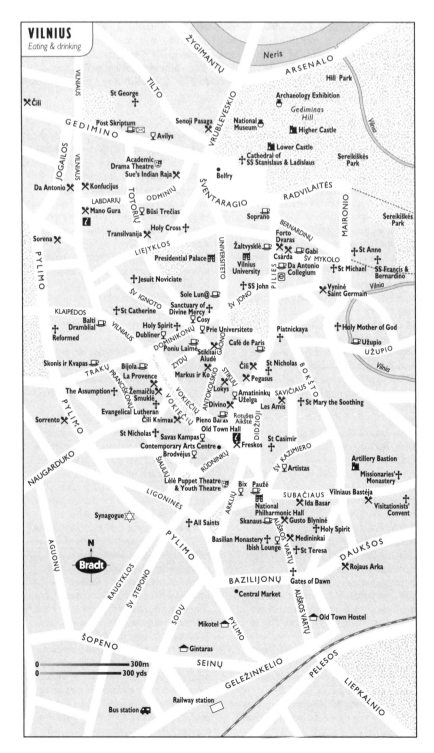

VILNIUS
Eating & drinking

ŽYGIMANTU

Neris

ARSENALO

Hill Park

VILNIAUS
TILTO
VRUBLEVSKIO

✗Čili

St George ✝

Archaeology Exhibition

Gediminas Hill

Post Skriptum
GEDIMINO

Senoji Pasaga ✗

National ✗
Museum

🏰 Higher Castle

♟✉ ♟Avilys

🏰 Lower Castle

Sereikiškės Park

JOGAILOS
VILNIAUS

Academic
Drama Theatre
Sue's Indian Raja ✗

Cathedral of
✝ SS Stanislaus & Ladislaus

Da Antonio ✗   ✗ Konfucijus

● Belfry

SVENTARAGIO

RADVILAITĖS

MAIRONIO

LABDARIŲ
✗ Mano Gura
ℹ

ODMINIŲ
TOTORIŲ

♟Būsi Trečias

Soprano ♟

Sereikiškės Park

Sorena ✗

PYLIMO

Transilvanija ✗

LIEJYKLOS

Holy Cross ✝

BERNARDINŲ

Forto
Dvaras

✝ St Anne

Presidential Palace 🏛

UNIVERSITETO

Žaltvykslė ♟
Csárda ✗✗ ♟Gabi
SV MYKOLO

✝ St Michael

SS Francis &
Bernardino

✝ Jesuit Noviciate

Vilnius
University
🏛

Da Antonio
Collegium

Vilnia

SV IGNOTO

Sole Lun@ ♟

✝ SS John

Vyninė
Saint Germain

KLAIPĖDOS
Balti
Dramblial
Reformed ✝

✝ St Catherine

Sanctuary of
Divine Mercy ✝
♟Cosy

PILIES

VILNIAUS

Holy Spirit ✝
Dubliner ♟

Prie Universiteto ♟

Piatnickaya
✝

✝ Holy Mother of God

DOMINIKONŲ

Poniu Laime ✗

Café de Paris ♟

UŽUPIO

♟Užupio

Skonis ir Kvapas ♟

TRAKŲ
FRANCISKONŲ

Bijola ✗
La Provence ✗

ZYDŲ

Stikliai ✗
Aludė

STIKLIŲ

Čili ✗
✗ Pegasus

St Nicholas
✝

Vilnia

The Assumption ✝ ✗ Žemaičių
Smuklė ✗

VOKIEČIŲ

Markus ir Ko ✗

Lokys ✗

ANTOKOLSKIO

Amatininkų
Uželga ✗

SAVIČIAUS

Les Amis ✗

✝ St Mary the Soothing

BOKŠTO

PYLIMO

Evangelical Lutheran

VOKIEČIŲ

✗ Divino

Čili Kaimas ✗

Pieno Daras ✗

Rotušes
Aikštė ♟
Old Town Hall 🏛

Sorrento ✗

St Nicholas ✝

Savas Kampas ♟

Contemporary Arts Centre ●
Brodvėjus ♟

ŠAULIŲ

RŪDNINKŲ

DIDŽIOJI

♟ Freskos

St Casimir
✝

SV KAZIMIERO

♟Artistas

Artillery Bastion
🏰

NAUGARDUKO

Lėlė Puppet Theatre 🏛
& Youth Theatre

LIGONINĖS

ARKLIŲ

Bix Paužė
♟ ♟

SUBAČIAUS

Missionaries' ✝
Monastery

Vilniaus Bastėja

✗ Ida Basar

Visitationists' ✝
Convent

Synagogue ✡

National
Philharmonic Hall

Skanaus ♟✗

✗ Gusto Blyninė

✝ Holy Spirit

AGUONŲ

N

Bradt

✝ All Saints

PYLIMO

Basilian Monastery ✝
Ibish Lounge

AUŠROS VARTŲ

✗ Medininkai

✗ St Teresa

DAUKŠOS

✗ Rojaus Arka

RAUGYKLOS

ŠV STEPONO

BAZILIJONŲ

● Central Market

✝
Gates of Dawn

AUŠROS VARTŲ

SODU

0 ──────── 300m
0 ──────── 300 yds

Mikotel 🏠

PYLIMO

🏠 Old Town Hostel

SEINŲ

🏠 Gintaras

ŠOPENO

GELEŽINKELIO

PELĖSOS

LIEPKALNIO

Railway station 🏠

Bus station 🚌

Hotel Europa Royale. The menu has a shortish but well-chosen selection of reasonably priced Lithuanian dishes. In summer, tables are set outside in the peaceful courtyard.

✗ **Pas Rudolfą II** Gedimino 48. New Town restaurant serving typically hearty Czech cooking & beers.

✗ **Pegasus** Didžioji 11. This presents fusion cooking, drawing on a range of Asian traditions. In the late evening, it becomes a cocktail bar.

✗ **Rojaus Arka** Daukšos 3. The 'Arch of Paradise' occupies part of a block of houses in the Viennese Secessionist style, the only examples of this type of architecture in the city, & is named after its splendidly curvaceous doorway. This leads to a suite of intimate little dining rooms, where a short but attractive menu of starters, fish & meat dishes awaits. There are regular exhibitions of paintings & photographs.

✗ **Rytai** Naugarduko 22. An authentic Chinese eatery, situated in the eastern part of the New Town.

✗ **Senoji Pasaga** Vrublevskio 2/Tilto 1. The 'Old Horseshoe' is a country-style tavern, complete with a cellar & a back garden with fountain, & serves a typically Lithuanian menu.

✗ **Sorena** Islandijos 4. This Azerbaijani speciality restaurant serves tasty chargrilled kebabs, spicy stews & marinated vegetables & fruits.

✗ **Sorrento** Pylimo 21. This is now probably the best & most expensive Italian restaurant in Vilnius. Reasonably priced pizzas are made in a wood-fired oven; the seafood, veal & beef dishes are predictably much more expensive. A well-selected wine list is also featured.

✗ **Stikliai Aludė** Gaono 7. This small restaurant has a predominantly local menu & makes a much cheaper but still highly recommendable alternative to the posh French restaurant in the hotel next door.

✗ **Sue's Indian Raja** Odminių. After a period of closure, this has returned in a new location, & is deservedly a big favourite with the local English-speaking community for its authentically spiced curries prepared by Punjabi chefs.

✗ **Transilvanija** Totorių 24. Romanian restaurant cum bar, offering a rare opportunity to sample local specialities of Transylvania & Moldovia.

✗ **Vandens Malūnas** Verkių 100. Occupying a converted 19th-century watermill in the Verkiai Park, this is a popular excursion destination, particularly in summer, when a large outdoor terrace is open. Traditional Lithuanian fare is served, & there is a good line in freshwater fish dishes.

✗ **Vilniaus Bastėja** Subačiaus 15/2. A new venture with high gastronomic ambitions; it serves international fare & is among the most expensive in the city.

✗ **Vyninė Saint Germain** Literatų 9. French restaurant cum wine bar tucked away down an Old Town alley.

✗ **Žemaičių Smuklė** Vokiečių 24. An amazing warren of a place, the 'Samogitian Tavern' offers a choice of dining experiences, ranging from the dark intimacy of the cellars (which are adorned with a series of fantastical murals) to the airy al fresco atmosphere of the courtyard's upper storey. A special strong beer is brewed exclusively for the tavern, which serves many traditional dishes & has live folk bands at w/ends.

Cafés

▭ **Balti Drambliai** Vilniaus 41. A cellar with garden, 'White Elephants' is currently Vilnius's only purely vegetarian eatery, presenting a wide range of meat-free cuisine.

▭ **Bijola** Vokiečių 28. Small café attached to an Old Town bakery.

▭ **Café de Paris** Didžioji 1. Café-restaurant attached to the French Cultural Centre; it has a predictably good choice of crêpes.

▭ **Collegium** Pilies 22. There is no more convenient place for public internet access in central Vilnius than this cybercafé, which charges 6Lt/hr. ⊕08.00–midnight.

▭ **Gabi** Šv Mykolo 6. A delightful café with a rustic interior & a side courtyard, right next door to the Amber Museum. One of the few places in the city to have adopted a strict no-smoking policy, it offers a full menu of homely Lithuanian dishes.

▭ **Kalvarijų I** Kalvarijų 1. Pleasant café in the imposing setting of the pseudo-castle to the north of the Green Bridge.

▭ **Magdė** Basanavičiaus 3. A small country-style café-restaurant at the eastern edge of the New Town.

▭ **Pauzė** Aušros Vartų 5-1. Located at the front of the Filharmonija building, this café is part of the Stikliai chain, whose very name is a byword for quality. It serves salads & other snacks, but is primarily recommendable for its cakes & desserts.

▭ **Pieno Baras** Didžioji 21. Seemingly belonging to a bygone age, this traditional milk bar serves hot milk & home-baked cakes at very low prices.

▭ **Ponių Laimė** Stiklių 14-1. 'Ladies' Happiness' is yet another Skiliai establishment, occupying recently expanded premises across the street from the hotel.

▭ **Post Skriptum** Gedimino 7. Drolly named café adjoining the Main Post Office. It has outside seating in summer.

▭ **Skanaus** Aušros Vartų 9. This café attached to a bakery is primarily of interest for its cakes & sweets, though savoury dishes are also available.

⌸ **Skonis ir Kvapas** Trakų 8. Set in a delightful suite of rooms off an old courtyard, this exquisitely furnished café presents a marvellous selection of teas & coffees from around the world, & also serves full meals.

⌸ **Sole Lun@** Universiteto 4. Situated alongside the university, this Italian café is a particularly recommendable choice for a summertime al fresco drink or snack, which can be enjoyed in the irregularly shaped triple-tier Baroque courtyard to the rear.

⌸ **Soprano** Pilies 2. This is Vilnius's first genuine Italian-style ice-cream parlour. In addition to a mouth-watering array of different ices, it serves excellent coffee & snacks.

⌸ **Užupio** Užupio 2. Predictably, the 'local' of Vilnius's bohemian quarter is a favourite with artists & students. Idyllically set by the River Vilnia, it has a spacious beer garden (the only one in Vilnius) & a contrastingly cosy interior.

⌸ **Žaltvysklė** Pilies 13. A very reasonably priced café-restaurant serving both Hungarian & local dishes.

Pubs, bars and nightclubs

♀ **Amatininkų Užeiga** Didžioji 19/2. Plenty of inexpensive Lithuanian dishes, including a wide range of tasty starters, are available in this rambling bar with a snug cellar. ⏱until 05.00.

♀ **Artistas** Šv Kazimiero 3. The main draw here is the large courtyard, one of the most attractive spots for outdoor imbibing in the Old Town.

♀ **Avilys** Gedimino 5. This home-brew pub has 3 products: Avilio, a standard light beer; Medaus, which is made with honey; & Korio, a dark ginseng beer. Plenty of other drinks, including a wide range of Tibetan teas, are also available, & there is a long menu which includes plenty of typical Lithuanian fare.

♀ **Bix** Etmonų 6. Founded by the eponymous Lithuanian band as a rock music bar, though it also has a cellar with a more sedate atmosphere.

♀ **Brodvėjus** Mėsinių 4. The beer tap in the guise of a saxophone is the most eye-catching piece of décor in this pub, which presents all kinds of live music, from rock to classical, each evening at 20.00.

♀ **Būsi Trečias** Totorių 18. A pleasantly rustic bar on 2 floors. In the basement is Vilnius's first boutique brewery, whose single product can either be enjoyed neat, or mixed with perfumed cordial to make a 'cherry beer'.

♀ **Cozy** Dominikonų 10. Currently one of Vilnius's hippest addresses, this serves creative modern cooking & also has a basement nightclub (⏱Wed–Sun) where there are different musical themes each evening.

♀ **Dubliner** Dominikonų 6. After a gap of several years, Vilnius once again has an Irish pub. It is predictably popular with expats, & serves a range of homely Irish, British & international dishes.

♀ **Ibish Lounge** Aušros Vartų 11. This is best known as a late-evening cocktail bar, though it functions as a normal restaurant at other times.

♀ **Prie Universiteto** (also known as 'The Pub') Dominikonų 9. The Old Town sister establishment to the above. Although the food served is a bit more downmarket, it has the advantage of an attractive galleried courtyard.

♀ **Savas Kampas** Vokiečių 4. This popular bar serves a wide range of food, including tasty lunchtime hotpots on w/days. An atmospheric cellar is open in the evening, while in summer a large pavilion is rigged up outside.

OTHER PRACTICALITIES
Currency exchange
Parex Geležinkelio 6. ⏱24hrs.

Pharmacy
Gedimino Vaistinė Gedimino 27. ⏱24hrs.

Post
✉ **Central Post Office** Gedimino 7. ⏱Mon–Fri 07.00–19.00, Sat 09.00–16.00.

Medical services
✚ **Baltic–American Medical & Surgical Clinic** Nemenčinės 54a; ☏ 5 234 2020; e bak@takas.lt; www.baclinic.com. This is the only hospital in the Baltic states offering fully Western standards.

✚ **Medical Diagnostic Centre** Grybo 32, ☏ 5 270 9120; e mdc@medcentras.lt; www.medcentras.lt. There are English-speaking doctors on the staff.

Embassies The following is a selection of the foreign embassies in Vilnius. A complete list can be found on the website of the Lithuanian Ministry of Foreign Affairs (*www.urm.lt*).

Ｅ Belarus Mindaugo 13; ☎ 5 266 2200 or 266 2211; f 5 662212; e bpl@post.5ci.lt, www.belarus.lt

Ｅ Belgium Kalinausko 2b; ☎ 5 266 0820; f 5 212 6444; e vilnius@diplobel.org; www.diplomatie.be/vilnius

Ｅ Canada Jogailos 4; ☎ 5 249 0950; f 5 249 7865; e vilnius@canada.lt; www.canada.lt

Ｅ Denmark Kosciuškos 36; ☎ 5 264 8760; f 5 231 2300; e vnoamb@um.dk; www.ambvilnius.um.dk

Ｅ Estonia Mickevičiaus 4a; ☎ 5 278 0200; f 5 278 0201; e sekretar@estemb.lt; www.estemb.lt

Ｅ Finland Klaipėdos 6; ☎ 5 212 1621; f 5 212 2441; e sanomat.vil@formin.fi; www.finland.lt

Ｅ France Švaro 1; ☎ 5 212 2979; f 5 212 4211; e ambafrance.vilnius@diplomatie.gouv.fr; www.ambafrance-lit.org

Ｅ Germany Sierakausko 24/8; ☎ 5 210 6400; f 5 210 6446; e info@wilna.diplo.de; www.deutschebotschaft-wilna.lt

Ｅ Italy Vytauto 1; ☎ 5 212 0620; f 5 212 0405; e ambasciata.vilnius@esteri.it; www.ambvilnius.esteri.it

Ｅ Japan Čiurlionio 82b; ☎ 5 231 0462; f 5 231 0461.

Ｅ Latvia Čiurlionio 76; ☎ 5 213 1260; f 5 213 1130; e embassy.lithuania@mfa.gov.lv

Ｅ Netherlands Jogailos 4; ☎ 5 269 0072; f 5 269 0073; e vil@minbuza.nl; www.netherlandsembassy.lt

Ｅ Norway Mėsinių 5/2; ☎ 5 261 0000; f 5 261 0100; e emb.vilnius@mfa.no; www.norvegija.lt

Ｅ Poland Smėlio 20a; ☎ 5 270 9001; f 5 270 9007; e ambpol@tdd.lt; www.polandembassy.lt

Ｅ Russia Latvių 53/54; ☎ 5 272 1763; f 5 272 3877; e post@rusemb.lt; www.rusemb.lt

Ｅ Sweden Didžioji 16; ☎ 5 268 5010; f 5 268 5030; e ambassaden.vilnius@foreign.ministry.se; www.sweden-abroad.com

Ｅ Ukraine Teatro 4; ☎ 5 212 1536; f 5 212 0475; e ukrembassy@post.5ci.lt

Ｅ UK Antakalnio 2; ☎ 5 246 2900; f 5 246 2901; e be-vilnius@britain.lt; www.britain.lt

Ｅ USA Akmenų 6; ☎ 5 266 5500; f 5 266 5510; e mail@usembassy.lt; www.usembassy.lt

Cultural institutes

America Centre Akmenų 7; ☎ 5 266 5300; f 5 266 5310

British Council Jogailos 4; ☎ 5 264 4890; f 5 264 4893; e mail@britishcouncil.lt; www.britishcouncil.lt

Jewish Tolerance Centre Naugarduko 10/2; ☎ 5 231 2357; f 5 2231 2351

English-language church services

✝ **Grace International Baptist Church** Verkių 22; www.church.lt. Service every Sun at 11.00.

✝ **International Church of Vilnius** Vokiečių 20; www.icvilnius.org. An ecumenical service is held in the Lutheran Church every Sun at 09.30.

✝ **SS Francis & Bernardino** Maironio 8. Roman Catholic Mass every Sun at 09.00, with confessions beforehand on request.

SHOPPING Shopping in Vilnius has been revolutionised in the past few years by the creation of several large suburban shopping malls. These have resulted in the demise of the old Soviet-era department stores, which can still be found in other Lithuanian towns. Thankfully, the Old Town has been relatively unaffected by these developments, and many fine traditional shops still survive there.

Amber

Amber Gallery Šv Mykolo 8. The excellent gallery has a shop alongside where authenticated pieces of amber & amber jewellery can be purchased.

Amber Sculpture Museum Aušros Vartų 9. This specialises in elaborate objects made of amber.

Lino ir Gintara Studija Didžioji 10. As its name suggests, the Linen & Amber studio produces artistic examples of both linen & amber goods. There are several more specialised branches scattered throughout the Old Town.

Bookshops

Akademinė Knyga Universiteto 4. An academic bookshop with a selection of English-language paperbacks, though the stock is mainly of textbooks more specifically for Lithuanians.

Gedimino 2 & Gedimino 50 The first of these is much the largest bookshop in central Vilnius, with substantial English-language sections.
Littera Šv Jono 12. With its elaborate frescoed interior, the bookshop within the university complex is undoubtedly the most attractive in the city, & has a decent representation of English-language books about Lithuania.

National Museum of Lithuania Arsenalo 1. The bookstall at the cash desk sells the wonderful coffee-table books published by the museum (see pages 93–4).
Pilies Pilies 22. This stocks plenty of locally produced books in English on Lithuanian subjects.
Rūdninkū Knygynas Rūdninkų 20. In addition to books, the stock here includes a good selection of English-language magazines & CDs of Lithuanian music.

Chocolates

Šokoladas Pausalis Didžioji 40. One of a number of manufacturers of handcrafted chocolates to have sprung up in Vilnius in the last few years, this also has a tiny café area where hot chocolate is served.

Šokolado Namai Trakų 13. Another specialist in handmade chocolates.

Shopping malls

Akropolis Ozo 25. A major retail development in the north of the city, with over 200 shops, around a dozen restaurants, an ice rink & a bowling alley.

Europa Konstitucijos 7a. This showpiece scheme immediately north of the Neris is the obvious place to come for the modern shopping experience, with plenty of international as well as Lithuanian chains in evidence.

Souvenirs

Contemporary Arts Centre Vokiečių 2. This sells paintings, amber & ceramics, & also has a large selection of art books, including many in English.
Dailė Žydų 2/2. Sells a wide range of Lithuanian handicrafts.
Mano Niša Basanavičiaus 3. Makes beautiful enamel objects; there are demonstrations Tue 13.00–17.00.

Sauluva Literatų 3. This sells ceramics, glassware, woodcarvings, leather goods & many other traditional artefacts, including candle houses which are made to order.
Stiklas Didžioji 38. Stylish examples of all kinds & sizes of contemporary Lithuanian glassware can be bought in this specialist outlet.

ENTERTAINMENT AND NIGHTLIFE
Theatres

🎭 **Lėlė Puppet Theatre** Arklių 5; 🕿 5 262 8678; www.teatraslele.lt. Housed in the Baroque Oginskis Palace, this presents entertaining shows, mostly for children, though with a few pitched at an adult audience.
🎭 **Lithuanian National Drama Theatre** Gedimino 4; 🕿 5 262 9771; www.teatras.lt. The city's main venue for straight dramatic fare, offering both traditional & avant-garde productions.
🎭 **Opera & Ballet Theatre** Vienuolio 1; 🕿 5 262 0727; www.opera.lt. A varied programme of operas,

operettas & ballets is staged in this huge concrete & glass building from the 1970s.
🎭 **Russian Drama Theatre** Basanavičiaus 13; 🕿 5 262 0552; www.rusdrama.lt. As its name suggests, it presents Russian-language performances.
🎭 **Youth Theatre** Arklių 5; 🕿 5 261 6126; www.jaunimoteatras.lt. Housed in the same building as the Puppet Theatre, this company has gained a high reputation for its innovative stagings, & has made successful tours to the West.

Music In addition to the concert halls listed below, concerts and organ recitals are held in several Old Town churches, especially the Cathedral, SS John, St Catherine and St Casimir. At the last-named, live music is normally performed every Sunday immediately after the last morning Mass ends at around 13.00. Open-air concerts – which take place in the courtyards of Vilnius University and the Chodkevičius Palace, among other venues – are a regular feature of the city's musical life in summertime.

🎵 **Concert & Sports Palace** Rinktinės 1; 🕿 5 272 8964. The main venue for large-scale pop concerts.

🎵 **Congress Centre** Vilniaus 6/14; 🕿 5 261 8828; www.lvso.lt. Between mid-Sep & mid-Jun, there are

regular concerts by the Lithuanian State Symphony Orchestra, usually on Fri evenings.
♪ **Music Academy** Gedimino 42; ✆ 5 261 2691. In term-time, there are usually several public recitals every week by students & staff.
♪ **National Philharmonic Hall** Aušros Vartų 5; ✆ 5 266 5216 or 266 5233; www.filharmonija.lt. The country's leading concert hall presents an enticing programme of orchestral, choral & chamber concerts & organ, piano & song recitals by both Lithuanian & foreign artists. There are regular concerts by the Lithuanian National Symphony Orchestra on Sun at 19.00.

Festivals Vilnius hosts an extremely varied programme of festivals throughout the year, including the following:

Užgavėnės (*www.etno.lt*) The climax of the Carnival season celebrations is held on Shrove Tuesday (variable date in Feb or Mar on Tauro Hill).

St Casimir's Market The feast-day of Vilnius's very own saint is on 6 March. Associated with it is a handicrafts market in the Old Town which lasts for several days.

Cinema Spring (*www.kinopavasaris*) A two-week long festival of international non-commercial films in March and April.

Skamba skamba kankliai (*www.etno.lt*) A colourful annual festival of folk-song and dance, held throughout the city, usually on the last weekend in May. It features invited groups from abroad as well as performers from all over Lithuania.

Rasos The midsummer solstice, is celebrated on 23 June on the White Bridge.

St Christopher Summer Music Festival (*www.vilniusfestivals.lt*) Throughout July and August, there is a wide range of concerts of all types of (predominantly classical) music. They take place at a variety of venues, many in the open air, with the majority given by Lithuanian performers.

World Lithuanian Song Festival (*www.dainusvente.lt*) This massive six-day event is held in early July, usually at four- or five-yearly intervals; the last was in 2007, but another is planned for 2009 in association with the European City of Culture celebrations. The first two days are mainly devoted to rehearsals; on the third, the participating groups assemble in Sereikiškės Park for informal performances. Each of the last three days climaxes in a spectacular open-air concert: the first, held in the Hill Park, is given by song and dance ensembles; the second, in the Žalgiris Stadium, by dance troupes (with no singing); the third, in Vingis Park, by choirs (with no dancing). The last-named makes an awesome climax, featuring up to 12,000 singers on the Song Dome stage at a time.

Day of Statehood On 6 July there is a solemn military procession with banners, followed by an open-air concert of patriotic songs and operatic arias with orchestral accompaniment.

Vilnius International Summer Fair and Street Events Festival (*www.vilniusfestivals.lt*) The week-long fair in mid-August features a crafts market, complete with an ethnographic village, in Sereikiškės Park. During the last four days, pageants and street theatre are held throughout the Old Town.

Three Days Three Nights A three-day beer festival on the last weekend of August or the first weekend of September in Vingis Park.

Banchetto Musicale A festival of early music, held in September and October.

Film Festival A week-long cinematic festival in mid-September.

Fire Sculptures Festival (*www.etno.lt*) A celebration of the 21 September autumn equinox in Kalnu Park.

Jazz Festival (*www.vilniusjazz.lt*) A festival of avant-garde jazz, held over three days in the first half of October.

WHAT TO SEE AND DO

Old Town Vilnius's Old Town (Senamiestis) is among the most extensive in Europe, occupying a total of 255 hectares, and including over 1,000 protected monuments, among them outstanding masterpieces not only of Baroque, but also of Gothic, Renaissance and Neo-Classical architecture. A great deal of cleaning and other restoration work has been carried out since independence was achieved, though many fine buildings languish in a semi-derelict state, a situation which is likely to persist for many years to come.

There are two distinct parts to the Old Town. The site of the original settlement, which includes the castles, the cathedral and the areas of greenery surrounding them, is no longer inhabited, and now forms an island of calm in the midst of the city centre. Across the bustling Šventaragio and Radvilaitės streets lies the much larger part of the Old Town, which came into being after the threat from the Teutonic Knights had been eliminated. Although it has become a tourist magnet in recent years, it is far from being a museum-piece. Some of it is still residential, it retains the main university campus, has plenty of shops and offices, and is well-endowed with places to eat and drink. It preserves its chaotic medieval layout, in which twisting narrow alleys are juxtaposed with a central thoroughfare divided into three distinct parts and several huge open squares. Almost every street is worth a look, and a detailed exploration of all the important sights requires several days. Much of the Old Town is either pedestrianised or has severe restrictions on vehicular access, so it can really only be seen on foot.

Cathedral of SS Stanislaus and Ladislaus The Cathedral of SS Stanislaus and Ladislaus occupies the site of an ancient pagan temple dedicated to the god Perkūnas, and originally lay within the fortification system of the Lower Castle. Following the ostensible conversion of King Mindaugas around 1251, the first church was built on the site. When the nation officially reverted to heathen ways, the Perkūnas temple was re-instated, but was replaced by another church when Christianity was introduced in 1387 following the royal union with Poland. Under Vytautas the Great, this was supplanted by a more splendid Gothic cathedral, which underwent repeated alterations down the centuries, before being almost totally rebuilt between 1783 and 1801 to plans by Laurynas Gucevičius. Even if its Neo-Classicism makes it something of an outsider in the predominantly Baroque townscape of Vilnius, it is a majestic building none the less, one of the most important churches in the style anywhere in Europe. Under the Soviets, it served as an art gallery for 32 years, but in 1989 was restored to its role as the seat of the local archbishop.

The façade has a portico of six Doric columns and a rosette-encrusted vault. On the tympanum above is a carving depicting *The Sacrifice of Noah* by an Italian sculptor, Tommaso Righi, who was also responsible for the five small reliefs and the niche statues of the four apostles and the patriarchs Abraham and Moses on the entrance wall. Atop the tympanum, and visible from afar, the figures of SS Stanislaus and Casimir flank St Helena, who bears the gilded True Cross. These huge statues, which were put in place in 1996, are reproductions of the originals, which were destroyed by Soviet decree. The north and south sides of the cathedral are closely harmonised with the façade. Both have colonnades with six columns, with the former having niche statues of saints, the latter of Grand Dukes.

The interior is laid out in the form of a spacious hall, with a grand central area and narrow aisles with chapels. Its focal point is the high altar, which is shaped like the front of a classical temple, and shelters a large painting of *The Martyrdom of St Stanislaus* by Franciszek Smuglewicz, the founding director of the Vilnius School of Art. On the altar table is an exquisite gilded silver tabernacle from the 1620s, whose panels depict *Christ Washing the Disciples' Feet* and *The Last Supper*. A complete series of the apostles by Smuglewicz hangs on the columns of the nave. In the west gallery is the organ, which preserves a splendid 18th-century case; most of the pipework dates from 1969, though some 19th-century registers survive.

It is sometimes possible to visit the vaults underneath the cathedral on application to the shop, which is currently located off the south aisle. The best time to try is around 11.00, when pre-booked groups are often escorted round, though it is easy enough to tag discreetly along whenever one of these is in the building. On view are altars used for pagan worship, as well as fragments of the medieval churches which occupied the site. Particularly intriguing is a late 14th-century fresco of *The Crucifixion with the Virgin and St John*, the oldest surviving monumental painting in Lithuania. Several royal coffins can also been seen, among them that of the highly esteemed Barbora Radvilaitė, the second wife of Zygmunt August and herself a member of one of Lithuania's most powerful families.

Of the small chapels off the aisles, the third on the south side is of particular note. It belonged to the Goštautas family, and contains a 17th-century painting of miracle-working properties, *The Adoration of the Virgin Mary by SS Francis and Bernardino*, and two magnificent tombs by 16th-century Italian Renaissance masters. The monument to Albertas Goštautas, Chancellor of the Grand Duchy and Governor of Vilnius Province, was carved by Bernardo Zanobi, and is the oldest memorial sculpture in Lithuania. That to Bishop Povilas Algimantas Alšėniškis is by the most celebrated of the Italians who dominated artistic life at the Polish–Lithuanian court, Giovanni Maria Mosca, 'Il Padovano'. The first chapel on the same side houses a painted wooden crucifix from the early 18th century, while the second chapel on the north side, which was the property of the Valavičius family, features some impressive stuccowork.

The **Chapel of St Casimir**, which is entered via a resplendent portal from the southern aisle, is the only important part of the previous cathedral which survives in an unaltered state. In order to integrate it into his new design, Gucevičius added a sacristy on the northern side which copies its distinctive outline of a square lower storey surmounted by an octagon supporting a cupola with lantern. The chapel was built between 1622 and 1636 by the Italian Constantino Tencalla in order to house the mortal remains of St Casimir (1458–84), Lithuania's patron saint. Work on the sumptuous interior, which is faced with luxuriant black, white and coloured marble, continued for a century after its construction. Much is by itinerant Italian masters. Hiacinto Campana painted the ceiling frescos, Michelangelo Palloni the side frescos of *The Opening of the Coffin of St Casimir* and *The Miracle of the Coffin of St Casimir,* while Pietro Peretti (or Perti) created the lavish stucco backdrop to the silver shrine. In front of the shrine is a curious little portrait of the saint, dating from the 1520s, in commemoration of his beatification.

The Vilnius Cathedral Treasury occupies an honoured place in the cultural heritage of the Lithuanian capital. Its history has been nothing if not eventful. Over the centuries, monarchs, nobles, bishops and clergymen endowed it with masterpieces of decorative art made in some of the most prestigious European workshops. It suffered many losses in the 17th-century wars against the Russians and Swedes, but continued to be augmented by important new gifts. In 1939, it was bricked up for safekeeping in a false wall of the cathedral, and for several decades was believed lost. However, it was found in 1985 by three local men who kept their discovery secret from the Soviets for fear it would be carted off to Moscow; only in 1998, when the country's independence was reckoned to be fully secure, was the public officially informed. From 1999 until 2003 it formed the centrepiece of the great millennium exhibition Christianity in Lithuanian Art at the Museum of Applied Arts, and its contents were described and illustrated in a sumptuously produced book (see page 246). In 2005 it became part of the new Church Heritage Museum, which staged its first temporary display in the National Museum the following year. A permanent home is being established in the former Church of St Michael and the adjoining convent (see page 96), and this is due to open in 2009.

The treasury's oldest artefact is a 14th-century French ivory diptych of four scenes from the life of Christ. This was, it is believed, given by Pope Urban to Grand Duke Jogaila on the occasion of the latter's marriage and baptism in 1386, and subsequently donated to the cathedral at the time of its foundation. The earliest of the many chalices was made in the 15th century in Danzig (Gdańsk); the stipula or ritual stick used by the cathedral's precentor is of the same era. From the following century are a huge gilded monstrance and a crystal cross-reliquary, both of which were given by the Goštautas family. A particularly rich group of 17th-century artefacts includes a gold monstrance studded with precious stones and enamels given by Bishop Jurgis Tiškevičius, and three pieces donated by Bishop Mikalojus Steponas Pacas – the reliquary of St Mark Magdalene dei Pazzi from Florence, and the spectacularly florid monstrance and chalice made in the German city of Augsburg. Of special note among the 18th-century objects is the sarcophagus-reliquary of Josaphat Kincevitius, a martyred Uniate archbishop.

The only painted sections uncovered by the intricate 18th-century silver frame are Casimir's head – and three hands. Other 18th-century additions to the chapel are the eight niche statues of Lithuanian Grand Dukes, and the unusual moveable pulpit, which is shaped like a goblet.

Katedros aikštė (Cathedral Square) is a vast paved space on the south and west sides of the cathedral which makes an ideal starting or finishing point for parades and processions. Since 1996, it has been the setting for the **Monument to Grand Duke Gediminas** – a particularly appropriate location, as it must be close to the spot where he had his legendary dream about the iron wolf. The commission for the statue was entrusted to the veteran sculptor Vytautas Kašuba, who had spent most his career in America and died soon after the monument was erected. That Gediminas is shown with his sword in his left hand is an allusion to his supposed preference for diplomacy over war – though in reality he used both to achieve substantial territorial gains for the Grand Duchy.

The focal point of the square is the **Belfry**, a combined bell and clock tower which is a favourite local rendezvous point. It has had a curious history. Its round lower storey, which is pierced by numerous gunports, dates back to the 14th century and belonged to the fortification system of the Lower Castle; indeed, it is the only part of this which survives to this day. In the 1520s it was converted into the cathedral's bell tower by the addition of two octagonal tiers. The following century, a fourth tier was added to house a clock which still preserves its original mechanism. In 1893 it finally assumed its present appearance when it was crowned with a small steeple.

Lower and Higher Castles The **Lower Castle**, which in the 16th century was transformed into a splendid Renaissance-style royal palace for Zygmunt the Old, was the main residence of Lithuania's Grand Dukes. Unfortunately, the finest parts of the complex, which had a stately triple-tiered courtyard as its centrepiece, were pulled down by the Tsarist authorities in 1802, leaving only a number of ancillary buildings. However, highly fruitful archaeological excavations have been carried out on the site over the past decade, uncovering the foundations of the palace. For a time, these were accessible to the public, but they are currently off-limits pending the completion of the ambitious and highly controversial project to reconstruct the building. Work on this is well underway, and by the end of the decade it is likely to become one of the city's major tourist attractions.

A path to the rear of the cathedral leads up the 48m-high Gediminas Hill to the **Higher Castle** on its summit; the lazy alternative to this is the new funicular which runs up the northern slope. The original wooden fortress was replaced in the late 14th century and early 15th century with a brick and stone Gothic castle which featured three towers, a palace, a chapel and various other buildings. Badly damaged in the wars of 1655–61, it was thereafter abandoned, only to be revived as a fortress by the Russians following the 1831 uprising. A wooden superstructure containing an optical telegraph was built on top of the truncated western tower, the only one of the three which was retained. This was removed in 1930, and replaced by a reconstruction of one of the two octagonal storeys which had previously been lopped off.

Nowadays designated the **Castle Museum** (⊕*May–Sep 10.00–19.00 daily, Oct–Apr 10.00–17.00 Tue–Sun*), the tower contains displays of historic arms and armour, plus models showing the changing appearance of Vilnius's medieval fortification system. However, the main attraction is the wonderful view from the observation platform on top. As all the main landmarks of the Old Town are clearly visible (the only publicly accessible place where this is so), it makes an ideal place to begin or end a tour of the city. Normally, the best light for photography is in the later part of the day. Other than the tower, little remains of the Higher Castle, save for the ruins of the palace and fragments of the outer walls.

National Museum of Lithuania Just to the north of the cathedral, fronted by a statue of King Mindaugas, is the 18th-century New Arsenal, which now houses the National Museum of Lithuania (*www.lnm.lt;* ⊕*May–Sep 10.00–17.00 Tue–Sat, 10.00–15.00 Sun; Oct–Apr 10.00–17.00 Wed–Sat*). The history of the Grand Duchy is evoked in a display of portraits, weapons, books, textiles, prints, liturgical objects, coins and sundry other artefacts. Those of particular aesthetic appeal include the 15th-century treasury door of the nearby Bernardine Friary, the Baroque banner of the Handcraftsmen's Guild, the 17th-century vestments of a Uniate bishop, the embossed leather sleigh of the Tiškevičius family, and a Meissen vase decorated with coats-of-arms honouring the dynastic union of

Saxony and Lithuania. Also on display are the artefacts discovered in 2001 in the mass graves in Verkiai Park of 4,000 soldiers from Napoleon's retreating army: these include parts of uniforms (buckles, belts, brooches, shoes and caps) as well as such personal effects as rings, chains, crosses and both French and Russian coins. There is also an extensive folk art section, which is grouped by region and features iron crosses, wooden statues, painted chests, embroidery, costumes, pottery, masks, lace, baskets and decorated Easter eggs. Note that, because of a shortage of display space, the temporary thematic exhibitions which are often mounted in the museum result in the closure of large parts of the permanent collection.

Next door, in the 17th-century western extension to the Old Arsenal, is the **Archaeology Exhibition** (⊕*same times*), which was inaugurated in 2000, using fully modern display techniques. The exhibits are arranged chronologically in two large rooms, the first of which ranges from the Paleolithic era of the 11th millennium BC up to the time of Christ. Šventoji, the Baltic port which is now part of Palanga, has yielded some particularly rich finds from the 3rd and 4th millennia BC, including a metre-long upturned boat, a clay bowl in the shape of a vessel, a wooden pole statue, ceremonial sticks and ladles with animal and bird heads, and amber jewellery. Upstairs, the era leading up to the formation of the Lithuanian state is documented by thematic displays on barter, agriculture, metallurgy, pottery, horse and rider, arms, spinning and weaving, and silver, all of which are copiously illustrated with excavated objects. There are several impressive silver hordes, notably one consisting of brooches, necklaces and ingots from Štakliškės. The culture of the various different tribes who lived in and around the territory that is now Lithuania is imaginatively illustrated by means of dummies decked out with reconstructions of the clothes, weapons and jewellery they wore, while the intact contents of several excavated graves of the period are also on view. Finally, in the entrance hall is a horde of 15,950 coins, mostly Lithuanian and Polish copper shillings of the 17th century, which were probably stowed away by a local merchant when the Swedes occupied Vilnius in 1702, and only rediscovered in 1999.

Museum of Applied Arts The original Old Arsenal, a hybrid Gothic-Renaissance building of the 16th century, is now home of the Museum of Applied Arts (*www.ldm.lt;* ⊕*11.00–18.00 Tue–Sat, 11.00–16.00 Sun*), one of the constituent parts of the Lithuanian Art Museum. From 1999 until 2003 its premises were entirely given over to the really marvellous exhibition Christianity in Lithuanian Art, which celebrated both the new millennium and the 750th anniversary of King Mindaugas's coronation in 1253. This gave Vilnius the world-class museum it otherwise lacks, and its official closure was a sad loss, not least because the wonderful Vilnius Cathedral Treasury (see boxed feature on page 92) subsequently went back into storage.

However, many of the other objects in the exhibition were the property of the Lithuanian Art Museum, and they remain on view: indeed, the top floor displays have been left largely intact. The gallery of paintings is mostly devoted to lesser-known masters, though there are a few outstanding works, including two prime examples of Netherlandish Mannerism: *St Ursula and the Martyrs* by Bartholomeus Spranger, court artist to Emperor Rudolf II in Prague; and *An Allegory of the Old and New Testaments*, a Protestant tract by Cornelis van Haarlem. There are also some characteristic 17th-century Italian canvases, such as *Christ in the Tomb* by Lodovico Carracci, *St Paul the Hermit* by Salvator Rosa, *Mater Dolorosa* by Carlo Dolci; a few Spanish works, including *Head of the Crucified Christ* by Luis Morales and *Penitent Mary Magdalene* by Francisco Ximenez; and a fine *Lot and His Daughters* by the leading exponent of Austrian Baroque, Johann Michael

Rottmayr. Several large and archetypally Baroque altarpieces which the Polish artist Szymon Czechowicz painted for various Vilnius churches are also on view; the most notable are *The Holy Trinity* and *The Vision of St Ignatius Loyola*. A display of icons includes examples from Orthodox, Old Believers and Uniate congregations.

Also on this floor is an outstanding display of folk art in all its many religious manifestations. This is dominated by numerous examples of the wooden crosses which are such characteristic features of rural Lithuania. Around a score of those on view are by the acknowledged master of the genre, Vincas Svirkis (1835–1916), who spent his whole life moving continually from village to village and farm to farm, leaving behind crosses which typically incorporate high reliefs of saints or religious scenes clearly influenced by the Baroque art of the 18th century. A set of four dozen coloured drawings by Kazys Šimonis show crosses in their original locations. The pomp associated with local religious festivals is evoked by some splendid processional banners and lanterns mounted on poles, while smaller devotional figures, paintings, embroideries and miscellaneous liturgical objects further illuminate the sheer diversity of the Lithuanian tradition.

On the floor below, some of Vilnius Cathedral's collection of French and Flemish tapestries – which include mythological and genre scenes as well as religious subjects – can be seen. There are usually a couple of small temporary exhibitions in the museum. That on artefacts earmarked for display in the rebuilt Lower Castle is scheduled to remain here until the end of 2008.

Bernardine churches At the extreme eastern edge of the Old Town, on the far side of Sereikiškės Park, which stretches south from Gediminas Hill, is the **Bernardine Friary**. An offshoot of the Franciscan Order, the Bernardines arrived in Vilnius in 1469. They initially built a wooden church on the site, which was granted to them by Grand Duke Kazimierz, but this was destroyed by fire.

Its replacement, the brickwork **Church of SS Francis and Bernardino**, was erected at the beginning of the 16th century under the patronage of the Radvila (Radziwiłł) family. Unusually large by the standards of medieval Lithuania, it is in the hall church style (with nave, aisles and chancel of equal height), and features some spectacular examples of late Gothic vaulting. Following repeated damage by fire and in war, the church was given a twin-turreted Renaissance façade, though the single tower on the southwest side was restored to its original Gothic form. The Baroque Chapel of the Three Kings, which is used for weekday services, was added in 1632. Among several impressive funerary monuments in the nave is that to Stanislovas Radvila by Willem van den Block, the leading Renaissance sculptor of Danzig (now Gdańsk). In the Soviet era, the church was allowed to fall into a dilapidated state. It is now back in Franciscan hands, and for some years past has been the subject of what will be a very long-term restoration programme.

The much smaller and better-preserved **Church of St Anne** (⊕ *May–Sep 10.00–18.00 Tue–Sun, otherwise only for services*) in front is undoubtedly the most celebrated building in Lithuania. According to an oft-quoted tradition, Napoleon was so captivated by it that he declared his wish to carry it back to Paris in the palm of his hand, and it has long been an inexhaustible source of inspiration to local painters and photographers. No fewer than 33 different shapes of brick were employed in the construction of its unforgettable Flamboyant Gothic façade, which is symmetrical in appearance, being twice as high as it is broad. Its decoration is a bravura medley of extravagant ogee arches, narrow oriel windows, slender pinnacles, openwork octagonal towers and crocket-studded steeples. When lit by the setting sun, the upwardly sweeping lines take on a truly incandescent appearance.

For all its fame, the church is something of a mystery, there being no general agreement as to exactly what its function was in relation to the friary, nor exactly when and by whom it was built. According to one theory, it was constructed by German masters at the very end of the 15th century. Indeed the design is sometimes attributed to Benedict Rejt, who is securely documented as the architect of some marvellously distinctive buildings in Prague. However, others claim that the façade, at least, was not built earlier than the mid-16th century, and is the work of local craftsmen.

Directly across the street is the former **Church of St Michael**, built between 1594 and 1625 by order of Leonas Sapieha, Chancellor of the Grand Duchy of Lithuania, to serve as a convent for Bernardine nuns, as well as a mausoleum for his own aristocratic family (also known as Sapiega or Sapiegos). The only important Renaissance building to survive in the city, the church has an elaborate façade with a massive central pediment, twin turrets, and pilasters with capitals bearing stylised depictions of leaves of the rue (*rūta*), the national flower of Lithuania. In the early 18th century, a wall was constructed round the church in order to create an enclosed courtyard for processions. Entry to the complex is now via a sturdy Baroque tower which serves as both belfry and gateway.

Most of the furnishings of the hall-like interior, which boasts a richly stuccoed vault, were stripped away by the Soviets, but several Sapieha memorials remain. The most prominent is a 10m-high red marble monument commemorating the founder and his two wives; also of note is that to Stanislovas Sapieha, which has an eccentric location above the sacristy doorway. For more than three decades, the church housed the now defunct Museum of Lithuanian Architecture. Together with the adjoining conventual buildings, it is now undergoing restoration in preparation for the installation of the new **Church Heritage Museum**, which is due to open in 2009. This will provide a permanent home for the Vilnius Cathedral Treasury (see page 92), as well as other artefacts from throughout the archdiocese.

Rest of the northeastern quarter Bernardinų, which follows a winding northwesterly course from the Church of St Michael, is one of the best-preserved streets of the Old Town, lined with many splendid urban mansions. The **Mickiewicz Museum** (◔ *10.00–17.00 Tue–Fri, 10.00–14.00 Sat–Sun*) at Bernardinų 11 has been set up in the courtyard building where the great Romantic poet Adam Mickiewicz (known to Lithuanians as Adomas Mickevičius), who had previously spent four years in Vilnius as a student at the university, lodged for two months in 1822. It was during this stay that he wrote the Byronic verse tale *Gražyna*. Old editions of Mickiewicz's main works are on display in the museum, as well as paintings and engravings showing Vilnius as it was in the poet's day. A memorial to Mickiewicz can be seen nearby, just a few paces to the south of the Bernardine Friary. Designed in 1984 by Gediminas Jokubonis, this shows the influence of the Socialist Realist style of which the sculptor had long been a favoured practitioner. Just to the north is the gleaming white Orthodox **Church of the Holy Mother of God.** There has been a church on the site since the late 14th century, though the present building dates mainly from the 1850s.

At No 8 on Šv Mykolo, an atmospheric old street running west from the Church of St Michael, is the **Amber Gallery** (*www.ambergallery.lt;* ◔ *10.00–19.00 daily*). Like its pioneering counterpart in Nida, which is owned by the same family, this offers informative displays on the geology of 'Baltic gold', as well as temporary exhibitions of amber jewellery. The recently excavated cellars are open to view; among the objects which have been discovered are two 15th-century kilns. There is also a shop selling fully authenticated pieces of amber and amber artefacts.

Both Bernardinų and Šv Mykolo terminate at Pilies, the northern part of the Old Town's central axis. Stalls selling handicrafts can be found all along the street, and these increase greatly in number and quality whenever a festival is taking place. Of particular note among a picturesque jumble of buildings of various dates are the Renaissance mansion at Pilies 4 and the gabled Gothic houses at numbers 12 and 14. Pilies 26 is now designated the **House of the Signatories** (⊕ *10.00–17.00 Tue–Sat, also May–Sep only 10.00–15.00 Sun*), as it was there, on 16 February 1918, that Lithuania's declaration of independence was signed. On the second floor is a small museum devoted to the event. Due to the lack of any surviving original material, it has to improvise, displaying some furniture of the period plus a set of modern portraits of the signatories based on old photographs. The first and ground floors both have exhibition rooms where temporary artistic and photographic displays are held. The downstairs section of the **Šlapelis Museum** (⊕ *11.00–16.00 Wed–Sun*) at Pilies 40 is a recreation of the pioneering Lithuanian bookshop established in 1906 by Jurgis Šlapelis and his wife Marija Šlapelienė. Displayed in the couple's flat above, which is entered from the courtyard, are books and other objects associated with the national cultural revival they did so much to promote. Backing on to the western side of Pilies is the sprawling university campus whose main public entrance is from Universiteto, the next street to the east.

Vilnius University It is fitting that Vilnius University is by far the largest and most prominent complex of buildings in the Old Town, as it has played a key role in the life of the city since its foundation in 1570, despite suffering many vicissitudes at Russian hands over the past two centuries – it was closed down altogether between 1832 and 1919, and for most of the Soviet period was forced to tailor its activities to Marxist–Leninist dogma. Grouped around no fewer than 12 courtyards is a picturesque huddle of structures of widely varying dates and aesthetic merit. In a somewhat opportunistic attempt to extract money from the many visitors to the complex, the authorities have introduced what are supposedly set opening times (⊕ *09.00–17.00/18.00 Mon–Sat*) and an entrance charge. However, the only benefit gained by buying a ticket is the woefully inadequate sketch map available in several languages from the cash desk. In practice, anyone can, as before, wander in and look around discreetly.

Payment of the entry fee does not even result in access to the **University Library**, which is entered via the doorway labelled Vilniaus Universitetas on the south side of the courtyard opening directly on Universiteto. Officially, this is now only open to pre-booked groups, though a sympathetic attendant may grant individual access to the oldest room (reached by taking two consecutive left turns then descending a short flight of stairs), which is known as Smuglevičius Hall in honour of the Neo-Classical painter Franciszek Smuglewicz, who frescoed the vault. The central scene shows the Holy Trinity blessing the Madonna of Mercy, who shelters a group of Jesuits under her cloak. On the spandrels above the windows are monochrome *trompe l'oeil* busts of distinguished scholars of classical antiquity. A small selection of the library's most valuable books and manuscripts is displayed in the show-cases.

Immediately behind the library is the **Astronomical Observatory**, the fourth oldest surviving example of its type in the world. Built between 1753 and 1773 by Tomas Žebrauskas (Thomas Žebrowski), the Professor of Mathematics and Astronomy, it is actually two separate observatories, one of which occupies the entire length of the building, with a smaller one above. No longer in use, the interior is not generally accessible, but the peaceful courtyard to the rear offers a fine view of the building's façade, with its handsome portal, twin turrets and frieze of zodiacal symbols.

A gateway at the northeastern corner of the Library Courtyard leads into the Sarbievijus Courtyard, which is named in honour of Maciej Kazimierz Sarbiewski (1595–1640), who served as Professor of Rhetoric, Philosophy and Theology but is better known as a prolific writer of both sacred and secular Latin verse. At the far end is the **Littera Bookshop**, whose interior is covered with a colourful fresco scheme painted by Antanas Kmieliauskas in 1978–79. Inspired by the Vatican frescos of Michelangelo and Raphael, this pays symbolic tribute to the subjects which have loomed largest in the university's history.

A small hall on the first floor of the **Centre for Lithuanian Studies** next door is decorated by an even more ambitious fresco cycle entitled *The Seasons*, which Petras Repšys completed in 1985 after nine years' work. There are over a hundred different scenes, illustrating episodes from Lithuanian history and mythology as well as work, pastimes and popular customs. Also worth seeking out is the classically inspired coloured stucco frieze of *The Nine Muses* by Rimtautas Gibavičius which can be found on the first floor of the **Philology Department** in the Daukantas Courtyard immediately to the north.

A large archway on the southern side of the Sarbievijus Courtyard leads into the **Great Courtyard**, which is also known as the Skarga Courtyard in honour of Piotr Skarga, the Jesuit scholar who was the university's first rector. The academic buildings lining three of its sides were erected in the early 17th century in the Mannerist style which marks the transition from Renaissance to Baroque. All along their lower storey are open arcades which impart a sunny Mediterranean flavour, even if the local climate is only occasionally warm enough for them to be enjoyed to best advantage. Between the pilasters are faded 18th-century frescos portraying important figures in the history of the university.

The eastern side of the Great Courtyard is closed by the **Church of SS John**, which was founded by Grand Duke Jogaila immediately after his conversion to Christianity and completed in 1426. A presbytery and apse were added to the original hall church after it was allocated to the Jesuit college in 1571, and much of the Gothic fabric is clearly visible underneath the overlay added between 1738 and 1749 by Jan Krzysztof Glaubitz, the presiding genius of the final phase of Vilnius Baroque. The monumental façade, in which the plain horizontal rustication of the lowest storey forms a dramatic counterpoint to the sweeping vertical emphasis of the elaborately contoured tiers above, ranks among the greatest achievements of the style. Almost equally impressive is the assemblage of ten interconnected altars which together make up the high altar. There are memorials honouring, among others, Adam Mickiewicz, Tadeusz Kościuszko and Stanisław Moniuszko, the Polish composer who served as the church's organist from 1840–58. Of the six side chapels, the most elaborate is that dedicated to St Anne, which has both an ornate portal and a carved altar of *Christ as the Tree of Life*.

Nowadays, the building has a curious double life, serving as the university church once again, yet still retaining its communist-era role as the **University Science Museum** (◷ *10.00–17.00 Mon–Sat*) – hence the scattering of cases displaying old scientific tracts. The detached **Belfry**, one of the Old Town's most prominent landmarks, was built in the first decade of the 17th century and raised to its present height as part of the programme of Baroque renovations.

Northwestern quarter Daukanto aikštė, the triangular space immediately west of the university, is dominated by the vast pile of the **Presidential Palace**. The bishop's palace which had stood on the site since the 14th century was remodelled to serve as the residence of the Russian governor-general, and Tsar Alexander I and Napoleon both held court there in the fateful year of 1812. Between 1824 and 1832 this was expanded and rebuilt by a Russian architect, Vassily Stasov, in late Neo-Classical style. In Soviet times it served as the artists' palace and was the French Embassy in the first years of independence, before assuming its present role, following a costly refurbishment, in 1997. In August 2000 the palace started opening on Fridays and Saturdays for pre-booked groups. A tour showing the main reception rooms, the president's office and the gardens takes about 45 minutes. The furnishings are entirely modern, but the designs are from the early 19th century. Oak and birch are the main woods used. One room has four large portraits of the previous Lithuanian presidents, three from the 1920–40 period and one of Algirdas Brazauskas, in office 1993–98. An even larger painting shows Vytautas the Great riding into the Black Sea, when the Polish–Lithuanian Commonwealth stretched that far in the mid-15th century.

Opposite stands the modest little **Church of the Holy Cross**, a foundation of the Bonifratrian Order, which came to Vilnius in 1635. The original building was remodelled in the course of the first half of the 18th century, and the twin towers, pediment, porch and exterior fresco of *The Madonna and Child* all date from this period. The Soviets renamed it the Baroque Hall and used it for concerts, but it now functions as a place of worship once more. Beside the church is a monument to Laurynas Gucevičius, architect of the Cathedral and Town Hall.

At Vilniaus 22, towards the far northwestern edge of the Old Town, is the **Radvila Palace** (*www.ldm.lt;* ⊕*12.00–18.00 Tue–Sat, 12.00–17.00 Sun*). Built in the 17th century for Jonušas Radvila, Grand Hetman of Lithuania, this splendid urban palace has been much altered subsequently, and now serves as a branch of the Lithuanian Art Museum. One room is devoted to a gallery of 165 portrait engravings of members of the dynasty commissioned by Mykolas Kazimieras Radvila from an amateur artist, Herszek Leybowicz (1700–70). Apart from an unexpected collection of Oceanic art, the rest of the display space – unless occupied by a temporary exhibition – is given over to old master paintings, graphics, furniture and decorative art. Most of the former are by little-known artists; among the few works of special note are *Venus and Cupid* by Antoine Pesne, the French-born court painter to Frederick the Great of Prussia, and several fine examples of 17th-century Dutch painting, including *The Allegory of the Owl and the Birds* by Melchior d'Hondecoeter, *The Old Mill* by Meindert Hobbema and *The Waterfall* by Jacob van Ruisdael.

A little further up the same street is the **Church of St Catherine**, which originally belonged to a Benedictine convent founded in 1618. Following a series of fires, it was rebuilt between 1741 and 1753 by Jan Krzysztof Glaubitz. In order to overcome the restricted nature of the site, he adopted an audacious design based on a nave which is as high as it is long. The exterior features an elaborate rear-facing gable as a counterbalance to the majestic twin-towered façade; the interior is richly furnished, and has only been partially restored, as the church is now a venue for small-scale concerts, and no longer used for worship. A statue of Stanisław Moniuszko stands in the garden in front of the church.

Diagonally opposite is a long, low-lying Baroque palace which was formerly another of the Radvila properties. For the first 15 years of Tsarist rule, it housed the municipal theatre; nowadays it contains the **Lithuanian Theatre, Music and Cinema Museum** (⊕*12.00–18.00 Tue–Fri, 11.00–16.00 Sat*). This offers a mixture of temporary exhibitions and permanent displays on the history of the performing arts in Lithuania.

Šv Ignoto, a block to the east of Vilniaus, is named after the Church of St Ignatius, part of the former **Jesuit Noviciate**, a vast 17th- and 18th-century Baroque complex with three large courtyards. Following the suppression of the Order in 1773, the buildings served successively as a seminary and a barracks; they are now home to, among others, a commercial art gallery and a technical library.

Šv Ignoto leads to Dominikonų, which takes its name from the Dominican friary established there in 1501. Its **Church of the Holy Spirit**, one of the most extravagant manifestations of Vilnius Baroque, was one of the few churches kept open during the Soviet years, and is nowadays the principal place of worship for the Polish-speaking community. Although retaining some of the fabric of its fire-ravaged 17th-century predecessor, its main features – the dome, the side gables and the sumptuous array of furnishings and decoration which give the interior an almost Rococo appearance – date from the second half of the 18th century. A sculptor of German origin, Franz Ignatius Hoffer, designed the assemblage of 16 artificial marble altars and the curious pulpit, which is combined with the confessionals below in a single unit. The elegant tribune gallery houses an organ whose richly carved case with statues of King David and angel musicians still shelters the original 18th-century pipework. As the only genuine Baroque organ to survive anywhere in Lithuania, it is regarded with enormous pride, and it should sound splendid when it returns to action on the completion of the current restoration, which has been ongoing for several years.

A little further down the same street is the **Sanctuary of Divine Mercy**, which has recently been restored and re-opened as a place of worship, having lain derelict for several decades. Gothic by origin, this little church was remodelled in Baroque style in the mid-18th century, when the twin towers on the street frontage were added. On the high altar is a small painting depicting St Faustina Kowalska's vision of Christ. It was painted in 1934 by Eugeniusz Kazimirowski from descriptions supplied by the mystic herself, and was recently moved from its former home in the Church of the Holy Spirit.

Didžioji The Old Town's central thoroughfare changes its name from Pilies to Didžioji at a little square which has become an open-air gallery. Forming a backdrop to this is the **Piatnickaya Orthodox Church**, the favoured place of worship of the younger members of the Russian community. Although the church's present appearance is the result of a remodelling carried out in the 19th century, it was originally built in 1345 for Marija, the wife of Grand Duke Algirdas, and was the place where the grandfather of the great Russian poet Alexander Pushkin was baptised.

Immediately to the rear is the Baroque Chodkevičius Palace, which was adapted to house the **Vilnius Picture Gallery** (*www.ldm.lt;* ◷ *12.00–18.00 Tue–Sat, 12.00–17.00 Sun*), a branch of the Lithuanian Art Museum, when the latter was forced to vacate its previous premises in the cathedral. The early 19th-century interiors on the first floor form a setting for period furniture, *objets d'art* and paintings, including portraits of Mickiewicz by Valentinas Vankavičius, and of the arts patron Duke Mykolas Oginskis by François Xavier Fabre. One room on the floor above is devoted to portraits of leading lights of 18th-century Lithuania, including that of Chancellor Jonas Sapieha by Silvestre de Mirys, an artist born in France to Scottish Jacobite exiles. There then follows a large collection of paintings by Franciszek Smuglewicz; sacred works predominate, though his love of the exotic is expressed in a pair of canvases evoking the courtly and diplomatic life of the ancient world. His successors at the Vilnius Academy of Arts are likewise well represented, while there is also an illuminating display of architectural drawings by Laurynas Gucevičius. The final rooms of the circuit are often used for loan displays. At other times they feature works by participants in the celebrated exhibitions of Lithuanian art in the first decade of the 20th century, with the little paintings entitled *Storm* and *Mountains* by Čiurlionis being among the very few works by him outside his memorial museum in Kaunas.

A few paces further on, just before the point where Didžioji broadens out to form Rotušės aikštė (Town Hall Square) is the Orthodox **Church of St Nicholas**, which was originally built in a hybrid Gothic–Byzantine style in 1514. In 1609, the church was granted to the Uniates, remaining in their hands until 1827. Extensive renovations were carried out in the 1860s, when a Neo-Byzantine façade and belfry were erected and a new iconostasis added to the interior.

Tucked away in a courtyard at Savičiaus 11, the next street to the south, is the **Čiurlionis House** (🕘 *10.00–16.00 Mon–Fri*), the home of the composer-artist during his residency in Vilnius. It often hosts recitals of his music, but unfortunately contains no original paintings by him – only a copy of the theatre curtain he made for the Rūta society, plus photographic reproductions of his finest works. A little further along the same street stands the **Church of St Mary the Soothing**, which was formerly part of an Augustinian friary. Built between 1746 and 1768, it was among the last of Vilnius's great series of Baroque churches, and is dominated by its elegantly tapering single tower which displays clear classicising tendencies. Now in a totally decrepit state, it is awaiting a much-needed restoration.

Coincidentally, the nearby Jesuit **Church of St Casimir** at the southern end of Didžioji marked the debut of the Baroque style in the city. It was begun in 1604, just two years after Casimir's canonisation, and completed in 1618. Although probably designed by the Italian Giovanni Maria Bernardoni, it was built by a local architect, Jan Prochowicz. Despite being modelled on the Jesuits' much-imitated mother church of Il Gesù in Rome, the addition of twin towers (which are now lower than when first built) give it a distinctive Lithuanian accent. The crown atop the lantern of the central dome was added as recently as 1942 in recognition of St Casimir's royal lineage. In 1966, in a humiliating affront to Lithuania's Catholics, the Soviet authorities installed a Museum of Atheism in the church's bare interior. However, it was returned to the Jesuits in 1988, and a strong musical tradition, in which a new German-built organ plays a key role, has since been established. The altars are a somewhat brash mix of the old and the new.

Immediately opposite, its grand Doric portico fronting the square named after it, is the **Old Town Hall**. Designed by Laurynas Gucevičius, it was built between 1781 and 1799 on the site of its medieval predecessor. The municipal offices have long since moved elsewhere, though the building is still used for receptions. It also functions as an 'artists' palace', and as such its foyer is regularly used to show-case contemporary Lithuanian arts and crafts.

Southwestern quarter Vokiečiu, which leads northwest from the Town Hall, was widened considerably as part of a 1950s planning project, and now has a pedestrianised area down the middle. The new layout necessitated the demolition of part of the former **Ghetto** to the east, including the 17th-century Great Synagogue on Žydu, which lost its roof during the Nazi occupation period but otherwise survived largely intact. In recent years, there has been talk of re-instating it. A monument on Žydų commemorates Eliyyahu ben Shelomoh Zalman (1720–97), otherwise known as the Gaon of Vilna, one of the greatest Talmudic scholars of all time and a virulent opponent of the revivalist Hasidic movement.

At the head of Vokiečių, right alongside the Town Hall, is the concrete and glass **Contemporary Art Centre** (*www.cac.lt;* ⊕ *12.00–19.30 Tue–Sun*). Although an ugly blot on the face of the Old Town, it provides much-needed display space for exhibitions which are predominantly, but not exclusively, of the works of living artists. Upstairs is a permanent display on *Fluxus*, the experimental art movement founded in the United States by the Lithuanian-born George Maciunas.

Hidden away at the back of a courtyard at Vokiečių 20 is the **Evangelical Lutheran Church**. Vilnius's first Protestant church was established on the site in 1555. The present building, a plain Baroque preaching hall which is whitewashed both inside and out, was built in the 1740s by Jan Krzysztof Glaubitz, with the Neo-Romanesque belfry being added in 1872. The focal point of the interior is the high altar, which adapts traditional Catholic forms to the requirements of Lutheran doctrine, giving a prominent role to the carved depiction of The Last Supper.

Šv Mikalojaus, the little street immediately to the east, is named after the **Church of St Nicholas** at its far end. An unassuming example of the Gothic brickwork style, it is the oldest intact church in Lithuania, and the only one pre-dating the official adoption of Christianity in 1387, having been built earlier in the century to serve the German merchants and artisans who had made the city their home.

According to tradition, the **Church of the Virgin Mary**, situated a short distance to the northwest on Pranciškonų, was founded by Franciscan missionaries before the mass conversion of Lithuania. However, the present building, constructed between 1773 and 1785, is in a classicising Baroque style, and while it incorporates a few fragments of its Gothic predecessor (notably the façade portal and the crystalline vaults of the south aisle), these appear to be 15th century in date. Having been closed since 1949, the church was handed back to the Franciscans in 1998, leaving them with the massive task of repairing the worn fabric and bringing the faded frescos back to life.

On Rūdninkų, close to the now-vanished western gate to the Old Town, is the **Church of All Saints**, formerly part of a Carmelite friary. The main body of the church was built in 1620–31 and is modelled on the Jesuits' Il Gesù. The single bell tower was not added until 1743 and is somewhat more elaborate in appearance, but none the less blends in well. What would otherwise be a rather plain interior is enormously enlivened by the kaleidoscopic colours of the somewhat folksy carvings and paintings adorning the altars.

Southeastern quarter The southernmost section of the Old Town's central axis is known as **Aušros Vartų** ('Gates of Dawn') after the gateway at which it terminates. On the western side of the street, the first major landmark is the **National Philharmonic Hall**, which was built in 1902. The massive street frontage, built in the fin-de-siècle eclectic style, seems rather out-of-scale in comparison with the concert hall itself, which is of very modest dimensions. None the less, it is the most important venue in the country for classical music, and has also hosted some fateful political meetings, including the 1940 'application' for Lithuania to be admitted to the Soviet Union.

A bit further up the same side of the street is the **Basilian Monastery**, which takes its name from the Uniate monks who settled there in 1608. Access from the street is via the entrance gateway, a swaggering Baroque masterpiece built in 1761 to designs by Jan Krzysztof Glaubitz. Its gable bears a carved depiction of the Holy Trinity, this being the dedication of the now very dilapidated church in the courtyard behind, which was originally built in 1514 but much altered down the centuries. A congregation of Ukrainian-speaking Uniates currently worships there. For six months in 1823–24, Adam Mickiewicz was imprisoned in a cell in the monastery for anti-governmental activities, and was shortly afterwards deported from Lithuania, never to return.

Across the street, again in a secluded courtyard, is the Orthodox **Church of the Holy Spirit**. It is the most important Orthodox church in the country, though its external appearance differs markedly from all the others, being very obviously a product of the Vilnius Baroque style, with only the merest traces of Russian influence. Indeed, it is in large part the work of Jan Krzysztof Glaubitz, who was entrusted with rebuilding the original 17th-century church following a fire in 1749. Glaubitz is also believed to have designed the colossal lurid green iconostasis, which incorporates Baroque paintings of the life of Christ in addition to traditional icons. In front of the altar, a baldachin shelters the miraculously preserved bodies of SS Anthony, Ivan and Eustachius, whose feet can be seen peeking out from under their shrouds. The trio were servants at the court of Grand Duke Algirdas but were martyred for their faith in 1347 as a result of a militant pagan backlash against the previous policy of religious tolerance.

Back on the street a short distance beyond stands Vilnius's most Italianate building, the **Church of St Teresa**, which was designed for the Discalced Carmelites by Constantino Tencalla, and built between 1633 and 1652. The façade, the only part erected under Tencalla's direct supervision, is a strikingly vertical composition culminating in a pediment adorned with the coat-of-arms of the aristocratic Pacas (Pac) family, who provided funds for the construction. Following a fire in 1760, the interior was provided with a new set of furnishings, and the walls were frescoed by Mateusz Sluszczański. The scenes he painted in the nave illustrate the life of the church's patron, the Carmelite mystic St Teresa of Avila.

A covered stairway to the rear of the church, up which pious penitents hobble on their knees, leads to the so-called **Gates of Dawn**, Lithuania's most famous place of pilgrimage. Disabled people and beggars can almost invariably be found outside the gateway, which once formed part of the city wall and is the only one of the nine it formerly had which survives. When viewed from the south its original defensive function is still obvious, but the northern side looks completely different, having been revamped in Neo-Classical style in 1829 in order to provide a chapel to house the reputedly miraculous image of *The Madonna of Mercy*. Despite adopting the form of a traditional icon, this was probably painted in the early 17th century and was later provided with a gold and silver setting which covers the entire picture except for the face and hands. Densely hung ex-votos left by grateful pilgrims are attached to the wall panels of the chapel.

The other significant surviving fragment of the municipal defences is the **Artillery Bastion** (⊕ *10.00–17.00 Tue–Sat, also May–Sep only 10.00–15.00 Sun*), which is reached by following Šv Dvasios in a northeasterly direction. This was built in the early 17th century in order to provide extra protection for the nearby Subačius Gate. It consists of three parts: a tower on a round base, a horseshoe-shaped gallery for firing cannon, and an underground tunnel. The bastion encloses a natural hillock, from which there is a good, albeit partial, view over the Old Town.

New Town In the 19th century, the New Town (Naujamiestis) was built immediately to the west of the Old Town, in the process engulfing a few older buildings which had hitherto stood in isolation. In addition to serving as the commercial and administrative heart of the city, it is also a residential area, its streets lined with large tenements which were originally thrown up to house a rapidly growing population.

Pylimo Pylimo is the street which marks the boundary between the Old and New Towns. Near its southern end, at the corner with Bazilijonu, is the rather cramped **Central Market**. Downhill, on the left-hand side of the street, is the **Synagogue**, the only survivor of the hundred or so Jewish temples Vilnius had prior to World War II. Built at the turn of the 20th century, it is modelled on Moorish architecture. Above the doorway is a depiction of the tablets of the Ten Commandments.

Somewhat further down, on the opposite side of the street, is the **Reformed Church**, which was built in 1830–35 by Karol Podczaszyński, the leading local practitioner of the late Neo-Classical style. It is fronted by a giant Corinthian portico surmounted by a tympanum carved with a scene representing *Christ Preaching to the People*. The interior, which was converted into a cinema in 1958 but has now been returned to the local Calvinists, is a large hall covered with a coffered wooden vault. Normally it is only open for services (usually on Sundays at 18.00).

Housed in a tenement building at Pylimo 4, a short distance to the north, is the **Lithuanian State Jewish Museum** (*www.jmuseum.lt; ⊕09.00-13.00 Mon–Fri*). On the first floor are displays of liturgical objects, dolls used for theatrical performances during the Feast of Purim, prints and drawings of Vilnius's Great Synagogue, and photographs, supplemented by a few tantalising fragments, of the wonderfully elaborate wooden synagogues, all now destroyed, which once graced several Lithuanian towns. Two rooms on the floor above are dedicated to a photographic record of memorial sites throughout Lithuania to victims of Nazism, and to a gallery honouring those who sheltered or otherwise saved Jews.

Round the corner, at Paménkalnio 12, the wooden **Green House** (⊕*09.00-17.00 Mon–Thu, 09.00-16.00 Fri*) serves as an annexe of the museum, with a documentary display focusing on Jewish culture and life in Vilnius and Lithuania immediately before World War II, and its destruction during the Holocaust. Outside stands a monument entitled *Moonlight*, which commemorates Chiune Sugihara (see feature on pages 156–7), the Kaunas-based Japanese diplomat who is credited with rescuing up to 6,000 Jews.

Gedimino Gedimino, the New Town's central boulevard, stretches for 1.75km along a straight east–west line. Its name has changed many times since it was laid out in the early 1850s, with the appellations chosen almost invariably reflecting the nationality and ideology of the authorities of the time. Indeed, the present honouring of Grand Duke Gediminas, a historical figure with impeccable Lithuanian credentials, is as politically motivated as some of the names (which include those of Piłsudski, Hitler, Stalin and Lenin) bestowed on the street in the past.

The easternmost of the three large squares which open out from the northern side of Gedimino is Savivaldybės aikštė. On its northern side is the **Government building**, which was formerly the seat of the central committee of the Lithuanian Communist Party, while on the eastern side are the **Municipality** headquarters. Incorporated within the latter complex is a secluded courtyard, round which are the Baroque buildings of a former convent of the Discalced Carmelites, centred on the **Church of St George**. Designed by Franz Ignatius Hoffer, this lacks a tower, but has a striking tiered façade; the interior is unfortunately not accessible at present.

Just off the south side of the square, at Totoriu 2, is the **Bank of Lithuania Museum** (⊕ *09.00–12.00, 13.00–14.30 Wed/Thu, but closed in 2007 for restoration work*), which has two exhibition rooms. The first of these displays coinage of the Grand Duchy of Lithuania, the earliest dating back to the late 14th century, plus a few maps and plans. In the second room are Ostmarks issued by the German occupying forces during World War I, the currency of the inter-war republic, Soviet-era roubles and the trial printing sheets for the Litas banknotes which were introduced in 1993. Excellent documentary information in English on all the exhibited material is provided free of charge.

The next square to the west, Lukiškių aikštė, was where the leaders of the 1863 rebellion were executed. On the far northern side is the Baroque **Church of SS Philip and James**, which was begun in 1690 but not completed until 1748, when the twin towers were raised to their present height. A Dominican foundation, the church has a strikingly geometric appearance, with its single nave being exactly as high as it is long.

A statue of Lenin once stood in the little park in the middle of the square, facing the KGB headquarters. The latter, originally built in 1899 by the Tsarist authorities to serve as a courthouse, is now designated the **Museum of Lithuanian Genocide Victims** (*www.genocid.lt;* ⊕ *10.00–17.00 Tue–Sat, 10.00–15.00 Sun*). In due course, it is intended to present a full documentary record on Soviet repression against Lithuania (particularly the Siberian deportations), and on the resistance to it. In the meantime, the cells in the basement, which were used for the imprisonment and torture of political opponents until 1991, can be visited. These include an isolation cell which has neither heating nor windows, a special padded and soundproofed cell for suicide risks, and two cells where water torture was administered in order to keep prisoners constantly awake. There is documentary material on some of the most prominent victims, while sacks of incriminating documents shredded by the KGB in the final three years of Soviet rule are also on view.

Towards the eastern end of Gedimino is Nepriklausomybės aikštė. Despite its name ('Independence Square'), it is dominated by two of the most prominent buildings of the communist era. The **National Library**, which is built in a debased modern version of Neo-Classicism, is a typical example of the cultural 'gifts' Moscow was wont to bestow on subsidiary republics and satellites. Ironically the **Seimas** (Parliament) alongside, which is no more distinguished from an architectural point of view, has gained an honoured place in the Lithuanian consciousness, being the place where the restoration of national independence was declared on 11 March 1990.

Outside the city centre Vilnius's suburbs have a generous endowment of sights, and while most of these lie off the beaten tourist track, a few rank among the best-known landmarks of the city.

Rasos, Paupys and Markučiai The **Rasos Cemetery**, which takes its name from the district in which it lies, is about 1km southeast of the Gates of Dawn, on the opposite side of the rail tracks. Its leafy, undulating site, which looks particularly wistful in autumn, contains the graves of some of Lithuania's most revered citizens. The tombstone of the composer-painter Čiurlionis is directly uphill from the main entrance, while that of Jonas Basanavičius, cultural guru and founder of the newspaper *Aušra*, is just across from the chapel. More controversially, the heart of Józef Piłsudski, who bears the primary responsibility for Poland's annexation of Vilnius in 1920, is buried in the family plot to the left of the entrance; the rest of his body lies in the Polish national pantheon in Cracow's Wawel Cathedral.

Rasų leads from the western side of the cemetery to the district of Paupys and the former **Visitationists' Convent**, which directly overlooks the Old Town. At the heart of the complex is the domed Church of the Heart of Jesus, the only one of Vilnius's Baroque churches built to a Greek-cross design. Although a prominent feature of the city's skyline, the church can only be seen from afar, as the whole convent is currently a prison enclosed within a high wall topped with barbed wire.

The former **Missionaries' Monastery** opposite is now a hospital and is likewise inaccessible, although at least good close-up views can be had of the exterior of its Church of the Assumption, which was begun in 1695 and remodelled by Jan Krzysztof Glaubitz in 1750–54. As with the Church of St Catherine in the Old Town, which he worked on at the same time, the architect concentrated attention on the monumental façade, so giving the building a sense of grandeur which belies its small size. The slender five-storey twin clock towers are unlike any others in Vilnius, being clearly influenced by those of the German-speaking lands.

Subačiaus leads eastwards from the Missionaries' Monastery to the residential district of Markučiai, at the far end of which is an extensive park in which stands the **Pushkin Memorial Museum** (⊕ *10.00–17.00 Wed–Sun*), a large wooden homestead which belonged to Alexander Pushkin's son Grigorij (1835–1905) and his wife Varvara (1855–1935). The ground floor is furnished according to Russian upper-class taste of the time, with a large ceramic stove being a feature of each of the main public rooms. Upstairs is a small exhibition on the works of Pushkin and their dissemination in Lithuania.

Užupis North of the Missionaries' Monastery, just across the River Vilnia from the Old Town, is the district of Užupis, the city's bohemian quarter. It is often, albeit fancifully, compared with the Paris suburb of Monmartre, with which it established official ties in conjunction with its declaration of 'independence' in 1998. The tumbledown 19th-century tenements and courtyards are much favoured by artists and members of the 'alternative' set, and several collective galleries and craft workshops have been established there. In the southeastern part of Užupis, directly above the river, is the tranquil **Bernardine Cemetery**, the last resting place of, among others, many university luminaries. At the junction of Užupio and Malūnų is a curious column originally topped by a large egg; this duly 'hatched', as planned, into the angel which can now be seen.

The wooded **Hill Park** (Kalnų Parkas), which stretches northwards from Užupis to the Neris embankment, is one of the city's most popular recreation areas. Towards its northeastern end is the Song Valley, an open-air auditorium which is regularly used for a variety of folklore events. In medieval times, the Crooked Castle, one of the city's trio of fortresses, crowned the 91m hill above, one of the city's highest points. In its place are the **Three Crosses**, which first appeared there in the 17th century. According to tradition, they were erected to commemorate early missionaries of the Franciscan Order who were martyred for their faith. Substitute concrete crosses were erected in 1916, but these were destroyed by the Soviets in 1950. The present crosses were put in place on June 14 1989 to coincide with the inauguration of the annual festival of the Day of

Mourning and Hope, which commemorates Lithuanians deported to Siberia after World War II.

Church of SS Peter and Paul Situated in splendid tree-framed isolation at the edge of the Antakalnis district, immediately east of the Hill Park, is the Church of SS Peter and Paul, which was founded in 1668 by Mykolas Kazimieras Pacas (Michał Kazimierz Pac), Grand Hetman of Lithuania and Governor of Vilnius, and granted to a congregation of Lateran Canons. The design of the church, whose main external features are a squat, twin-towered façade and a large central dome, was entrusted to a Polish architect, Jan Zaor, who supervised the construction work for several years before being replaced by Giambatista Frediani, who worked simultaneously on the Pacas dynasty's other prestige project, the Pažaislis Monastery outside Kaunas.

When the fabric was completed in 1675, local sculptors were commissioned to make the façade statues. Pacas was dissatisfied with the results, and accordingly invited two masters from the Lake Como region of northern Italy, Pietro Peretti (or Perti) and Giovanni Maria Galli, to take charge of the decoration of the interior. Between 1677 and 1685 the Italian duo created a stuccowork scheme of stupendous richness and variety, in the process transforming the pleasant but unexceptional shell of the building into a High Baroque masterpiece, one which has been regarded ever since as among the crowning glories of Lithuania's cultural heritage.

There are over 2,000 human figures, each of them differently characterised, though these form but a small part of the overall scheme, which also features carvings of plants (including accurately depicted local species), flowers, trees, mythological creatures, grotesques and purely decorative elements. The iconographic programme behind the decoration is highly complex and often symbolic. For example, the many battle scenes are a reference to Pacas's status as Lithuania's most senior soldier, while the recurrent fleur-de-lis was his family emblem, and several of the saints depicted in hagiographic fashion were those with whom his dynasty had a special affinity.

Instead of aisles, there are two chapels on either side of the nave. Those on the north are dedicated to the Holy Queens and to St Augustine, the patron of the Lateran Canons; those to the south to the Warrior Martyrs and to St Ursula and the Virgin Martyrs. The last-named chapel, with its coolly beautiful statue of St Mary Magdalene alongside a virtuoso relief of a palm tree, stands out even among the magnificence all around it. To appreciate the decoration to the full, it is necessary to come on a sunny day, when the shafts of light penetrating the clerestory and dome windows illuminate the stuccowork in a magical series of ever-changing reflections.

Among the church's most notable furnishings are the pulpit and the main chandelier, both of which adopt the form of a boat. At the entrance to the chancel is another curiosity, an impassioned *Ecce Homo* statue in the Spanish manner, which was carved in Rome in the late 17th century. A large painting of *The Parting of SS Peter and Paul* by Franciszek Smuglewicz has taken the place of the original unfinished high altar.

Antakalnis Antakalnis itself was formerly the estate of another prominent dynasty, the Sapieha family. A short distance to the north along Antakalnio are the two main buildings, both dating from the 1690s: the **Sapieha Palace**, an Italianate *palazzo*, and the **Church of Our Lord Jesus**, which formed part of one of the city's two Trinitarian foundations. The latter is a domed octagon fronted by a porch flanked by two towers placed at strikingly oblique angles. It apparently still preserves stucco decoration by Pietro Peretti, but there is little prospect of seeing this as the building is boarded up with no sign of any much-needed restoration work.

The **Antakalnis Cemetery** to the east encapsulates Vilnius's complicated modern history. Close to the entrance are rows of identical tombstones of Polish soldiers killed in World War I. At the heart of the complex is a large circular memorial containing the graves of the nationalist martyrs of the 1991 standoffs with the Red Army at Vilnius's TV tower and the border post of Medininkai. Further on, colossal Socialist Realist statues guard an eternal flame which no longer burns, while a pantheon of the leading lights of Soviet Lithuania is laid out in tiers alongside.

Šnipiškės From the New Town, the **Green Bridge** (Žaliasis tiltas) leads across the River Neris to the district of Šnipiškės. Adorning each of its four corners are Socialist Realist sculptures of happy workers and peasants. These now seem somewhat comical, but have been left in this prominent location as a deliberate reminder of the 'heritage' of the communist era.

Just over the bridge is the **Church of St Raphael**, which was built by the Jesuits in the first decade of the 18th century. A typical example of the Baroque architecture of the period, it has a monumental high altar with a large painting of the archangel Raphael by Szymon Czechowitz. The church now stands at the edge of a pedestrian precinct which was something of a Soviet-era show-piece. Its facilities include the **Planetarium** (*shows 09.30–18.00 Mon–Fri, 12.00–16.00 Sat*) and two gargantuan hotels. Both of the latter have undergone makeovers – which in the case of the transformation of the old Lietuva by the Reval chain has been nothing short of startling.

Immediately to the north, on the opposite side of the busy thoroughfare recently renamed Konstitucijos, is the new business quarter, which features three new skyscrapers and a huge multi-level shopping mall, somewhat ironically known as **Europa**. That such a brash, American-inspired showpiece development – which has significantly altered the city's skyline – came into being little more than a decade after the fall of communism has to be accounted a remarkable fact. However, it certainly does not meet with universal approval among locals: many see it as a potent symbol of the abandonment of so many traditions in the headlong rush to embrace the ways of Western capitalism.

Just west of the Reval Lietuva are the custom-built premises of the Revolutionary Museum of the Lithuanian Soviet Socialist Republic, which has been supplanted by the **National Gallery**. For a while, this building displayed the modern collections of the Lithuanian Art Museum, notably a varied cross-section of the output of Vytautas Kašuba, donated by the sculptor himself. These include large wall reliefs, classically inspired female portraits, erotic medallions of the Lithuanian Grand Dukes, and humorous hollowed-out carvings. However, the gallery has been closed for the past decade because of stalled renovation work. It should reopen in 2009.

At the foot of Rinktinės, just over 0.5km east of the Green Bridge, the **Žalgiris Stadium** and the **Concert and Sports Palace** occupy the site of the city's main Jewish cemetery. This was levelled by the Soviets in 1950 in order to make way for the stadium, which hosts large-scale open-air events, including international football matches and the dance programme of the Song Festival. Its indoor counterpart, which is two decades younger, stages everything from basketball tournaments to rock concerts.

A short distance further north, with entrances on Rinktinės and Kalvarija, the long street running northwards from the Green Bridge, is the **Calvary Market**

(⏱ *06.30–16.30 Tue–Sun*). Like all the best Lithuanian markets, this has an almost bazaar-type atmosphere. Although dominated by stalls offering a huge choice of fresh fruit and vegetables, hardware items and clothing can also be bought, while a poignant touch is added by the people who stand in rows day after day, and somewhat desperately try to sell individual plastic bags or a few odd garments.

Northern suburbs From Kalvarija, buses 26, 35, 36 and 50 run to the northern suburbs, which are primarily high-rise housing estates separated by large areas of greenery. In the district of Jeruzalė, some 5km north of the market, the **Calvary Church of the Rediscovery of the Holy Cross** can be seen on a hillock to the right of the road. One of Lithuania's most important pilgrimage sites, this one-time Dominican priory was among the few Vilnius churches kept open during the Soviet era. In its present form, it was built between 1755 and 1772, and features a characteristic twin-towered façade and a richly decorated interior. The most notable features of the latter are the combined pulpit and font and the illusionistic ceiling frescos on the theme of the Holy Cross and its rediscovery by St Helena, mother of the Emperor Constantine. Outside the church are four pilgrimage chapels, the only original ones remaining from the 19 which, together with a ceremonial archway which also still survives, formed a processional way similar to that in Žemaičių Kalvarija (see pages 198–200).

The others, which were razed by the Soviets but are gradually being reinstated, were scattered along a route which leads 1.5km southeast through the woods to the **Trinapolis Convent**, a Trinitarian foundation overlooking the River Neris. Designed by Pietro Putini, one of the architects of the Pažaislis Monastery, it was built between 1695 and 1709. It has been re-settled by a small community of nuns, and is now a popular retreat centre. Although the façade of its Church of the Holy Trinity is a characteristic example of Lithuanian Baroque, the interior, an irregular octagon with highly complex spatial arrangements, is untypical, being modelled on the Trinitarian church of San Carlo alle Quattro Fontane in Rome by Francesco Borromini.

The landscaped **Verkiai Park**, a former estate which nowadays functions as Vilnius's Botanical Garden, can be reached from the Trinapolis Convent by the road alongside the Neris, or from the Calvary Church by continuing northwards along Kalvarija. At its heart is the **Verkiai Palace**, a late 17th- century complex remodelled in Neo-Classical style by Laurynas Gucevičius as a summer residence for the Vilnius bishops. Unfortunately, the main building was demolished in the 1850s, but the two wings, which are themselves of palatial dimensions, both survive. One serves as the headquarters of the Botanical Institute, and is not accessible to the public. However, regular art exhibitions are held in the other, whose reception rooms were plushly decorated in the late 19th century with oak panelling, marble and stuccowork.

Bus 36 continues northwards from Verkiai to the **Green Lakes**, a hugely popular recreation area. On summer weekends especially, it swarms with day trippers who come to go boating or swimming in the chain of lakes and to have a relaxing picnic or barbecue by one of the shores.

Western suburbs The setting for many of the big nationalist rallies during the final years of Soviet rule, the **Vingis Park** is bounded on three sides by a loop of the River Neris, and to the east by the New Town, one of whose major thoroughfares, Čiurlionio, leads straight to the main entrance. In the middle of the park is the **Song Dome**, whose covered auditorium, which can seat 20,000 people, can serve two completely different functions. On the last day of the four-yearly Song Festival, it serves as the stage for the concert by the massed choirs, which the audience watches from the field alongside. However, the roles can be reversed, in order to have open-air performances watched by an audience seated under cover.

A footbridge at the northern end of the park leads to **Žvėrynas**, a residential suburb of wooden houses and grand villas, which can also be reached from the New Town via the bridges at the end of Gedimino and Jasinskio. Just west of the latter, on Liubarto, is the **Kenesa**, an early 20th-century temple whose vaguely Oriental appearance reflects the exotic origins of the Karaites (see page 113) who worship there.

In 1957 a Jewish graveyard, the only one in Vilnius, was established within the **Saltoniškių Cemetery** in Viršuliškės, the next suburb to the west, which can be reached by trolleybuses 11 (from the city centre), 16 (from the station) and 19 (from Žvėrynas). This contains tombs brought from razed Jewish cemeteries, notably the large burial chamber of the Gaon of Vilna, though many gravestones were pillaged in the Soviet era and recycled as masonry in the construction of new buildings.

Lithuania's tallest building, the 326m-high **Television Tower** (*www.lrtc.lt;* ⊕ *10.00–22.00 daily*), rises above the apartment blocks of Karoliniškės, the suburb immediately south of Viršuliškės, which is likewise on the routes of trolleybuses 11 and 16. Outside the entrance, crosses commemorate the 14 unarmed civilians who were mowed down by Soviet tanks on January 13 1991 in the single most tragic episode in the run-up towards independence. A lift goes up as far as the observation deck at 165m, which rotates slowly on its own axis and offers sweeping views over the city.

The **Gariūnai Market**, which lies just off the Kaunas highway, 10km west of the centre, is by far the most notorious in the country. All manner of secondhand and imported goods are sold there, and it is best-known for its huge array of used motor vehicles (not all of which have an impeccable provenance). Trading takes place every morning except Monday, and minibuses run out from the stands in front of the bus station.

Paneriai The name of the southwestern suburb of Paneriai has become synonymous with the killing fields of the Nazis, who murdered around 100,000 people there, including almost all of Vilnius's large Jewish population, between 1941 and 1944. There are several memorials to the dead. The earlier of these adopt the communist practice of paying tribute to 'Soviet citizens' massacred as a result of 'Fascist terror'; the more recent, which date from 1990, make proper acknowledgement of the fact that 70,000 of the casualties were local Jews. A path round the site leads to the pits where the dead bodies were burnt, and to another where the bones where crushed. There is also a branch of the **Lithuanian State Jewish Museum** (⊕ *11.00–18.00 Mon/Wed/Fri/Sun*), which contains a photographic record of the site, as well as some of the retrieved personal effects of the victims.

By far the quickest and easiest way to reach the site is by rail. All trains to Trakai and Marcinkonys, and most of those to Kaunas, stop at Paneriai station. From there, it is a straight ten-minute walk onwards along a dead-end road which runs parallel to the rail tracks.

TRAKAI HISTORICAL NATIONAL PARK

The one unmissable short excursion from Vilnius is to the Trakai Historical National Park. With an area of just 8,000 hectares, this is by far the smallest of the country's national parks and – as the additional word 'Historical' in its title implies – it differs markedly from its four counterparts. Whereas the conservation of the landscape is their primary purpose, this one is mainly concerned with preserving the monumental heritage of Trakai, Lithuania's best-known and most impressive small town. That said, the scenery is an integral part of Trakai's charm, and is archetypally Lithuanian, with forests accounting for 33% of the park's area, lakes for 18%.

TRAKAI Although its current population is a modest 7,000, Trakai has played an important role in Lithuanian history and is one of the country's oldest towns, perhaps dating back to the 12th century. The original settlement was the capital of one of the duchies into which early medieval Lithuania was divided, and at one time it rivalled Vilnius in importance. Indeed it may have served as capital of the whole country for a couple of years during the reign of Grand Duke Gediminas. Now known as Senieji (Old) Trakai, it lies 4km southeast of the replacement town founded some time around the middle of the 14th century by one of Gediminas's sons, Duke (later Grand Duke) Kęstutis. This occupies a highly strategic site on a peninsula bordered to the west by Lake Totoriškiai, to the east by Lake Luka (or Bernardinai), and to the north by the islet-strewn Lake Galvė. These lakes, and others beyond, are interconnected by narrow channels.

Trakai fell briefly to the Teutonic Knights in the internecine wars which led to Kęstutis's death. Under his son, Grand Duke Vytautas the Great, it was transformed into one of the strongest fortresses in Europe. Vytautas also encouraged Karaites, with whom he had made contact during his eastern military campaigns, to come and settle in the town, and they have made a distinctive mark, retaining a presence there to this day.

Trakai's multi-ethnic character was boosted in the 16th century, when Jews arrived in numbers. However, the 17th-century wars with Russia left the fortresses in ruins. As a result it lost its strategic importance and went into economic decline, becoming just another small provincial town. Only in the late 19th century, when the nationalist movement stimulated interest in Lithuania's medieval past, did it begin to make something of a come-back.

Getting there and around

🚌 **Bus station** Vytauto 90; ☎ 528 51333. Located immediately south of the peninsula. There are over 30 services daily to Vilnius, 2 direct to Kaunas via Rumšiškės, & 7 to Prienai via Aukštadvaris & Birštonas.

🚆 **Railway station** Vilniaus 5; ☎ 528 51055. Situated a short walk south of the bus station, this is the terminus of a branch line from Vilnius via Paneriai, on which there are 8 trains on w/days & 6 at w/ends in each direction.

Information and maps

Historical National Park Administration Centre Karaimų 5; ☎ 528 55776; f 528 51528. This publishes a 1:50,000 map of the Historical National Park, with a panorama of the town on its reverse.

Tourist office Vytauto 69; ☎/f 528 51934; e trakaitic@is.lt; www.trakai.lt. Accommodation in private houses can be arranged; some English is spoken. ⊕ May–Sep 09.00–17.15 Mon, 09.00–18.00 Tue–Fri, 10.00–15.00 Sat–Sun; Oct–Apr 08.00–17.00 Mon–Thu, 08.00–15.45 Fri.

Where to stay

🏠 **Apvalaus Stalo Klubas** Karaimų 53a; ☎ 528 55595; f 528 51760; e info@asklubas.lt; www.asklubas.lt. In summer 2007 a hotel was opened as an adjunct to Trakai's classiest restaurant, which overlooks the Island Castle & has a strong line in fish dishes. It also operates an annex in an old Karaite house. $$$
🏠 **Salos** Kranto 5b; ☎ 528 54100; f 528 54101; e salos@salos.lt; www.salos.lt. This brand-new hotel

offers good-value accommodation, & has a sauna, restaurant & nightclub on the premises. $$, suites $$$
🏠 **Trakų Sporto Bazė** Karaimų 73; ☎ 528 55501; f 528 55387; e sportocentras@mail.lt; www.sc.trakai.com. This large hotel, originally intended for sportsmen, lies just north of the peninsula. A gym, sauna & swimming pool are among the facilities. $$

6

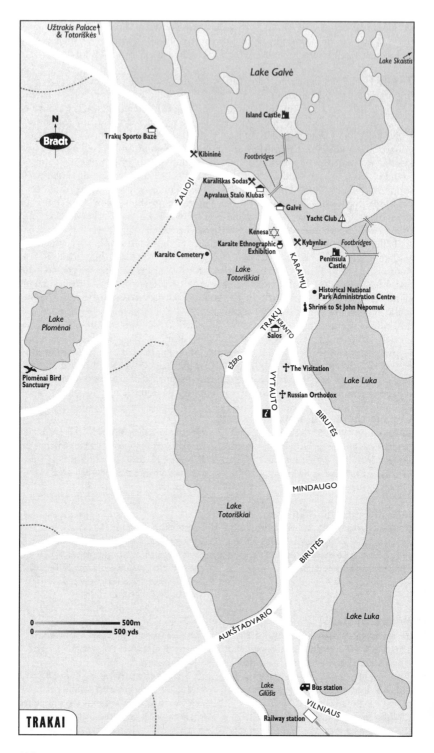

Užtrakis Palace
& Totoriškės

Lake Skaistis

Lake Galvė

Island Castle

N

Bradt

Trakų Sporto Bazė

Footbridges

Kibininė

ŽALIOJI

Karališkas Sodas

Apvalaus Stalo Klubas

Galvė

Yacht Club

Kenesa

Kybynlar

Footbridges

Karaite Ethnographic
Exhibition

Karaite Cemetery

Peninsula
Castle

KARAIMŲ

Lake
Totoriškiai

Historical National
Park Administration Centre

Shrine to St John Nepomuk

TRAKŲ KRANTO

Lake
Plomėnai

Salos

EŽERO

Plomėnai Bird
Sanctuary

✝ The Visitation

VYTAUTO

Lake Luka

✝ Russian Orthodox

i

BIRUTĖS

MINDAUGO

Lake
Totoriškiai

BIRUTĖS

Lake Luka

0   500m
0   500 yds

AUKŠTADVARIO

Lake
Gilūšis

Bus station

VILNIAUS

TRAKAI

Railway station

112

✖ Where to eat

✖ **Karališkas Sodas** Karaimų 57. This restaurant in a wooden building with a covered terrace offering good views of the lake has a moderately priced menu of Lithuanian cuisine.

✖ **Kibininė** Karaimų 65. The Karaite restaurant has a decent drinks list, including a freshly made gira, but there are just 2 dishes to choose from (with only the former always being available): kibinai, which is a meat pie resembling a Cornish pasty, & troškinta mėsa, a meat & vegetable stew.

✖ **Kybynlar** Karaimų 29. Although not actually run by Karaites, this restaurant opposite the Kenesa offers a far more extensive menu of Karaite dishes than the Kibininė, including a warm beer, Jazma.

✖ **Židinys** Vytauto 91. This basic town-centre café-restaurant, which serves standard Lithuanian fare, has a small terrace overlooking Lake Totoriškiai.

Festivals The Island Castle makes a dramatic backdrop for a number of annual events, including the Medieval Festival in late May, the Festival of Lithuanian National Opera and Ballet throughout July, and the Trakai Festival in August. On a weekend in early July, the Peninsula Castle is the setting for the Archaeology Festival, with demonstrations of knightly combat and medieval handicrafts.

The town Trakai's peninsula is bisected by a snaking main street. The southern part of this, known as Vytauto, leads past the 19th-century **Russian Orthodox Church** to the **Church of the Visitation**, which is set in splendid isolation on a hillock overlooking the street. One of Lithuania's oldest churches, it was founded by Grand Duke Vytautas around the turn of the 15th century. It was originally fortified, but was remodelled in the Baroque style in 1718. Inside, the high altar has as its centre-piece a venerated image usually known as *The Madonna of Trakai*. This was painted in the 16th century, though the gilded silver surround – which is sometimes placed over the image, at other times displayed on the adjacent wall – was only added in the 18th century. From the church, Vytauto sweeps round to the east, terminating in what is effectively an open square, in the centre of which is another Baroque monument, a pillar topped by a **shrine to St John Nepomuk**.

By the lakeside immediately to the east is the **Peninsula Castle**, the outer part of the elaborate defensive system begun by Kęstutis and completed by Vytautas. Destroyed by the Russians in 1655, it has been left as a ruin, though one of the towers, a gateway and the lower parts of the walls have all been restored. Within the grounds is the former chapel of a Dominican convent, which now houses a **Museum of Sacred Art** (*www.trakaimuziejus.lt*; ⊕ *10.00–18.00 Wed–Sun*).

Yachts, rowing boats and water bicycles can be hired at the various quaysides to the north of the castle or from the **Yacht Club**, which lies on the opposite side of the channel between Lake Luka and Lake Galvė. By road, it is several kilometres away, but it can be reached in a couple of minutes via a rustic wooden footbridge which commands fine views over the town and its lakes.

The northern section of Trakai's main street is named Karaimų in honour of the Karaite settlers, and is lined with their colourful wooden houses. At Karaimų 22 is the **Karaite Ethnographic Exhibition** (*www.trakaimuziejus.lt*; ⊕ *10.00–18.00 Wed–Sun*), a permanent display on the life of the community. The Karaites' military background is evoked in a collection of swords, knives, daggers, helmets, armour, shields and guns; other aspects of their culture are illuminated by displays of historic photographs, books, costumes, textiles, household goods and liturgical objects. A little further up the street is the Karaite prayer house or **Kenesa**, a late 18th-century building with a distinctively Oriental look. It was recently given a thorough restoration, and a volunteer from the local community regularly makes it accessible to the public during the

6

THE KARAITES (KARAIM)

Founded in the 8th century, the Karaite sect is often regarded as an offshoot of Judaism, adhering as it does to the authority of the Old Testament. In reality, it differs considerably, rejecting both Talmudic interpretations of the Word and oral religious laws. Moreover, the Lithuanian Karaites are not a Semitic people. They are of Turkish origin, and spread from their original base in the Byzantine Empire into the Crimean Peninsula. There, some were taken to Lithuania by Vytautas as prisoners-of-war, while others came of their own volition.

Granted freedom to practise their own religion, they were settled in Trakai, where they served as guardians of the fortresses and as Vytautas's personal bodyguards. In 1441, Vytautas's successor, Grand Duke Kazimierz, granted the Karaites the right to administer their own affairs, a privilege most unusual in medieval Europe for a non-Christian denomination. Although Lithuania's Karaite community remained small, it retained its own faith, language and identity and produced several distinguished scientists and writers. However, in the 20th century numbers declined sharply, and with a population now under 300 there are fears that it will die out within a generation.

summer. The focal point of the interior is the gilded wooden altar in the Neo-Classical style. Its upper tier bears an Old Testament inscription: 'Behold the eye of the Lord is upon them that hear Him', while the Ten Commandments are written on the framed tablets to the sides.

Karaimų continues northwards across the bridge at the tip of the peninsula which spans the channel between Lake Galvė and Lake Totoriškiai. The wooden building at Karaimų 65 houses **Kibininė**, a Karaite restaurant which has gained cult status, in spite of its abbreviated menu (see page 113). Just before it, Žalioji leads up to the **Karaite Cemetery**, which overlooks Lake Totoriškiai, with a fine view back towards the Kenesa. The older tombs are scattered among the grass on the higher ground, while the more recent graves are clustered more closely together on a promontory by the lakeshore.

Island Castle One of Lithuania's most famous sights, Trakai's Island Castle (*www.trakaimuziejus.lt;* ⊕*May–Sep 10.00–19.00 daily, Oct–Apr 10.00–17.00 Tue–Sun*) occupies almost the whole of one of the islets in Lake Galvė, and is linked by footbridge to the tiny Karaite Isle, from where another footbridge provides a connection to the eastern shore of the peninsula. The most secure and prestigious part of the town's medieval fortification system, it suffered the same fate as the Peninsula Castle in the mid-17th-century wars with the Russians, and was left as a ruin, albeit a substantial one, whose relatively isolated setting meant that it survived in better shape than any of the country's other medieval castles. Plans to rebuild it were mooted in the late 19th century, and brought to fruition between 1951 and 1962, although it seems positively bizarre that the Soviet authorities were prepared to countenance the phoenix-like reappearance of a monument symbolising Lithuania's past as a great military power.

Although this type of conjectural restoration is now very unfashionable, it is hard to judge the result as anything other than a spectacular success. When seen from across the water – and there are marvellous views from all over Lake Galvė's shoreline – it looks an awesome sight, one which must have struck fear into the heart of any medieval attacker. Close up, it is not quite so impressive, mainly because of the very obvious difference between the original bricks and rough stonework of the lower parts of the walls, and the modern machine-made bricks used to reconstruct the missing sections.

There are two parts to the fortress, which has a highly irregular ground-plan. The **Outer Castle**, whose walls are up to 3.9m thick, is entered via a gateway with drawbridge. This is flanked by massive towers, with a third tower guarding the northwest corner. All round the trapezoid-shaped inner courtyard are casements, which were used as residential quarters and storage rooms. Those on the western side now contain a somewhat quirky collection of applied art, including furniture, amber, ceramics, snuff-boxes and pipes.

A short bridge connects the Outer Castle to the **Palace**, whose dominant feature is a 25m-high keep. From its inner courtyard, there are steps down to the basement, where the treasury was housed, and stairways to the upper chambers, including the Great Hall on the first floor. These contain displays on the castle (including a series of archive photos showing how it looked prior to and during the reconstruction work), plus sundry historical artefacts.

In summer, a cruise ship departs hourly from the jetty in front of the Island Castle for a circular voyage around Lake Galvė (10Lt).

ELSEWHERE IN THE HISTORICAL NATIONAL PARK Outside Trakai itself, the main set-piece attraction in the Historical National Park is the 19th-century **Užtrakis Palace** on the eastern shore of Lake Galvė. Built in Neo-Renaissance style for the Tiškevičius (Tyszkiewicz) dynasty, it is set in a formal park laid out by the French landscape gardener Edouard André, whose work for the same family can also be seen in Palanga. The quickest way to reach Užtrakis from Trakai by road involves circumnavigating the entire shoreline of Lake Galvė in an anticlockwise direction from the northern tip of the peninsula; approximately 7km in total.

Just to the west of Lake Totoriškiai is the **Plomėnai Bird Sanctuary**. This consists of the small, almost circular Lake Plomėnai, together with the much larger area of marshland to the west.

Where to stay

Slėnyje Slėnio 1; \f 528 53880; e kempingasslenyje@one.lt; www.camptrakai.lt. This campsite, one of the few in Lithuania to be open to caravans & camper vans, is on the north shore of Lake Galvė, 7km by road from Trakai. Chalets $, guesthouse rooms $$.

OTHER DESTINATIONS IN VILNIUS COUNTY

Besides Trakai, there are a few other places in Vilnius County which make suitable day or half-day excursions from the capital.

THE CENTRE OF EUROPE The point which the French National Geographic Institute deemed in 1989 to be the centre of Europe lies some 25km north of Vilnius, down a signposted dirt track from the main A101 road to Molėtai. There is now a large sundial to mark the spot.

A far more substantial attraction inspired by the Centre of Europe theme is the **Europe Park** (*www.europosparkas.lt;* ⊕ *daily 09.00–sunset*), which lies much closer to the city, some 5km north of the Green Lakes. It can be reached by a 3km-walk from the terminus of bus 36, but a better alternative is to take a bus bound for Skirgiškės from the Žalgirio terminal (one stop north of the Calvary Market). This stops at the side road leading to the park entrance and runs ten times on weekdays, five at weekends.

The Europe Park is an open-air museum of modern sculpture in a woodland and meadow setting, with exhibits specially created for the site by around 100 different artists from 30 countries around the world. Founded in 1991, it is the brainchild of the Lithuanian sculptor Gintaras Karosas, who had conceived the idea a few years earlier while still a teenager, and who did much of the preparatory work of clearing the site with his own hands. He created the pivotal *Monument of the Centre of Europe*, which features a pyramid and indications of the direction and distances to a range of worldwide capitals, of which the furthest away is Wellington in New Zealand. Karosas was also responsible for the heavily symbolical *Infotree* by the park entrance, which has gained an entry in the *Guinness Book of Records* for being the world's largest artwork of TV sets. There are 3,000 in all, arranged (when viewed from above) in the shape of a tree, with a decaying statue of Lenin in the middle.

Chair Pool by the American Dennis Oppenheim is the most popular work – and also the most humorous, its subject being exactly what the title suggests, a giant chair with a small pool instead of a seat. The success of this led to the commissioning of a second composition from Oppenheim, *Drinking Structure with Exposed Kidney Pool*, consisting of a hut dipping down towards the water. Other sculptures which are guaranteed to catch the eye are Magdalena Abakanowicz's *Space of Unknown Growth*, a group of 22 concrete boulders; Jon Barlow Hudson's *Cloud Hands*, which consists of four granite blocks seemingly suspended in the air; and the 6m-high *Woman Looking at the Moon* by the Mexican Javier Cruz.

KERNAVĖ Kernavė, which lies on a terrace high above a bend on the River Neris, 40km from Vilnius down a minor road, is nowadays an insignificant village of just over 300 souls. However, its now-vanished medieval predecessor, which was situated by the riverside and abandoned in 1390 following repeated sackings by the Teutonic Knights, was almost certainly Lithuania's original capital, a status it may have gained under King Mindaugas, and is securely documented as having held throughout the reign of Grand Duke Traidenis (1269–82). Its importance to the country's history was given due international recognition in 2004, when it became the third place in Lithuania to gain admittance to UNESCO's World Heritage List.

At the southern end of the present-day village is its dominant monument, a bloated Neo-Gothic parish church completed in 1920. Alongside is the entrance to the **Historical and Archaeological Museum-Reserve** (*www.kernave.org; guided tours Apr–Oct 09.00–17.00 Tue–Sat*), the only one of its type in Lithuania. From the observation platform there is a magnificent view over the protected area, with its five large mounds, and the Neris valley beyond. The mounds, which can be ascended via wooden stairways, were formerly girded with ramparts and fortifications, and formed a unified defensive system. To the southeast of the platform is Castle Mound, which according to legend was linked by an underground tunnel to Trakai and Vilnius. However, the ducal castle was actually situated on the central Hearth Mound (the oldest of the group), which lies immediately south of the platform; its name comes from the tradition that a pagan temple formerly stood there. The nearby mound is known as Mindaugas's Throne, as it is believed to have been the setting for the king's coronation; the others are the steep Lizdeika Mound, which protected its approaches, and Kriveikiškis Mound, which is further to the southeast, on the right bank of the Kernavelė stream.

Kernavė, which was first settled around 9000BC, has proved to be a fruitful hunting ground for archaeologists. Many of the artefacts they have unearthed are on view in the exhibition building, though this is likely to be closed for renovations until 2009. These range from Stone Age arrowheads via Bronze and

Iron Age tools to medieval cult objects and jewellery. The extensive trade networks are well illustrated by a string of 400 beads of Russian origin which also includes ten shells which originated in the Maldive Islands in the Indian Ocean.

In honour of Kernavė's status as the likely setting for the coronation of King Mindaugas in 1253, the Living Archaeology Days festival is held there over a weekend in early July, around the time of the public holiday commemorating the event. It consists of a series of tableaux re-creating different aspects of life from the Stone Age to medieval times, and the emphasis is firmly hands-on, with visitors given the opportunity to sample ancient methods of cookery, metalwork, handicrafts and even fighting.

There are usually three daily buses to Kernavė from Vilnius, and also several minibuses which stop *en route* to Širvintas. A full timetable is published on the museum's website.

AUKŠTADVARIS REGIONAL PARK West of the Trakai Historical National Park lies another very pretty protected landscape, the Aukštadvaris Regional Park. Within its boundaries are no fewer than 77 lakes, and it is seen at its best in September or October when cloaked in glorious autumnal colours. Buses from Vilnius to Alytus, or from Vilnius to Birštonas and Prienai, travel all the way through the middle of the park, enabling a good cross-section of its scenery to be seen. *En route* they pass through the village of **Aukštadvaris**, which lies on the northern shore of Lake Nava and has a fine twin-towered wooden parish church. In the woods some 4km to the north, and reachable by footpath, is the so-called **Devil's Cave**, a mysterious hole 40m deep and 200m in diameter which has been the inspiration for a host of legends.

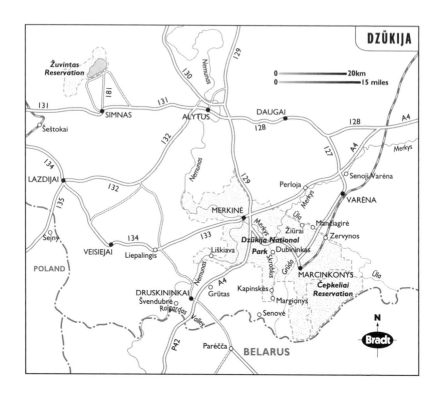

7

Dzūkija

The southeasternmost part of Lithuania is known as Dzūkija, and is recognised as a distinctive ethnographic region in its own right. Its borders are roughly similar to the modern administrative county of Alytus, its capital and main town. With the single exception of the health resort of Druskininkai, one of Lithuania's most popular destinations, it sees very little tourism. None the less, it is undoubtedly among the most fascinating and rewarding parts of the country, particularly for nature lovers, as it boasts two strictly maintained reserves in addition to a national park. Predominantly rural, it has many attractive old villages where traditional work and lifestyle patterns are maintained defiantly.

NORTHERN DZŪKIJA

Dzūkija's most obvious attractions lie in the southern part of the province, but there are several places in the north which lie, if sometimes unwittingly, on the tourist trail.

ŠEŠTOKAI The village of Šeštokai is many visitors' first glimpse of Lithuania. Regrettably, it is not at all an auspicious introduction, as it is an unremarkable little place in every respect, save for the fact that it happens to be a major railway junction important enough to feature on international railway timetables, its significance stemming from the fact that its line south to the Polish border, which was opened in 1993, is the only one in Lithuania using the standard European gauge, as opposed to that of the former Soviet Union. Currently, there is one daily daytime service, plus one overnight on alternate days, between Warsaw and Vilnius. These all involve changing trains at Šeštokai, but are still far more convenient than the now-suspended alternative route via Grodno in Belarus, which entailed not only a noisy gauge change but also the purchase of an outrageously expensive transit visa.

ŽUVINTAS RESERVATION Lithuania's longest-established protected landscape, the Žuvintas Reservation, lies 12km north of the small town of Simnas, which is 15km east of Šeštokai on the road to Alytus. By public transport, the easiest means of access is via Alytus; four daily buses run from there to Žuvintai and stop at the turn-off to the reservation, about 3km before the terminus. Established in 1937 through the initiative of the celebrated naturalist Tadas Ivanauskas, founder of the Zoological Museum and Zoo in Kaunas, it exists to provide protection for Lake Žuvintas, which was formed during the last glacial period, and the marshes to the west. Sadly, the lake has been silting up gradually for the past 10,000 years, and it is reckoned it will disappear altogether in a few hundred years' time. None the less, it is one of the most important ornithological sites in the country. Of the 255 species which have been identified, 195 breed there. There are large populations of swans, marsh harriers and cranes, with up to 1,000 of the last-named settling there in autumn. Between 55% and 60% of the surface of the lake is covered with plants at any one time, though the picture changes markedly in the course of the year. In summer, for example, the islets and vegetation merge, leaving green meadows. Tench, pike, perch, carp and roach are among the 19 species of fish living in the lake; there are also four types of reptiles and nine amphibians, while there are 37 sorts of mammals in the reserve.

The administration building contains the **Žuvintas Reservation Museum** (⊕*daily in summer 08.00–12.00 and 12.45–17.00, closed weekends the rest of the year*), which presents a small exhibition on the local flora and fauna, with some information in English. It is also possible to go up the observation tower on top of the building for a panoramic view over the lake. Some parts of the nearby lakeshore are used by locals for swimming and sunbathing, though other parts are difficult to access because of the heavy vegetation. Boats are available for hire, but – in line with the fact that this is a research institute rather than a tourist attraction – there are no organised trips of any kind.

⌂ Where to stay

⌂ **Administration Centre Guesthouse** \/f 315 49540; e zuvintas@takas.lt; www.zuvintas.lt. 3 sgl rooms & 3 suites are at the disposal of visitors in the administration building for 20Lt per head. Note that no meals are served, & that there are no shops in the vicinity, so it is essential to bring adequate supplies.

ALYTUS Capital of both the historic province of Dzūkija and the modern administrative county which takes its own name, Alytus lies 30km east of the Žuvintas Reservation, straddling both banks of the Nemunas. As the river has often made a convenient frontier in the past, Alytus has sometimes been divided. In the early 19th century, for example, the main part of town on the western bank was successively part of the semi-autonomous Grand Duchy of Warsaw and the Congress Kingdom of Poland, while its counterpart belonged to the Vilnius province of the Russian Empire. Nowadays the sixth largest town in Lithuania with a population of about 70,000, Alytus is predominantly industrial.

The town's name has become virtually synonomous with the sparkling wines produced by the Alita factory, one of the most notable success stories of the post-communist economy. Ten different varieties are made, using a mixture of imported wines and employing a biochemically altered version of the traditional French *méthode champenoise* which reduces the production period from three years to three months. The drinks are so popular in Lithuania that almost all the output is consumed internally, though the quality is high enough to have won several international awards. Alita also produces brandy, as well as wines made from berries and other fruits.

Alytus has a very modest roster of sights. The most interesting historic monument is the **Church of the Guardian Angels**, which stands in its own quiet grounds just off Savanorių, a short walk north of the main square, Rotušės aikštė. This rustic-looking wooden church with detached belfry dates from the 1830s, though in both design and decoration it looks like a product of the Baroque era of the previous century. In the cemetery are the graves of 114 volunteers who fought for Lithuania's independence after World War I. At Savanorių 6, the **Museum of Regional Ethnography** (⊕*09.00–18.00 Tue–Sat*) documents the history of Dzūkija. A block to the north, at the eastern end of Kauno, is the late 19th-century **Synagogue**, which preserves its shell intact, though is clearly derelict inside. Fine views over the Nemunas can be enjoyed from the bridge which spans the river. Just over the other side, on Panemuninlkėlių, is Alytus's oldest building, the **Church of St Louis**. However, little more than the foundations remain of the original edifice of the 1520s, which was rebuilt in the 19th century in Neo-Classical style and is primarily of note for its imposing façade.

Tourist information
🛈 **Tourist office** Rotušės aikštė 14a; ☎ 315 52010; f 315 51982; e info@alytus-tourism.lt, www.alytus-tourism.lt. Situated on the main square; some English spoken. ⏲ Jun–Aug 08.00–18.00 Mon–Fri, 10.00–14.00 Sat; Sep–May 08.00–17.00 Mon–Thu, 08.00–16.00 Fri.

Getting there and around
🚌 **Bus station** Jotvingių 5; ☎ 315 52333. This lies immediately west of Rotušės aikštė. There is generally at least 1 bus per hr to both Kaunas & Vilnius; other daily services include 11 to Druskininkai, 5 to Varėna, 3 to Panevėžys, 2 to Trakai, 2 in season to Palanga, 1 to Klaipėda, 1 to Šiauliai & 1 to Anykščiai.

Where to stay
🏠 **Dzūkija** Pulko 14; ☎ 315 51345; e hoteldzukija@takas.lt; www.hoteldzukija.lt. Located on the main north–south thoroughfare, just to the rear of the bus station. $$

🏠 **Senas Namas** Užuolankos 24; ☎ 315 53489; f 315 51643; e info@senasnamas.lt; www.senasnamas.lt. A small hotel with a restaurant, situated a couple of blocks north of Rotušės aikštė. $$

Where to eat
✗ **Dzūkų svetainė** Rotušės aikštė 16. Offers a typical Lithuanian menu, including many of the local wines.

✗ **Palermo** Rotušės aikštė 2a. Serves good pizzas & other Italianate fare.

VARĖNA The curious feature of Varėna, which lies 45km southeast of Alytus and 75km southwest of Vilnius, is that it is a town of two distinct sections which lie 6km apart. Senoji (Old) Varėna stands with its back to the River Merkys, beside the main A4 highway linking the capital with Druskininkai. Following the construction of the Warsaw–Vilnius–St Petersburg railway in 1862, a second settlement, which soon became the main part of town, grew up around the station.

Varėna's other claim to fame is as the birthplace of the composer and painter Mikalojus Konstantinas Čiurlionis (see pages 122–3), whose father served as organist of the parish church prior to taking up a similar appointment in Druskininkai. Badly damaged in World War I, when it was the scene of bitter fighting between the Germans and Russians, Varėna has no tourist attractions of its own, but is none the less quite a convenient base for exploring the surrounding region. The main annual event is a mushroom festival on the last Saturday of September.

Getting there and around
🚌 **Bus station** Savanorių 5; ☎ 310 31636. Located in the south of town. Daily services include 7 to Vilnius, 5 to Alytus & 3 to Druskininkai.

🚂 **Railway station** Savanorių 3; ☎ 310 53284. There are 4 trains daily to Vilnius, 3 to Marcinkonys.

Where to stay
🏠 **Alrimta** Vasario 16-osios 5; ☎/f 310 52572; e info@ekoratas.lt; www.ekoratas.lt. A small hotel in the town centre, not far from the station. $, suites $$.

Where to eat
✗ **Didysis Kunigaikštis** Vytauto 12. An inexpensive town-centre restaurant offering typical Lithuanian dishes.

'Lithuania's great man' was how the French composer Olivier Messiaen described Dzūkija's favourite son. Despite his short life, Čiurlionis ranks as Lithuania's most esteemed composer, as well as its only painter with a definite claim to genuine international standing.

Čiurlionis was born in Varėna, the eldest of 11 children. His father, of peasant stock, was an organist and choirmaster; his mother, though the child of German immigrants, was steeped in the lore and folk songs of the region. In 1878 the family moved to Druskininkai, where he spent his boyhood, becoming proficient on both piano and organ by the age of ten. From 1889–93 he lived at Plungė under the patronage of Duke Mykolas Oginskis, serving as flautist in the ducal orchestra and singing in the choir.

In 1894 Čiurlionis began five years of study at the Warsaw Institute of Music. While there he wrote many (mostly small-scale) works for piano. Although more severe in style, these show an obvious debt to Chopin in their melancholy mood, and in the penchant for repetitive bass figures, a favourite device throughout Čiurlionis's career. He also composed a set of variations for string quartet and the cantata De Profundis. Čiurlionis stayed on in Warsaw for two years after graduation, earning his living by giving private lessons, and writing the first-ever symphonic composition by a Lithuanian, the tone poem In the Forest. In 1901–02 he studied composition and counterpoint at the Leipzig Conservatoire, and composed keyboard canons and fugues strongly influenced by Bach, plus a string quartet.

Čiurlionis then returned to Warsaw where he resumed his freelance teaching activities, this time to finance the study of painting and drawing. In 1903, he produced the first of his many cycles of pictures, albeit in pastel rather than the tempera he used for the bulk of his output. Entitled Funeral Symphony, it marked the beginning of his highly idiosyncratic attempts at synthesising music and painting by bringing to the latter some of the forms and principles (especially thematic development) of the former. Although classifiable as a Symbolist, it was only in his early paintings that Čiurlionis can really be described as an adherent of that movement. His preoccupation with music, philosophy and cosmology, and his roots in the Lithuanian folk tradition, mark him out as a supreme artistic individualist.

When the new Warsaw School of Art opened in 1904, Čiurlionis enrolled as a student, and branched out into creating designs for stained glass and book covers in an Art Nouveau style. He also continued to compose, developing a tougher, more personal manner in his piano miniatures, adopting a form of serial technique at around the same time as Schoenberg. By the following year, he was irresistibly drawn to the Lithuanian Movement, declaring in a letter written early in 1906 his decision 'to dedicate all past and future work to Lithuania'. Although he began to spend a great deal of time travelling, he helped organise the First Exhibition of Lithuanian Art in Vilnius in 1907; among the

The Čiurlionis Road In 1975, to celebrate the centenary of Čiurlionis's birth, a series of wooden poles, variously arranged singly or in groups, was erected along the road between Varėna and Druskininkai; in time, this popularly became known as the Čiurlionis Road (*Čiurlionio Kelias*). The carvings, the work of sculptors who practise the folk idiom which influenced so much of Čiurlionis's own output, are inspired by a mixture of musical themes and subjects from the artist's paintings. Surprisingly, the project has generated a fair amount of controversy; some critics

top left **Old Town Hall, Kaunas** (GMcL) page 149
top right **Kaunas Castle** (GMcL) page 149
above left **Aleksotas funicular railway, Kaunas** (GMcL) page 157
above right **Windmill at Kleboniškiai** (GMcL) page 182

above **View of Žemaičių Kalvarija**
(GMcL) page 198

lleft **Pažaislis Monstery, Kaunas**
(GMcL) page 158

above **Pilgrimage at Feast of the Visitation, Žemaičių Kalvarija** (GMcL) page 33

below **Orvydas Garden, near Salantai** (GMcL) page 203

above **Beach, Palanga** (GMcL) page 207

below **Tiškevičius Palace (Amber Museum), Palanga** (GMcL) page 214

top Mouth of the River Danė during Sea Festival, Klaipėda
(GMcL) page 222

centre Kopgalis Fortress (Maritime Museum), Klaipėda (GMcL) page 226

right Witches' Hill, Juodkrantė
(GMcL) page 231

Dead dunes, near Juodkrantė (GMcL) page 232

paintings he exhibited were the cycles *The Creation of the World* and *The Storm*. The same year he completed his musical masterpiece *The Sea*, a 30-minute symphonic poem for large orchestra. He also executed the first two of his seven Sonatas, his most ambitious paintings with musical titles, and an enchanting cycle, *The Zodiac*.

While living in Vilnius, Čiurlionis met the writer Sofija Kymantaitė, whom he later married. Together they planned to write the first Lithuanian opera, *Jūratė*, but in the meantime his musical energies became concentrated on the Vilniaus Kanklės choir, the first officially sanctioned society of Lithuanian music. He served as its conductor and wrote numerous folk-song harmonisations for it. Čiurlionis played a major role at the Second and Third Exhibitions of Lithuanian Art in 1908 and 1909, and in the latter year created some of his most memorable paintings, including a series – notably *The Fairy Tale of the Kings* – inspired by Lithuanian legends, as well as such powerful visions as *The Knight Prelude*, *The Altar* and *Rex*. He also penned his main prose work, *On Music*, for his wife's book of articles, *In Lithuania*. (Čiurlionis's first language was Polish, and his imperfect command of Lithuanian severely curtailed his long-cherished literary ambitions.)

Towards the end of the year, Čiurlionis was overcome by depression, racked by overwork and by continued financial problems, his frequent trips to St Petersburg having failed to secure any prestigious permanent employment. In 1910 he was brought back to Druskininkai, then placed in a private nursing home near Warsaw. His health improved following the birth of his daughter, but he later relapsed, and died the following year of pneumonia.

Soon afterwards, the Lithuanian Fine Arts Society set about preserving almost his entire output of paintings *en bloc*, stating that they 'represent the soul of the whole nation'. They went on what was intended to be permanent display in Vilnius in 1913, but on the outbreak of World War I were sent to Moscow for safekeeping, to be recovered in 1920 and purchased by the Lithuanian state two years later. In 1925 they were put on show in a temporary gallery in Kaunas. A permanent home was built in the same city in 1936, and re-organised as the MK Čiurlionis Gallery in 1944.

Despite having some ardent champions, Čiurlionis is little-known in the West. Lithuania's independence leader, Vytautas Landsbergis, has been an indefatigable propagator through books, recordings and recitals, but Čiurlionis has not yet attracted a celebrity virtuoso who could make his piano pieces internationally popular, while wider appreciation of his paintings is hampered by their fragility and concentration in one location. None the less, concerted attempts are being made to raise his international profile: the 1998 exhibition in Cologne, the first ever in the West, has been followed by others at Paris's Musée d'Orsay and elsewhere.

have attacked it as being a debased derivative of genuine Lithuanian folk art, in which a religious element is an essential component. Moreover, many of the poles weathered very quickly and have needed a lot of repair work.

PERLOJA Best known for its quirky history, Perloja, a village of wooden houses clustered around a Neo–Gothic brick church, lies 9km from Senoji Varėna along the road to Druskininkai. It was granted a charter in 1387 by Vytautas the Great, who promised that none of its inhabitants could ever become a serf. This immunity duly survived down the centuries, and took a sudden and dramatic twist at the end of World War I. With the Soviet Union and the revived states of Poland and Lithuania locked in combat over vast tracts of disputed land, the Perlojans took matters into their own hands and declared the establishment of their own republic on November 23 1918. A president, prime minister, finance minister and interior minister were all elected, and an army set up, which could count on 300 men from the surrounding area. Although Polish sovereignty over the area was recognised internationally by 1920, the Perlojans abandoned their village whenever the Poles tried to occupy it, and their republic survived until 1923, when it finally became clear that not even their fellow-Lithuanians would recognise the existence of their state.

The statue of Grand Duke Vytautas on the main square is the only one of the great Lithuanian hero which survived the Soviet years, having defeated an attempt by the authorities in 1957 to demolish it with tanks and explosives. It proved so resistant because the cunning villagers, resentful of the foreign rule to which they had been subject for so long, had reinforced the statue with steel rail sleepers, and its pedestal with concrete.

DZŪKIJA NATIONAL PARK

Occupying 55,900 hectares between the towns of Varėna and Druskininkai is the Dzūkija National Park, the largest protected landscape in Lithuania. Set up in 1991, it aims to preserve the nature, culture and economy of the Dainava ('Singing') land, as well as to encourage a discreet amount of eco-tourism. From an ethnographic point of view, it is by far the most interesting of the country's national parks. Within its boundaries there are, discounting the innumerable isolated farmsteads, more than a hundred villages and hamlets, all of which preserve a traditional rural lifestyle centred on farming and forestry which has changed relatively little in centuries. Major monuments may be few in number, but fine examples of folk architecture, notably large-scale farmsteads, are legion. Although the landscape is seldom very dramatic, the majestic valley of the River Nemunas apart, the clear streams, forests, marshes, inland dunes and tiny lakes all have an undeniable beauty of their own.

INFORMATION AND MAPS The National Park runs information centres at its headquarters in Marcinkonys and in Merkinė, the only settlement which has the status of a town; see the appropriate sections below for the addresses. It publishes an excellent booklet about the park, richly illustrated with colour photographs. A good-quality map (1:120,000) is also available, and is an essential companion for anything more than a superficial visit; regular new editions of this are planned in order to incorporate more detail, and to document changes to the roads and trails.

TOURISM AND TRANSPORT As the tourist infrastructure is very basic, and will be kept so, a trip to the Dzūkija National Park profits from careful planning. For those who do not wish to camp, there is only one small hotel plus one youth hostel, though accommodation in farms can also be arranged via the information centres. Lying only a few kilometres from the park's southwestern edge, Druskininkai makes an alternative base. For anyone travelling by car, it is a more than adequate centre for covering the whole park, but only the places along the western edge are readily accessible on day trips by the decent, if somewhat sporadic, bus service. There is no longer a regular bus service across the park, or along its eastern edge.

However, some of the villages in the latter area lie on the Vilnius–Druskininkai railway line. This currently terminates at Marcinkonys because of operational difficulties with the last stage of the journey. As a result of the collapse of the Soviet Union, the service took on a quasi-international aspect, as the route between Marcinkonys and Druskininkai includes a short stretch of track within the frontiers of Belarus. For the years it continued to operate, the train itself was deemed to be in Lithuanian territory, but its exits and entrances were carefully policed by Belarussian border guards for the entire period it passed through land under their jurisdiction. Moreover, as it could be boarded by Belarussian nationals at both the frontier and the small town of Paréčča, it was itself subject to a Lithuanian customs inspection before disembarkation was permitted at Druskininkai. The experience is certainly worth sampling if it is ever re-instated, which unfortunately seems unlikely in the foreseeable future: now that the Lithuanian border with Belarus has become a frontline of the EU, it is among the most tightly controlled on the entire continent.

The road network, on the other hand, is being improved all the time, and the main routes are all covered (or soon will be) with asphalt. Otherwise – and even within the villages themselves – dirt roads are the norm, often providing serious tests of a vehicle's suspension. Cycling is obviously a more satisfactory way of seeing the scenery, even if the forest tracks often make for bumpy rides. Walking is best of all, the relatively large distances being the only drawback. As yet, there are only a few colour-coded hiking trails, but it is planned to increase the provision of these. The placid streams are ideal for exploration by canoe; indeed, this is the only way of appreciating them to the full.

Note that there is no more than a handful of restaurants and cafés within the park, and that only the biggest villages are able to support a food store.

GEOGRAPHY Two-thirds of the park's territory consist of a sandy plain whose most remarkable feature is the presence of dune massifs which came into existence around 30,000BC following the second stage of the glacial period. In contrast, the northwestern part of the park features a landscape of low morainal hills. The altitude varies little, the highest point being 168m, the lowest 66m above sea level, with the average around 100m. Forests predominate, accounting for a total of 43,700 hectares.

The western edge of the park lies in the middle valley of the Nemunas, while the plain is drained by a major tributary, the Merkys; by the latter's tributaries the Ūla, Grūda and Skroblus; and by more than two dozen rivulets. These meandering, slow-flowing streams are nourished by ground water and are wonderfully fresh and clear.

There are a number of small lakes, mostly round or oval in shape, in the plain. Formed long after the glacial period, they are usually overgrown and difficult to access. A denser concentration of lakes, which are typically narrow and deep, can be found among the morainal hills. Various patches of marshland lie within the park, particularly in the south.

FLORA Pines make up 92% of the trees in the forests. Black alders are concentrated along the banks of the streams and near the marshes; elms can likewise be found in the river valleys, while there are also spruce and birch groves within the park. No more than 2% of the total number of trees can be considered mature, the average age being 60 years. The pine forests are rich in lichen, and 212 different sorts have been identified.

A wide variety of plant species, some of them rare, grow in the different landscapes of the park. Herbs, berries and nuts can be found in abundance, and can be picked. However, the Dzūkija National Park is best-known for having the best yield of wild mushrooms in Lithuania. There are around 300 different species, ten of which are under protection. The most popular edible varieties are the boletus and chanterelle, and searching the forests for crops is a popular activity with weekend visitors as well as locals. In season, mushrooms can be bought at many farms and wayside stalls which will certainly be a better option for visitors who may be in doubt as to which varieties are safe to eat and which may be harmful.

FAUNA Around 150 species of birds live in the park, about a fifth of which are classified as rare. Chaffinches, pied flycatchers, crested tits, thrushes and black woodpeckers are the commonest species within the pine forests; tree pipits, woodlarks and nightjars inhabit glades and cleared spaces; while black storks, lesser spotted eagles, black kites, honey buzzards, eagle-owls and owls tend to keep to the remoter parts of the woods. Stock doves and various different types of woodpeckers live in trees along the river banks; kingfishers and goosanders favour the larger rivers; while reed buntings and river, sedge and great reed warblers settle around the lake shores and overgrown river valleys. Rollers, hoopoes and green woodpeckers are attracted to the vicinity of the villages which are set deep in the forests. Meadow pipits, whinchats and snipes inhabit marshy meadows, while the more remote marshland is populated by cranes, capercaillies and black grouse.

Of the 40 or so species of mammals, the most common are elk, roe and red deer and wild boars. Wolves, foxes, racoons, badgers, pine martens, mountain hares and dormice are also found, while otters, beavers and mink inhabit the rivers. The rivers teem with fish, including trout, bream, carp, tench, eel, pike and perch. Nine species of amphibia live within the park, plus all seven species of reptilia found in Lithuania. Among the many insects are numerous butterflies, ten of which are classed as rare, while the presence of no fewer than 217 types of bee is responsible for bee-keeping being a long-established, but now much declined, component of local culture.

ETHNOGRAPHY Historically, there were few large estates within the area that is now the Dzūkija National Park, which meant that the area escaped both serfdom and then compulsory collectivisation. Instead, a pattern of small farm-holdings evolved, with strong communal bonds. To this day, cattle are grazed jointly, and several farms may share the same horse for such diverse purposes as ploughing, moving timber, and to draw a carriage for visiting family and friends. There is even a modern twist to this tradition in the tendency to pool the use of cars.

The villages and hamlets consist primarily of groups of fenced-in farms, which often lie far away from their associated plots of arable land and meadows for grazing. Additionally, there are many isolated farmsteads, some located deep in the forests. Few concessions are made to modernity in the labour-intensive style of agriculture practised. Apart from the use of horses for the heavy work, almost everything – including harvesting with sickles, threshing hay, and grinding with millstones – is done by hand. Life is lived firmly at the subsistence level, and this has, not surprisingly, led to severe depopulation, with over half the current population of the park being above the official retirement age. Many farms have been abandoned altogether, while others are now relegated to the status of holiday or weekend retreats by owners who have moved to the cities. One of the most challenging tasks facing the National Park authorities is to reverse, or at least halt, the pattern of rural decay.

Generally speaking, saws and nails are eschewed in the construction of the characteristic wooden farm buildings, the axe being the only tool used. The woodcarving tradition finds expression in the many wayside crosses (which are often double in shape) and shrines with statuettes of saints, though these are far less elaborate than in Samogitia. Among the handicrafts practised are candle-making, textile-weaving, basket-making, clog-making and ceramics. Ethnographic song and dance ensembles are active in many of the villages, while Margionys is home to a barn theatre. The bee-keeping tradition has left a distinctive mark on the landscape in the form of numerous hollowed-out pine trees which the keepers had to climb in order to collect the honey.

ZERVYNOS AND THE ŪLA VALLEY Although situated only just within the northern boundaries of the park, **Zervynos** is the most atmospheric of its villages, and is so well preserved that it has been proposed as a candidate for inclusion on UNESCO's prestigious World Heritage List. It is 12km southwest of Varėna, or one stop away by train. The station (actually no more than a small shelter) lies immediately before an impressive bridge which carries the railway high above the River Ūla, the most beautiful of the park's streams. From the northern end of the platform, a dirt track runs down into the village, which spreads out on both sides of the Ūla, while a few hundred metres north of the station is a road which runs northwestwards from Zervynos along the Ūla valley.

Zervynos has preserved its 18th- and 19th-century street pattern and layout intact. It consists of 48 farmsteads, eight of which are considered to be of monumental character and are outstanding examples of the wooden folk architecture of the region. The whole village, indeed, resembles a living and working open-air museum, yet has absolutely nothing artificial about it. There are no shops, nor a church, though there is a peaceful shaded cemetery at the southern edge, an ancient oak tree and some hollowed-out pines where bees were kept.

Where to stay

🏠 **Youth hostel** 🔌 310 52720; e svirnelis@ hotmail.com. Heavily promoted by the management of the Vilnius Old Town hostel, this is easy to find, despite being unmarked. It is one of the buildings in the first farmyard down the track from the station. Canoe trips on the Ūla can be arranged. Normally ⏰ 15 May–15 Sep. Simple home-cooked meals can be taken at a nearby farmhouse. 💲

Ūla valley A short distance southeast of Zervynos is the **Povilnis Reserve**, one of three strict nature reserves which should only be visited in the company of an official of the National Park. It consists of the source and upper canyon of the eponymous rivulet, a tributary of the Ūla.

More readily accessible is the downstream section of the Ūla, though the road between Zervynos and **Mančiagirė**, 5km to the northwest, lies some way back from the river. The latter, another well-preserved village, was the home of the area's best-known woodcarver, Tomas Miškinis (1876–1962), five of whose crosses can be seen in the cemetery.

A couple of kilometres onwards is the valley's most remarkable natural feature, the spring **Ūlos Akis** ('Eye of the Ūla'), an oval lake 4.4m by 3.4m with constantly boiling black sand underneath. It was formerly much more powerful than it is today; the older inhabitants of Mančiagirė can remember when it could be heard from the village itself. **Žiūrai**, a further 3km downstream from the spring, dates back at least as far as the early 18th century, and is nowadays best known for its ethnographic ensemble, the first to be established in the region.

MARCINKONYS Marcinkonys, 8km southwest of Zervynos and one stop away by train, is the second largest settlement in the park, with a population which presently stands at about 870, having once been over 1,200. It is the headquarters not only of the National Park itself, but also of the separately administered Čepkeliai Reservation, a far more strictly preserved wilderness area between the southeastern boundaries of the park and the River Katra, at the point where the

Dzūkija **DZŪKIJA NATIONAL PARK**

7

latter doubles as the frontier with Belarus. Occupying one of the largest areas of any Lithuanian village, Marcinkonys consists of one 2km-long main street, Miškininkų, running northwards from the station, plus a few smaller streets, including one on the opposite side of the rail tracks, and many isolated farms.

First documented in 1673, Marcinkonys expanded from being a small community of foresters after the railway was constructed in 1862, and the part of the village adjacent to the station dates from this time. Until World War II it had a sizeable number of Jewish residents. A short distance up the street is the **Ethnographic Museum**, which occupies a pre-World War I wooden house which belongs to the site. In the grounds (not its original location) can be seen an example of a pine tree used for bee-keeping, while among the many objects displayed inside is an example of the type of rope ladder formerly used for gathering the honey. Other simple yet ingenious local inventions on show are a torch which helped make night-time river fishing safe and efficient; and an 'old man', a device for illuminating the home during the long winter evenings. A barn has been brought to the grounds and re-assembled in order to provide extra display space. The museum does not have regular opening hours, and it may be necessary to ask at the National Park information centre further up the street in order to arrange a visit.

At the very end of the street is the wooden **Church of SS Simon and Judas Thaddeus**. The present building, resplendent with twin towers and a central cupola, was built around 1880. A couple of decades later it was ringed with a stone wall on which are placed shrines illustrating the Stations of the Cross. Inside, the church is divided into nave and aisles by means of slender pillars, while the main and side altars are fine pieces of folk art. Unfortunately, it is usually only possible to gain access at the times of Masses, the only regular ones being on Saturday evening and Sunday morning.

From the large double cross in front of the church enclosure, a path leads along the side of the cemetery and past several picturesque agricultural buildings to one of the inland dunes characteristic of the National Park.

A couple of undemanding colour-coded nature trails have been established in and around Marcinkonys, and there are plenty of enticing longer walks which can easily be made, notably in the valley of the Grūda, which flows just west of the village, and to fringes of the Čepkeliai Reservation. Lake Kastnis, a popular picnic and camping spot, lies about 1km northeast of the station on the far side of the rail tracks.

Park administration centres

Dzūkija National Park Miškininkų 62; ✆ 310 44641; f 310 44437. Located about halfway along the main street.

Čepkeliai Reservation Šilagelių 11; ✆ 310 44684; f 310 44428; e cepkeliai@takas.lt; www.cepkeliai.lt Located at the southwestern edge of the village.

Tourist information

🛈 **Dzūkija National Park** Miškininkų 61; ✆ 310 44466/44467; f 310 44471; e info@dzukijosparkas.lt; www.dzukijosparkas.lt. ⏰08.00–12.00 & 13.00–17.00 Mon–Sat. In addition to providing information, the centre organises tours & angling, hunting & canoeing permits (the last-named being necessary for the Ūla, on which only 5 parties are allowed to take to the water at any one time). There is also a small gallery with changing exhibitions of local arts & crafts. English spoken.

Where to stay

🏠 **Eglis** Miškininkų 61; ✆ 310 44466; f 310 44471. The National Park's own guesthouse occupies the rear of its information centre, which was built as a retirement residential home but shortly afterwards converted to its present purpose. The rooms are very quiet, comfortable & modern & all have private facilities & satellite TV.

Meals can be provided if arranged in advance, or if a group is also staying there. $$, suites $$$
🏠 **Sakalų sodyba** Naujalių 15; 📞 615 34305;
📧 marcinkonys@centras.lt;

www.marcinkonys.infoseka.lt. 2 rooms are available for rent in this log cabin located alongside the farmhouse of its owners, who offer guests courses in local handicrafts, music & dancing. $

Camping This is only allowed in designated areas in the park marked with pictures of a tent. Camping places must be registered and paid for at the park headquarters. 5Lt for a tent, 2Lt for a car; tents and sleeping bags can be rented for 5Lt each.

✗ Where to eat The grocery store located close to the station on Miškininkų has a small and sometimes quite boisterous bar alongside with its own unmarked entrance door. Basic hot meals are available there. There is another bar further up the same street.

ČEPKELIAI RESERVATION The 10,752 hectares of the Čepkeliai Reservation are not technically part of the national park, but are actually under far more stringent environmental control, being an uninhabited wilderness. It is the largest state reserve in Lithuania, and was established in 1975 to protect the country's most extensive area of mire, which accounts for 5,858 hectares of the total area. A varied landscape includes high marshes, sedge marshes, swamps, pine forests, 21 small lakes and some 80 'islands' of dry land. There are around 2,500 different species of plant (including many more characteristic of the nearby dune landscape), 36 of mammal, and 178 of bird. The marshland is particularly important as an ornithological breeding ground, especially for capercaillies, black grouse and cranes.

Access to the mire itself is only permitted in the company of a guide from the National Park or the Reservation itself, and is normally banned altogether from April 1 to June 1 when hatching takes place. Nevertheless, there is unrestricted access to the observation platform which provides a grandstand view over the northern part of the reservation. This can be reached by walking or driving for 4km down the signposted forest track at the extreme southwestern edge of Marcinkonys, then continuing eastwards on foot for a further 1km.

MARGIONYS AND THE SKROBLUS VALLEY Margionys, which lies 10km southwest of Marcinkonys, is the fifth largest settlement in the National Park, though its population does not even reach three figures. From a cultural point of view, it is best known for its Barn Theatre, which was founded in 1929, and directed from 1941 until his death by Juozas Gaidys (1908–93), a self-taught local man who gained it a national reputation. The present theatre, erected by the National Park authorities in 1993, still puts on performances of Gaidys's plays and productions, though its star is somewhat on the wane. Gaidys's grave can be seen in the cemetery, close to a pine formerly used for bee-keeping.

At the southeastern edge of the village is the source of the Skroblus, which is geologically the most remarkable rivulet in the park, with a much faster flow than the larger Ūla and Grūda. The yield of eight litres per second produced by the spring has risen to 700 litres per second, having been boosted by several other springs and tiny brooks, by the time the stream joins the Merkys after a journey of just 17.3km. An extraordinarily rich flora flourishes on its banks, and the area between the villages of Kapinskės, 1.5km north of Margionys, and Dubininkas, a similar distance south of the confluence, is a strict nature reserve.

MERKINĖ Lying a short way back from the Vilnius to Druskininkai highway, 100km from the former and 33km from the latter, Merkinė boasts an illustrious history a world away from that of the villages on the eastern side of the National Park. Its favourable setting at the confluence of the Nemunas and Merkys recommended it to Paleolithic peoples, who first settled there in the 9th or 10th century BC. In the Middle Ages it was the site of one of the most important Lithuanian castles. It was granted town rights in 1569 by Zygmunt August, King of Poland and Grand Duke of Lithuania, and developed into a trading centre. One of his successors, Władysław Waza (or Vasa) – who was also titular King of Sweden – died there in 1648. Soon afterwards Merkinė went into decline; the castle was destroyed by the Russians in 1655, and the town itself was also badly damaged, never recovering its former importance. Its present-day population is just 1,600, but it still proudly preserves its status as a municipality.

Although nothing remains of the structure itself, the **Castle Hill**, reached by a path from the parking place beside the Nemunas Bridge, commands a fine panoramic view of the great river and its tributary at the point of their convergence. In a surprisingly unassuming position on the slopes of the nearby hill on which the town itself is situated is the major surviving monument, the **Church of the Assumption**. This was built in the early 15th century, and is a hall church with nave, aisles, presbytery and triple apse, a design not found anywhere else in Lithuania. Most of its Gothic features – windows, wall buttresses and octagonal pillars supporting ribbed vaults – survive intact. However, the façade, with its picturesque three-storey gable, and the entrance gateway, which doubles as a belfry, are in late Renaissance style, and were added in the 17th century. The much-venerated *Madonna of Merkinė* inside the church combines Gothic and Byzantine elements, and was probably painted in the 16th century.

On the central square further uphill, a Russian Orthodox church was built in 1888 on the foundations of the Town Hall erected immediately after Merkinė gained its municipal rights. Now deconsecrated, it serves as the home of the **Merkinė Local Lore Museum** (⊕ *11.00–19.00 Wed–Sun*). A few minutes' walk to the northwest is a small **Hill of Crosses**, commemorating partisans killed in the post-war resistance to Soviet rule.

Tourist information

🖪 **Dzūkija National Park** Vilniaus 2; 📞/f 310 57245; e merkine@dzukijosparkas.lt. Located at the edge of the main square. ⊕08.00–12.00 & 13.00–17.00 Mon–Thu, 08.00–12.00 & 13.00–15.45 Fri. B&B can be arranged in any one of about 30 farmsteads in the vicinity; no other accommodation is available locally.

✗ **Where to eat** At least three places in and around the main square have served as cafés at one time or other, and one should be operational. Otherwise, there are several grocers and general stores to choose from, and an even wider choice of outlets selling wild mushrooms.

LIŠKIAVA At the extreme southwestern corner of the Dzūkija National Park is Liškiava, another place with a disproportionately grand air in relation to the minute number of inhabitants who now live there. It lies on the back roads bus route between Merkinė and Druskininkai, and in summer is the goal of excursion boats (see page 136) along the Nemunas from the latter. At the southern end of the village is **Castle Hill**, which was first fortified in the 3rd century BC and now preserves the scanty remains of a never-completed medieval fortress. Alongside it is **Church Hill**, below which are two pagan stones. Both hills offer fine views over the river and valley.

Liškiava is dominated by the **Church of the Holy Trinity**, one of the most beautiful places of worship to be found anywhere in rural Lithuania. Built between

1704 and 1741 as part of a Dominican priory, it has a Greek-cross plan with two small towers flanking a huge central dome consisting of four large and four small segments. The dome's interior is particularly singular, with two tiers of galleries, and *trompe l'oeil* frescos painted in imitation of framed pictures. These show saints and leading figures of the Polish–Lithuanian Commonwealth on the drum, members of the Dominican Order on the dome, and the Holy Trinity on the lantern. More frescos, depicting a choir and orchestra of angels, can be seen above the organ gallery. There are seven altars, whose brightly coloured frames completely overshadow the paintings they contain. Of particular note are the high altar, which occupies the entire width of the choir, and the altar which forms a single unit with the pulpit. The latter shelters a venerated image of the Madonna and Child adorned with ex-votos arranged in the shape of a cross. In the churchyard are a detached belfry erected in 1884 and a pillar topped with a statue of St Agatha.

Note that the church is opened during the times when the excursion boats visit, but is otherwise normally kept locked, except for services.

DRUSKININKAI

Druskininkai, Lithuania's premier spa and southernmost town, lies close to the Belarus border, some 130km southwest of Vilnius. Picturesquely set over an expansive tract of land immediately south of the Nemunas, and surrounded by pine forests with wonderfully fresh, scented air, it is a delightful place to spend a restful few days. With nine large sanatoria and a growing stock of hotels it is extremely well equipped for tourism, and can handle up to 4,000 guests at any one time. The town's name derives from *druska*, the Lithuanian word for salt, in recognition of the high saline content of its seven mineral springs, which are used to treat cardiac, blood vessel, gastro-intestinal, gynaecological and nervous system disorders.

Druskininkai's history as a health resort began in 1794 as a result of a decree promulgated by Stanisław August Poniatowski – the last man to hold the combined office of King of Poland and Grand Duke of Lithuania – asserting the curative properties of the local waters. Between 1821 and 1835 extensive research work on the therapeutic values of the springs was carried out under Professor Ignacy Fonberg of Vilnius University. The first sanatorium was opened in 1838, and by 1843 2,000 patients a year were being treated, this figure rising to 18,000 by the outbreak of World War I. Between 1920 and 1939 the town belonged to Poland and was much favoured by the country's leaders, including its Lithuanian-born military strongman and de facto dictator, Marshal Piłsudski. In the Soviet period several huge new sanatoria were built, and the annual volume of visitors, many from Russia, increased to 40,000. Lithuanian independence led to a virtual end to the flow of Russian guests, but it was quickly rediscovered by the Poles, who flock there in large numbers. More recently, expensive refurbishments have been carried out with the aim of attracting a wealthier clientele from the West. The success of this policy was given due recognition in 2003, when the American magazine Newsweek ranked Druskininkai among the ten leading spa towns of Europe.

GETTING THERE AND AROUND

Bus station Gardino 1; ☎ 313 51333. There are up to 12 daily buses to Kaunas, 10 to Vilnius (one of which continues on to Utena), 4 to Merkinė via Liškiava, 2 to Vaėna via Liškiava, 2 to Šiauliai, 1 in season to Palanga, 3 to the Belarussian town of Grodno (Gardinas), 1 to Warsaw & 1 to Kaliningrad. Currently minibuses are used for the majority of these services.

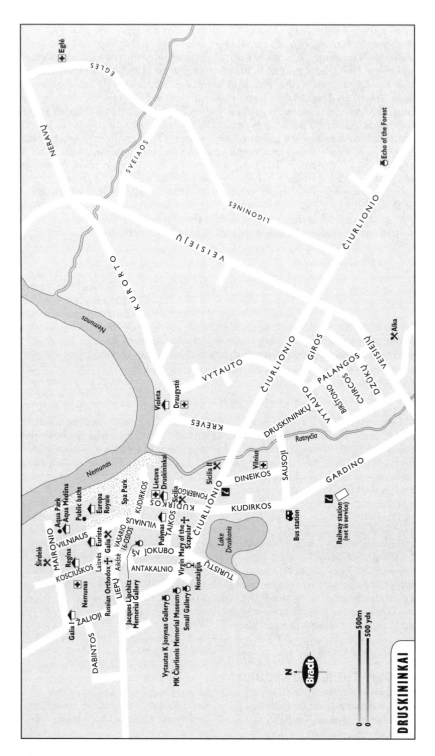

DRUSKININKAI

Bradt

N

0   500m
0   500 yds

Egle

NERAVŲ
EGLÈS
SVEIKOS

KURORTO

Nemunas

Echo of the Forest

ČIURLIONIO

LIGONINĖS

VEISIEJŲ

VYTAUTO

ČIURLIONIO
GIROS
CVIRKOS
PALANGOS
DZŪKŲ
VEISIEJŲ

Alka

BIRŠTONO
VYTAUTO

KRĖVĖS

Draugystė
Violeta

DRUSKININKŲ

Ratnyčia

Vilnius
Sicilia II
FONBERGO

Lietuva
Druskininkai

DINEIKOS
SAUSOJI
GARDINO

KUDIRKOS

Lake
Druskonis

Bus station

Railway station
(not in service)

Nemunas

Aqua Park
Aqua Medūna
Public baths

Spa Park

Europa
Royale

KUDIRKOS

Sicilia

TAIKOS

ČIURLIONIO

Širdelė
MAIRONIO
VILNIAUS
Regina
Eurista
Galia

VASARIO
16-OSIOS

Pušynas
VILNIAUS

Virgin Mary of the
Scapular

TURISTŲ

Laisvės
KOSCIUSKOS
Russian Orthodox
LIEPŲ
Aikštė
ŠV. JOKŪBO
ANTAKALNIO
Nostalgija

Nemunas
Galia I
ŽALIOJI
DABINTOS

Jacques Lipchitz
Memorial Gallery

Vytautas K Jonynas Gallery
MK Čiurlionis Memorial Museum
Small Gallery

TOURIST INFORMATION

Tourist office Gardino 3; ☎ 313 60800; f 313 52784; e information@druskininkai.lt; www.druskininkai.lt or www.druskonis.lt. ⏰08.30–12.15 & 13.00–17.15 Mon–Fri. The railway station building, which became redundant following the closure of the line through Belarus, has been converted to serve as the headquarters of the tourist office. More convenient is the branch at Čurlionio 65; ☎/f 313 51777; ⏰10.00–13.00 & 13.45–18.45 Mon–Sat, 10.00–13.00 & 13.45–17.00 Sun, reduced hours out of season.

WHERE TO STAY
Druskininkai has a good choice of hotels, but anyone wanting to enjoy the town to the full should stay in one of the sanatoria.

Hotels

Aqua Medūna Vilniaus 13-1; ☎ 313 59195; f 313 59194; e aquameduna@stamita.lt; www.aquameduna.lt. This hotel forms part of the new Aqua Park complex. Everything is pristine, if somewhat functional, & there are certainly better value options in town. $$$, suites $$$$, apts $$$$$

Europa Royale Vilniaus 7; ☎ 313 42221; f 313 42223; e druskininkai@europaroyale.com; www.europaroyale.com. This growing chain has renovated a 19th-century spa building for its Druskininkai operation. It offers luxurious rooms complete with AC & heated bathroom floors, as well as a restaurant, café & bar. $$$, suites $$$$, apts $$$$$

Violeta Kurorto 4; ☎ 313 60600; f 313 60602; e info@violeta.lt; www.violeta.lt. Another new establishment, albeit built in a traditional style, with an enticing setting directly above the Nemunas. Steam baths, a swimming pool, whirlpool & massage are among the facilities, & there is a fine restaurant. $$$, suites $$$$

Regina Kosciuškos 3; ☎ 313 59060; f 313 59061; e reservation@regina.lt; www.regina.lt. A swish new hotel with restaurant, which represents something of a departure in this very traditional town. $$$

Druskininkai Kudirkos 43; ☎ 313 52566; f 313 51345, e reception@hotel-druskininkai.lt; www.hotel-druskininkai.lt. What was until recently a very faded hotel has undergone a spectacular transformation, with the new glass-fronted balconies giving it a singular exterior appearance. The daily room price (which varies according to season) includes 1hr each in the Turkish bath, the mineral water jacuzzi & the training hall. A range of European dishes is served in the restaurant. $$, suites $$$, apt $$$$

Pušynas Vilniaus 3; ☎/f 313 56666; e info@pusynas.lt; www.pusynas.lt. A curvaceous, surrealistic apt block with balconies – one of the wackiest of Druskininkai's Soviet-era buildings – has been converted into a mid-range hotel with restaurant. $$, suites $$$

Galia I Maironio 3; ☎ 313 60511; f 313 60512; e hotel@galia.lt; www.galia.lt. Occupies a modern wooden building in the north of the town centre with stained glass windows & well-appointed wood-panelled bedrooms, of which only the cheapest have shared facilities. Rooms of similar standard are available in 3 other buildings; all 4 have a café on site. $, suites $$

Eurista Vilniaus 22; ☎/f 313 52318; e eurista@one.lt. A small hotel, likewise in the centre; the facilities include a sauna, 2 bars & a disco. $

Sanatoria
Needless to say, the sanatoria are interested primarily in long-stay guests, though they are also prepared to accept passing trade. Only a selection is listed below, all of which are well geared to Western tourism. Typically, the facilities available include physiotherapy, massage, acupuncture, baths, gymnastics, dance and music in addition to specialist medical cures. The pricing structure is quite complicated, being determined not only by type of room chosen, the length of stay and the kind of treatment taken, but also by season. Three dietary meals and at least one treatment are included in the daily rates, though some of the sanatoria also offer full board or bed and breakfast terms only. For more details, consult the websites, which all give comprehensive information in English.

Vilnius Dineikos 1; ☎ 313 51454/53811; f 313 52046; e info@spa-vilnius.lt; www.spa-vilnius.lt. A high-rise block just southeast of the centre whose main speciality is its range of baths: herbal, iodine-bromide, carbonic, pearl & vertical. $$$

🏠 **Draugystė** Krėvės 10; 📞 313 53132; f 313 53118; e sandraugyste@is.lt; www.draugyste.lt. Winner of an international tourism award in 1996, this very traditional sanatorium offers de-luxe bedrooms in 2 villas as well as apts in its main building just east of the town centre. $$, apts $$$
🏠 **Eglė** Eglės 1; 📞 313 60220; f 313 60238; e info@sanatorija.lt; www.sanatorija.lt. Large modern complex at the eastern end of town, with mud baths among the treatments on offer. $$, apts $$$

🏠 **Lietuva** Kudirkos 45; 📞 313 52833; f 313 55490; e info@sanatorijalietuva.lt; www.sanatorijalietuva.lt. This large modern building is the most centrally sited of the sanatoria, & specialises in a wide variety of massages. $$, apts $$$
🏠 **Nemunas** Kosciuškos 6; 📞 313 51660; f 313 51085; e nemunas@office.vilja.lt; www.druskonis.lt/sanatorijos/nemunas. Lithuania's biggest sanatorium, providing a wide variety of treatments, is situated in the north of town. $$

Camping

🏕 **Campsite** Gardino 3a; 📞 313 60800; f 313 52984. Conveniently located just south of the town centre, close to the former railway station, this has chalets as well as spaces for tents & camper vans. $

✖ **WHERE TO EAT** As most guests take all their meals in their hotel or sanatorium, there is a relatively limited choice of alternative places to eat.

✖ **Alka** Veisiejų 13. A café-restaurant best known for its truly wacky interior (see page 136), but also serves a wide range of traditional Lithuanian cuisine.
✖ **Galia** Vilniaus 20. This complex incorporates a very formal dining room as well as a bar which itself serves full meals.
♀ **Nostalgija** Čiurlionio 55. A café-bar with a balcony overlooking Lake Druskonis.

✖ **Sicilia I** Taikos 9. Serves decent pizzas & pasta, as well as a few other dishes.
✖ **Sicilia II** Čiurlionio 56. There is now a second branch of the pizzeria down the street, which has the advantage of a large terrace outside.
✖ **Širdelė** Maironio 16. Occupies a charming old wooden house with a garishly decorated interior; the food is tasty & inexpensive.

ORIENTATION Despite having only 20,000 inhabitants, Druskininkai is spread over quite a large area. To the north, it is bounded by one of the many loops in the Nemunas, while a small tributary, the Ratnyčia, divides the town into distinct eastern and western parts. The commercial 'centre' is actually towards the northwestern end of the built-up area. Its main streets are the pedestrianised Vilniaus and Kudirkos, which continues south towards past Lake Druskonis – where wonderful sunsets can often be seen – to the bus and train stations, changing its name there to Gardino and continuing on as the main road leading eventually to the Belarus border. Kudirkos is bisected by Čiurlionio, which sweeps in a southeasterly direction right through the town and then onwards through the woods to the outlying village of Ratnyčia.

WHAT TO SEE AND DO The Spa Park beside the Nemunas is a peaceful area dotted with a number of late Neo-Classical pavilions. Alongside its now redundant predecessor is the new **Pump Room** (⊕ *11.30–13.00 & 15.30–19.30 Mon–Fri, 10.30-13.30 Sat*), which is fitted out with colourful stained glass windows. Water from two of the local springs can be sampled there. Dominating the town-centre skyline to the south is the slender octagonal belfry of the **Church of the Virgin Mary of the Scapular**, a redbrick Neo-Gothic building standing in its own shady grounds between Vilniaus and Kudirkos. It was erected in 1931 as a direct replacement for its mid-19th-century predecessor, where Čiurlionis's father was organist. A highly stylised statue of Čiurlionis himself can be seen at the top end of Kudirkos.

On Vilniaus are some examples of the Futuristic tendency in Soviet architecture, which provide a startling contrast with the wooden houses all around. The most prominent is the erstwhile Physiotherapy Centre at Vilniaus 11 which, together with the huge new glass extension behind, houses the spectacular **Aqua Park** (*www.aquameduna.lt;* ⊕ *10.00–22.00 Mon–Thu, 10.00–23.00 Fri–Sun*). This has a wide choice of aquatic attractions. One block contains a large indoor swimming pool with jacuzzis on the artifical cliffs which form its banks, plus five saunas, six Roman baths, a Turkish bath and two outdoor bath houses separated by a small pool. The other part of the complex is devoted to watery entertainments, and features six slides (one of which is 212 metres long), a 'wild' river, an outdoor pool with warm water and an indoor pool with artificial waves.

Just to the south, the recently renovated **Public Baths** (*www.gydykla.lt;* ⊕ *08.00–20.00 daily*), a colonnaded green building directly overlooking the Spa Park at Vilniaus 11, offer around a score of different water treatments, ranging from a turpentine bath to a 'Scottish shower'.

At the corner with Vasario 16-osios is a recognisably post-independence monument to King Mindaugas. This street leads west to a landscaped square, in the middle of which stands the **Russian Orthodox Church**, a predominantly wooden building with six cupolas painted in blue and white. The date of construction, 1865, can be seen above the main doorway. The eaves shelter small pentagonal paintings on religious themes while, inside, the iconostasis bears rather saccharine paintings, though more traditional icons, as well as works showing distinct Roman Catholic influence, are hung elsewhere in the church.

Occupying an intricately carved yellow house a short distance south at Šv Jokūbo 17 is the **Jacques Lipchitz Memorial Gallery** (⊕ *Tue–Thu 12.00–17.00*), a branch of the Lithuanian State Jewish Museum. It commemorates the eponymous sculptor (known as Žakas Lipšicas in Lithuania), a native of Druskininkai, which once had a sizeable Jewish community. Lipchitz (1891–1973), who emigrated to France in 1909, then to the USA in 1941, gained an international reputation for his instantly recognisable transparent sculptures. The gallery does not own any original examples, but displays documentary material on his career, as well as work by other Jewish artists, such as the sculptor Michal Kapelovich and the painter Adomas Jacovskis.

A short walk to the southwest is a small artistic quarter, centred on the **MK Čiurlionis Memorial Museum** (⊕ *11.00–17.00 Tue–Sun*), at Čiurlionio 41. This occupies three wooden houses, two of which are furnished as they were when the composer-painter lived in them as a boy. The third contains posters of exhibitions in which Čiurlionis took part, reproductions of his most important paintings, plus a stained glass window recently made from one of his hitherto unexecuted designs. In summer, there are regular piano recitals which usually include some of Čiurlionis's compositions. A feature of these is that the pianist sits in the house and plays through the open window to the audience seated in the garden outside (in poor weather the venue is switched to the ticket-office building).

At Čiurlionio 37, directly to the rear, is the **Small Gallery** (⊕ *12.00–17.00/18.00 Wed–Sun*), which hosts changing exhibitions. Alongside, at Čiurlionio 45, is the **Vytautas K Jonynas Gallery** (⊕ *11.00–17.00 Tue–Sun*), containing works donated by Vytautas Jonynas (1907–98), a versatile graphic and watercolour artist, sculptor and stained glass designer who emigrated to West Germany in 1946, then to the USA in 1951. His works on display range from the highly regarded German postage stamps he designed to studies for the large decorative projects he carried out for several American churches.

OUTSKIRTS In a wooded setting about 2km east of the town centre at Čiurlionio 102 is the **Echo of the Forest** (*Girios Aidas;* ⊕ *10.00–18.00 Wed–Sun*), a remarkable wooden house designed by local forester, naturalist and inventor Algirdas Valavičius. The original building of 1971 rested on an oak tree stump and gave the impression of floating above the ground. This was totally destroyed by fire in 1992, but a replacement was erected within two years. It gives a similar illusion to its predecessor, but has a glass-enclosed room at the rear for extra stability. The interior is intended as a living evocation of the forest, complete with trees, plants, animals, birds and fish. Its centre-piece, which grows through two of the floors, is an oak tree adorned with sculptures of fairy-tale characters. Behind the house a trail leads past various wooden sculptures with subjects from history and myth.

The **Sun Path** (*Saulės Takas*) follows a 7km route upstream along the Ratnyčia, though in the initial stages there is not always a walkway along the waterside. Just beyond the far bank of the first large pond (and actually only a few minutes' walk away from the Echo of the Forest) is another eccentric building, the café-restaurant **Alka**. This has a plain exterior, but the interior is a riot of elaborate woodcarving, with what must be some of the most outrageous tables and chairs ever made. Back on the other side of the stream, the path leads to a popular bathing and recreation area adorned with more whimsy in the shape of little bridges, benches and picnic shelters by another local carver, Vytautas Urnevičius.

AROUND DRUSKININKAI

A deservedly popular out-of-town excursion is the steamboat cruise along the Nemunas to Liškiava run by the travel agency Gelmė, whose office is in the Hotel Druskininkai. Departures are from the jetty in the Spa Park, and advance reservations are advisable, as the number of tickets available is fixed. Normally there are sailings between June and early September at 14.30 every day except Monday. The return trip, which costs 28Lt, takes just under three hours and allows ample time for seeing the sights of Liškiava.

Švendubrė, 5km southwest of Druskininkai, is a Dzūkijan village reminiscent of those in the eastern part of the National Park, with an impressive main street of fenced-in wooden farmsteads. At its northern edge is a huge boulder known as the Devil's Stone, which features in many legends. The same is true of the **Raigardas valley** east of the village, a large hollow formed around 5,000 years ago when the Nemunas changed course. It forms the subject of one of the few pure landscapes painted by Čiurlionis, a triptych which can be seen in Kaunas. The best view over the valley is from a vantage-point very close to the Belarus border. This is reached in a minute or so from the footpath which begins at the end of the A4 road, and continues all the way through the woods back to Druskininkai.

Some 8km northeast of Druskininkai, by the main road to Vilnius, is the hamlet of **Grūtas**. This lay in total obscurity until 2000, when it suddenly became a focus of international attention – the first time the global media had shown much interest in Lithuania since the dramatic events leading up to the achievement of independence a decade before. The cause of this interest was the bitter controversy surrounding the establishment of the **Grūtas Park** (*www.grutoparkas.lt;* ☉*09.00–17.00/20.00 daily*) on a wooded site 1km to the south of the hamlet. Lithuania's first ever theme park, the only one in the world specifically devoted to the communist-era experience, is the brainchild of the flamboyant local businessman Viliumas Malinauskas, a former wrestler and collective farm manager who made his fortune in the immediate post-Soviet years by exporting fresh and pickled wild mushrooms to the West.

Malinauskas acquired the monuments to Marx, Lenin and innumerable stalwarts of Soviet Lithuania which were removed from positions of eminence in the country's towns and cities at the beginning of the 1990s. In due course, he accumulated the world's largest private collection of Soviet statues, and dreamed of using these to form the basis of a full-scale 'Stalin's World' theme park which would re-create the full horrors of the Gulag. He hoped to buy railway track from the government and transport visitors to the park in the sort of tightly packed cattle trucks which were used to transport Lithuanians to Siberia during and after World War II. Staff were to be hired to man Soviet-era watchtowers, while authentic prison-camp meals of thin gruel were to be served up in the canteen.

Not surprisingly, these plans provoked outrage, not least among the many surviving Lithuanian citizens who had first-hand experience of the Gulag. The whole idea of the park was condemned as tasteless, and Malinauskas was widely vilified as an out-and-out hypocrite – a man who had himself prospered under the communist system, yet who was exploiting its demise for his own private profit while claiming to be doing so for the public good. The entrepreneur and his supporters dismissed their critics as woolly minded liberals, and claimed that, far from trivialising the sufferings of the Lithuanian people under Stalinism, the park would help to ensure that this traumatic period in the nation's history would never be forgotten by future generations.

Despite some determined parliamentary opposition, the park duly opened, albeit in a form radically different from what was initially intended. All the obviously tasteless elements have been dropped – the trains are kept stationary, there are no make-believe Soviet guards, and instead of a prison canteen there is a restaurant which serves a range of delicious wild mushroom dishes in addition to the usual Lithuanian fare.

The first part of the circuit round the park follows the course of the Grūtas stream, on one side of which are unmanned watchtowers which eerily evoke the totalitarian atmosphere of the past. Most of the statues in this section are of high-profile Soviet heroes – Lenin is particularly ubiquitous – whereas those in the second part of the circuit are generally of obscure (and often very young) Lithuanians, many of whom died in the communist cause – and are thus now regarded as traitors. The peaceful woodland setting – so very different in character from the original locations – serves as an appropriate 'graveyard' for the redundant statues, and helps to spotlight the sheer artistic sterility of their Socialist-Realistic style. Supplementing the outdoor displays is an information centre jam-packed with all kinds of bric-à-brac from the Soviet period.

All in all, the park in its present form seems a huge if at least partially inadvertent success, and has proved popular with both Lithuanian and foreign visitors. The hope must be that it will remain much as it is, rather than as originally envisaged. There is a direct connection between the park and the centre of Druskininkai via local bus 2, but beware that this has several different routes, and on weekdays there are only four services daily which run the whole way. Otherwise, plenty of inter-urban buses stop in Grūtas itself.

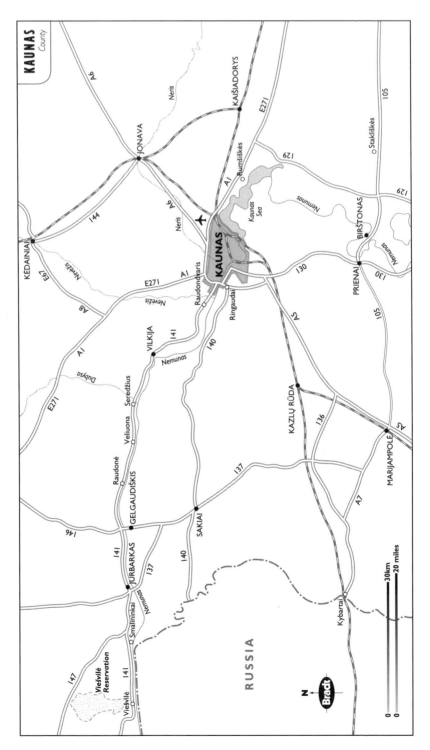

KAUNAS County

KAIŠIADORYS

E271

105

Staklškės

Neris

A6

129

JONAVA

129

Rumšiškės

Kaunas Sea

Nemunas

144

A6

A1

Neris

KAUNAS

E67

KĖDAINIAI

Nevėžis

BIRŠTONAS

Nevėžis

E271

A1

Raudondvaris

PRIENAI

Nemunas

A8

Ringaudai

130

130

A1

VILKIJA

141

140

105

Dubysa

Nemunas

A5

E271

Serėdžius

Veliuona

KAZLŲ RŪDA

Raudonė

GELGAUDIŠKIS

137

136

MARIJAMPOLĖ

A5

146

ŠAKIAI

A7

141

JŪRBARKAS

137

140

Nemunas

Smalininkai

30km

20 miles

147

141

Viešvilė Reservation

Viešvilė

Kybartai

RUSSIA

N

Bradt

0

0

8

Kaunas County

Kaunas (formerly known as Kowno or Kovno) is Lithuania's second city and the capital of the county which bears its name. It lies at the confluence of Lithuania's two major rivers, the Nemunas and the Neris, just 98km west of Vilnius. Despite its proximity to the national capital, it is of a markedly different character. Whereas Vilnius is multi-national and multi-cultural, Kaunas is doggedly Lithuanian, with only 8% of its inhabitants belonging to ethnic minorities. Vilnius consists of a hilly city centre surrounded by flat suburbs; Kaunas has precisely the reverse. While Vilnius has had a long history as an administrative and academic centre, Kaunas's past has been dominated by trade – hence the saying that Vilnius is the queen of Lithuania, Kaunas its merchant prince.

Even if it has to be admitted that Kaunas is, as it nearly always has been, in Vilnius's shadow, it has traditionally had little of the sense of malaise or inferiority felt by so many of the world's second cities. Indeed, in many spheres it rivals and even surpasses the capital. A key element in this is its status as the city with the highest ethnic Lithuanian population – not just proportionally, but also in absolute terms. An even more important factor was its period as capital of the inter-war Lithuanian state. During the 19 years Vilnius languished as a Polish provincial city, Kaunas was developed into a showpiece capital and the home of a host of new institutions, many of which have remained there ever since. Thus Kaunas still has some of Lithuania's most important museums (including the pick of its few old masters and virtually the whole of the output of the revered artist Čiurlionis), its only zoo, and finest botanical garden. Its dominance also extends to the sphere of the national sport of basketball, Žalgiris Kaunas being the country's representative in the European League. That said, the past few years have seen a noticeable diminution of the city's self-confidence: while both Vilnius and Klaipėda have successfully capitalised on their multi-national make-up to forge ahead economically, Kaunas has been left lagging in their wake.

Kaunas's administrative county is dominated by the city, but includes some enticing tourist destinations. Among them are Lithuania's premier open-air museum, its best-preserved middle-sized town and its second spa, as well as a spectacular serpentine stage in the flow of the River Nemunas.

KAUNAS

The city of Kaunas has a population of around 358,000 (having been as high as 420,000 a few years ago), making it easily the largest non-capital in the Baltic region. It occupies an area of 121km², of which 18 are green and 12 water. Over 30% of the workforce is employed in industry, notably food products, textiles and construction-material concerns; a further 20% work in the retail sector. The well-preserved Old Town is situated on the tongue of land between the Nemunas and Neris. It is joined seamlessly to the east by the much larger New

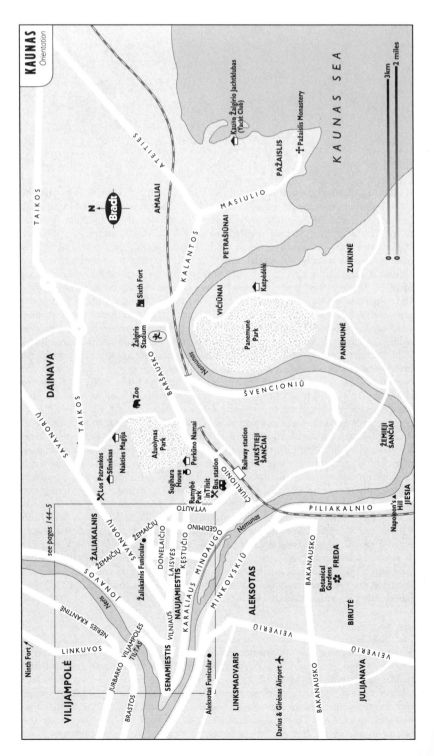

KAUNAS SEA

Kauno Žalgirio Jachtklubas
(Yacht Club)

PAŽAISLIS

† Pažaislis Monastery

ZUIKINĖ

MASIULIO

PETRAŠIŪNAI

3km

2 miles

0

0

ATEITIES

TAIKOS

AMALIAI

KALANTOS

VIČIŪNAI

Katpėdėlė

Panemunė
Park

PANEMUNĖ

ŠVENCIONIŲ

Nemunas

Sixth Fort

DAINAVA

Žalgiris
Stadium

BARŠAUSKO

SAVANORIŲ

TAIKOS

Zoo

Ąžuolynas
Park

Sfinsksas

Nakties Magija

Los Patrankos

Perkūno Namai

Sugihara
House

Ramybė
Park

in Tilsit

Bus station

Railway station

AUKŠTIEJI
ŠANČIAI

ŽEMIEJI
ŠANČIAI

JIESIA

ČIURLIONIO

VYTAUTO

PILIAKALNIO

Napoleon's ▲
Hill

see pages 144–5

ŽALIAKALNIS

Žaliakalnis Funicular

ŽEMAIČIŲ

SAVANORIŲ

DONELAIČIO

LAISVĖS

KĘSTUČIO

GEDIMINO

MINDAUGO

Nemunas

Railway station

BAKANAUSKO

Botanical
Gardens   FREDA

BIRUTĖ

Ninth Fort

VILIJAMPOLĖ

LINKUVOS

Neris

NERIES KRANTINĖ

JONAVOS

JURBARKO

VILIJAMPOLĖS
TILTAS

BRASTOS

SENAMIESTIS

NAUJAMIESTIS

VILNIAUS

KARALIAUS

MINKOVSKIŲ

ALEKSOTAS

VEIVERIŲ

VEIVERIŲ

BAKANAUSKO

JULIJANAVA

LINKSMADVARIS

Aleksotas Funicular

Darius & Girėnas Airport ✈

N

Bradt

Town, the modern commercial and cultural heart of the city. There are also a number of major sights in the suburbs, including the killing fields of the Ninth Fort and the city's most impressive historic monument, the Pažaislis Monastery.

HISTORY The origins of Kaunas are lost in legend. According to one tradition, its name derives from the pagan god Kaunius; according to another, from a Roman named Kunus, one of three brothers who came with their father Palemonas to the River Nemunas region and built a castle there. In fact, there was certainly a settlement on the spot long before this, perhaps as early as the 7th century BC. The official date for the founding of the present city remains much disputed. Some historians place it at AD1030; for others, the earliest documentary reference is that by the Arab traveller and geographer Ibn Indrisis, who mentioned a settlement named Kanigu in 1140.

It is not until the time of the wars with the Teutonic Knights that more detailed and reliable information becomes available. What is certain is that the early history of Kaunas was closely tied up with that of the castle at the confluence of the Nemunas and Neris. This was destroyed by the Knights in 1361, but rebuilt the following year. It changed hands several times before a more peaceful era was ushered in by the decisive victory of the combined army of Poland and Lithuania over the Order at the Battle of Žalgiris in 1410. Two years before this Kaunas had been given municipal status, and it developed as a trading crossroads and port, profiting from the navigability of the Nemunas all the way to the Baltic Sea. Under Grand Duke Vytautas, Tatars, Karaites and German merchants were encouraged to settle. In 1441 the Hanseatic League, the powerful German-dominated trading alliance, opened an office in the city. Kaunas's economy remained continuously strong and stable for a full quarter of a millennium, and it eventually became the seat of the Grand Duchy's mint. The first school was established by 1473, the first college by the Jesuits in 1648.

A long period of decline began in 1665, when the city was razed by the Russians. It suffered several more times from war, fire and plagues, most disastrously during the Napoleonic Wars, when at one point the population dropped from 28,000 to 300. Kaunas was a major centre of resistance to Russian rule in the uprisings of 1831 and 1863, and as a result was subject to repressive measures. None the less, the local economy began to revive as a result of the building of the railway in 1862, and by the digging of a canal linking the Nemunas with the Dnieper. This ushered in a period of industrialisation, in which the first factories appeared. However, this process was checked by Tsar Alexander II's decision to make Kaunas the strongest point of the Russian Empire's western border. Between 1882 and the start of World War I, a series of forts, interconnected by underground passageways, was built to encircle the city. The successful German assault on these in 1915 was a military disaster for the Russians, and a turning-point in the events which led to Lithuanian independence three years later.

When Vilnius finally fell to Poland in 1920, Kaunas, as the largest city left in the newly revived Lithuania, was given the status of 'temporary' capital. This role, however, quickly assumed what seemed at the time to be a rather more permanent aspect as Kaunas was transformed into a modern European capital city whose grandeur belied its relatively modest population of around 150,000. Not only were government offices and foreign embassies established there, so were a new archbishopric and a host of cultural institutions, while numerous prestige projects were initiated, including the building of two funiculars, bridges over the Nemunas and Neris, and a series of important public buildings in what was intended to be a distinctive national architectural style, one combining the concepts of functionality and aesthetics. Notwithstanding the many problems faced by the inter-war Lithuanian state, it was truly a golden age for Kaunas.

This era came to a swift end in 1939, when Vilnius was restored to Lithuania as its capital as part of the Mutual Assistance Pact with the Soviet Union. Two years later, the invading German forces ushered in the most inglorious chapter in the city's history by making it the site of a concentration camp in which around 80,000 people were murdered. Kaunas's Jewish population of 37,000 was reduced to just 2,500 by the time the Soviets re-captured the city in 1944.

In the post-war period, firstly under the Soviets and later in the revived independent Lithuania, Kaunas has had to settle for the role of a second city, though it has grown markedly in size by the building of new residential and factory districts. The construction of a hydro-electric power plant, which became operational in 1959, led to an important topographical change in the creation of the so-called Kaunas Sea, a huge artificial reservoir which has since become a popular recreation ground. In 1972 the city was the scene of the first major protests against communist rule, when riots followed the self-immolation of a 19-year-old student, Romas Kalanta, and it later played a prominent role in the successful drive towards independence.

GETTING THERE AND AROUND Separate tickets are required for the buses and trolleybuses which cover virtually every corner of the city. These can be bought in advance from kiosks (currently 0.90Lt) or from the driver (1Lt); they then have to be punched in one of the on-board machines. Perhaps the most useful services are trolleybuses 1, 5, 7 and 13, which travel all the way through the city centre, from the railway station via the bus station to the edge of the Old Town. Because of the one-way system, they go westwards along Kęstučio, Kanto, Nemuno and Gimnazijos, and eastwards along Ožeškienės and Donelaičio. Numerous fixed-route minibuses also cruise the streets, and can be hailed anywhere; the fare (1.50Lt in the day, 3Lt at night) is paid to the driver. To call a taxi, dial ✆1444, ✆333111, ✆333333, ✆341111, ✆366666 or ✆76666

By car
🚗 **Litinterp** Gedimino 28-7; ✆/f 37 228718;
e kaunas@litinterp.com; www.litinterp.com

By bus
🚌 **Bus station** Vytauto 24; ✆ 37 409060. There are usually a couple of buses an hour to Vilnius & approximately hourly services to Šiauliai & Panevėžys. Direct daily services run to most other Lithuanian towns, including 11 to Druskininkai, 12 to Klaipėda, 9 to Palanga (seasonal) & 4 to Ignalina. International services include 3 daily to Kaliningrad, 3 daily to Minsk, 3 daily to Rīga, 3 daily to Warsaw, 1 or 2 daily to Amsterdam & Brussels, 1 daily to Grodno (Gardinas), 6 weekly to Suwałki, 6 weekly to Tallinn, 5 weekly to Vienna, 4 weekly to Prague, 3 weekly to London, 3 weekly to Dublin, 3 weekly to Paris, between 1 & 3 weekly to many German cities. The bus station is equipped with a left-luggage counter.

By train
🚃 **Railway station** Čiurlionio 16; ✆ 37 221093, 292260. There are up to 16 trains daily to Vilnius, including a couple of expresses which are much faster than any bus. There are also 3 to Šeštokai, one of which continues to Warsaw, & 2 to Kaliningrad. New computerised left-luggage lockers have been installed in the station.

By air
✈ **Karmėlava Airport** ✆ 37 399307; www.kaunasair.lt. Located 12km north of the city & connected with the centre by minibus 120, this former Soviet military airport is the Lithuanian base for

Ryanair, which has 1 or 2 flights daily to London Stansted, 6 weekly to Dublin, 2 weekly to Shannon & 2 weekly to Glasgow Prestwick. The only other scheduled services are 2 weekly to Vaxjo (Sweden) with Stockholmplanet.

INFORMATION AND MAPS The *Kaunas In Your Pocket* listings magazine, produced annually by the *Vilnius In Your Pocket* office, is the most useful guidebook to the city. The free *Exploring Kaunas* offers similar practical information, but much less in the way of reviews. There is a good 1:25,000 map of the city – supplemented by a 1:10,000 section of the centre and a panorama of the Old Town – with full street and other listings. It is published by Briedis and is available from bookshops and some kiosks.

TOURIST INFORMATION

🄸 Kaunas Regional Tourist Information Centre Laisvės 36; 🕾 37 323436; ⅃/f 37 423678; e turizmas@takas.lt; www.kaunas.lt. This provides information on the whole of Kaunas County, & also has a counter for booking international bus tickets. ⏰May & Sep 09.00–18.00 Mon–Fri, 10.00–15.00 Sat; Jun–Aug 09.00–19.00 Mon–Fri, 10.00–13.00 & 14.00–18.00 Sat, 10.00–15.00 Sun; Oct–Apr 09.00–18.00 Mon–Thu, 09.00–17.00 Fri. From Jun to Aug the branch at Kaunas Castle (Pilies 17) is open daily 10.00–18.00, while a counter at the airport is opened to coincide with the arrival of Ryanair flights.

WHERE TO STAY The provision of accommodation in Kaunas lags well behind that of Vilnius in terms of both quality and quantity, but there is something to suit most tastes and pockets. At least one more upmarket hotel should re-open within the lifetime of this edition, as the former Intourist flagship, the Neris, Donelaičio 27, has been acquired by the Reval chain and is undergoing a total refurbishment. Contact details should appear on the website www.revalhotels.com in due course. Basic English and/or German is spoken in most places.

Hotels

🛏 Daniela Mickevičiaus 28; 🕾 37 321505; f 37 321632; e daniela@danielahotel.lt; www.danielahotel.lt. A swanky new hotel aimed primarily at business travellers, featuring some truly audacious colour schemes in both the bedrooms & public rooms. The highly regarded restaurant is particularly strong on fish & seafood dishes. $$$$, suites $$$$$

🛏 Kaunas Laisvės 79; 🕾 37 323110; f 37 323301; e kaunas@kaunashotel.lt; www.kaunashotel.lt. A fine new business-class hotel in a renovated old building in the very heart of Kaunas's famous pedestrian boulevard. A conference centre, swimming pool & fitness room are among the facilities. The restaurant, 55°, has quickly become one of the most popular in town; it serves a wide-ranging menu & has its own home-made spirit, *samanė*. $$$$, apts $$$$$

🛏 Santakos Gruodžio 21; 🕾 37 302710; f 37 302702; e office@santaka.lt; www.santaka.lt. The first hotel in Lithuania to be admitted to the Best Western group, which gives it a 4-star rating, this occupies a 19th-century brick building on the border of the Old & New Towns. All rooms are equipped with telephone, satellite TV & minibar, while a buffet b/fast in the cellar café-restaurant is included in the price. $$$$, apts $$$$$

🛏 Daugirdas Daugirdo 4; 🕾 37 301561; f 37 301562; e hotel@daugirdas.lt; www.daugirdas.lt. New business-class hotel under the same management as the long-established Perkūno Namai, occupying a historic & a modern building linked together by a glass pavilion. The restaurant occupies a suite of Gothic cellars, while the cocktail bar is a winter garden immediately below the roof. $$$$

🛏 Babilonas Raseinių 25; 🕾 37 202545; f 37 209156; e babilonas@hotel.lt; www.babilonas.lt. A modern, 10-room hotel with a restaurant in the Žaliakalnis district. Each room has a refrigerator, satellite TV, minibar & hairdryer; those on the upper floors command a fine view over the city. $$$, suites $$$$

🛏 Perkūno Namai Perkūno 61; 🕾 37 320230; f 37 323678; e hotel@perkuno-namai.lt; www.perkuno-namai.lt. The first privately owned hotel to be opened in Kaunas, this is a spanking new Scandinavian-style design situated in its own manicured grounds with old

143

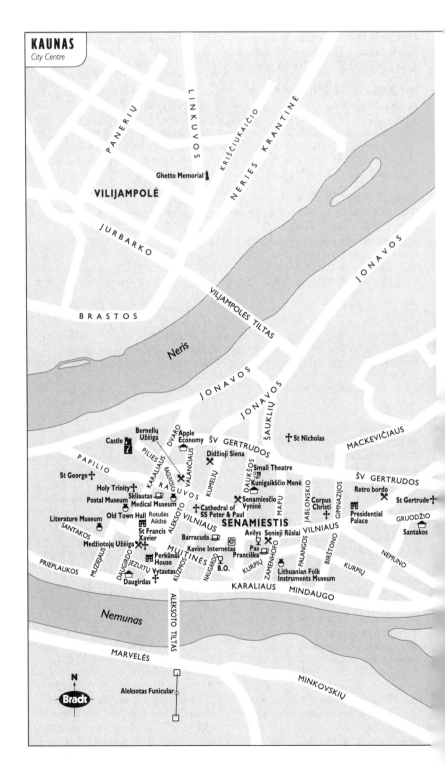

KAUNAS
City Centre

VILIJAMPOLĖ

Ghetto Memorial

LINKUVOS

KRIŠČIUKAIČIO

NĖRIES KRANTINĖ

PANERIŲ

JURBARKO

BRASTOS

VILIJAMPOLĖS TILTAS

JONAVOS

Neris

JONAVOS

JONAVOS

ŠAUKLIŲ

MACKEVIČIAUS

Castle

Bernelių Užeiga

Apple Economy

ŠV GERTRUDOS

✝ St Nicholas

PAPILIO

DVARO

VALANČIAUS

Didžioji Siena

PILIES

St George ✝

RAGUVOS

KARALIAUS

Holy Trinity ✝

KUMELIŲ

Small Theatre

DAUKŠOS

ŠV GERTRUDOS

Kunigaikščio Menė

Retro bordo

St Gertrude ✝

Postal Museum

Skliautas

Medical Museum

ALEKSOTO

Senamiesčio Vyninė

MAPU

JABLONSKIO

Corpus Christi

GIMNAZIJOS

Presidential Palace

GRUODŽIO

Literature Museum

Old Town Hall

Rotušės Aikštė

✝ Cathedral of SS Peter & Paul

VILNIAUS

SENAMIESTIS

VILNIAUS

Santakos

SANTAKOS

St Francis Xavier

Barracuda

Avilys

Senieji Rūslai

BIRŠTONO

NEMUNO

Medžiotojų Užeiga

MUITINĖS

Kavine Internetas

Pas Pranciška

ZAMENHOFO

PALANGOS

KURPIŲ

PRIEPLAUKOS

MUZIEJAUS

DAUGIRDO

Perkūnas House

JEZUITŲ

KUŠZMO

NAUGARDO

B.O.

KURPIŲ

KARALIAUS

MINDAUGO

Vytautas ✝

Daugirdas

Lithuanian Folk Instruments Museum

Nemunas

ALEKSOTO TILTAS

MARVELĖS

MINKOVSKIŲ

N

Bradt

Aleksotas Funicular

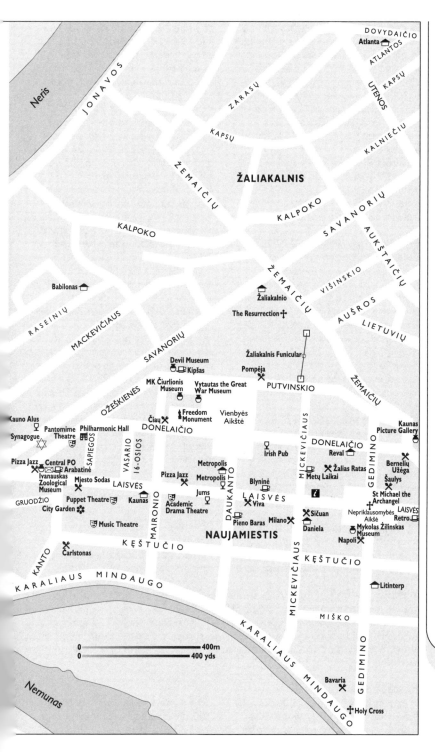

Neris

JONAVOS

DOVYDAIČIO

Atlanta

ATLANTOS

ZARASŲ

UTENOS

KAPSŲ

KAPSŲ

KALNIEČIŲ

ŽEMAIČIŲ

ŽALIAKALNIS

KALPOKO

SAVANORIŲ

AUKŠTAIČIŲ

KALPOKO

ŽEMAIČIŲ

VIŠINSKIO

Babilonas

MACKEVIČIAUS

RASEINIŲ

Žaliakalnio

AUŠROS

LIETUVIŲ

The Resurrection ✝

SAVANORIŲ

ŽEMAIČIŲ

Devil Museum
Kipšas

Žaliakalnis Funicular

MK Čiurlionis
Museum

Pompėja

PUTVINSKIO

Vytautas the Great
War Museum

OŽEŠKIENĖS

Čiau ✗

Freedom
Monument

Vienbyės
Aikštė

Kaunas
Picture Gallery

Kauno Alus

Pantomime Philharmonic Hall
Synagogue Theatre

DONELAIČIO

MICKEVIČIAUS

DONELAIČIO
Reval

Pizza Jazz
Central PO
Arabatinė
Ivanauskas
Zoological
Museum

SAPIEGOS

VASARIO
16-OSIOS

Irish Pub

Žalias Ratas
Metų Laikai

GEDIMINO

Bernelių
Užėga
Šaulys

Mjesto Sodas

Metropolis

St Michael the
Archangel

Pizza Jazz

Metropolis

Blyninė

GRUODŽIO

LAISVĖS

Jums

LAISVĖS
Viva

Puppet Theatre

Kaunas

MAIRONIO

Academic
Drama Theatre

DAUKANTO

i

Sičuan

Neipriklausomybės
Aikštė

LAISVĖS

Retro

City Garden

Music Theatre

Pieno Baras

Milano ✗

Daniela

Mykolas Žilinskas
Museum

NAUJAMIESTIS

Napoli ✗

Carlstonas

KĘSTUČIO

MICKEVIČIAUS

KĘSTUČIO

KANTO

KARALIAUS

MINDAUGO

Litinterp

MIŠKO

MICKEVIČIAUS

GEDIMINO

0   400m
0   400 yds

KARALIAUS

MINDAUGO

Bavaria ✗

GEDIMINO

Holy Cross ✝

Nemunas

oak trees on the western edge of Ąžuolynas Park. All rooms have telephone & satellite TV, while those facing south have balconies. There is also a fine restaurant with an international menu. $$$, suites $$$$

⌂ **Sfinksas** Aukštaičių 55; ☎ 37 301982, f 37 301983; e hotelsfinx@takas.lt; www.sfinksas.lt. This classy new hotel in the residential Žaliakalnis district has just 12 rooms, all of them different, plus a restaurant, sauna & swimming pool. $$$, suites & apt $$$$

⌂ **Kunigaikščio Menė** Daukšos 28; ☎ 37 320800; f 37 320877; e mene@takas.lt; www.hotelmene.lt. A modern, 8-room hotel in an atmospheric location on a cobblestoned Old Town street. It has both a café & a restaurant, the latter being in a 17th-century cellar. $$$

⌂ **Nakties Magija** Skroblų 3; ☎ 37 797923; f 37 795832; e nmagija@takas.lt; www.naktiesmagija-hotel.lt. A modern villa in a residential quarter immediately north of Ąžuolynas Park. It only has 10 rooms, & prides itself on the personal touch. All rooms have a minibar, & there is a small restaurant. $$$

⌂ **Sandija** Jonavos 45; ☎ 37 734462; f 37 254804; e hotel@sandija.lt; www.sandija.lt. A modern motel in the north of the city, just off the Vilnius–Klaipėda highway. All rooms have satellite TV & minibar. The restaurant is among the best in the city, featuring some exotic & correspondingly expensive items on its menu. $$$

⌂ **Žaliakalnio** Savonorių 66; ☎ 37 321412; f 37 733769; e zaliakalnis@greenhotel.lt; www.greenhotel.lt. A fully modern hotel in a converted factory in the Žaliakalnis district. It numbers a restaurant, conference room, business centre & even a panoramic viewing platform among its facilities. $$$

⌂ **Alanta** Alantos 33; ☎ 37 731142; f 37 733871; e hotel@alanta.lt; www.alanta.lt. A small guesthouse in a quiet residential area to the north of the city centre. All bedrooms have satellite TV & a minibar; other facilities include a café & a billiards room. $$, suites $$$

⌂ **Apple Economy Hotel** Valančiaus 19; ☎/f 37 321404; e info@applehotel.lt; www.applehotel.lt. A new venture which aims to offer modern standards of hotel comfort at bargain rates. $$, apts $$$

⌂ **Baltosis burės** Gimbutienės 35; ☎ 37 370422; f 37 370467; e jachtclubas@takas.lt; www.jachtklubas.lt. The yacht club's hotel is right beside the Kaunas Sea, 1km north of Pažaislis Monastery, & within walking distance of the termini of trolleybuses 4, 5, 9 & 12. There is a café-restaurant with a terrace overlooking the harbour, & yachts & motorboats can be hired. The cheaper doubles, triples & quadruples are unrenovated rooms & exclude b/fast; the other rooms are renovated & include b/fast in the price. $$

⌂ **Metropolis** Daukanto 21; ☎ 37 205992/208081; f 37 206269; e sales@greenhotel.lt, www.greenhotel.lt. A pleasantly faded hotel from the early Soviet years, with nice touches such as the revolving entrance doorway, the panelled lobby & the stained-glass window over the staircase. Its location, on a quiet pedestrian precinct just round the corner from Laisvės alėja, could not be bettered. Now with a new name & under new management, many of the rooms have been refurbished, though this is not reflected in the prices, which remain very reasonable, particularly as they include a substantial buffet b/fast. $$

Bed and breakfast

⌂ **Litinterp** Gedimino 28-7; ☎/f 37 228718; e kaunas@litinterp.com; www.litinterp.com. ⊕08.30–17.30 Mon–Fri, 09.00–15.00 Sat. As well as having its own small guesthouse, this arranges B&B in private houses in central Kaunas, & can make advance bookings for the same in Vilnius, Klaipėda, Palanga & Nida. Bike & car hire, interpreting & translating services are also available. $$

✗ **WHERE TO EAT** Kaunas comes much nearer to matching Vilnius in its wide variety of places to eat and drink. Many of the best places are conveniently located on or just off the pedestrianised Vilniaus–Laisvės axis, and are thus able to offer outside seating in summer. Note also that several of the hotels listed above have good restaurants, and that most of the cafés and bars listed later also serve full meals.

Restaurants

✗ **Bernelių Užeiga** Valančiaus 9 & Donelaičio 11. Both of these evoke the atmosphere of traditional Lithuanian country inns, with cuisine to match. The former occupies 2 buildings, each with a courtyard, in the Old Town; the latter a wooden building in the New Town.

✖ **Bravaria** Karaliaus Mindaugo 47. This German-style beer hall is the most enticing of the restaurants grouped around the ice rink on the top floor of the new Akropolis shopping mall.

✖ **Čarlstonas** Kęstučio 93. Although nominally Spanish, this very formal restaurant serves dishes influenced by a range of different cuisines, notably French. There are exotic & correspondingly expensive items on the menu as well as reasonably priced roast meats in fruit sauces.

✖ **Čiau** Donelaičio 66. A pizzeria whose main dining area is reminiscent of a conservatory. It is a particularly convenient place to break for lunch when visiting the concentration of museums nearby.

✖ **Didžioji Siena** Kumelių 7. An authentic Chinese restaurant in the heart of the Old Town.

✖ **inTilsit** Vytauto 32. Located in a small shopping centre with windows overlooking Ramybė Park, this is a theme restaurant whose walls are hung with photos of the old Prussian city of Tilsit – nowadays Sovetsk in the Kaliningrad *oblast* – & whose menu features both German & Lithuanian dishes.

✖ **Medžiotojų Užeiga** Rotušės aikštė 10. An extensive Lithuanian menu, including many game dishes, is served in the cosy interior, with the alternative of outside tables overlooking the Town Hall in summer.

✖ **Miesto** Sodas Laisvės 93. This large glass palace with an even larger summertime patio offers an international menu, including a good salad bar. There is live music every evening, & the complex incorporates the Siena nightclub.

✖ **Milano** Mickevičiaus 19. Incongruously located within the army officers' club, this is a pizzeria, though it also offers the full range of Italian cuisine.

✖ **Napoli** Gedimino 33. Attached to a wine merchant's shop, this offers a small but well-chosen menu of Italianate dishes.

✖ **Pizza Jazz** Laisvės 68 & Laisvės 106. These are the most convenient branch of a small local chain which makes both thin- & thick-crust pizzas.

✖ **Pompėja** Putvinskio 38. The mock-antique clay plates & bowls, intended to evoke ancient Pompeii, might appear gimmicky, but this restaurant presents some of the most creative cooking in Kaunas, with a notable line in game, including elk & wild boar. There is live music on Fri & Sun.

✖ **Retro bordo** Vilniaus 39. This advertises itself as a steak house & as such serves succulent cuts, though the menu is actually wide-ranging.

✖ **Šaulys** Nepriklausomybės aikštė 5. Something of a hybrid between a restaurant, serving pizzas as well as tasty Lithuanian dishes, & a whisky bar.

✖ **Senamiesčio Vyninė** Daukšos 23. The Old Town's principal wine bar-cum-restaurant.

✖ **Senieji Rūsiai** Vilniaus 34. A classy new formal restaurant in medieval cellars. It serves both Lithuanian & international cuisine & is reasonably priced.

✖ **Sičuan** Mickevičiaus 30. Another Chinese restaurant, offering spicy dishes from the Szechuan region as well as the usual fare.

✖ **Žalias Ratas** Laisvės 36b. Despite its address, this old wooden country-style tavern lies well back from the main thoroughfare, tucked away behind the Hotel Neris. It serves some of the tastiest local fare in the city, & features live folk bands on Fri & Sat evenings.

Cafés

▱ **Arabatinė** Laisvės 100. A strictly vegan daytime tearoom, run in tandem with a pharmacy. Closed Sun.

▱ **Barracuda** Vilniaus 14-4, entrance from Naugardo 15. A pleasant, inexpensive café with minimalist décor. It serves full meals, including many fish dishes.

▱ **Blyninė** Laisvės 56. As the name implies, this specialises in pancakes.

▱ **Kavinė Internetas** Vilniaus 24. This cybercafé offers light meals & charges 4Lt/hr for internet access. ⊕08.00–22.00 Mon–Sat, 09.00–21.00 Sun.

▱ **Kipšas** Putvinskio 64. The café in the basement of the Devil Museum offers gargantuan main dishes & desserts.

▱ **Metų Laikai** Mickevičiaus 40b. A fine choice for well-prepared local dishes, especially meats grilled over lava stones. In summer the courtyard offers an enticing alternative to the rather dank interior.

▱ **Pas Pranciškų** Zamenhofo 11. A homely Old Town cellar restaurant offering a good choice of Lithuanian cuisine.

▱ **Pieno Baras** Daukanto 18. An old-style milk bar near the corner of Laisvės. Inexpensive coffee, ice-cream, milk-shakes & gooey sweets & pastries are served to those unfazed by the calorie count; the health-conscious can have hot milk.

▱ **Retro** Laisvės 15. This small café at the quiet eastern end of the main thoroughfare is a good choice for b/fast or a snack.

▱ **Skliautas** Rotušės aikštė 26. A dimly lit café with a contrastingly bright summertime courtyard, renowned as a favourite haunt of local poets & chess enthusiasts.

Bars and café-bars

♀ **Amerika Pirtyje** Vytauto 71. A raucous Wild West theme bar-cum-disco.

♀ **Avilys** Vilniaus 34. This homebrew cellar pub currently makes only 2 beers – the light Avilio & the honeyed Medaus. It also has a wide-ranging menu.

♀ **B.O.** Muitinės 9. A youthful favourite, a rock music pub with painted furniture.

♀ **Irish Pub** Donelaičio 65. A favourite of flash local yuppies, with Guinness among the beers on draught.

♀ **Jums** Laisvės 61. A designer-style café-bar with distinctive pod chairs. It serves a good selection of light meals & sweets.

♀ **Kauno Alus** Savanorių 11. A bar for serious drinkers, situated alongside the splendidly old-fashioned premises of the eponymous brewery (formerly known as Žalsvytis), which makes 7 different beers, all with an alcohol content of at least 5%. 4 of these are available on tap, the others in bottles.

♀ **Los Patrankos** Savanorių 124. This huge bar & disco complex on 3 floors is Kaunas's hippest nightspot. ⏰21.00–04.00 Tue–Fri, 21.00–06.00 Fri/Sat.

♀ **Metropolis** Laisvės 66. This cavernous bar has a predominantly young clientele; it has an eclectic menu & features live music & dancing in the evenings.

OTHER PRACTICALITIES
Pharmacy
✚ **Lucerna** Vytauto 2. ⏰24hrs.

Post
✉ **Central Post Office** Laisvės 102. ⏰07.00–19.00 Mon–Fri, 07.00–17.00 Sat.

SHOPPING
Bookshops
Alėja Laisvės 29. A general bookshop with a deliberately old-fashioned appearance.

Centrinis Knygynas Laisvės 81. A general bookshop with a travel/maps section.

Humanitas Vilniaus 11. The university bookstore.

Pegasus Laisvės 75. A smart new general bookshop.

Shopping mall
Akropolis Karaliaus Mindaugo 47. Opened in 2007, this shopping mall follows in the wake of its Vilnius & Klaipėda namesakes. Clothing shops predominate, though the top floor has an entertainment complex & several restaurants along with some truly wacky decor.

Souvenir shops
Dailė Rotušės aikštė 1. Sells all kinds of modern Lithuanian folk art, notably carvings, ceramics & baskets.

Suvenyrai Vilniaus 36. Sells a variety of art work, including jewellery & pictures.

ENTERTAINMENT AND NIGHTLIFE
Theatre and music Theatrical and musical performances tend to begin very early in Kaunas, with 18.00 being the norm.

🎭 **Academic Drama Theatre** Laisvės 71; ☏ 37 224064; www.dramosteatras.lt. Independent Lithuania's first theatre, founded in 1920, puts on a mixed programme of classics & contemporary plays.

♪ **Kaunas Philharmonic Hall** Sapiegos 5; ☏ 37 222558, www.kaunofilharmonija.lt. The main concert hall, meeting-place of the inter-war parliament, is of modest dimensions & thus best suited to chamber & instrumental recitals, though it also hosts orchestral & choral events.

🎭 **Music Theatre** Laisvės 91; ☏ 37 200933; www.musikinisteatras.lt. Operas, operettas & musicals are performed at this theatre, which was founded in 1940 in premises originally built in 1891.

🎭 **Pantomime Theatre** Ožeškienės 12; ☏ 37 225668. A specialist pantomime stage. It is claimed language is no barrier to enjoyment of the productions.

🎭 **Puppet Theatre** Laisvės 87a; ☏ 37 209893 or 227158; www.kaunasleles.lt. Established in 1948, this was Lithuania's first puppet theatre. The performances are intended exclusively for children.

📺 Small Theatre Daukšos 34; ☎ 37 206546 or 226090; www.mazasisteatras.omnitel.net. A chamber theatre staging a programme of contemporary & classic modern plays.

Festivals Kaunas holds a four-day jazz festival (*www.kaunasjazz.lt*) each spring; most events are held at Vytautas the Great University, Daukanto 28. The Pažaislis Music Festival (*www.pazaislis.lt*), which takes place from early June until late August, features a series of classical music concerts, including some in the open air outside the Pažaislis Monastery. There are many outdoor folklore events throughout the year, many in the Song Valley arena in Ąžuolynas Park. An annual festivals schedule is published in *Kaunas In Your Pocket*.

WHAT TO SEE AND DO

Old Town Kaunas's Old Town (Senamiestis) is quite modest in size, but is none the less liberally endowed with historic monuments – a castle, numerous churches, monasteries, palaces and mansions. No longer the hub of commercial life, it is fairly quiet and sedate, and much of it is pedestrianised, making it ideal for exploration on foot. Since independence, a large proportion of the buildings have been cleaned and restored, though reconstruction work will continue for some years on the more dilapidated survivals. The wooden telephone booths and iron street lamps have been designed to melt into their historic surroundings, while loving care is evident even in the specially made cobblestones and pavement slabs.

Around the Castle The **Kaunas Castle**, situated south of the Neris just before it flows into the Nemunas, is the oldest building in the city, and the obvious place to begin a tour. Its exact age is uncertain, but it had certainly been in existence long before it was first mentioned in the chronicles of the Teutonic Knights following its destruction in 1361. The present ruins belong to the building constructed immediately after that incident. This originally had four towers and was surrounded by a moat. Ironically, it was eventually the River Neris which left the castle in its ruinous state. Repeated flooding demolished the north wall and all but one of the towers. In the 1920s the municipal authorities landscaped the area around the surviving fragment, and its appearance has remained the same since, save for the protective roofs installed in 1989. A small museum was established in the tower, though this has not been accessible in recent years.

Just south of the castle is the **Church of St George**, built in the 15th century as part of a Bernardine friary, and a typical example of the spare brick Gothic architecture favoured by mendicant orders. Under the Soviet regime it was allowed to fall into a semi-derelict state, and its tall lancet windows were bricked up. Restoration work has now begun, but will take many years to complete. The Baroque high altar is an impressive sight, filling the entire apse, but, like its smaller counterparts, it has been stripped of its original paintings and sculptures. Immediately to the east is the seminary, the only one in Lithuania which remained open in the Soviet era. It incorporates the **Church of the Holy Trinity**, which was built in Renaissance style with some archaic Gothic elements in the late 16th and early 17th centuries. The interior was destroyed by fire in 1668 and subsequently given a Baroque makeover, but most of the furnishings were lost when the church was converted into a dance studio in 1963.

Rotušės aikštė At the heart of the Old Town is Rotušės aikštė (Town Hall Square), with the **Old Town Hall** itself, something of a symbol for the city, standing in splendid isolation in the middle. The building was begun in 1542, remodelled in the 1630s, then again in 1771–80 by a Bohemian architect, Jan

Mattekier. This last project saw the addition of the final stage of the gracefully tapering tower – which rises for five storeys above its base to a height of 53m – and bestowed a classically influenced late Baroque appearance to the whole exterior. Painted a gleaming white, the highly distinctive shape of the building has led to the inevitable nickname of the 'White Swan'. In the 19th century, the Town Hall served successively as an Orthodox church, an artillery warehouse, a residence for the Tsar, a theatre and then the seat of the local administration. The two main floors now serve as a Palace of Weddings and are thus freely accessible, though sightseeing is not encouraged. In the vaulted Gothic cellars is a **Ceramics Museum** (⊕ *11.00–17.00 Tue–Sun*), which has changing exhibitions of work by contemporary artists in the field.

On the south side of the square is the Jesuit Monastery, centred on the **Church of St Francis Xavier**. This was begun in 1666 but burned down two years later, and was only completed in 1698. The twin towers, added in 1725, make a splendid sacred foil to the single tower of the Town Hall. The church was converted to Russian Orthodox use in 1825 and re-named in honour of Alexander Nevsky; in 1843 it was raised to cathedral status. It was returned to the Jesuits after World War I, but confiscated again by the Soviets, who used the complex as a school, with the church sanctuary serving as a sports hall. Although now back in religious use, it is hardly surprising, after all these vicissitudes, that the interior is stark and rather bare.

On the western side of the square is a pensive **statue of Maironis**, otherwise known as Jonas Mačiulis (1862–1932), a Roman Catholic priest regarded by many commentators as the finest-ever poet to write in the Lithuanian language, and a key figure in the nationalist movement which won the country back its independence in 1918. In his capacity as Rector of the Seminary, Maironis lived from 1911 until his death in the splendid Baroque palace to the rear, which is entered via a Neo-Classical portal. It now houses the **Maironis Lithuanian Literature Museum** (*www.maironiomuziejus.lt;* ⊕ *09.00–17.00 Tue–Sat*). On the ground floor is a documentary exhibition, complete with many first editions, on the entire history of literature in Lithuania, regardless of what language it was written in. Maironis's private apartments on the first floor, which have been well restored, can also be visited.

Likewise on the west side of the square, a little to the north, are the 19th-century postal buildings, which now house the **Museum of Posts and Telecommunications** (⊕ *10.00–18.00 Wed, Thu, Sat & Sun*). There are displays on the establishment of the postal system in Lithuania, the postal services of the inter-war period, radio and telecommunications and equipment from the late 19th century onwards, and the philately of the two Lithuanian republics. A modern reproduction of a postal coach is kept in the former stables to the rear.

The northern and eastern sides of the square are lined with a number of fine old mansions of various dates, which in the main were formerly the residences of the city's most prosperous merchants. No 28 is now home to the **Museum of the History of Lithuanian Medicine and Pharmacy** (⊕ *10.00–18.00 Tue–Sat*), which contains a collection of historic medical equipment from the 16th century onwards, including a complete 19th-century pharmacist's shop.

Cathedral of SS Peter and Paul A short way down Vilniaus, which leads east from Rotušės aikštė, is the **Cathedral of SS Peter and Paul**, by far the largest Gothic church in Lithuania, and the only one with a basilican plan. It was probably constructed at the time of the Christianisation of Samogitia in the early 15th century, and Grand Duke Vytautas may have been the founder. The building has repeatedly been damaged by fire, hence the predominantly

Renaissance and Baroque aspect of the interior, though the single-towered brick exterior has been restored to something like its original form. It only gained cathedral status, along with its current dedication, when the headquarters of the bishopric of Samogitia was transferred to Kaunas in 1864. It was raised to the rank of a papal basilica in 1921, and in 1926 became the seat of the archbishopric of the new Lithuanian ecclesiastical province.

Inside the cathedral are some impressive Baroque furnishings created by artists from several different countries. The gigantic high altar by the Pole Tomasz Podhayski features a theatrical *Crucifixion* scene with statues of the apostles. At the end of the north aisle is an elaborate carved and gilded wooden altar sheltering a painting of *The Assumption* by the German Johann Gotthard Berchoff. Another feature of special note is the Chapel of St John the Baptist adjoining the south aisle, one of the most elegant examples of Neo-Gothic architecture in the country. Bishop Motiejus Valančius (see page 202) is buried underneath the cathedral, while the tomb of Maironis can be seen outside on the southern wall.

Rest of the Old Town Immediately to the rear of the Jesuit Monastery is the mysterious late 15th-century building known as the **Perkūnas House** (⊕ *08.00–17.00 Mon–Thu, 08.00–15.45 Fri*). This name dates only from the 19th century, when a statue of the thunder god Perkūnas was found embedded in a wall, fuelling speculation that the site had formerly been occupied by a temple dedicated to him. The extravagant Gothic brickwork, with its ogee arches, pinnacles and finials, recalls that of the Church of St Anne in Vilnius; indeed, it is the only structure which is at all reminiscent of Lithuania's most famous building. Although its early history is unknown, it is likely that it was originally the combined home and office of a prosperous Hanseatic merchant. It has served many functions over the centuries; currently there is a public library on the top floor, an exhibition space below.

A few steps away, perilously close to the Nemunas whose floods have often endangered it, is another highly picturesque example of Gothic brickwork, the Church of the Assumption. Formerly part of a Franciscan friary, it is popularly known as the **Vytautas Church** in honour of its founder. A modern painting inside illustrates the story (which may or may not be true) behind its foundation. Vytautas' army was defeated by the Tatars in 1398, but the Grand Duke himself escaped, having promised that he would endow a church in honour of the Virgin in return for his safe deliverance. Some credence is lent to this tale by evidence that the church appears to date back to around 1400, making it one of the oldest in the country. The tower, idiosyncratically perched over the porch, and only assuming an octagonal shape in its two uppermost storeys, is more than a century younger.

Three blocks to the east, at Zamenhofo 12, the **Lithuanian Folk Instruments Museum** (⊕ *09.00/10.00–17.00/18.00 Tue–Sat*) occupies a couple of houses in a courtyard. On display are examples of the country's most popular musical instruments, including reed pipes, whistle flutes, clay whistles, trumpets, horns, bells, zithers, accordions, concertinas and bandoneons. There are also a few offbeat items, the most improbable being a musical washing board, and a small selection of folk instruments from other countries. Tapes featuring many of the instruments are played as background music.

Back on Vilniaus, a couple of blocks further east is the Baroque **Church of Corpus Christi**, formerly part of a Dominican convent. Over the road the former **Presidential Palace** (*www.istorineprezidentura.lt;* ⊕ *11.00–17.00 Tue–Sun*) has recently been converted into a museum of the history of the inter-war Lithuanian state. In its gardens are statues of the three presidents who lived there – Antanas Smetona, Aleksandras Stulginskis and Kazys Grinius.

A little further on, Gruodžio leads off Vilniaus towards the **Church of St Gertrude** at the extreme eastern edge of the Old Town. This little building is in many ways reminiscent of the Church of Vytautas, notably in its unconventional tower, though it is less elaborate. It has Baroque furnishings, including a pulpit which the priest can enter directly from the sacristy. In an enclosure on a hillock at the far northern end of the Old Town is the final example of Gothic brickwork, the much-altered **Church of St Nicholas**, once part of a Benedictine monastery.

New Town The New Town (Naujamiestis) was laid out in the late 19th century as a planned grid immediately east of the Old Town. It is the hub of the city's banking, business and administrative sectors, the main shopping area and the location of the most important museums and places of entertainment.

Laisvės alėja The central axis of the New Town is the 1.6km-long Laisvės alėja ('Freedom Avenue'), a dead-straight tree-lined boulevard which may not quite match the Champs Elysées in Paris or Unter den Linden in Berlin, yet is an impressive and distinctive feature of the city nevertheless. Since 1982 it has been free of traffic along its entire length, though little-used cycle lanes have been introduced and vehicles can cross it at the intersections with Maironio and Mickevičiaus. For many years, smoking was strictly prohibited at any point on the avenue, but in 2000 this restriction was lifted by a decree of the ruling mayor, and the signs enforcing the ban were taken down. Laisvės is firmly established as the retail heart of Kaunas; it has acquired many ritzy shops in recent years and is also well-endowed with trendy restaurants, cafés and bars.

Towards the western end, at Laisvės 106, is the **Tadas Ivanauskas Zoological Museum** (⊕ *11.00–19.00 Tue–Sun*), the only specialist natural history collection in the country. Tadas Ivanauskas (1882–1970), who dedicated his life to the study, documentation and protection of Lithuania's fauna, established it in 1919. In addition to arrays of stuffed and preserved animals, birds, reptiles, amphibians, insects, butterflies, fish, molluscs and shells from around the world, there are some charmingly old-fashioned dioramas, a display of postage stamps with zoological themes, information on the career of the founder and a rather incongruous roomful of hunting trophies. Some of the labels, albeit a minority, are translated into English.

A little further along, at Laisvės 102, is the **Central Post Office**, a typical example of the sort of Bauhaus-inspired official architecture sponsored during Lithuania's inter-war independence. Inside is a display on the country's philatelic history. Beyond it is a **statue of Vytautas the Great**, in which the Grand Duke is shown trampling on four defeated enemies – a Pole, a Tatar, a Teutonic Knight, and a Russian. Directly opposite is the **City Garden**, a small area of greenery in front of the Music Theatre. It was the scene of the suicide of Romas Kalanta in 1972. A memorial of 19 stones, one for each year of his life, was unveiled on the 30th anniversary of his death.

At the far eastern end of Laisvės is the massive Neo-Byzantine bulk of the **Church of St Michael the Archangel**, erected in 1891–93 as a custom-built place of Orthodox worship for the local garrison – and as a visual symbol of Russian hegemony over the city. Services were suspended under the Soviets, though the building was kept open as a museum of stained glass. It became a Roman Catholic church in 1990.

Mykolas Žilinskas Art Museum Across from the church, at Nepriklausomybės aikštė 12, is the Mykolas Žilinskas Art Museum (⊕ *11.00–17.00 Tue–Sun*), built in 1989 to house the foreign collections of the MK Čiurlionis State Art Museum. It is fronted by Petras Mozūras's statue of the Greek god Nike, whose unabashed eroticism unleashed a public furore which lasted several years. The ground floor of the museum is devoted to decorative arts, with the emphasis on ceramics. This is dominated by a fine collection of Meissen porcelain, a legacy of the former dynastic links between Lithuania and Saxony. There is also a small display of antiquities from classical civilisations, notably Egypt.

Paintings and sculptures are displayed on the two upper floors. Among the Italian Renaissance works are *Madonna and Child with SS Margaret and Roch* by Palma Vecchio and a curious *Nativity* by Parmigianino. The pride of the collection is a small *Crucifixion* by Rubens; set against a dark sky, with a low horizontal view towards Jerusalem, it is the only canvas by the prolific Flemish master in the country. Hung in the same room are two rare works by the short-lived Utrecht artist Dirck van Baburen; one is a study for an altarpiece in a church in Rome, while *Democritus and Heraclitus* depicts the laughing and crying philosophers of ancient Greece. Ribera's *Diogenes with the Lamp* is another notable 17th-century work with a classical theme.

A decent representation of French 19th-century painting includes two fine portraits of children of the Oginskis family by François Xavier Fabre, as well as works by Corot, Courbet, Monticelli, Renoir and Cézanne. There are also three works by the Danish Neo-Classical sculptor Berthel Thorwaldsen, good examples of the German Impressionists Max Liebermann and Lovis Corinth, and, as a legacy of an inter-war exhibition, a large number of paintings by early 20th-century Belgian artists.

Vienybės aikštė Vienybės aikštė (Unity Square) lies immediately beyond Donelaičio, a block north of Laisvės. It faces the headquarters of both Vytautas the Great University, re-established in 1990 after a 50-year hiatus, and the rather larger Technical University. On the square itself stands the **Freedom Monument**, built to commemorate Lithuania's inter-war independence; this was removed by the Soviets but reinstated in 1989. A hall of fame, featuring busts of nationalist statesmen and writers, leads to an eternal flame surrounded by carved crosses in honour of those who gave their lives in the struggle.

To the rear, in custom-built premises complete with bell tower, is the **Vytautas the Great War Museum** (⊕*May–Sep 11.00–17.00 Tue–Sun, Oct–Apr 11.00–17.00 Wed–Sun*), founded in 1921 to display items pertaining to the (general rather than purely military) history of Lithuania. It contains archaeological finds and a valuable collection of old weapons, but by far the best-known exhibit is the mangled wreck of the *Lituanica* aeroplane in which the pilots Steponas Darius and Stasys Girėnas – both of whom were Lithuanian-born, though residents of the USA – crashed to their deaths over Pomerania, just 775km from their intended destination of Kaunas, while attempting to break the world record for the longest non-stop transatlantic flight in 1933. Their bloodstained shirts are displayed in a glass case alongside. Despite their failure, they immediately assumed the status of posthumous national heroes, and remain so to this day, with streets named after them in almost every Lithuanian town, and their portraits adorning the front of the 10Lt banknote. (The 20Lt note depicts the museum itself.)

MK Čiurlionis State Art Museum In the rear part of the same building as the War Museum, at Putvinskio 55, is the MK Čiurlionis State Art Museum (*www.ciurlionis.lt;* ⊕*10.00/11.00–17.00 Tue–Sun*). Its extension, built in 1969 and refurbished according to the most modern museum standards in 2001–03, contains virtually the entire painted output, numbering around 300 works, of Mikalojus Konstantinas Čiurlionis (see pages 122–3), though the artist-composer had no more than a fleeting connection with Kaunas. Because the finished paintings are nearly all pastel or tempera on paper, they are extremely delicate, and fewer than half are on view at any one time in the upper-floor galleries.

Although little-known outside Lithuania, Poland and Russia, Čiurlionis is a major figure whose legacy is remarkable for one whose painting career lasted just seven years. He is generally classed as a Symbolist, but is also considered a pioneer of Abstraction, as well as a precursor of the Futurists and Surrealists. One of his most original achievements was the introduction into his paintings of musical concepts such as thematic development, tempo, rhythm, harmony and counterpoint; many of his paintings have musical titles, including a series of seven named and numbered sonatas, each of which is arranged in three or four 'movements'.

The Knight Prelude, showing a horseman riding through the air above a cityscape closely resembling Vilnius, is a 'musical' work which also shows another of Čiurlionis's preoccupations, Lithuanian folklore. His best-known work in this field is *The Fairy-Tale of the Kings*, the only painting he himself explained: the two kings find a small object radiating sunlight in a fantastical forest; this turns out to be a Lithuanian village shining to the world its distinctive culture. His few directly representational paintings, such as *Lithuanian Graveyard* and *Wayside Crosses of Samogitia*, are loving tributes to the country's folk art tradition. However, in many ways Čiurlionis's most remarkable paintings are his impenetrable cosmic visions, above all the extraordinary *Rex*, which shows a barely discernible deity sitting on a throne suspended between the globe and the heavens.

Čiurlionis's largest painting, a theatre curtain for the Rūta society, can be seen in the music hall on the floor below. This is occasionally used for live chamber and instrumental performances; at other times, recordings of Čiurlionis's music are played, and it is possible to request to hear particular pieces. In the basement is extensive documentation on his life and work in both Lithuanian and English. Autograph musical manuscripts, sketchbooks, drawings, vignettes, book designs, photographs, postcards and letters help to illuminate the diversity of his creative activity.

The older part of the museum contains collections of folk art, including iron crosses; of old Lithuanian art, predominantly portraiture; and of works by other 20th-century Lithuanian artists. Prominent among the last-named are the works of Čiurlionis's close associate Petras Rimša (1881–1961), including the portrait medals – Realistic in his early period, with more decorative stylisation later on – for which he is best known. There is also a model for an unexecuted monument to Darius and Girėnas. Very different are the eccentric sculptures of Elžbieta Paškauskaitė-Daugvilienė (1886–1959) inspired by the 1863 rebellion in which her grandfather took part. The artist gathered the bark of trees in springtime, soaked them in liquids, then dried them out; she later sewed separate carved pieces of bark on to a canvas with a needle and strong thread.

Devil Museum Diagonally opposite, at Putvinskio 64, is the Devil Museum (☉ *10.00/11.00–17.00 Tue–Sun*), established in 1966 as the first of its kind in the world, and still one of only two in existence. It has its origins in the private collection of the painter Antanas Žmuidzinavičius (1876–1966), who was a leading light, along with Čiurlionis and Rimša, in the pioneering exhibitions of Lithuanian art in the first decade of the 20th century. Žmuidzinavičius claimed, perhaps only half-jokingly, that his longevity was due to his obsession with collecting representations of the devil. In his lifetime, he amassed no fewer than

260, or 20 devil dozens. The museum is in two distinct parts. That to the right of the entrance is Žmuidzinavičius's own house, with one floor furnished as he knew it, and the other two floors hung with a selection of his landscapes (of the Curonian Spit, the Nemunas and other Lithuanian beauty spots, as well as of the USA and various European countries), portraits and genre scenes.

The extension displays around 700 of the museum's devils which, thanks to continued donations, now number around 2,000. On the first two floors, they are almost exclusively Lithuanian. In the local pagan folklore, the devil was not a simple demon, but a guardian of the dead, fertility and animals. After the introduction of Christianity, he came to be an evil spirit, albeit an unsuccessful one who tried to trick people, but instead found himself outwitted. The devils on display are shown in many guises, including celebrating weddings, tempting victims with drink, watching over the dying, snatching souls and taking them to hell. There are also some which are overtly political, including one, made for the 50th anniversary of the Molotov–Ribbentrop Pact, which shows a devil with the features of Stalin chasing another with the features of Hitler out of Lithuania. On the top floor are devils from all over the world plus displays of Lithuanian witches (who ride on beehives as an alternative to broomsticks) and carnival masks.

Žaliakalnis Eastwards along Putvinskio, at the junction with Mickevičiaus, is the lower station of the Žaliakalnis (Green Hill) funicular. The first of two such railways in Kaunas, it was built in 1932 to a German design, and travels 140m on a 20° incline. Although intended as a useful addition to the city's public transport facilities, the modest size of the hill suggests that there was always a prestige element attached to the project, and within five years there was a proposal to demolish the adjacent steps in order to force an increase in the number of passengers. This was never done, however, and the funicular – which nowadays is protected by its status as a historic technological monument – continues to operate daily from morning until early evening, except for an hour-long lunch break.

A short walk from the funicular's upper station is Kaunas's single most prominent building, the **Church of the Resurrection**. This geometric modernist building was begun in 1932 as a symbol of national revival, and was the most ambitious of the prestige projects of the inter-war years. However, it was still unfinished when it was confiscated by the Soviets in 1940. After wartime service as a warehouse for the Nazis, it was turned into a workshop for a radio plant. Although handed back to the Catholic Church in 1988, restoration work was stalled repeatedly on the grounds of cost, and only completed at the end of 2004. A gleaming whitewash now covers both the exterior and interior brickwork. The terrace (⊕ 11.30–18.30 Mon–Fri, 11.00–16.30 Sat–Sun), which can be reached by steps or lift, commands a fine view over the city.

Eastern fringe At Donelaičio 16, at the extreme northeastern edge of the New Town, is the **Kaunas Picture Gallery** (⊕ 11.00–17.00 Tue–Sun), which offers changing exhibitions of work by contemporary Lithuanian and émigré artists. It also owns a collection of artefacts of North American native tribes, but this is not always on view.

About halfway down Vytauto, which marks the eastern boundary of the New Town, is Ramybė Park. At its northern end is the small **Tatar Mosque**, built in the 1930s. On the western edge is the **Museum of Exiles and Political Prisoners** (⊕ 10.00–16.00 Wed–Sat), a photographic commemoration of those who fought against Soviet rule. To the southeast are the two very modest-sized **Russian Orthodox cathedrals**. Towards the far end of Vytauto, squeezed into a restricted site between the bus and train stations, is a typical open-air market.

The spectacular success of the film *Schindler's List* has led to renewed interest in other people – often of far more obviously admirable qualities than the deeply flawed German industrialist Oskar Schindler – who risked their lives or careers to save large numbers of Jews from the Holocaust. Among them is Chiune Sugihara, a Japanese career diplomat and Christian convert who in March 1939 was sent to open a one-man consulate in Kaunas, which was strategically placed for gathering information about the war plans of both Germany and the Soviet Union.

In July 1940 the occupying Soviet authorities ordered all diplomats to leave the city. Most went immediately, though Sugihara and his Dutch counterpart Jan Zwartendijk were permitted to remain for another month. Together they hatched a plan to help Jews who wished to flee from the advancing Nazis. Those with Polish passports were able to travel through the Soviet Union on transit visas, provided they were equipped with visas for another destination. It turned out that the Jews would be allowed to enter the Dutch Caribbean colonies of Curacao and Dutch Guiana (now Surinam), but would need transit visas for Japan in order for the journey to be possible.

Sugihara tried to gain official permission from the foreign ministry in Tokyo to issue the visas, but when this was refused outright he decided to do so anyway. He spent his last four weeks in Kaunas writing out visas by hand, processing

A few minutes' walk to the northwest, at the corner of Mindaugo and Gedimino, is the **Church of the Holy Cross**. This twin-towered Baroque building was once part of the former Carmelite Convent alongside, the place Napoleon lodged during his stay in Kaunas in June 1812.

Jewish Kaunas Before World War II, Kaunas's Jewish population was around 37,000, and there were 37 synagogues, including two, now empty shells, which can be seen on Zamenhofo, directly opposite the Lithuanian Folk Instruments Museum. Nowadays just over 1,000 Jews live in the city, many of them non-practising, and the only functioning **Synagogue** is by the northwestern fringe of the New Town, at Ožeškienės 17. Built in 1871, it has galleries on three sides, and a fine gilded wood *bimah*, which was restored a few years ago. To the rear is a monument to the approximately 1,600 Jewish children murdered during the Nazi occupation.

Jews traditionally settled in the Slobodka district (known to Lithuanians as Vilijampolė) directly across the Neris from the centre, but from the mid-19th century spread themselves all over the city. In 1941, however, the Nazis ordered them back to Slobodka, which became the enclosed **Kovno Ghetto**. This functioned until 1944, when it was liquidated. Much of the area remains derelict to this day, though a memorial has been erected on Kriščiukaičio.

Most of Kaunas's Jews, along with many others from throughout Lithuania and elsewhere in Europe, were murdered at the **Ninth Fort** (⊕*Apr–Oct 10.00–18.00 Wed–Mon, Nov–Mar 10.00–16.00 Wed–Sun; buses 23 and 35, which start from the terminal beside the castle, pass nearby*) at the extreme northwestern edge of the city, overlooking the Klaipėda highway. As with all such places of mass execution, the precise number of victims is much disputed, but may have been anything up to 80,000. In contrast to the largest Nazi death factories, such as Auschwitz–Birkenau and Treblinka, many of the assassinations were carried out with handguns, rather than by gassing.

around 300 per day, and continued doing so up to the moment his Berlin-bound train pulled out of the station on September 1, whereupon he handed over his consular stamp to a refugee, who was able to use it to issue yet more visas.

It is estimated that as many as 6,000 Jews were able to escape from the Holocaust as a result of Sugihara's actions: if so, it was the second or third highest total saved by a single individual. Although he continued to work for the Japanese diplomatic service for the duration of the war, Sugihara was sacked in 1945. In her memoir *Visas for Life*, his wife Yukiko claimed this was a retrospective punishment for having deliberately disobeyed orders, but it seems far more likely that Sugihara was merely one casualty among many in a programme of redundancies implemented as a result of the new peacetime conditions. His subsequent working life, firstly as a freelance translator, latterly in a managerial position with an export company, was spent in obscurity. Not until 1969 did one of the people he saved manage to get in contact with him. In 1985, following the receipt of many testimonies from all over the world, he was granted Israel's highest honour, the designation of a 'Righteous among the Nations'. He was too ill to attend the ceremony, but his wife – whose claims to have played a crucial role in helping him prepare the visas in 1940 have since been called into question – accepted it on his behalf.

A museum by the entrance details the history of the fort, which was originally constructed as part of the 19th-century Russian defensive system, and was used after the Nazi defeat by the Soviet secret police as a prison and execution place of Lithuanian partisans. Part of the display is given over to works of art inspired by the various atrocities. One of the prison buildings still survives, with some of the cells preserved as they were during the time of terror, complete with the graffiti scrawled by many of the prisoners prior to their execution. '*Nous sommes 5,000 Français*' ('We are 5,000 Frenchmen') wrote one, providing telling evidence of the scale of the crimes. Outside, the site of the mass graves is marked by a huge, jagged concrete memorial sculpture impressive in its starkness and simplicity.

Another key feature of the city's Jewish heritage trail is the **Sugihara House** (⊕*Jun–Sep 10.00–17.00 Mon–Fri, 11.00–16.00 Sat–Sun; Oct–May 12.00–15.00 Mon–Fri*) at Vaižganto 30 in the villa district on the high ground between the Ramybė and Ažuolynas Parks. This is the building in which the Japanese diplomat Chiune Sugihara (see boxed feature above) established his consulate, and the one room open to the public contains the table at which he wrote out the visas which saved thousands of Jewish lives.

South of the Nemunas Directly facing the Old Town from the opposite side of the Nemunas is **Aleksotas Hill**, which was equipped with a similar funicular railway to that on Žaliakalnis in 1935. It operates in much the same way as its counterpart, and it is noticeable that students attending the music academy on the summit tend to use the stairs. Near the upper station is a belvedere commanding what is easily the best panoramic view of the city.

About 1km south of the hill, at Veiverių 132, is the **Darius and Girėnas Airport**. This was the city's international airport during its period as the national capital, and was where huge crowds gathered in July 1933, firstly to wait in vain for the arrival of the *Lituanica*, then a few days later to meet the German plane bringing the dead bodies of the two pilots back to their homeland. Nowadays, the airfield is used for recreational flights only. The terminal building houses the **Lithuanian Aviation Museum** (*www.lam.lt;* ⊕ *09.00–17.00 Tue–Sat*).

Another 1km to the southeast is the **Botanical Garden** (⊕ *10.00–20.00 or dusk daily; buses 7 and 12, plus various minibuses, run from the city centre*), one of the pleasantest and most peaceful spots in Kaunas. Among its features are an orangery (⊕ *10.00–15.30 Mon–Fri, 11.00–17.30 Sat–Sun*) with tropical plants, a tree-lined pond with an ornamental bridge, a rose garden and a dendrological park.

From there, it is a walk of about 1.5km southeast through a residential district of predominantly wooden houses to **Napoleon's Hill** (or Piliakalnio), a viewpoint directly overlooking the Nemunas which the French emperor ascended in order to survey the city. Unfortunately, the view nowadays is almost totally obscured by trees.

East of the centre
Not far east of the New Town is the 90-hectare **Ąžuolynas Park**, a popular recreation ground still preserving features of the oak wood it once was. Along its western fringe are, from north to south, a monument to Darius and Girėnas, a sporting complex named after the two pilots, and the Song Valley, an open-air arena where folklore events are often held.

In the northeastern part of the park is the **Zoo** (*www.zoosodas.lt;* ⊕ *daily Apr–Sep 09.00–19.00, Oct–Mar 09.00–17.00*), the only one in Lithuania. Founded by Tadas Ivanauskas in 1938, it currently has some 1,200 animals representing around 250 different species. Although it has had some recent successes, notably in the breeding of tigers, it is desperately run-down and underfunded, encapsulating all the faults anti-zoo campaigners are prone to protest about.

Further south is the **Girstupis valley**, which was much loved by the poet Adam Mickiewicz, who sang its praises in the epic poem *Grażyna*:

> I once saw near Kowno a beautiful vale
> Where water nymphs' hands in spring and July
> Scatter colourful flowers on meadow and trail;
> No lovelier valley exists anywhere.

About 1.5km to the east, past the Žalgiris Stadium which is home to the basketball team of the same name, is the site of the **Sixth Fort**. In the Soviet period a tank was placed there to commemorate 'Freedom from Fascism'. This was removed in 1991, and a miniature Hill of Crosses, which continues to grow, has taken its place.

Pažaislis
In a secluded woodland setting close to the Kaunas Sea at the eastern edge of the city is one of the country's greatest architectural and artistic treasures, the **Pažaislis Monastery** (⊕ *10.00–13.00 & 14.00–17.00 Mon–Sat, Sun for Mass at 11.00 only*). In summer, trolleybus 9 runs to the nearby marina, and excursion boats run on Sundays to Rumšiškės. During the rest of the year, it only goes as far as the main terminus about 1km to the north, which can be reached directly from the centre by trolleybus 5.

Founded by Kristupas Žygimantas Pacas (Krzysztof Zygmunt Pac), Grand Chancellor of Lithuania, Pažaislis was granted to 12 monks of the Camaldolese order, an idiosyncratic Benedictine offshoot which aimed at a compromise solution between the communal monastic tradition and a solitary eremitical way of life. The Polish–Lithuanian Commonwealth was one of the few countries outside its Italian homeland where it found favour. There is also a well-preserved but now uninhabited Camaldolese monastery at Lake Wigry (historically part of the Grand Duchy but now just over the Polish border) and another, still active, in Kraków.

Building work began in 1667 under an Italian architect, Giambatista Frediani, who retired at the time of the consecration of the church seven years later, perhaps to become a member of the original monastic community. The buildings were completed over the next two decades by his fellow-countrymen, the brothers Carlo and Pietro Putini, though work on the sumptuous interior decoration scheme continued until 1712.

Exactly a century later, the monastery was desecrated by Napoleon's troops. It was closed down in 1832 as one of the punitive measures following the anti-Tsarist revolt the year before, and re-settled by Russian Orthodox monks, who removed the altars and painted over some of the frescos. They left in 1914, taking the archives and many moveable furnishings to Russia. Following service as a German military hospital in World War I, the complex was given in 1920 to the Chicago-based Sisters of St Casimir. The order's founder, Maria Kaupaitė, came to Pažaislis with four other sisters and initiated a programme of opening schools and kindergartens throughout Lithuania. In 1948 the nuns were expelled, and the monastery was used successively as an archive, a residential home for the elderly, a psychiatric hospital and a museum. The sisters were invited back in 1992, and nowadays run a retreat centre, summer camps and seminars, while classical music concerts are often held in the grounds.

Pažaislis adopts the classic Camaldolese plan, and is the only Baroque complex in Lithuania built according to axial principles. From the imposing entrance gateway to the west (sadly no longer in use), a path leads up a narrow enclosed space to the guesthouse. At the other side of the lawn behind, at the very heart of the monastery, is the **Church of the Visitation**, flanked by two cloisters. To its rear are the cottages – of which only three survive – where the monks lived in solitude, only coming together for services and feast-day meals. Beyond the orchard-cum-market garden, at the far eastern end, the belltower stands in splendid isolation.

Nowadays, the visitors' entrance is by a small doorway to the left of the guest house, which leads round the side of the administration building to the lawn in front of the church. This is planted with oaks and has several graves, including that of Aleksei Fyodorovich Lvov, composer of the Tsarist national anthem quoted by Tchaikovsky in *The 1812 Overture*.

The church is highly distinctive; the façade has a concave central section and twin towers crowned with small open cupolas. Behind rises the massive main dome, hexagonal in shape and illuminated by a lantern. The central space is surrounded by four chapels, and has a vestibule at one end, a presbytery and monks' choir at the other, with the sacristy and chapter house on either side of the choir. At the high altar is a much-loved oval painting of *The Virgin and Child in a Garden of Flowers* by an unknown 17th-century Flemish master. This was donated to the monastery at the time of its foundation, but was transferred to Kaunas Cathedral by the communists and only recently returned. A fresco of *The Coronation of the Virgin* by Giuseppe Rossi fills the dome. Elsewhere, the walls are covered with costly red and black marble, delicately moulded white stucco work, and frescos by Michelangelo Palloni of scenes from the lives of, among others, the Virgin, Christ, St Benedict and St Romuald, with those on the vaults adopting virtuoso *trompe l'oeil* effects.

AROUND KAUNAS

The administrative county of Kaunas contains a number of destinations which can be the subject of day or half-day trips from the city, or else as stopovers on the way to destinations in other parts of the country.

RUMŠIŠKĖS By far the most popular excursion from Kaunas is to Rumšiškės, which lies 25km to the east, just south of the main highway to Vilnius. The original settlement, which dated back to the 14th century and had municipal rights, was drowned in 1959 when the Kaunas Sea was created. A village of the same name was established to replace it, though only the early 18th-century wooden church and belfry were saved and brought to the new location.

The **Lithuanian Open-Air Museum** (*www.llbm.lt;* ⊕*Easter–30 April 14.00–18.00 Fri, 10.00-18.00 Sat–Sun; May–Sep 10.00–18.00 Tue–Sun; Oct 10.00–15.00 Tue, 10.00–17.00 Wed–Sun*), by far the largest and best of its type in the country, was set up in 1966 on 175 hectares of land between Rumšiškės and the Kaunas Sea. Some 180 redundant buildings (a total which is continually being added to) have been re-erected on the site, and they contain around 60,000 artefacts which provide a comprehensive picture of the lifestyles of rural inhabitants from all over Lithuania from the 18th to the early 20th century. The buildings are arranged in groups according to the country's four ethnographic divisions, and the presence of farmyard animals (including Samogitian horses, which are bred on the stud farm), and the planting of fruit trees and both kitchen and floral gardens ensure that the original settings are reproduced as accurately as possible. A 6.5km asphalt path goes all the way round the museum; three hours is the absolute minimum amount of time needed for even a relatively superficial visit, and there is certainly enough to see to justify a full-day outing.

The circuit begins with the exhibition of traditional folk sculpture in the gallery just behind the ticket office. This gives the opportunity to compare 19th-century works with those produced today by carvers working in the same style. The path then leads straight ahead to the bridge over the Praviena stream, at the point where it enters the Kaunas Sea. On the opposite side, it can be followed in either a clockwise or anticlockwise direction. Heading clockwise, it loops round to the largest section, that of Samogitia (Žemaitija), which features a manor-house, a windmill and a sawmill as well as several farmsteads, while in the woods to the south is an inn where Lithuanian cuisine can be sampled. In a secluded setting away from the traditional wooden farms is a *numas*, an earthwork house invented by Bronze Age peoples, which survived in the region until recent times, latterly as an auxiliary agricultural building.

The path continues on to a partial re-creation of a Lithuanian village, whose houses are used for practical demonstrations of traditional handicrafts, such as woodcarving, weaving, basket-making and pottery. A left and then a right turn lead to the small Suvalkija section, from where the path continues straight ahead to the Aukštaitija section. This features a number of farms grouped together as on a village street, plus an octagonal wooden church with a steeply pitched roof containing a large collection of carved crucifixes. Originally the church stood in a cemetery; nowadays, in a neat turn of fate, it is a popular venue for weddings. The circuit is completed by a loop down to the Dzūkija section, in which several farms are picturesquely grouped in the Praviena valley.

Getting there and around There are seven buses a day running directly between Kaunas and Rumšiškės. Alternatively, it is a 2km walk from the Rumšiškės stop on the Kaunas–Vilnius highway, on which there are regular services in both directions. On summer Sundays, there are cruises between Pažaislis and Rumšiškės.

THE LOWER NEMUNAS VALLEY Following its confluence with the Neris at Kaunas, the Nemunas changes from its hitherto serpentine course, and follows a relatively direct route towards the Curonian Lagoon. Although the river is not at its most picturesque in its lower valley, it is majestic none the less. Up until 2000, it was possible to travel from Kaunas all the way to Nida by hydrofoil: there was a return service daily except Monday from June 1 to September 1. This was by far the longest cruise that could be taken within Lithuania, and its demise is a sad loss. It is to be hoped that some means will be found of re-instating the service. Until that happens, a car is the best means of exploring the area.

Many castles can be seen along the valley, legacies of the period when the Nemunas was the border between Lithuania and the lands of the Teutonic Knights. Because of the area's turbulent history, the castles were often destroyed, though some were rebuilt in the 19th century. An example of this is **Raudondvaris**, just a few kilometres out of Kaunas at the confluence with the Nevėžis. Once the property of the Radvilas, it passed to the Tiškevičius dynasty, who commissioned the Italian architect Cesare Anichini to reconstruct it in Neo-Gothic style.

A further 35km downstream, at the point where the Dubysa flows into the Nemunas, is the village of **Seredžius**, above which is an ancient hill fort. According to legend, this was either the sanctuary of the goddess Romava, or the stronghold of Duke Palemonas, father of the founder of Kaunas. The next castle, 10km on at **Veliuona**, is reputed to be the burial place of Grand Duke Gediminas, who was killed there by the Teutonic Knights. It is then 10km to **Raudonė**, once the property of the Kirchensteins, a German mercantile family, and in the 19th century of the Faria de Castro family from Portugal. The main tower was rebuilt as recently as 1968. On the south bank, a similar distance on, is **Gelgaudiškis**, once the seat of the Gelgaudas family, ancestors of the British actor Sir John Gielgud.

The first bridge spanning the Nemunas comes another 14km downstream at **Jurbarkas**, a small industrial town at the confluence with the Mituva. Before World War II it was an important Jewish centre, boasting a synagogue which was recognised as a masterpiece of wooden architecture. Sadly, this was totally destroyed prior to the massacre of the community itself.

After a further 10km, the river becomes the international border with the Kaliningrad oblast of Russia (which, prior to 1945, was the German province of East Prussia) and remains so all the way to the delta near its mouth. Another 12km on, the Nemunas is joined by the Viešvilė at the village of the same name. Immediately to the north of the latter is the **Viešvilė Reservation**, a strictly controlled area notable for its large populations of birds and fish. The smallest of Lithuania's four state nature reserves, it embraces most of the river's 21.4km length, together with the surrounding swampy moorland and forest.

Among the places subsequently passed on the Russian side is **Sovetsk**, a grimy industrial centre of smoking haystacks which is the largest town in the oblast after Kaliningrad itself. In German times, it was called Tilsit, and is best known for the humiliating treaty signed there in 1807, when Napoleon forced Prussia's King Friedrich Wilhelm III to cede half his country's territory and population. The bridge over the river was named in honour of Friedrich Wilhelm's wife, Queen Luise, who unsuccessfully petitioned the French emperor for lenient terms. It was destroyed, the grandiose gateway apart, by the retreating Nazis in 1944, but subsequently rebuilt by the Soviets.

PRIENAI Prienai, which is 40km south of Kaunas on the main road to Alytus and Druskininkai, stretches over both banks of the Nemunas at the far end of one of the most extravagant loops in the river, where it travels some 20km while moving its course by little more than 1km. There are good views upstream and downstream from the bridge linking the two parts of the town. The dominant monument is the wooden **Church of the Epiphany** on the left bank, a fine example of folk architecture inspired by the monumental Baroque style. In its present form, it dates back to 1750, though the two chapels, which transformed the ground-plan into a Greek cross, were not added until 1875. The façade, which has a triangular pediment topped with a turret flanked by twin towers, is particularly imposing, while the interior is furnished with a carved pulpit, altars and other decoration. A wooden house at Martišiaus 9 is home to the local history collections of the **Prienai Area Museum** (⊕ *08.00–17.00 Mon–Thu, 08.00–16.00 Fri, 10.00–15.00 Sat*).

Getting there and around
🚌 **Bus station** Vytauto 11; ☎ 319 52333. There is usually at least 1 bus per hr to Kaunas & to Alytus, around 2 per hr to Birštonas, 9 daily to Druskininkai & 7 daily to Vilnius via Aukštadvaris & Trakai.

BIRŠTONAS Birštonas, Lithuania's second-ranking spa resort, is 7km southeast of Prienai, near the narrowest point of the isthmus formed by the Nemunas loop. As might be expected from its strategic position, it is a place of some antiquity, having been settled as far back as the 4th or 3rd century BC. It was mentioned in the chronicles of the Teutonic Knights in 1382 as the site of a Lithuanian castle; this was converted into a hunting lodge in more peaceful times, but no longer exists.

After several centuries of decline, Birštonas revived in the 19th century, when saline springs were discovered; the first sanatorium was built in 1855 and soon attracted visitors from all over the Russian Empire. Badly damaged in World War I, it was placed under the control of the Lithuanian Red Cross in 1924 and soon afterwards entered its golden era. As Druskininkai had been annexed by Poland, Birštonas was developed as Lithuania's showpiece health resort. New spa buildings, hotels and a hydropathic and mud-cure house were built; the bottling of the mineral waters Vytautas and Birutė for general sale was initiated; the spa orchestra gave two concerts daily; and not only Lithuanians but also Germans from neighbouring East Prussia flocked to take cures. In the Soviet period, Birštonas went into decline, but revived again in the late 1960s. Nowadays, about 2,000 patients annually are treated in two sanatoria, and in even-numbered years a springtime jazz festival is held.

The **Birštonas Museum** (⊕ *10.00–17.00 Wed–Sun*) occupies a wooden house at Vytauto 9, in the residential district west of the Spa Park. It contains archaeological finds, a carriage from 1903, old photographs and medical equipment, and documentary material (most translated into English) about the history of the town. A branch, the **Sacred Art Museum** (⊕ *10.00–17.00 Wed–Sun*), is at Birutės 8. Otherwise, there are no obvious sights, though there are plenty of pleasant places to go for a stroll, whether along the Nemunas promenade or the footpaths through the adjacent woods. In summer, motorboat cruises are run, and rowing boats can be hired.

Getting there and around
🚌 **Bus station** Vaižganto 10; ☎ 319 56333. Located in the western part of town. Service frequencies are similar to those from Prienai, except that there are not so many direct buses to Kaunas & Alytus.

Tourist information
ℹ **Tourist office** Jaunimo 3; ☎/f 319 65740; e turizmas@birstonas.lt; www.visitbirstonas.lt. ⊕ 09.00–18.00 Mon–Fri, 10.00–18.00 Sat.

Where to stay

Sanatoria These are geared principally to long-stay guests, but also cater to those making a short visit. Room rates, which include three dietary meals, are slightly higher in summer than at other times.

Tulpė Sruogos 4; ☏ 319 65525; f 319 65520; e santulpe@mail.lt; www.tulpe.lt. Accommodation is in low-rise flats in the park close to the Nemunas. $$

Versmė Sruogos 25; ☏/f 319 65663; e registratura@is.lt; www.versme.com. As well as the usual spa facilities, it offers car & bike hire, tennis courts & sports halls. $$

Where to eat

✗ Birštono Seklytėlė Prienų 10. A riverside restaurant with a pleasant terrace.

STAKLIŠKĖS

Stakliškės, which lies 10km east of Birštonas, just north of the main road to Vilnius, is best known for the production of mead, which was revived, using age-old recipes and techniques, in 1959. Fourteen different varieties are made at present, including the reddish *Šventinė*, in which the honey is mixed with the juice of cranberries, cherries and blueberries, and *Suktinis*, a powerful mead balsam. The Baroque **Church of the Holy Trinity**, built in the 1760s to replace its wooden predecessor, has a monumental façade with twin towers and Corinthian columns framing the doorway and window.

KĖDAINIAI

Some 55km north of Kaunas is Kėdainiai, which has suffered more than its share of wartime destruction down the centuries, but is none the less the only medium-sized town in Lithuania which still preserves something of the feel and appearance of the melting-pot tradition that was once so characteristic of the country. First documented in 1372, Kėdainiai was associated with the powerful Radvila (Radziwiłł) family from 1445, and reached its zenith after they gained control over the whole of the town in 1614. Under Kristupas II Radvila (1585–1640) – whose grandfather Mikalojus Radvila 'the Red' and father Kristupas I Radvila 'the Thunderer' rank among Lithuania's greatest military heroes, both having led the nation's armies to victories over Russian forces which were several times larger – it became a centre of Renaissance culture and the Protestant faith, and continued as such under his son Jonušas (1612–55). Splendidly monumental public buildings were constructed; the first Lithuanian print-house was set up in 1651; and Calvinists from Scotland were encouraged to settle.

In 1655 Kėdainiai was the setting for the signing of a treaty with Sweden which would have broken Lithuania's long-standing political ties to Poland. However, this met with a good deal of internal opposition and was in any case forestalled by a Russian invasion in which the town was laid waste. Kėdainiai's influence also declined sharply as a result of the success of the Jesuit-led Counter-Reformation from Vilnius. Not until the coming of the railway in 1871 did it begin to recover from more than two centuries in the doldrums, developing as an industrial and trading town. It was badly damaged by the Germans in 1944 and hastily reconstructed with the usual Soviet indifference towards aesthetic considerations. Since independence, a welcome reversal of this policy has been initiated. Nowadays, with a population of 35,000, Kėdainiai has a mixed industrial base, including chemicals, metals, sugar refining, grain processing and electrical equipment.

Getting there and around

Bus station Basanavičiaus 93; ☏ 347 60333. This is located only just within the town's southern boundary. There are 1 or 2 services per hr to Kaunas, & approximately 1 per hr to both Šiauliai & Panevėžys.

Railway station Dariaus ir Gireno 5; ☎ 347 52333. Still preserving its original building, this is at the opposite side of town, just west of the top end of Basanavičiaus. It is on the Vilnius–Šiauliai line, with 4 daily trains in each direction.

Where to stay

Grejaus Namas Didžioji 36; ☎ 347 51500; f 347 67154; e hotel@grejausnamas.lt; www.grejausnamas.lt. 'Gray's House', which was built in the 18th century for a Scottish settler, has recently been converted into a midrange hotel with restaurant. Bathing facilities are planned for the future. $$, suites $$$

Aroma Rex Didžioji 52; ☎/f 347 55555; e hotel@aroma.lt; www.aroma.lt. New 5-room hotel in the town centre. $$

Where to eat

Ritmas Didžioji 44. This small & inexpensive café is the best option among a very limited choice of places, other than the hotels, to have a full meal.

What to see and do

The town A long street, Basanavičiaus, runs all the way through the town in a general northwest to southeast direction, roughly paralleling the course of the River Nevėžis somewhat to the north. Most of the Old Town is bordered by Basanavičiaus, the south bank of the Nevėžis and by the latter's tributary, the Smilga. However, several historic buildings lie beyond these boundaries, including the Gothic **Church of St George**, the oldest in town, which is on the opposite side of the Nevėžis.

Dominating the town centre is the massive, austere bulk of the **Reformed Church** (*guided tours ⊕09.00–17.00 Mon–Fri by application to the Kėdainiai Area Museum*), one of the most imposing Calvinist temples ever built. Constructed in late Renaissance style between 1631 and 1653, it has a fortress-like appearance, the plain walls enlivened only by the tympana above the tall windows and by the turrets, two square and two octagonal, at each corner. A detached belfry was erected alongside in the 18th century. In the communist period, the church's rectagonal ground-plan recommended it for ready conversion into a sports hall; it was subsequently used for concerts and large-scale events, but was eventually returned to the small congregation of Calvinists remaining in the town. Of the original furnishings, the splendid oak pulpit still survives minus its stairway, as do a number of panels made from the same wood. In the crypt is the only extant ducal mausoleum in Lithuania. The oldest sarcophagus, which is Renaissance in style and made of pewter, is of Kristupas I Radvila 'the Thunderer', who actually had no more than a fleeting connection with Kėdainiai. Alongside is the magnificent gilded silver tomb of Jonušas Radvila, which was made in the royal workshops. The four small sarcophagi are of his children Elžbieta, Jurgis, Mikalojus and Steponas, all of whom died young.

To the rear of the Reformed Church is the main market square, Didžioji rinka, on which stand some impressive gabled merchants' houses and the **Town Hall**, part of which is now an art gallery (⊕09.00–17.00 Tue–Sat) hosting temporary exhibitions of paintings, sculptures and photography. More fine mansions can be seen on Senoji, on the opposite side of the Reformed Church, among them the rector's house of 1650 at Senoji 2–4. This was the residence of the head of the high school or gymnasium, which was established in 1625 at the southern end of Didžioji, the Old Town's main axis.

At Didžioji 19 is the former conventual building of the Carmelite Friary, which was established in the early 18th century as part of an attempt to return the town to the Roman Catholic fold. A few years ago it underwent a highly successful conversion to become the new home of the **Kėdainiai Area Museum** (*www.kedainiumuzuejus.lt;* ⊕ *09.00–17.00 Tue–Sat*). The eclectic displays, which are mostly well labelled in English, include a wide-ranging group of archaeological finds; the sash of Kristupas II Radvila and the robe of Jonušas Radvila; an astonishing set of English-made 19th-century furniture decorated with stags' heads which formerly adorned Apytalaukis, a nearby stately home; and an imposing group of wooden crosses, most of which were carved by Vincas Svirkis.

Jews, who made up over half Kėdainiai's population in the 19th century, lived in the west of the old town. A number of their wooden houses can be seen on Senoji and Smilgos, which leads off it to the south. At the end of the former street is a square on which stands the recently restored **Old Synagogue**, whose architecture is similar to that of the Reformed Church. A smaller synagogue alongside serves as an exhibition centre, while a third, at Smilgos 13, is now a hardware shop.

On Radvilu, which runs parallel to Didžioji to the east, is the main Catholic place of worship, the **Church of St Joseph**. A twin-towered wooden construction with detached belfry, it is of a type usually associated with Lithuanian villages, though it originally served the friary. It is decorated inside in a folksy manner, and has an appropriately rustic setting in its own enclosure.

The **Lutheran Church**, a plain Renaissance building with three small chapels in its grounds, was built between 1629 and 1640 on a hillock just to the southeast of the Old Town, and is clearly visible from Basanavičiaus. Its original congregation was predominantly German in origin, and numerically small in comparison with Kėdainiai's Calvinist community – hence its relatively modest dimensions. Until a few years ago, it served as an exhibition hall where local handicrafts could be purchased, but it is now once again used for worship. Further up Basanavičiaus, facing the southern end of Didžioji, is the **Russian Orthodox Church**.

In an isolated park setting at Basanavičiaus 45, on the far side of the Smilga stream, is the former home of the Kėdainiai Area Museum. This is now known as the **Janina Monkutė-Marks Museum-Gallery** (*www.jmm-muziejus.lt;* ⊕ *10.00–18.00 Wed–Fri, 12.00–15.00 Sat–Sun*) in honour of its founder, an émigré artist who has donated a collection of her own works and also provided funds for changing exhibitions of Lithuanian contemporary art. Further along the same street, a larger park straddles both banks of the Dotnevėlė, another Nevėž tributary. In it stands the **Kėdainiai Minaret**, a folly built by Count Totleben, the then local lord, in commemoration of his service in the Tsarist army in the 1877–78 war against the Turks.

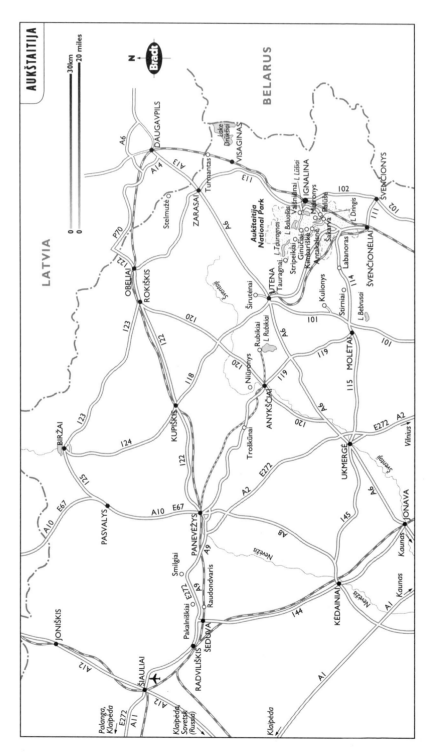

AUKŠTAITIJA

9

Aukštaitija

Aukštaitija, Lithuania's 'Highlands', is one of the country's four ethnographic regions, but its boundaries are not at all precise. In its widest sense, the term refers to the territory of the most dominant of the original Lithuanian tribes, who united with the neighbouring Samogitians to the west to form the medieval Grand Duchy. Under this definition, Aukštaitija incorporates the whole of the eastern part of the country, including Vilnius and even Dzūkija. However, the term is also used in a narrower sense to refer to the northeastern part of the country – comprising the modern counties of Utena and Panevėžys, plus small parts of the counties of Vilnius and Šiauliai – and it is this area which forms the subject of the chapter.

AUKŠTAITIJA NATIONAL PARK

The 40,570-hectare Aukštaitija National Park, founded in 1974 to protect the finest lake and forest landscapes of the so-called Lithuanian Highlands, is by far the oldest in the country. It has also been something of a model for the others, in that it covers a relatively large area incorporating numerous villages, hamlets and farms, with strictly controlled nature reserves accounting for only a tiny percentage of the total. To a certain extent, a traditional rural way of life based on labour-intensive farming has been preserved, though this has been diluted more than in, for example, the Dzūkija National Park. The great attraction of the park is its wonderful sense of stillness. Outside the summer tourist season, at least, it is possible to walk for hours without meeting anyone, while the only noises likely to be encountered are the rustling of the trees and the occasional bird call.

INFORMATION AND MAPS The National Park's own 1:65,000 map is generally quite serviceable, but it is not quite detailed enough for the purposes of serious hiking – although many of the paths are shown, others are not. Given that there are no wayside markings this can, amid the labyrinthine network of tracks in the depths of the forests, pose serious orientation problems for the unwary.

TOURISM AND TRANSPORT Having been established so long, the Aukštaitija National Park has far more facilities than any of its counterparts, with the obvious exception of the Curonian Spit, and has an enormous tourist base – virtually amounting to a holiday village – beside its headquarters in Palūšė. There are also 18 officially designated camping places throughout the park – all clearly marked on the maps – which can be used on payment of a small registration fee to the authorities. Being easily accessible from Vilnius, the park attracts a large number of day trippers as well as those taking a full-length vacation. However, it is very much a summertime destination; the numbers fall to a trickle in other seasons, and most of the people who visit do so at weekends only. Of these, many come solely to pick mushrooms or berries, though others prefer to go hiking or sailing

GETTING THERE AND AROUND The easiest method of approaching the Aukštaitija National Park is to take a Turmantas-bound train from Vilnius (there are six daily) to the industrial town of Ignalina, which lies immediately outside its eastern boundary, just 5km from Palūšė. *En route*, the train passes through the southeastern part of the park, entering it just north of Švenčionėliai, and subsequently travelling along the western side of Lake Kretuonas, the park's largest.

Unfortunately, bus services to complete the journey are very scarce. There are six daily services in each direction between Ignalina and Palūšė, of which three are part of long-distance routes, while three are on ancient little local buses whose other terminus is the village of Antalksnė in the west of the park. No further buses run northwards from there, though the north of the park can be reached from Utena, there being four daily buses to Tauragnai, just outside the far northwestern boundary.

By car/bike For those travelling by car or bike, there are small and large circular routes round the park on serviceable if sometimes rather rough roads, enabling a good cross-section of the scenery to be seen in a short time. In a clockwise direction, the shorter route travels southwest from Ignalina via Palūšė to Šakarva, which is situated between Lake Šakarvai and the 12km-long, finger-like Lake Žeimenys. From there, it goes northwest via Antalksnė to Kimbariškė, then passes northwards along the narrow strip of land separating Lakes Linkmenas and Ūkojas to Ginučiai. It continues east along the southern sides of the small Lake Jaskutis and the much larger, isle-strewn Lake Baluošas to Vaišniūnai on the north shore of the heavily indented Lake Dringis, finally passing down the eastern side of the last-named to return to Ignalina.

The larger loop follows the same route to Kimbariškė, but then continues northwestwards, for the most part just outside the boundaries of the park, to Tauragnai. It then goes eastwards along the north shoreline of Lake Tauragnas, Lithuania's deepest lake, continuing onwards to Šeimatis. From there, it continues southeast to Daunoriai, where there is the opportunity of making a detour south to Stripeikiai. The main road, however, maintains its southeasterly direction and passes Strazdai on the eastern bank of Lake Baluošas before joining up again with the shorter route at the junction just before Vaišniūnai.

Many of the forest paths are also passable for cars and bikes – they are, after all, treated as roads by the local farmers and foresters – but are only recommendable to those who do not mind bumpy rides.

By boat/foot The two best ways of travelling in the park are by boat and on foot. The former is a particularly pleasant way to see a great deal of otherwise inaccessible scenery, and is an efficient method of transport thanks to the presence of numerous channels and rivulets linking one lake to another. All the readily navigable water routes are marked on the maps of the park.

A reasonable portion of the park can be seen on day-long hikes from Palūšė, particularly if walking is supplemented by judicious use of the local buses. For those wanting to do more ambitious trekking, the ubiquity of the campsites makes it is easy to undertake a longer linear or circular trip lasting several days.

GEOGRAPHY The Aukštaitija National Park is a post-glacial landscape which began to assume its present appearance around 16,000 years ago. Its highest hills are over 200m in altitude, though the average height is around 150m. The hollows left by the glaciers are filled with crystalline lakes; there are over 100 in the park, accounting for more than 15% of its total area. Only ten lakes are of more than 100 hectares, whereas there are 36 of less than 5 hectares; these tend to be shallow and to have swampy shorelines. Some 70% of the park is forested, with pines predominant. The average age of the trees is around 60 to 70 years, though some are as much as 200 years old.

FLORA AND FAUNA The undulating relief of the park encourages the growth of a wide variety of flora. Indeed, nearly 60% of all Lithuania's indigenous species grow there, a remarkable total given that the area of the park occupies only 0.5% of the country as a whole. Many very rare plants are to be found, including a lobelia which grows in only two other locations in Lithuania. At the other end of the scale, there are no fewer than 628 species of fungi, including 112 types of edible mushrooms.

The park's fauna are typical of that of the country as a whole. Among the 50-odd mammals are roe deer, red deer, elks, mountain hares, brown hares, wolves, wild boar, foxes, pine martens and racoons, while a solitary brown bear was spotted in 1991. Beavers and mink live in the waterways. There are also 11 species of amphibian and 29 of fish, the most common being pike, perch, roach and bream. Of the 193 species of birds which have been recorded in the park, 135 breed there. Some of them are rare. It is, for example, the only place in Lithuania that bramblings' nests have been found. In the migratory period, white-tailed and golden eagles visit, as do large numbers of snipes and peregrines. A particularly rich variety of insects includes around 500 beetles and 60 butterflies.

ETHNOGRAPHY Around 2,000 people live within the Aukštaitija National Park. They are spread over 116 different settlements, of which little more than a handful have a population of over 100, with Kaltanėnai, the largest, numbering around 300 inhabitants. Most of the hamlets are groupings of several farmsteads, but there are also a few so-called street villages. In the latter, the houses are laid out along both sides of a single thoroughfare, with the narrow side of the living quarters facing the street, and the auxiliary agricultural buildings to the rear. The northern part of the park is very sparsely populated, with isolated farmsteads being the norm.

Although the style of farming is very traditional, with much heavy work done by hand, and horses still the favoured means of ploughing the land, there is an increasing use of tractors. The presence of these, and of cars and other mod cons, provides evidence that the general standard of living is now well above the old subsistence level.

IGNALINA Justifiably, the boundaries of the National Park have been drawn so as to exclude **Ignalina**, a nondescript town which grew up around the railway, part of the Warsaw–St Petersburg line. Nevertheless, it is hard to avoid, being the hub of local communications and transport. It is also worth considering as an accommodation base.

Where to stay

⌂ **Žuvėdra** Mokyklos 11; ✆ 386 52314; e info@zuvedra.com; www.zuvedra.com. New hotel by the southern shore of Lake Paplovinis, in the northwestern part of town. It has a restaurant, sauna & various bathing facilities. $$, suites $$$

⌂ **Žiemos Sporto Centras** Sporto 3; ✆ 386 54193. This winter sports centre, which is open all year round, is reached by crossing the railway tracks & continuing straight ahead for 1.5km. $

PALŪŠĖ Palūšė has a pretty setting on the eastern shore of Lake Lūšiai, and the northern edge of the village is a wonderful vantage point for sunsets, offering as it does an uninterrupted view westwards over the waters to a low horizon. The **Church of St Joseph**, situated on a little hillock in the heart of Palūšė, is undoubtedly the most famous of all Lithuania's multitude of wooden churches, thanks in large part to its appearance on the reverse of the now withdrawn 1Lt note. Built between 1747 and 1757, it is a plain, very geometrical design, with a rectangular nave and a pentagonal apse. The detached belfry, which doubled as the entrance to the enclosure prior to the erection of a separate gate alongside, is somewhat fancier, featuring an upper storey of open arcades covered by a pyramidal roof. Inside the church (which is normally open for Mass every morning except Saturday), slender pillars divide the nave from the aisles. There are also many folksy furnishings, including three altars, a pulpit with an elevated doorway to the sacristy, confessionals, and a set of processional banners.

In the immediate outskirts of Palūšė is what seems to be the only walking route in the Aukštaitija National Park identified with waymarkings. Dubbed the botanical trail, it begins at the very northern end of the village, following a circular 5km-long route through the pine woods to a tiny overgrown lake, then along the northern shore of Lake Tarama to the dirt road at its far end. It is well worth following this a short distance south for a lovely view over Lake Dringykštis to the west. However, the waymarked path doubles back through the wood high above the south shore of Lake Tarama, before arriving back at Lake Lūšiai just west of the starting-point.

Tourist information

🛈 **Aukštaitija National Park** ☏ 386 52891; e info@paluse.lt; www.paluse.lt. In addition to selling maps, this office rents canoes, rowing boats, water cycles, windsurfing boards, bikes & sleeping bags, & offers guided tours on foot or by bus.

🏠 Where to stay

🏠 **Tourism & Recreation Centre** ☏ 386 21404, 47430; f 386 53135; e info@paluse.lt; www.paluse.lt. Simple rooms equipped only with beds & wardrobe are available within the administration building, slightly more appealing rooms with shared private facilities in the chalets in the grounds. $ This is also the place to book the more luxurious rooms which are available in the Ecology Education Centre on the north shore of Lake Lūšiai ($) & in the watermill in Ginučiai ($$).

✗ Where to eat

✗ **Aukštaičių Užeiga** Located directly in front of the Tourism & Recreation Centre, this outwardly unimposing building has an extraordinary interior dotted with a whole series of snug imitation log cabins. A wide range of good & inexpensive Lithuanian dishes is on offer.

ELSEWHERE IN THE NATIONAL PARK From the northern end of Palūšė, the trail along the shore of Lake Lūšiai passes a number of folk sculptures *en route* to **Meironys**, 2km away. One of the most characteristic of the street villages, it is situated by the channel which links Lake Lūšiai with Lake Asalnai. A dirt road goes all the way through Meironys, and continues on through the woods to the north of Lake Asalnai, which can be glimpsed occasionally through the trees. Some 2km from the end of the village, the second main forest track to the right leads after a further 2.5km to a strict nature reserve centred on Lake Baltys.

Alternatively, just a little way beyond, a footpath on the left-hand side leads up to the hamlet of **Puziniškas**, from where there is a superb backwards panorama over Lake Asalnai, then, a little further on, another fine view over the smaller Lake Asalnykštis to the west.

Backtracking a little, a path leads northwards then west down to the bridge over the rivulet linking Lakes Asalnykštis and Linkmenas, then swings round to the left to reach **Salos II**, a well-preserved example of the hamlets made up of several farmsteads. The smaller **Salos I** is a dead-end, situated on higher ground a few hundred metres to the south. A further 2km to the northwest is Ladakalnis, a wooded hill offering a view over several lakes.

About 4km north is **Ginučiai**, a fine old village with a 19th-century watermill, which the National Park authorities have converted into a small guesthouse and exhibition centre, laid out along the land separating Lakes Stravinaitis and Almajos. This can also be reached more directly by following the main dirt road all the way from Meironys, which is some 8km away. A signposted path leads from the village to an early medieval defensive mound, which can be ascended via wooden steps and offers a sweeping panoramic view.

Another road leads northwest from Ginučiai to **Stripeikiai**, 5km away. This hamlet, which has apparently been inhabited since the 14th century, is the home of the **Ancient Bee-keeping Museum** (⊕*1 May–15 Oct 10.00–19.00 Tue–Sun*), which is claimed as the only one of its type in Europe. It displays over 400 exhibits illustrating Lithuania's diverse bee-keeping traditions, including many examples of the old log and straw hives (which are still a feature of many of the farmsteads of the park), as well as modern frame hives.

UTENA COUNTY

While the star tourist attraction of Utena County is undoubtedly its share of the Aukštaitija National Park (a part of which lies within Vilnius County), there are various other places in the province of more than passing interest.

VISAGINAS Lithuania's newest town is Visaginas, which lies 35km northeast of Ignalina, close to the borders with Belarus and Latvia. Founded in 1975, it was originally named Sniečkus in honour of the long-time leader of the Lithuanian Communist Party, and was built to house the workforce of the Ignalina nuclear power plant, which was built between 1978 and 1983 on the southern shore of Lake Drūkšiai, 2km to the east. This is equipped with two antiquated reactors which supply 80% of Lithuania's electricity, thereby making it more dependent on nuclear power than any other country in the world. The reactors are of the same type as the one at the Ukrainian plant of Chernobyl which exploded in 1986, causing disastrous fall-out effects. There was immediate concern about the safety of Ignalina, and plans to install two further reactors there were abandoned in 1988 following massive public protest. A huge amount of foreign aid has been spent in attempts to ensure the safety of the existing reactors, one of which is due to shut down in 2005, with the other following suit by the end of the decade.

Visaginas itself is an eerie place which none the less has a certain curiosity value as a living example of the ideal town of the Soviet mindset, with a largely working-class population housed in identikit high-rise apartment blocks. Only around 15% of the 28,000 inhabitants are Lithuanian; the vast majority of the others are Russian, and most signs are bi-lingual. Even the simple act of arriving has an air of unreality. The main transport link with the outside world is the Vilnius–Ignalina–Turmantas railway, on which six trains run daily in each direction. However, the station looks like that of a rural hamlet: there are no houses behind, only buses waiting to begin their circular route down the deserted highway to the town.

Where to stay
🏠 **Aukštaitija** Veteranų 9; ☎/f 386 74858, 75025. Predictably, this high-rise hotel, which has the town's only fully-fledged restaurant, is typically Soviet in style & appearance. $$, suites $$$

MOLĖTAI Immediately west of the National Park is another lake district, centred on the town of Molėtai, which lies 62km north of Vilnius. The town itself is built around the interconnected Lakes Pastovelis and Pastovis; immediately to the east is the much larger Lake Siesartis; while to the south are Lakes Luokesai, Kirneilis and Bebrusai, the last of which is a hugely popular holiday and recreation area. Molėtai is known to have existed since at least 1387, though it preserves little in the way of historic monuments. The **Church of SS Peter and Paul** at the eastern end of Vilniaus, the main street, is a Neo-Baroque building of 1905. Of similar vintage are the redbrick shops on the market square just to the west, which were originally the property of Jewish traders.

Tourist information
🔲 **Tourist office** Inturkės 4; ☎/f 383 51187; e turizmas@moletai.lt; www.infomoletai.lt. Located within the local administration building, immediately south of the main square. Offers a booking service for accommodation in local farms or campsites; English spoken. ⊕08.00–18.00 Mon–Thu, 08.00–17.00 Fri, 10.00–14.00 Sat.

Getting there and around
🚌 **Bus station** Vilniaus 2; ☎ 383 51333. Situated at the extreme northeast edge of town. There is usually at least 1 bus per hr to Utena, as well as upwards of 12 daily to Vilnius, three to Ignalina via Palūšė & 3 to Panevėžys via Anykščiai.

 ## Where to stay
Molėtai's only hotel has been converted for other purposes. However, there are plenty of chalets with rooms to let in the following campsites on the eastern bank of Lake Bebrusai, 5km southeast of town. The snag is that they are served by only a couple of buses per day in each direction on the Molėtai–Žydavainiai route, though most of the sites have bikes for rent, while taxis can be picked up at the bus station for a nominal cost. Rates vary according to type of room and length of stay, but all are $.

🏠 **Bebrusai** ☎ 383 51578; e vizba@vilnius.balt.net; www.bebrusai.lt

🏠 **Papartis** ☎ 383 52120, 52110; f 383 527090
🏠 **Rūta** ☎/f 686 66750

✖ Where to eat
✖ **Lelija** Vilniaus 48a. A pleasant café-restaurant on Molėtai's main street, offering typical Lithuanian dishes.

LABANORAS REGIONAL PARK The most beautiful part of the lake district around Molėtai lies within the 50,000-hectare Labanoras Regional Park, whose western boundary stops just short of the town. A heavily forested area with patches of swamp, the park, the largest of its type in Lithuania, also boasts some pretty villages. Among these is **Labanoras** itself, 23km from Molėtai along the road to Palūšė, which has an 18th-century wooden church with detached belfry. About halfway between Labanoras and Molėtai is **Stirniai**, whose church is comprised entirely of fieldstones.

The park is best known for the set-piece attractions in the hamlet of **Kulionys**, which lies at the dead-end of a 4km-long road running northeast from the Molėtai–Utena highway, about 10km north of the former. Although there are bus stops along this road, there are only two buses per week in each direction (leaving Molėtai at 13.15 on Tue & Thu, and returning immediately).

The landscape around Kulionys is dominated by the weirdly futuristic towers of the **Ethnocosmology Museum** (*www.cosmos.lt;* ⊕*Apr-Oct 08.00–15.30 Tue–Sun, Nov–Mar 08.00-15.30 Tue–Sat*). Seemingly the only one of its kind in the world, it was founded in 1990 and is concerned with everything to do with cosmology, ranging from historic meteorological instruments and both astronomical and astrological calendars to music and art inspired by the subject. Unfortunately, arranging a visit is somewhat problematic; all visits are guided, and really need to be booked in advance by phoning ✆ 383 45424. It is possible to tag on to a pre-booked group, but turning up without a reservation invites the very real risk of finding the museum shut. The tour begins in a series of underground chambers, and ends up in the 45m-high observation tower, which gives a fabulous view over the surrounding lakeland.

A couple of hundred metres up the road is the **Molėtai Astronomical Observatory**, the most important in Lithuania. There are two telescopes, one of 165cm, the other of 63cm. Both daytime and night tours in English can be arranged, but advance booking is absolutely essential: ✆ 383 45444. In due course Kulionys will have a third attraction as an ethnographic open-air museum is in preparation.

UTENA The name of Utena, which lies 30km north of Molėtai, is synonymous with the Utenos brewery, which produces a wide variety of different styles of beer and is among the best and most popular in Lithuania. Unfortunately the town has little else to offer: although first documented in 1261, it has been destroyed repeatedly in war or by fire, most disastrously in 1871. The centre is pleasant enough, with lots of rustic-looking wooden houses, but almost the only sightseeing attraction is the **Utena Local Lore Museum** (⊕*10.00–18.00 Tue–Fri, 10.00–17.00 Sat*), on the corner of the main square at Utenio 1. This has the expected displays of local and natural history, ethnography and folk art.

Getting there and around
🚌 **Bus station** Basanavičiaus 52; ✆ 389 61740. Located in the centre. In addition to the approximately hourly service to Molėtai, there are around 12 daily buses to Vilnius, 4 to Širutėnai, 4 to Tauragnai & 3 to Daugavpils in Latvia.

Tourist information
ℹ️ **Tourist office** Utenio 5; ✆ 389 4346; www.utenainfo.lt; ⊕09.00–18.00 Mon–Fri, 12.00–13.00 Sat.

Where to stay
🏠 **Filomena** Basanavičiaus 101; ✆ 389 57776; f 389 05363; e filomena@tuzikieme.one.lt. This 6-room guesthouse is the only obvious accommodation option. 💲

ŠIRUTĖNAI In the small village of Širutėnai, 5km north of Utena, a round redbrick tower contains the privately owned **Bell Museum** (*no set opening hours*) of the sculptor Valentinas Simonelis. In the 1970s Simonelis travelled throughout Lithuania on a mission to save bells from the clutches of cultural commissars, who were keen to destroy them, along with sundry other religious artefacts, as being 'anti-communist'. He amassed a collection of around 300 bells of all sizes, and has supplemented this with an array of Soviet statues and other memorabilia, which are heaped up in a pile outside his workshop opposite the tower.

STELMUŽĖ In an isolated setting hard by the Latvian border, 60km northeast of Utena, Stelmužė is only readily accessible by car, which is rather a pity, as it is one of Lithuania's most remarkable villages. Not only does it have the country's oldest tree – an oak 11.9m in circumference which is believed to be anything from 1,000 to 1,500 years old – it also boasts an outstanding monument in the **Church of the Holy Cross** (⊕ *10.00–18.00 Tue–Sun*). Originally built in 1650 by the local landowner for Calvinist worship, it was reconstructed in 1713, with axes being the only tools used. In 1808, it was taken over by the Roman Catholics. The architecture of the church itself is plain and simple. In contrast to many of the country's other wooden churches, there is no attempt to imitate Baroque forms. However, the detached belfry is much grander than normal, with a hip roof protecting the open gallery which forms the upper storey. Even more notable are the church's rich furnishings, and the florid pulpit, featuring reliefs of the apostles on the basin and stairs and ethereal representations of cherubim and seraphim on the canopy, ranks as a true masterpiece of folk carving.

ANYKŠČIAI Anykščiai, which lies in the peaceful wooded countryside of the River Šventoji, 38km west of Utena and 44km northwest of Molėtai, is best known for its distinguished literary tradition. Above all, it was the inspiration for one of the seminal poems in the Lithuanian language, *The Anykščiai Grove* (sometimes known as *The Forest of Anykščiai*) which was written by Antanas Baranauskas (1835–1902) in 1858–59, during vacations in his studies for the priesthood. On one level it is a nature poem, a glorious evocation of the scents, sights and sounds of the local woodland; but it also has an impassioned nationalistic message, the forest serving as a metaphor for Lithuania, and its destruction a mirror of the sufferings of the nation under Russian rule.

The town's literary heritage is celebrated in the **Baranauskas and Vienuolis-Žukauskas Memorial Museum** (*www.baranauskas.lt;* ⊕*08.00/09.00–17.00/18.00 daily*), on the left side of the river at Vienuolio 4. There are two adjacent houses, one being the cottage where Baranauskas was born, and where he wrote *The Anykščiai Grove*. In 1922 this cottage was acquired by another distinguished author, Antanas Žukauskas, who wrote under the pseudonym of Vienuolis; he turned it into a museum and built a home for himself alongside. Baranauskas's house, now cocooned inside a protective glass building, documents his distinguished artistic and ecclesiastical career. He wrote some of Lithuania's most stirring patriotic songs, as well as many other poems and hymns, and he was also an enthusiastic musician who provided melodies for many of his own verses as well as harmonisations of Lithuanian folk songs. All the while, he rose in the Church hierarchy, eventually becoming Bishop of Seinai (now the Polish town of Sejny), where he translated the Bible into modern Lithuanian. Vienuolis, who is commemorated in the other house, was a short-story writer whose *Paskenduolė* tells the tragic tale of a young girl left with child while her lover leaves to seek his fortune in America. To the rear of the houses, and covered by the same entrance ticket, is an exhibition hall displaying Lithuanian landscapes (particularly of the Anykščiai region) by the local artist Stanislovas Petraška (b1935). He has a highly unusual technique, achieving a paint-like effect from the use of ground stones arranged in a similar way to mosaics.

Anykščiai's most prominent landmark, whose twin octagonal towers are visible from afar, is the redbrick Neo-Gothic **Church of St Matthew**, which stands high above the right bank of the Šventoji. Its large organ was brought in 1998 from Southampton's City Baptist Church. In the park outside is a monument to Baranauskas erected in 1993.

About 1km north of the town centre, at Vilties 1, is the **railway station**, the centrepiece of a remarkable period-piece complex from the early decades of the 20th century. In addition to the two-storey station itself, which was built in 1901, this features a storehouse, residential homes, a cobbled square, a water tower, a pump and a steel bridge over the River Šventoji. Oldest of all are the rails, some of which date back to 1878. A narrow-gauge railway exhibition (*www.baranauskas.lt;* ⊕*May–Oct 10.00–17.00 daily*) is gradually being developed throughout the complex.

There are also many possibilities for undemanding strolls along the river and into the hills, from where there are fine views of the valley. For a longer walk, the favourite destination is the **Puntukas boulder**, 5km to the southwest. Weighing around 265 tonnes, it is one of the largest of the many huge rocks deposited by glacial drift all over the Baltic region. A bas-relief of the ill-fated transatlantic pilots, Darius and Girėnas (see page 153), was carved on it in 1943.

Tourist information

🛈 **Tourist office** Gegužės 1; ☏/f 381 59177; e anyskciaiturinfo@erdvas.lt; www.antour.lt. ⊕09.00–17.00 daily.

Getting there and around

🚌 **Bus station** Vienuolio 1; ☏ 381 51333. There are approximately 7 buses daily to both Panevėžys & Kaunas, 5 to Utena, 4 to both Molėtai & Vilnius. Further connections to Vilnius can be obtained by taking a Kaunas-bound bus to Ukmergė & changing there.

🚆 **Railway station** Vilties 1; ☏ 381 51573. An intact period piece, located about 1km north of the bus station. See page 176 for details of the only services, on the narrow-gauge lines to Panevėžys & Rubikiai.

Where to stay

🏠 **Mindaugo Karūna** Liudiškių 19 ☏ 381 58520; f 381 58640; e info@mindaugokaruna.lt; www.mindaugokaruna.lt. This new hotel on the east side of town is by far the most luxurious option. The facilities include a restaurant, café-bar, sauna, swimming pool, tennis courts & a bowling alley. ⑂⑂

🏠 **Puntukas** Baranausko 8; ☏ 381 51345; f 381 51808. A town-centre hotel with a café. ⑂
🏠 **Šilelis** Vilniaus 80; ☏/f 381 58885, e an-silelis@post.omnitel.net; www.anyksciusilelis.lt. Located by the woods in the southern outskirts, this is a basic holiday & recuperation complex, likewise with a café. ⑂

NIŪRONYS The literary theme continues in the village of Niūronys, 6km north of Anykščiai, and connected to it by three daily buses, with the **Jonas Biliūnas Memorial Museum** (⊕*May–Aug 10.00–18.00 daily, Sep–Apr 08.00–17.00 Tue–Sat*). The short-lived Jonas Biliūnas (1879–1907) wrote tales with a philosophical bent, including one about a boy who dreams of becoming a brave hunter, but becomes remorseful after killing a cat with his bow and arrow.

Niūronys is also home to the **Horse Museum** (*www.arkliomuziejus.lt;* ⊕*08.00–17.00/18.00 daily*), a large collection of artefacts with an equine theme gathered by the agronomist and naturalist Petras Vasinauskas (1906–95). It is also possible to go horseriding (from 4Lt/km), or to hire a horse-drawn carriage (50–100Lt) for a trip around the surrounding countryside.

PANEVĖŽYS

Panevėžys, which lies midway between Vilnius and Rīga, is Lithuania's fifth largest city, with 114,000 inhabitants. Although it has been in existence since at

Established in 1899, the line between Panevėžys and Anykščiai is the only remaining part of Lithuania's once-extensive narrow-gauge railway network. Prior to 2001, it was still serviced by two daily passenger trains in each direction. Not the least of its attractions was that it was a wholly genuine local transport facility; although the journey could be accomplished far quicker by bus, the trains were well patronised, as the route passes through woodland and farmland which is otherwise served only by dirt roads, and it thus provided a vital link for the inhabitants of many hamlets and isolated farms. The only connotations with tourism concerned the line eastwards from Anykščiai to **Rubikiai**, which is situated at the northern tip of the lake of the same name. Previously, this was the first stage of the now broken connection to Utena, but was latterly serviced only by special excursion trains, generally on summer weekends.

Despite heavy passenger usage, the Panevėžys–Anykščiai line was expensive to maintain, and the decision was taken, despite widespread protests, to remove it from the regular network. Nevertheless, there was strong local determination that it would not be allowed to close down altogether, and, after a period of uncertainty, the line has been saved, albeit solely as a tourist attraction. It is possible to hire the entire train privately: prices range from 497Lt for Anykščiai to Rubikiai return by second class carriage, to 2,115Lt for Panevėžys to Rubikiai return by first class carriage, with numerous options in between.

Additionally, there are excursion services throughout the year which are open to anyone. These are most commonly on summer weekends, and are normally on the Ankyščiai to Rubikiai stage (12Lt return) only, though there are very occasional trips on the northernmost part of the line, from Panevėžys to the Kuzmiškio Forest (17Lt return). A full calendar of services is published annually; this can be accessed at www.siaurukas.eu, which also offers a full history and description of the line as well as news of the latest developments.

Of all the places along the route, the only one large enough to be considered a village is **Troškūnai**, which still preserves the form and appearance of a feudalistic estate settlement. It also has an imposing focal point in the **Church of the Holy Trinity**, which was built in 1789 in a style which bridges late Baroque and early Neo-Classicism. Unfortunately, Troškūnai lies on the section of line which is not currently covered by the excursion services.

least the early 16th century, it was a very modest-sized town prior to the Industrial Revolution, and the 20th century saw its population grow tenfold. It remains a major manufacturing centre, making dairy products, television tubes, compressors, electric cables, wire, flax, ceramics, glassware and beer, though it has one feature of potentially major interest to outsiders in the narrow-gauge railway to Anykščiai.

While the outer suburbs consist of a relentless series of high-rise apartment blocks, the centre, which is bordered to the north and east by the River Nevėžis, is far from unpleasant, with lots of old wooden houses in among the modern concrete. Panevėžys is well known for being bicycle-friendly, pioneering the special lanes for cyclists which are now common features of Lithuanian cities.

GETTING THERE AND AROUND

Bus station Savanorių 5; ℡ 45 463333. Situated in a cramped & very busy space right in the heart of the city, though the local council hopes to relocate it elsewhere. There are direct services to virtually all Lithuanian towns, including I or more per hr to Vilnius, approximately I per hr to Kaunas & Biržai, & 15 daily to Šiauliai, 4 of which continue to Klaipėda. There are also 5 buses daily to Rīga, 2 of which continue to Tallinn. Panevėžys is the first stop for travellers from Latvia who will find that the snack bar & kiosks at the bus station do not accept Latvian money. As there is no foreign exchange facility at the bus station, it may help to obtain some Lithuanian currency in Latvia before starting the journey.

Railway station Corner of Stoties & Kerbedžio; ℡ 45 463615. Located in the north of the city, a good 1.5km from the bus station. Its position as a passenger station is now precarious: apart from occasional excursions to Anykščiai, the only services are the 2 daily trains in each direction on the Šiauliai–Rokiškis line.

TOURIST INFORMATION

Tourist office Laisvės 11; ℡ 45 508081; f 45 508080; e pantic@takas.lt; www.panevezys.lt. ⊕ Apr–Sep 10.00–18.00 Mon–Fri, 09.00–14.00 Sat; Oct–Mar 08.00–17.00 Mon–Fri.

COMMUNICATIONS

Post office Respublikos 60.

WHERE TO STAY
The accommodation situation in the city has improved enormously, thanks to the opening of two new hotels; as an alternative, the tourist office has details of rooms in nearby farms.

Romantic Kranto 24; ℡ 45 584860; f 45 581162; e hotel.romantic@takas.lt; www.hotel.romantic.lt. A former mill overlooking the River Nevėžis has undergone a tasteful conversion into an upmarket hotel with restaurant. $$$

Panevėžys Laisvės 26; ℡/f 45 435117, e info@hotelpanevezys.lt; www.hotelpanevezys.lt. A huge tower block dominating the city centre, offering a largely undiluted Soviet-era experience. All rooms have private facilities, & a decent buffet b/fast plus hot dish in the first-floor café is included in the price. $$

Verso Klasė Smėltynės 104; ℡ 45 582032; f 45 582983; e verso.klase@takas.lt; www.versoklase.visiems.lt. New-build guesthouse with restaurant to the north of the city centre. $$

WHERE TO EAT
Panevėžys has a decent selection of places to eat, whether for a snack or a full meal.

Chili Laisvės 5. Recently opened branch of the Lithuanian pizza chain.

Galerija XX Laisvės 7. Popular café which serves inexpensive full meals. It is run in tandem with the commercial gallery next door, whose exhibitions are well worth a look.

Kakadu Laisvės 1. A good pizzeria on the main square.

Malūnas Ramygalos 121a. A cosy restaurant in an old mill in the south of the city.

Nendrė Vėjyjė Respublikos 6. Pleasant café which serves full meals.

Panevėžio Pienas Laisvės 25. Old-fashioned milk bar attached to a dairy shop.

Senvagė Laisvės 3a. Despite only billing itself as a café, this cellar restaurant is quite upmarket (though still reasonably priced), with a wide choice of dishes.

ENTERTAINMENT

Juozas Miltinis Drama Theatre Laisvės 5; ℡ 45 468691; www.miltinio-teatras.lt. This is the pride of Panevėžys's cultural scene, & is one of Lithuania's leading stages for straight drama.

Musical Theatre Nepriklausomybės 8; ℡ 45 584670. Presents concerts of all types as well as operas, operettas & musicals.

Puppet Theatre Respublikos 30; ℡ 45 460533. In summer, this company takes its children's shows on the road, touring Lithuania by horse-drawn wagon.

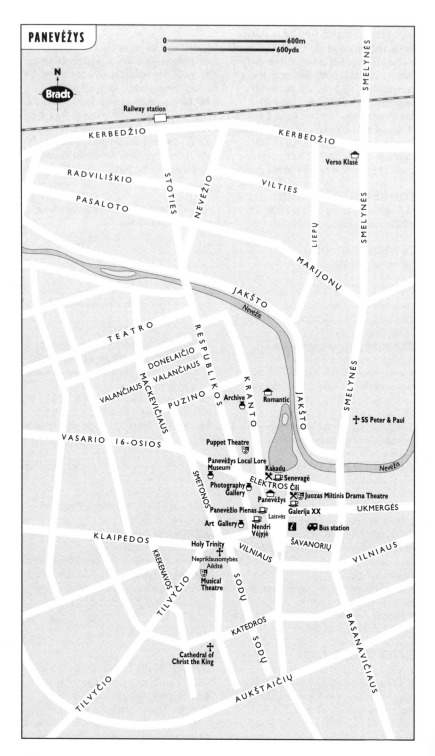

WHAT TO SEE AND DO

The city The centre of Panevėžys is a modern commercial district, with few obvious sights. Its oldest building, which dates back to the 17th century, is the former **Archive** at Kranto 21. In the past, it has contained a museum of folk art, but this has been closed for several years.

Just to the southwest, at Vasario 16-osios 23, is the **Panevėžys Local Lore Museum** (*www.paneveziomuziejus.lt;* ⊕*Jun–Sep 10.00–17.00 Tue–Sat, Oct–May 09.00–17.00 Tue–Fri, 10.00–15.00 Sat*). This features displays of archaeology, local history, natural history (especially butterflies) and costumes. A few paces to the east, at Vasario 16-osios 11, is the **Photography Gallery** (⊕*11.00–19.00 Wed–Sat, 11.00–18.00 Sun*), which features changing exhibitions. The **Art Gallery** (⊕*11.00–18.00 Wed–Sun*) is a block to the south at Respublikos 3. Every year, it hosts an international ceramics symposium, at the end of which the participating artists each donate a couple of works, which then form the basis of the next display.

Panevėžys has a number of prominent churches, the most important being the **Cathedral of Christ the King**, situated in its own quiet grounds at the end of Katedros in the southern part of the centre. It looks at first glance, both inside and out, to be a typical example of Lithuanian Baroque. Closer inspection reveals some of the tell-tale signs of a pastiche, and in fact the building was still under construction at the time Panevėžys was made the seat of a bishop in 1926.

A block further north, on Sodų, is the **Church of the Holy Trinity**, a small, simple building made from fieldstones. It ranks as the city's oldest place of worship, though it only dates from 1803. On the opposite side of the Nevėžis from the city centre is the **Church of SS Peter and Paul**, a large redbrick building of the 1880s strongly influenced by the Roman Baroque style.

BIRŽAI REGION

Nowadays part of Panevėžys County, the Biržai region is the northeastern-most part of Lithuania. It was an early stronghold of Protestantism, particularly of the Reformed tradition, which manages to maintain a visible presence even to this day. This is in large part because the region adjoins Protestant Latvia, and hence was less susceptible than other parts of the country to the influence of the Counter-Reformation led by the Jesuits in relatively distant Vilnius.

The region is also geologically unusual; the soil is rich in gypsum, and there are many underground rivers, lakes, caverns and caves, as well as 2,000 sinkholes. Some of the last-named are dry, while others are filled with water from underground. They range from the very small to craters which have caused fatal accidents.

The Biržai region is also renowned for its beer, which is generally considered among the best in Lithuania; however, the name connection is entirely coincidental, the word Biržai deriving from the Lithuanian for glade. A local dramatist, Borisas Dauguvietis, wrote an often-performed play, *Žaldokynė*, about a fictional Biržai brewer. In it, the hero warned about the strength of the local brews as follows:

> After two cups – singing, after four – you walk on your head, after six – fights, after seven – bitter tears, and after eight – dead silence.

BIRŽAI The town of Biržai is located at the confluence of the Apaščia and Agluona, 66km northeast of Panevėžys. It was first documented as a manor in

1455, when Radvila Astikaitis settled six peasants there. Asktikaitis's son Mikalojus adopted his father's Christian name as his own surname, and thereby founded the Radvila (Radziwiłł) dynasty, which before long became the most powerful in the Grand Duchy, and remained as Biržai's masters for 350 years. In 1586 Kristupas I Radvila 'the Thunderer', the Grand Hetman of Lithuania, began the construction of a fortress built according to the latest defensive theories. To provide extra cover, the two rivers were dammed, and a reservoir of 400 hectares, the first in the country, came into being. Now known as Lake Širvėna, it has been an important feature of the local landscape ever since. On completion of the project in 1589, Biržai was granted municipal rights, making it Lithuania's first privately owned town.

Although it prospered through trade, Biržai suffered its first major set-back in 1625 when the fortress was captured and destroyed by the troops of King Gustavus II Adolphus of Sweden, the greatest military commander of the age. A new castle was built in the 1660s, and in 1701 this was the setting for the signing of an anti-Swedish pact between Augustus the Strong, King of Poland and Grand Duke of Lithuania, and Tsar Peter the Great of Russia. However, in 1704 the Swedes again besieged and destroyed Biržai, whereupon the town went into decline. In 1811 the Radvilas sold out to the Tiškevičius family, who built themselves a grand new residence in the outskirts. Biržai grew rapidly after the building of a narrow-gauge railway from Šiauliai in 1921, but it was badly damaged in 1944 in battles between Soviet and German troops and many historic buildings were lost. Today it has around 17,000 inhabitants and is a small industrial centre, with two of the region's breweries, as well as factories making linen and dairy products.

Getting there and around
🚌 **Bus station** Basanavičiaus 1; ✆ 450 31333. This is situated just beyond the end of Vytauto. There is usually at least 1 service per hr to Panevėžys. Of these, 3 per day continue on to Kaunas, 4 to Vilnius; there are also 3 buses daily to Šiauliai.

Tourist information
ℹ️ **Tourist office** Janonio 2; ✆/f 450 33496; e tic@birzai.lt, www.birzai.lt. ⊕09.00–18.00 Mon–Fri. Very helpful; English spoken.

🏠 Where to stay
🏠 **Helveda** Janonio 7; ✆ 450 31150, 62051; e helveda@projektas.lt. 6-room guesthouse in the town centre. $$

🏠 **Tyla** Tylos 2; ✆ 450 31122/32741; f 450 32570; e info@tyla.lt; www.tyla.lt. Modern lakeside hotel with a swimming pool, situated just to the southeast of town. $$

✗ Where to eat
✗ **Agaro** Žiedas Vytauto 5. A restaurant offering a wide choice of local dishes.
✗ **Senas rūsys** Kęstučio 1. A café which also serves full meals.

✗ **Stumbras** Rotušės 22. A typically Lithuanian country-style bar & restaurant.

What to see and do The **Biržai Castle**, situated on a promontory overlooking Lake Širvėna, remained a ruin from 1704 until 1985, when the palace which formed its core was rebuilt. A fine example of late Renaissance architecture, it features two sturdy three-storey corner towers with attic, between which runs a wing fronted by a two-tier loggia. Inside are the local library and the **Sėla Museum** (⊕*May–Sep 10.00–18.30 Wed–Sat, 10.00–17.30 Sun; Oct–Apr 09.00-17.30 Wed–Sun, 09.00–16.30 Sun*). The latter contains extensive collections of archaeology, local history, natural history, religious art and artefacts, old books, handicrafts and musical instruments. Some historic photographs displayed on the landing show the castle's appearance prior to its reconstruction.

On either side of the castle are the two main churches. The one lying closer to the town centre, the gleaming white **Church of St John the Baptist**, serves the Roman Catholics, and is actually the sixth on the site. It was designed and built in 1857–61 by a Florentine, Lorenzo Cesare Antikini, and is in a distinctively Italianate late Neo-Classical style, with angular twin towers with three progressively smaller tiers. Closer to the lake, the redbrick Neo-Gothic **Reformed Church** is contrastingly severe and rather Germanic-looking.

Further east, the longest footbridge in Lithuania crosses Lake Širvėna at its narrowest point, and leads over to the **Astravas Palace**, the extravagant mansion of the Tiškevičius family, and nowadays the headquarters of the local linen-manufacturing company.

WEST FROM PANEVĖŽYS

Between Panevėžys and the major railway junction of Radviliškis, 55km to the west, are several notable historic sites. All lie within a couple of kilometres of the A9 road linking the towns, though it is necessary to keep a close watch out for the relevant signposts, which in several cases are not as prominent as they could be. Around a dozen buses a day travel along this stretch in either direction. This means that, while it is a definite advantage to have a car to visit the various places covered in this section, they are also easily accessible for anyone prepared to do a little bit of walking in between bus rides.

SMILGIAI Smilgiai, 24km from Panevėžys, is bypassed to the south by the A9. The focal point of the village is the wooden **Church of St George**, which was built in 1761 on the site of its predecessor. Its façade, with its twin towers capped by elegant cupolas and its curvaceous pediment, is a good example of the transfer of monumental Baroque forms to the realm of folk architecture. Inside, the most notable furnishing is the Rococo high altar, which spreads out to incorporate what would normally be two side altars. The village's other main attraction is the **Smilgiai Ethnographic Farmstead** (⊕*10.00–14.00 Tue–Sat*), consisting of a well-preserved 19th- century farm, complete with outlying barn, granary and bath-house, decked out with artefacts illustrating the life and customs of the times.

PAKALNIŠKIAI Just beyond Smilgiai, the road leaves the county of Panevėžys and passes into that of Šiauliai. Although the city of Šiauliai has always been considered part of Samogitia, the southeastern part of its modern administrative county, the Radviliškis region, traditionally belongs to Aukštaitija. Within the vicinity of the scattered village of Pakalniškiai, which lies 12km west of Smilgiai, are no fewer than three very different sites.

The first of these is the **Burbiškis Estate** (⊕*Apr–Oct 09.00–17.00 Tue–Sun*), whose impressive entrance gates, which face a statue of the Virgin Mary, are 1km down a side road leading north from the A9, approximately midway between Smilgiai and Pakalniškiai. Covering some 30 hectares, the estate is a fine Romantic-era landscaped park complete with formal floral gardens, footbridges, statues of Vytautas the Great and Adam Mickiewicz, and a number of outbuildings, including a picturesque little chapel with elaborate gables. The mansion house itself is under renovation, the aim being to convert one of its wings into a hotel.

About 5km further west, the **Kleboniškiai Rural Life Exhibition** (⏲*Apr–Oct 09.00–17.00 Tue–Sun*) is an open-air museum centred on an abandoned agricultural hamlet in the valley of the River Daugyvenė. This consists of a number of fenced-in farmsteads plus various other buildings, including a bath-house, a smoke-house, a smithy and, by the entrance to the complex, a windmill constructed in 1881. The buildings of the original settlement have been joined by others brought from elsewhere, and the collection continues to expand. In order to make the project more life-like, a couple of the farms have been re-inhabited; though these cannot be visited, most of the other interiors are accessible.

Some 1.5km up the road from the windmill, directly overlooking the Daugyvenė, is the **Raginėnai Archeological Reserve** (*free access at all times*), a mysterious series of mounds, sacred stones and graves which appear to date back to the 2nd or 3rd century. The largest, the Raginėnai Mound, is nicknamed Witches' Hill, and has inspired many local legends. Though it is unclear what its exact function was, it is likely that it had a defensive purpose, whereas some of the smaller mounds nearby were certainly used for burials.

RAUDONDVARIS Immediately south of the A9, some 2km west of the turn-off to Kleboniškiai and Raginėnai, is Raudondvaris, a well-preserved estate village. Formerly the property of magnates of German origin, the von Ropp (Ropas in its Lithuanian form) family, it is built round a small lake, and is a popular horseriding centre, with large and prestigious stables. It also makes a good alternative accommodation base to both Panevėžys and Šiauliai.

⌂ Where to stay

⌂ **Prie ežero** ☎ 422 44430; f 422 44436; e info@hotelprieezero.lt, www.hotelprieezero.lt. Located at the entrance to the village, directly overlooking the lake, this is a very professionally run hotel & restaurant, which aims to offer fully Western standards. German & some English spoken. $$, suites $$$.

ŠEDUVA Another 2km on is Šeduva, a little town of wooden houses which is under a preservation order, in its entirety, as a historic monument. The twin-towered **Church of the Discovery of the Holy Cross** is a surprisingly grand edifice in such a setting. Originally built in the 1640s in a style hovering between late Renaissance and early Baroque, it was given a partial Neo-Classical makeover in 1804 following a fire a few years earlier, and extended in 1905 by the addition of aisles. The high altar, featuring a painting of *The Crucifixion* flanked by statues of SS Peter and Paul, dates back to the initial construction period; also of note is the wooden pulpit, with figures of the apostles. Just off the main square, at Veriškių 9, an old leather-processing workshop has been converted to house the **Šeduva Local Lore Museum** (⏲*Apr–Oct 09.00–19.00 Tue–Sun*). This features archaeological finds, folk art, household articles and tools, plus documentation on the history of Šeduva and the surrounding area.

⌂ Where to stay

⌂ **Šeduvos Malūnas** Vytauto 89a; ☎/f 422 56300. This motel at the edge of town by the road to Kėdainiai adjoins an old windmill which contains its café-restaurant. $

10

Samogitia

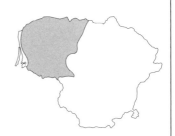

Samogitia (Žemaitija in its Lithuanian form) or Lower Lithuania is arguably the most ethnically distinctive area of the country, but it has not been a clearly defined political unit for hundreds of years and its exact boundaries are therefore a source of much dispute. A fairly generous interpretation is adopted here, though the Baltic coastal area has been omitted from consideration in order that it can be described in its entirety in the following chapter.

The early history of Samogitia is somewhat distinct from that of the rest of Lithuania. It originally had its own duke, and was on occasions at least partially occupied by the Teutonic Knights before becoming accepted as an integral part of the Grand Duchy after the Battle of Žalgiris in 1410. Not until 1413 did it finally abandon paganism, becoming the very last part of Europe to accept Christianity. As so often happens with late converts, it became fervently attached to its new faith, and its religious folk art is a very visible and still thriving feature of the province.

ŠIAULIAI

Šiauliai, some 220km northwest of Vilnius and 130km southwest of Rīga, is Lithuania's fourth largest city, with a population of around 128,000, of whom 85% are Lithuanian. While it is primarily an industrial and commercial centre, it is also firmly on the tourist trail, as its name has become synonymous with one of the country's most moving and popular visitor attractions, the Hill of Crosses, though this actually lies outside the municipal boundaries. The source of the city's name is something of a puzzle. It probably derives from the word *šaulys* ('hunter') in recognition of the fact that the original settlement was located beside a forest. An alternative explanation is that it comes from the word *saulė* ('sun'), which was an object of worship in heathen times; this latter definition is the source of its often-used nickname, *Saulės miestas* ('city of the sun').

HISTORY Although the site seems to have been inhabited since at least the 1st century, the first mention of the city, under the name of Saule, is in the *Rhyme Chronicle of Livonia*, written in Middle High German by an anonymous knight who was possibly a member of the Teutonic Order. The reference is to a battle fought in 1236 between the Samogitians and the Sword Brothers (properly the Brothers of the Knighthood of Christ in Livonia), a small but extremely ruthless monastic order under the patronage of the Bishop of Rīga which had initiated the German military crusades against the heathen Balts back at the beginning of the century. Having invaded eastern Samogitia, the Sword Brothers halted at Šiauliai, fearing for the loss of their horses in the swamps. The Samogitians thereupon launched a surprise attack, and the crusaders were, in the words of the chronicler 'cut down like women'. Master Folkwin, the leader of the Order,

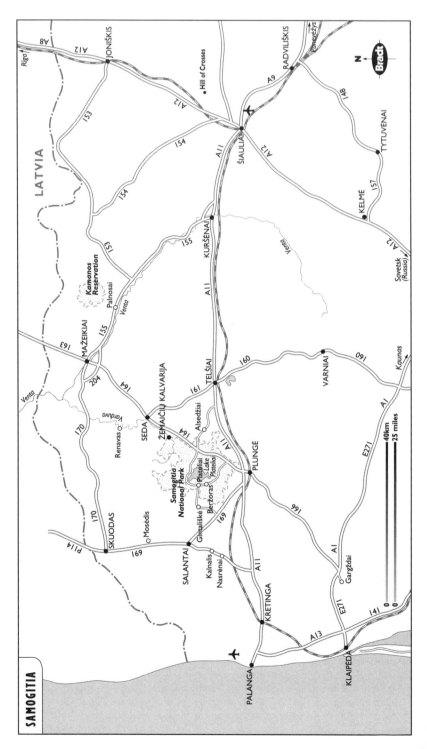

SAMOGITIA

LATVIA

Riga
A8
A12
JONIŠKIS
A12
153
154
154
153
155
Kamanos
Reservation
Palnosai
Venta
MAŽEIKIAI
E163
155
204
164
170
Venta
Varduva
Renavas
SEDA
ŽEMAIČIŲ KALVARIJA
164
Mosėdis
170
SKUODAS
169
P114
SALANTAI
Kalnalis
Nasrėnai
KRETINGA
A13
PALANGA
Hill of Crosses

ŠIAULIAI
A11
KURŠĖNAI
A11
155
Venta
A11
TELŠIAI
161
Alsedžiai
Plateliai
Beržoras
Lake
Plateliai
Samogitia
National Park
Gintališkė
PLUNGĖ
169
A11
991
Gargždai
A1
E271
141
E271
KLAIPĖDA

RADVILIŠKIS
Panevėžys
A9
148
A12
TYTUVĖNAI
KELMĖ
157
A12
Sovetsk
(Russia)

VARNIAI
160
091
Kaunas
A1
E271

N
Bradt

40km
25 miles
0
0

perished in the conflict along with a large percentage of his men. This marked the end of the somewhat inglorious history of the Sword Brothers, whose survivors were organised into a new Livoniai branch of the larger and more formidable Teutonic Knights. For the embryonic Lithuanian nation, it was an important watershed, being the first ever victory of any of its tribes over a powerful external enemy.

Šiauliai received its first (wooden) church in 1445, and in 1524 is mentioned as the administrative centre of the district. By the end of the 16th century, its population was in excess of 1,000. Civic rights and duties were classified in 1614; the first school was opened in 1617, and construction work begun on a splendid new church. Economic reforms introduced in the late 18th century by Antanas Tyzenhauzas, Treasurer of the Grand Duchy of Lithuania, mark the first steps in Šiauliai's development into a major manufacturing centre.

However, the city only began to grow rapidly when the construction of new road and rail links in the second half of the 19th century favoured the introduction of large-scale industrial enterprises. Among these was the prestigious Frenkel leather factory, whose 800-strong workforce was one of the largest in the Russian Empire. Its products were awarded the gold medal at the 1905 Paris Exhibition. Flax-processing, footwear, tile, tobacco and confectionery factories were also established before the end of the century.

Over half the city's buildings were destroyed in World War I, but in the early years of the inter-war independence period, when its population was still a relatively modest 23,000, it recovered to become the main economic and cultural centre of northern Lithuania. It suffered even more in World War II, when 80% of the buildings were damaged. As a result, the face of the city today is predominantly that of the Soviet period, when its population grew by leaps and bounds, reaching six figures in 1971. Latterly, Šiauliai became a centre of hi-tech Soviet industries, including electronics, radio engineering, the production of television sets and food processing. By 1990 30,000 people were employed in local industries, a figure which had fallen, as a result of the collapse of the old captive markets, to 12,000 in 1996.

None the less, the presence of a skilled and relatively cheap workforce is attractive to foreign investors, with the result that Šiauliai is facing the future with a reasonable amount of confidence. The initial phase of the redevelopment of the old Soviet military airport of Žokniai has been carried out by Philips, and it is the first in the Baltics capable of handling all types of aircraft, and of being operational round the clock, no matter how adverse the weather. It forms the centre-piece of a new free economic zone, where materials brought in or out for production, assembly or distribution are exempt from sales tax and customs duty.

GETTING THERE AND AROUND

Bus station Tilžės 109; ☎ 41 525058. Situated just south of the main shopping streets. There is usually at least 1 bus per hr to both Kaunas & Panevėžys, & up to 12 daily to both Vilnius & Mažeikiai. Other internal services include at least 10 daily to Telšiai, 7 daily to Palanga (in season), 5 daily to Klaipėda, & 3 daily to Biržai. There are also 4 buses daily to Rīga.

Railway station Višinskio 44; ☎ 41 203445. Located about 750m southeast of the bus station. There are 4 trains daily to Vilnius, 4 to Klaipėda via Telšiai, Plungė & Kretinga, 1 to Kaunas, 2 to Rīga & 1 to Moscow.

TOURIST INFORMATION

Tourist office Vilniaus 213; ☎ 41 521105/523110; f 41 523111; e tic@siauliai.lt; www.ticsiauliai.lt. Located right in the heart of the

central pedestrian precinct. Very well organised; English spoken. ⏰ 09.00–18.00 Mon–Fri, 10.00–16.00 Sat.

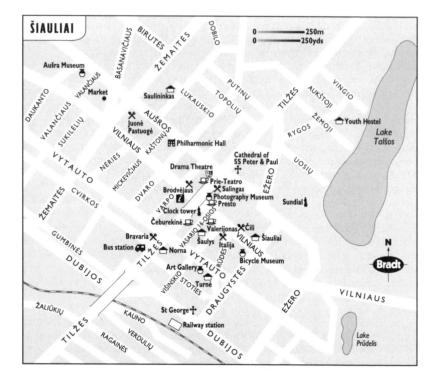

COMMUNICATIONS
✉ **Post office** Aušros 42.

🏠 **WHERE TO STAY** Šiauliai is now very well-off for hotels, and also has a youth hostel.

Hotels The following list is not exhaustive. It is worth contacting the tourist office before booking a room, as in some cases a discount on the normal price will be available.

🏠 **Šaulys** Vasario 16-osios 40; ☎ 41 520812; f 41 520911; e saulys.hotel@takas.lt; www.saulys.lt. This new, designer hotel is now the best address in town. All rooms have satellite TV, minibar & temperature regulators, while the other facilities include a restaurant, café, conference room, fitness room, sauna & swimming pool. $$$

🏠 **Norna** Tilžės 126c; ☎ 41 425594; f 41 429326. A newish & fairly upmarket small hotel with a recommendable restaurant, sited immediately opposite the bus station. $$

🏠 **Saulininkas** Lukauskio 5a; ☎ 41 436555; f 41 421848; e info@saulininkas.com, www.saulininkas.lt. A good, medium-range hotel with a restaurant. $$

🏠 **Šiauliai** Draugystės 25; ☎ 41 437333; f 41 438339; e info@hotelsiauliai.lt, www.hotelsiauliai.lt.

A Soviet-era tower block hotel which is one of the most prominent landmarks of the city centre. $$

🏠 **Turnė** Rūdės 9; ☎ 41 500150; f 41 429238; e hotel@turne.lt; www.turne.lt. A pleasant new hotel with a restaurant in a quiet residential street between the stations & the city centre. $$

🏠 **Vaivorykštė** Gytarių 25; ☎ 41 510502/540572, e info@vaivorykste.com, www.vaivorykste.com. A reasonably priced option in the southwestern outskirts of the city. Among the facilities are a restaurant, a bar & a swimming pool. $$

🏠 **Salduvė** Donelaičio 70; ☎ 41 553593; f 41 553590. Occupies a modern, box-like building in a quiet setting 4 blocks south of the train station. Full meals are available in the café. $

Hostel

⌂ **Youth hostel** Rygos 36; ☏ 41 523922; ℱ 41 523991; e sjtc@splius.lt. Offers basic but clean accommodation. Ⓢ

✗ **WHERE TO EAT** Šiauliai has a pleasingly diverse choice of places to eat and drink, all of them either inexpensive or moderately priced.

✗ **Bravaria** Tilžės 109. This German-style beer hall, one of a small chain, is among several restaurants in the new showpiece shopping centre adjoining the bus station. It offers several brews & hearty food.
✗ **Brodvėjaus** Vilniaus 146. A very hip bar-cum-pizzeria.
☕ **Čeburekinė** Tilžės 144. Pleasant café whose front section has panoramic windows commanding a grandstand view over the street.
✗ **Čili** Vilniaus 128. Šiauliai now has its own typically reliable branch of this pizzeria chain.
✗ **Italija** Vilniaus 167. An Italian-run pizzeria which makes its delicious pizzas in the most authentic way – in a wood-fired brick oven.

✗ **Juonė Pastuogė** Aušros 31a. Lithuania's only country music club, a modern cottage among the city centre tower blocks, also serves delicious local dishes & is a particularly good choice for summertime *al fresco* eating in its large courtyard. Live music is performed every evening Wed–Sun.
☕ **Presto** Vilniaus 134. Coffee shop with a good selection of cakes as well as a changing daily selection of hot dishes.
☕ **Prie Teatro** Tilžės 151. A small café serving tasty & inexpensive staples of Lithuanian cuisine.
☕ **Salingas** Tilžės 168. The city's Chinese restaurant.
✗ **Valerijonas** Vilniaus 173. A real rarity for Lithuania, a specialist vegetarian café serving dietary snacks & herbal teas. ⊕ 11.00–18.00 Mon–Fri.

ENTERTAINMENT AND NIGHTLIFE

🎭 **Drama Theatre** Tilžės 155; ☏ 41 523209. As its name suggests, this specialises in straight dramatic fare.

♪ **Philharmonic Hall** Aušros 15; ☏ 41 524458. The main music venue, home of the choir Polifonija, & often the setting for repeat performances of concerts or recitals held in Vilnius or Kaunas.

Festivals A week-long International Festival of Church Music is held in Šiauliai's churches around Easter. The Juonė Pastuogė restaurant organises the Lithuanian Country Music Festival, which also features a few invited groups from abroad, over two days in late June.

WHAT TO SEE AND DO One long street, Tilžės, runs all the way through Šiauliai in a general northeast to southwest direction, forming part of the A12 road which runs between the Latvian border (on the route to Rīga) and Kaliningrad. In the very heart of the city it is bisected by a similarly extended thoroughfare, Vilniaus, which to the west merges into the A11 to Palanga, to the east into the A9 to Panevėžys. Since 1975, Vilniaus has been pedestrianised for over 500m on either side of the junction with Tilžės, with the northern of these segments forming the hub of the shopping area.

Šiauliai's Old Town has all but disappeared, the sole surviving monument being the whitewashed **Cathedral of SS Peter and Paul**, which is towards the eastern end of the modern business centre. It was built between 1617 and 1634 in a late Renaissance style already showing a nod to the Baroque, and was intended for parish use, only becoming the seat of a bishop in 1997. The construction was financed in part by money donated by farmers from the sale of four-year-old oxen – hence the inclusion of an ox on the city's coat-of-arms (which also features a chained bear and the all-seeing eye of God). The steeple, which crowns an octagonal tower resting on a square base, reaches to a height of just over 70m, and has ranked as the highest in Lithuania ever since it was built.

However, it does not quite preserve its original appearance, as it had to be remodelled after being damaged by lightning in 1880. At one time the tower had a defensive function, as the gunports indicate. The interior of the cathedral, which is likewise painted in gleaming white, is disarmingly simple, consisting of a vast, sparsely furnished open space capable of accommodating 4,000 worshippers. Its most important recent acquisition is the organ, which was added in 1995.

A short distance southeast of the cathedral, at the junction of Ežero and Šalkauskio, is a large open square laid out in the manner of an amphitheatre. In the centre stands a huge **sundial** surmounted by a tall column crowned by a gilded sculpture of an archer. This was erected in 1986 to commemorate the 750th anniversary of the Battle of Saule, and neatly combines the two possible derivations of the city's name.

Just to the south, at Vilniaus 139, the **Bicycle Museum** (⊕*Jul–Sep 10.00–18.00 Wed–Fri, 11.00–17.00 Sat; Oct–Jun 10.00–18.00 Tue–Fri, 11.00–17.00 Sat*) celebrates Šiauliai's role as the two-wheel metropolis of the Baltic region. The exhibition starts on the top floor with mock-ups of some historic bikes, beginning with the German Baron von Drais's pioneering 'running machine' of 1816. It continues with original examples of most of the models produced by the Šiauliai factory throughout its history, displayed alongside contemporary models from elsewhere.

Immediately before the junction with Tilžės, at Vilniaus 140, is the **Photography Museum** (⊕*Jul–Sep 10.00–18.00 Wed–Fri, 11.00–17.00 Sat–Sun; Oct–Jun 10.00–18.00 Tue–Fri, 11.00–17.00 Sat*). On the first floor are regularly changing exhibitions of the work of both contemporary and early photographers, mostly from Lithuania. The second floor is devoted to old equipment and the history of Lithuanian photography. Outside the museum is a small clocktower, which is a favourite local meeting-point.

The pedestrianised section of Vilniaus ends at Žemaitės, on the other side of which is the central market. Round the corner from there, at Aušros 47, is the **Aušra Museum** (*www.siauliai.mok.lt;* ⊕*Jul–Sep 10.00–18.00 Wed–Fri, 11.00–17.00 Sat–Sun; Oct–Jun 09.00–17.00 Tue–Fri, 11.00–17.00 Sat*), the oldest in the city, founded in 1923 and named in honour of the first Lithuanian-language newspaper. Its ground floor has archaeological finds from throughout the Šiauliai region plus a section illustrating the history and economy of the city. Upstairs, the ethnographic department features displays of local costumes and other handicrafts.

A block south of the Bicycle Museum, the top floor of the splendid 1920s house at Vytauto 89 is currently home to the **Art Gallery** (⊕*09.00–17.00 Mon–Thu, 10.00–16.00 Sat*). This features works by Lithuanian painters and sculptors from the Renaissance period onwards, plus displays of folk art. The floor below has an exhibition on the house's original owners, the lawyer Kazimieras Venclauskis (1880–1940) and his actress wife, Stanislava Jakševičiūtė-Venclauskienė (1874–1958), who fostered no fewer than 124 orphans and other impoverished children.

Further south, diagonally opposite the train station, is the **Church of St George**. The second-oldest surviving church in the city, it was built in 1909 in traditional Russian Orthodox style to serve the local garrison. Allocated to the Roman Catholics after World War I, it was almost destroyed by fire in 1976. The underground press was able to inform the West that the firemen had deliberately failed to quell the blaze; this led to an outcry among Lithuanian communities abroad, as a result of which the authorities were prompted to authorise a full restoration.

Part of the modern administrative county of Šiauliai belongs historically to Aukštaitija and is covered in the previous chapter; the main highlights of the larger Samogitian section are described below.

HILL OF CROSSES One of the most potent symbols of Lithuanian nationhood, and the deep religious faith which is such a key element in it, the Hill of Crosses (or Jurgaičiai Mound, as it is officially known) is 12km northeast of Šiauliai, and 2km east of the main A12 highway. Buses bound for Rīga, Joniškis or Meškuičiai all stop at the turn-off (marked with the sign 'Kryžių Kalnas') to the tree-lined minor road leading to the hill.

There are many conflicting legends associated with the early history of the hill, which is actually quite a modest mound overlooking the left bank of the River Kulpė. According to the Livonian chronicles, it was the site of a wooden defensive fort built by the Lithuanians and destroyed by the Teutonic Knights. It may at one time have been a backdrop for pagan worship, though it is also possible that it was a holy place for early Lithuanian Christians, and it therefore could be the case that the first cross was planted there in the Middle Ages. However, it was not until relatively recent times that it began to assume any sort of major significance.

Although there exists no more than oral evidence to support the claim, it would seem likely that the first group of crosses was put up in memory of insurgents killed in the 1831 rebellion against Tsarist rule, and that this was followed by a second group commemorating those who died in the next failed revolt of 1863–64. Old photographs show that the crosses, which numbered no more than 130 in the late 19th century, were originally confined to the summit of the hill.

In the late 1950s Lithuanians returning from the Siberian Gulags began erecting crosses in memory of family and friends who had died in exile. Now that the country was under communist – and therefore atheist – rule, the symbolism associated with the hill became not merely one of nationalism, but of a belief system which was fundamentally opposed to that of the authorities. Determined to clamp down on outward expressions of Christianity, the Soviets bulldozed the hill in 1961. The wooden crosses were burnt, the iron ones melted down, the roads to the hill blocked off, and the site patrolled by the army and secret police. However, crosses soon started to re-appear in ever-increasing numbers. On at least three subsequent occasions the authorities razed the hill, but the Lithuanians always found ways of planting new crosses.

Since the fall of the Soviet Union, the number of crosses has continued to multiply, as pilgrims from all over the world have joined Lithuanians and Lithuanian émigrés in coming to the hill to plant a cross. Nowadays, many new crosses are added daily. The hill is now a truly extraordinary forest of crosses, looking like nothing else on earth, save for the much smaller replicas found elsewhere in the country. Through pressure of space, most recent additions have been planted in the meadows directly below the hill itself.

The crosses come in all shapes, sizes and materials. Most are of wood, but even these vary from two plain planks joined together to monumental figural representations. An example of the latter is the cross donated by Pope John Paul II (who numbered Lithuanians among his ancestors); the covered altar beside the hill is another legacy of his 1993 visit, as is the Italian-designed Franciscan Friary and Noviciate, which was built some 300m from the hill and consecrated in 2000. Many of the smaller crosses are piled on top of one another in their hundreds, to truly spectacular effect. Although many of the crosses are memorials to the deceased, others are simple expressions of faith or hope. Nor are crosses the only works of art to be seen – there are also figures of the Virgin Mary and the Man of Sorrows, as well as roofed poles ornamented with the characteristically Lithuanian mixture of Christian and heathen symbols, and piles of rosary beads (including many of amber).

The Hill of Crosses is perhaps seen at its most dramatic under a lowering sky accompanied by a strong enough wind to cause the crosses to sway and rattle, though it also looks stunning on bright, clear days. Easter sees the largest number of visitors, but there are group pilgrimages there all year round. A row of souvenir stalls beside the car park caters for those wanting to plant their own cross, however grand or modest.

TYTUVĖNAI Some 45km due south of Šiauliai is Tytuvėnai, which can be reached by either bus or train. The little town is centred on one of the country's most monumental monastic complexes, the Bernardine **Friary of the Blessed Virgin Mary**. This was founded by the local lord, Andrius Valavičius (Andreas Wołłowicz), holder of the title of Standard Bearer of the Grand Duchy of Lithuania, and built from 1614–39 under the direction of a Vilnius architect, Tomas Kasperas.

Although nominally Renaissance in style, the church has many archaic Gothic touches, notably the pointed windows and the high vaulting. Between 1759 and 1783 extensive additions were made to the complex. The church was given a new twin-towered façade with portico, and a spacious square cloister was built immediately in front, with a Chapel of the Holy Steps (an imitation of the stairway Christ ascended to hear Pilate's Judgement) placed within its garden.

Inside the church are many fine Baroque furnishings, including a high altar, side altars and pulpit. The tombstone of the founder in the right aisle is a fine piece of Renaissance carving made around 1640 in the workshop of Willem van den Block, a sculptor of Dutch origin who was a leading light in the artistic life of the wealthy city-state of Danzig (now Gdańsk).

KAMANOS RESERVATION (*Administration centre: Akmenės 2;* ✆/f *425 59285;* e *kamanos@takas.lt, www.kamanos.lt.*) One of Lithuania's handful of strictly preserved wilderness areas, the Kamanos Reservation is 5km north of the village of Palnosai, which is 65km northwest of Šiauliai on the road and rail lines to the oil refining town of Mažeikiai in the neighbouring county of Telšiai. Over half the reserve's total area of 3,650 hectares is taken up by the country's only intact bogland; the remainder is a mixed forest. From a botanical point of view, it is extraordinarily rich, featuring 526 different sorts of plants. It is also an important nesting ground for birds, including black storks, cranes and plovers. In order to gain access to the reservation, it is necessary to make an advance appointment for a guided visit.

TELŠIAI COUNTY

The county of Telšiai forms the central part of Samogitia. It is thinly populated, but contains several interesting towns and villages. In addition to the places described below, it includes the lion's share of the Samogitia National Park, the subject of the following section.

TELŠIAI Telšiai, which clusters along the northern shoreline of Lake Mastis, 77km west of Šiauliai, is no more than a modest-sized county town. That does not prevent it styling itself as the 'capital' of Samogitia – which is a perfectly legitimate claim in at least the spiritual and cultural spheres, particularly if the narrowest definition of the province (which excludes both Šiauliai and Klaipėda) is accepted.

Archaeological excavations in the bogs around the lake prove that Telšiai was first settled around 4,000BC. Its name appears in medieval maps and chronicles, but nothing survives from this period, and it was not until the second half of the 18th century that the town really began to prosper. A splendid Bernardine Friary was built in 1762–65, and in 1791 the town received a municipal charter. Between 1873 and 1940 it was the seat of a Jewish *yeshiva* which gained an international reputation for the quality of its Torah scholarship, attracting budding rabbis from all over Europe and America. Indeed, the inter-war independence period was a heady time for Telšiai, when it gained many important new buildings and institutions. The most important development came in 1926, when it became the seat of the Bishop of Samogitia (a role it retains to this day) as a result of the promotion of the see of Kaunas to the rank of archbishopric. A seminary was also established then, and although this was closed by the Soviets, it re-opened in 1989.

Getting there and around

Bus station Respublikos 48; ☎ 444 53333. There are 10 buses daily to Šiauliai, 9 to Klaipėda via Plungė, 6 (in season) to Palanga via Plungė & Kretinga, 2 to Mažeikiai via Seda, 5 to Varniai, 4 to Kaunas & 3 to Alšedžiai.

Railway station Stoties 35; ☎ 444 53553. Located in the north of town. There are 4 trains daily to Klaipėda via Plungė & Kretinga, & 4 to Šiauliai, 2 of which continue to Vilnius.

Tourist information

Tourist office Turgaus aikštė 21; ☎/f 444 5300; e turizmocentras@telsiai.lt; www.telsiaitic.lt. ⏱ 15 Jun–31 Aug 08.30–17.30 Mon–Thu, 08.30–16.15 Fri,

10.00–14.00 Sat;1 Sept–14 Jun 08.00–17.00 Mon–Thu, 08.30–15.45 Fri.

Where to stay

Branša A11, junction with E272; ☎/f 444 75455. This motel with restaurant at the edge of town by the main Šiauliai–Palanga road is the most attractive place to stay in Telšiai. $$

Pas Stefą Respublikos 49; ☎/f 444 74520; e sveciunamai@andernetas.lt, www.passtefa.lt. New guesthouse with sauna & cellar café. $$

Roneta Respublikos 59; ☎ 444 53597; f 444 69888, e roneta@andernetas.lt. A small hotel with a café on the main street which now charges a lot less than it once did. $$

Where to eat

Gotika Turgaus aikštė 19a. A bar-restaurant serving inexpensive daily specials.

Senoji Kvorta Respublikos 4. A cosy restaurant occupying the cellars of an old bakery.

What to see and do Telšiai's dominant monument is the Baroque **Cathedral of St Anthony of Padua**, which stands on a hillock overlooking the main street, Respublikos, and the lake beyond. It was built as the Bernardine Friary – hence its dedication, which would otherwise be highly unusual. A handsome triple gateway forms the entrance to the complex. The cathedral itself has an almost unrelievedly plain exterior, save for the lantern-topped octagonal tower above the façade, which was not added until 1864. Interest centres on the decidedly eccentric interior arrangement, which has two separate floor levels, whose central space is in the shape of an irregular dodecagon. A fully furnished upper church – complete with bishop's throne, stalls, confessionals, high and side altars – occupies what, in most cathedrals, would be empty galleries. Downstairs are more altars and an extravagantly carved pulpit featuring the Holy Spirit and the Four Evangelical Symbols on the canopy, the Four Doctors of the Church on the basin, and angels pulling back a curtain to reveal the preacher.

On a small rise at the far eastern end of Respublikos is the former **Russian Orthodox Church**. Built in the 19th century, it is a small whitewashed building built to a Greek-cross plan, with a tripartite apse and a flattened dome over the crossing.

At No 31 on Muziejaus, which leads southwards from the opposite end of Respublikos, is the **Samogitia Museum 'Alka'** (*www.zam.mch.mii.lt;* ⊕*09.00–17.00 Tue–Sat, 10.00–16.00 Sun*). Built in 1936–38, it is Lithuania's second oldest custom-designed museum, and is devoted to the archaeology, history, fauna, geology and ethnography of Samogitia, with an especially good collection of the distinctive local folk sculpture. Additionally, there is a gallery of paintings, including several with over-optimistic attributions to famous old masters such as Rembrandt. The most important canvas is the impressively large *Agrippina Carrying the Casket Containing the Ashes of her Husband Germanicus* by the Neo-Classical painter Franciszek Smuglewicz (who was partly of Samogitian descent).

About 1km further down the same street is the signposted turn-off to the **Open-Air Museum** (⊕*May–Oct 09.00–17.00 Wed–Sat, 10.00–16.00 Sun*), which is reached by bearing right when the side road comes to a fork. This contains over a dozen old rural buildings which have been moved to the site, including three farmsteads, a smithy and a windmill, whose interiors can all be visited in the company of the custodian.

VARNIAI Although Varniai, which is 33km south of Telšiai, is no bigger than the average village, it has had an illustrious history, having been the original seat of the Samogitia bishopric, which was founded in 1421 by Grand Duke Vytautas the Great, soon after the region finally accepted Christianity. In the same century, a municipal charter was granted and the first school founded. Its educational tradition was boosted in the 18th century with the establishment of a seminary. This was the only one in Lithuania which bucked the trend of promoting Polish language and culture, so it is not surprising that some of its alumni went on to become leading figures in the 19th-century nationalist movement.

The former cathedral, which was demoted to the status of the **Church of SS Peter and Paul** when the bishopric was transferred to Kaunas in 1864, was built between 1680 and 1691 on the site of its wooden predecessor under the patronage of Bishop Kazimieras Pacas, scion of one of Lithuania's leading dynasties. It is High Baroque in style, with a handsome façade dominated by two protruding square towers topped with steeples. The interior had to be reconstructed following its destruction by a fire in 1817, but it preserves some of the original furnishings, including the high altar, the stalls, and numerous portraits and epitaphs relating to the bishops who served there.

At Daukanto 6 is the former seminary building, which now serves as home of the **Museum of the Samogitian Diocese** (*www.varniai-museum.lt;* ⊕*08.00–17.00 Mon–Thu, 08.00–16.00 Fri, 11.00–17.00 Sat–Sun*). As its name suggests, it displays paintings, sculptures, treasury items and other religious artefacts collected from all over the diocese.

PLUNGĖ The linen-manufacturing centre of Plungė, 28km west of Telšiai, is also a busy market town, whose vast main square was formerly the most important place in Samogitia for the trading of agricultural products.

At the far end of this square is the **Church of St John the Baptist**, the successor to one built in 1617 under the patronage of Zygmunt Waza, the King of Poland and Grand Duke of Lithuania. The present brick building, a Neo-Romanesque monster with twin towers and a central dome, was erected in 1933. It completely dwarfs the stone belfry in front, which was built in Neo-Classical style in 1850.

Of far more interest is the 50-hectare **Palace Park** in the north of town, which can be entered via a grand Neo-Renaissance gateway opposite the train and bus stations. Within its grounds are the Babrungas stream, seven ponds, a small formal garden and many fine old trees, some 25m high, including the ancient Perkūnas oak which is believed to have marked a sacred site for the pagan Samogitian tribes. Among the estate buildings are a grand Neo-Gothic stable block and a pavilion built in imitation of the Palazzo Vecchio in Florence.

The **Palace** itself was commissioned by Duke Mykolas Oginskis (Michał Ogiński), a descendant of one of the great land-owning dynasties of the Polish-Lithuanian Commonwealth, as soon as he acquired the estate in 1873, and designed by a German architect, Karl Lorenz. Its architectural style is an eclectic one, borrowing freely from both Italian Renaissance and English Tudor models. Oginskis also established Lithuania's first musical academy in his palace, and this functioned until his death in 1902, its orchestra and choir providing music for receptions and religious services. Its most famous alumnus was M K Čiurlionis (see pages 122–3), who wrote his first musical compositions, which unfortunately have not survived, during his four-year stay there.

The palace's valuable library and art collections were dispersed after World War I, and the interior has lost all its original decoration. Since 1994 it has housed the **Samogitia Art Museum** (*www.oginski.lt;* ⊕ *10.00–17.00/18.00 Wed–Sun*). This includes a set of 30 somewhat crudely executed portraits of Samogitian bishops, plus examples of folk and religious art, and paintings by contemporary Lithuanian and émigré artists. One room is devoted to Čiurlionis memorabilia, including the Bechstein grand piano he played during his student days.

Getting there and around

🚌 **Bus station** Dariaus ir Girėno 29; ☎ 448 52333. There are approximately 8 buses daily to Seda via Žemaičių Kalvarija, 8 to Klaipėda, 6 to Telšiai, 6 to Plateliai, 6 to Palanga via Kretinga, 4 to Alsėdžiai & 3 to Mosėdis via Salantai.

🚆 **Railway station** Stoties 2; ☎ 448 52325/53271. There are 4 trains daily to Klaipėda via Plungė & Kretinga, & 4 to Šiauliai, 2 of which continue to Vilnius.

↑ Where to stay

🏠 **Beržas** Minijos 2; ☎/f 448 56840; e hotberzas@one.lt; www.berzas.service.lt. A reasonable town-centre hotel with restaurant. ⑂

ALSĖDŽIAI Alsėdžiai, a scattered village of wooden cottages and farmsteads on which several minor roads converge, is located 15km west of Telšiai and 20km northeast of Plungė. For several centuries, it was the residence of the Samogitian bishops, but is now a quiet agricultural community. On the hillock overlooking the main square is the **Church of the Immaculate Conception**, successor to a series of buildings which have occupied the site continuously since 1475. Erected in 1789–93, it is among the largest and most imposing wooden churches in Lithuania. The plain, angular appearance of the exterior is interrupted only by the little onion-domed turrets at either end. In contrast, the interior is richly furnished with altars and memorials to the local bishops. The detached belfry alongside the church houses a 191kg bell cast in Vilnius in 1679.

Getting there and around Although there are two bus stops, the only one which is operational is the shelter at the eastern edge of the village beside the Telšiai road. There are four buses daily to Plungė, three to Telšiai, two to Žemaičių Kalvarija and one to Klaipėda.

Where to stay

Norkienės sodyba Liepų 4; ☎ 448 48190. This large wooden private house is on the street beside the garage at the western end of the village, by the road to Plateliai. For anyone with their own transport, it makes an excellent central base for exploring Samogitia. The hostess speaks some German, Russian & Polish. A hearty cooked b/fast & a light supper are included in the price. ⑤

SEDA Seda, which lies on the banks of the serpentine River Varduva, 22km northwest of Telšiai, once had a sizeable Jewish population which was wiped out in World War II. Like Alsėdžiai, it is a meeting-point of several roads, and has a notable example of wooden architecture in the **Church of the Assumption**, which was built on the site of its predecessor in 1770. It boasts a fine array of art treasures; in addition to the altars made at the time of its construction, it has been fortunate enough to become heir to works from two redundant churches, plus a valuable collection of old ecclesiastical vestments formerly displayed in a museum in Kaunas which was closed down by the Soviets. The last-named are kept in the small detached chapel in the grounds, and can be seen on application to the priest.

One of the sacristies contains a monstrance made partly from amber and elephant tusk, which was donated in 1788 by General Benedictas Adamovičius. The other contains a cycle of paintings of the *Stations of the Cross* by Kazys Varnelis, a 'naive' artist active at the turn of the 20th century; these originally adorned the shrines in the churchyard, but had to be moved indoors for conservation reasons. Two 18th-century bells hang in the belfry beside the church.

RENAVAS Renavas, 8km north of Seda via a road which changes from asphalt to dirt track, is a one-time aristocratic estate which takes its name from the Lithuanian version of that of its former owners, the French Roenne family. The park, which is bisected by the River Varduva, features many old trees, including a fenced-off oak which is the biggest in Samogitia. Changing art exhibitions are held in the **Palace** (⊕ *10.00–18.00 Wed–Sun*), which was built in 1880 and is thus an exact contemporary of its counterpart in Plungė, though it is very late Neo-Classical, rather than Neo-Renaissance in style, and is somewhat better preserved. Despite its relative isolation, Renavas is a popular spot for weddings, largely because it makes such a picturesque backdrop for photos.

SAMOGITIA NATIONAL PARK

The 21,700-hectare Samogitia National Park was established in 1971 to preserve and manage a part of the province which is particularly rich in both natural and cultural interest. Centred on the heavily indented **Lake Plateliai**, one of the most beautiful stretches of water in Lithuania, it incorporates hills, woods and marshes in addition to fields and meadows which are still farmed in the traditional manner. Among a truly diverse range of historic monuments are the remains of numerous prehistoric settlements and burial mounds, many early medieval fortress hills, a couple of fine wooden churches, a major place of pilgrimage, and one of the Soviet Union's main missile bases.

INFORMATION AND MAPS There is an information centre in Plateliai, the little town on the western shore of the lake where the National Park has its administration headquarters. Here it is possible to purchase an English-language leaflet, on one side of which is a map (1:70,000) which is an indispensable companion for exploring the park. It shows the roads and paths clearly, has a legend listing all the attractions, and also has panoramic sketches of Plateliai and Žemaičiu Kalvarija. There are more detailed leaflets with maps of Plateliai and the nature trail immediately to the north, but these are in Lithuanian only.

TOURISM AND TRANSPORT Tourist facilities are quite reasonable, at least around Lake Plateliai. There is one hotel in Plateliai itself and another at Paplateliai on the eastern shore of the lake. Dotted around the lake are five campsites which can be used on payment of a modest registration fee to the park authorities; another can be found further south, beside the small Lake Ilgas. A number of farmsteads also offer rooms to rent. Curiously and inconveniently, there is currently no accommodation of any kind in Žemaičiu Kalvarija, the other main settlement and one of Lithuania's holiest places, despite the fact that comparable towns in Western Europe are chock-a-block with hotels and guesthouses to cater for the hordes of pilgrims. There are plans afoot to remedy this, in line with the town's status as the northern terminus of the new John Paul II Pilgrimage Route, which features 14 sacred sites throughout Lithuania.

On the other hand, Žemaičiu Kalvarija is the most readily accessible place in the park by public transport. It lies just 1km back from the main Plungė–Seda–Mažeikiai highway, and most of the many buses which ply this stretch make the short detour into town; the others stop at the crossroads. Extra services are laid on at the times of the major pilgrimages. There are usually six buses daily in each direction between Plungė and Plateliai, but only three across the park linking Plateliai and Žemaičiu Kalvarija.

For those travelling by car or bike, there is a decent paved road which loops round the central area of the park from the Plungė–Seda highway, passing along the south, west and north sides of Lake Plateliai. Elsewhere, some of the roads are mere dirt tracks, and the same is also true of the western approach from Salantai, which is very rough in its later stages, particularly in the vicinity of Gintališkė, a village with a fine but now disused 18th-century wooden church 6km from Plateliai. There is no road close to the eastern side of Lake Plateliai, so a complete circuit is possible only by foot or bike, and even this often strays far from the shoreline.

Boating and angling are popular activities, particularly on Lake Plateliai, though fishing is prohibited in many of the other lakes (which are clearly identified on the official map). It should be noted that there are very few places in the whole park where it is possible to have a full sit-down meal, though there are well-stocked groceries in both the main towns.

GEOGRAPHY The landscape of the park was formed around 12,000 years ago by a receding glacier. In comparison with the rest of Samogitia, it is quite hilly, with tops which typically range from 150m to 190m. Over 40% of the total area is wooded. With an area of 1,205 hectares, Lake Plateliai accounts for more than 5% of the park. Reaching to depths of up to 50m, it has clear and unpolluted waters, thanks in no small part to being fed by numerous short streams which have their sources in the nearby hills. The other 25 lakes in the park, many of which are minute, have a combined area of little more than 300 hectares.

FLORA AND FAUNA Spruce groves make up very nearly half of the woodland area of the park, with pines making up almost half the remainder. Birches are also quite common, as, to a lesser extent, are alders and oaks. Most of the trees are middle-aged; only 1.5% are mature. Berries are a distinctive feature of the local flora, with bilberries, cranberries and whortleberries being particularly numerous.

The park's mammal life is quite typical for Lithuania, including as it does elk, red deer, roe deer, wild boar, lynxes, wolves, racoons, badgers, foxes, mountain hares and pine martens. Otters, beavers, mink and small rodents live in the waters, which are also rich in fish, including salmon, perch, pike, roach, carp, tench, bream, lavaret, eel and crawfish. Around 170 types of birds live in the park, 23 of which are migrant, the others nesting. They include black storks, black grouse, ospreys, bitterns, peregrine falcons, curlews, black-throated divers and Montagu's harriers.

ETHNOGRAPHY The area of the Samogitia National Park has been inhabited more or less continuously since prehistoric times. There are no fewer than 32 archaeological sites, of which 15 are Stone Age settlements and burial mounds, the others castle hills or mounds from the age of the Samogitian tribes. Today, the park has around 3,000 inhabitants. Of these, just over 1,000 live in Plateliai, around 800 in Žemaičių Kalvarija; the rest of the population is spread among a host of villages, hamlets and isolated farmsteads.

Wooden farm buildings, including about 100 houses built in the late 19th century and early 20th century, are a characteristic feature of the park. There is also a generous representation of the wayside crosses and shrines which are so typical of Samogitia. These continue to be produced by a number of folk artists who still live and work in the area. By far the largest concentration of monuments of artistic value is to be found in Žemaičių Kalvarija.

PLATELIAI Plateliai, which lies some 25km north of Plungė, was founded back in the 14th century, but it was not until 1972 that it was granted the status of a town. On the main square, Didžioji, is a monument erected in 1928 to commemorate the tenth anniversary of Lithuanian independence. Just to the south, fronted by its detached belfry, is the **Church of SS Peter and Paul**, a typical example of 18th-century wooden architecture. Beyond stretches the Park, formerly part of an aristocratic estate, in which grow ancient chestnut, linden, ash and maple trees. One of the ashes, which is over 7m in diameter, has been given the status of a monument of nature. Little remains of the manor and its outbuildings, though the main granary has been reconstructed to serve as a cultural centre. A short distance to the west is Jazminai Hill, where there is a small cemetery with the graves of the Jews murdered there in World War II.

Towards the northeastern edge of town, down the side road just beyond the bus stop, a signposted path leads to a vantage point offering the best elevated view over Lake Plateliai. The car park near the start of the path marks the beginning of the circular 4km-long nature trail through the Šeirė wood then back along the shore of the lake. It is the only marked walking route in the park, but unfortunately is not identified with coloured waymarks, only numbers identifying the different trees (some of which are exotic species brought from around the world) along the way. It is thus advisable to invest in the map available from the information centre; although this is in Lithuanian only, it is simple enough to follow, with the single exception of the point where the route begins its loop back, which is quite easy to miss.

Near the end of the return leg of the nature trail is the yacht club, which can be reached directly by walking straight downhill from the vantage point. Yachts, rowing boats and water bicycles can be hired there in summer. The most popular destination is **Castle Island**, the second nearest islet to the jetty, and one formerly linked to the shore by a wooden bridge. It takes its name from the fortress which once stood there, a few traces of which still remain.

This has been a rich source of legends, for example that of the beautiful but cruel Princess Zigfrida. The story goes that, during a ball, the princess threw her jewelled hair clasp into the lake, promising that she would marry the man who would retrieve it for her. All were deterred by the danger of the task save for her manservant Gervazas, who duly plunged into the water. He was absent for such a long time that he was feared lost, but eventually emerged with the clasp. The princess thereupon threw a terrible tantrum, declaring that she would not give herself to a mere servant. Distraught, Gervazas jumped back into the lake and drowned himself. When his mother complained about what had happened, she was arrested and imprisoned.

More prosaically, the islet has also been dubbed 'Beggars' Island', as it was said that beggars repaired there immediately after the big pilgrimages to Žemaičių Kalvarija in order to feast and drink on their takings from pious pilgrims.

Park administration centre
Samogitia National Park Didžioji 10; \f 448 49337; e znp@zemaitijosnp.lt; www.zemaitijosnp.lt

Tourist information
Samogitia National Park Didžioji 8; \f 448 49231; e info@zemaitijosnp.lt. ⊕ Jul/Aug 08.00–17.00 Mon, 08.00–19.00 Tue–Fri, 10.00–17.00 Sat; Sep–Jun 08.00–12.00 & 12.45–17.00 Mon–Thu, 08.00–12.00 & 12.45–15.45 Fri. In addition to selling maps, this office issues camping & fishing permits, arranges accommodation & organises excursions (for example, to the former Soviet missile base).

Where to stay
Mikašauskienė sodyba (also known as Mortos Švecių Namai) Ežero 33; \ 448 49117. In addition to the 4 well-appointed rooms in the house itself, there are 5 chalets grouped beside a picturesque pond surrounded by flower beds. $, whole chalet $$

Šaltinėlis Ežero 44; \ 448 49315. Located at the far northern edge of town, this is a quite basic but none the less perfectly serviceable holiday hotel. $

Straksytė sodyba Zalioji 13; \ 448 49293. Another private house, this time with 3 rooms for rent. $

Where to eat
Jachtklubas Ežero 40. Open in summer only, the bar of the yacht club offers simple meals which can be eaten indoors or on the terrace.

Senas Ažuolas Ežero 3. Situated just off the corner of Didžioji, the 'Old Oak Inn' offers good local food at reasonable prices.

BERŽORAS Although less than 2km south of Plateliai, Beržoras is recognisably a quite separate village, which lies well back from Lake Plateliai, on the north shore of the small Lake Beržoras. The wooden **Church of St Stanislaus** is contemporary with its counterpart in Plateliai; it likewise has a detached belfry and is surrounded by 14 small shrines representing the Stations of the Cross. Just south of Lake Beržoras are the minute Lake Žiedelis and the somewhat larger Lake Ilgis. East of the former, on the opposite side of the road, is a peninsula jutting into Lake Plateliai where an ancient castle mound and another Jewish cemetery can be seen.

10

Where to stay

Rumšienės sodyba 🕿 448 41924. There are 6 rooms for rent in this farmhouse, one of 4 in the village to take guests. The hosts speak some English, French & Russian & can arrange the hire of horses, boats & bikes. $

PLOKŠTINĖ To the southeast of Lake Plateliai is the **Plokštinė Reservation**, one of two parts of the park which are strictly controlled nature reserves, and which should only be entered in the company of a member of staff. At its northern edge is the **Rocket Base**, an eerie place abandoned in 1978, which can now be visited in summer by guided tour. These normally take place between mid-May and mid-September (*10.00, 12.00, 14.00 & 16.00 Tue–Sat, 15.00 Sun*). Although the guide can sometimes be found on site, it is advisable to arrange a tour in advance at the National Park's information centre. A fair amount of scrambling around in dirty surroundings is involved, so it is best to wear old clothes. Built in 1960–62, this was the first underground missile base in the Soviet Union; one was built soon afterwards to the same system in Cuba. Each of the four giant rockets which can be seen above ground could carry a nuclear warhead many times more powerful than the Hiroshima bomb. They could travel up to 3,000km, though thankfully their accuracy was always somewhat suspect – an attack on West Germany would have carried the risk of hitting East Germany instead. To activate the system, two people had to press buttons simultaneously in the control room in the two-storey underground headquarters building. This is seen in the course of the tour, which also includes a walk round the interior of one of the rocket silos.

Where to stay

Linelis Paplateliai; 🕿 687 35058; f 448 49422; e info@linelis.lt; www.linelis.lt This former Soviet barracks was converted into a holiday centre in 1992; all rooms were renovated in 2003–04, & there is also a good restaurant. It lies north of the rocket base, & can be reached by a 5km forest track (which is comfortable enough for cars) from the main road round Lake Plateliai. $$, suites & apts $$$

ŽEMAIČIU KALVARIJA Žemaičiu Kalvarija, which lies 16km northeast of Plateliai via the back roads, is undoubtedly one of the most attractive and distinctive small towns in Lithuania. Under its original name of Gardai, it was first mentioned in the *Livonian Chronicles* of 1253. Its present designation derives from the decision made in 1633 by Jurgis Tiškevičius (Jerzy Tyszkiewicz), Bishop of Samogitia and later of Vilnius, to establish, along with a new Dominican Priory, a series of 19 chapels on the hillsides, each illustrating an episode in the story of Christ's Passion. The construction of such circuits, which are known as Calvaries after the hill where the Crucifixion took place, was common throughout Central and Eastern Europe. This was the first to be built in Lithuania, and is also the only one to survive intact. It soon became a popular pilgrimage site, and became even more so after a supposedly miraculous picture of *The Madonna and Child* was brought from Rome by one of the friars later the same decade.

The pilgrimages continue to this day at the times of all the major religious festivals, but are seen at their most spectacular during the ten-day celebration in early July of the Feast of the Visitation (the visit of the newly pregnant Virgin Mary to her aged cousin Elizabeth, who was expecting John the Baptist). On each of the days, following a midday Mass, there is a procession all the way round the circuit led by a group of high-ranking ecclesiastical dignitaries, who take turns to lead prayers or preach short sermons at each stop. They are accompanied by white-robed acolytes carrying banners and children dressed in colourful local costumes, while the miracle-working icon itself is borne in triumph in a gilded carriage. Most pilgrims, some of whom also don traditional garb, join the main procession. Others prefer to process later in smaller groups, perhaps bringing along an object of veneration such as a crucifix, or their own folk instruments, thereby giving the event a musical flavour.

Church of the Visitation The Church of the Visitation has the rank of a papal basilica; it was only the third in Lithuania to gain the honour, following the archdiocesan cathedrals of Kaunas and Vilnius. It is the fourth church the town has had, built in 1780–85 to plans by Augustinas Kasakauskas, and renovated in 1824. Although still Baroque in the fluidity of its outline, it also shows clear traces of the greater formality characteristic of the then emergent Neo-Classical style. While its dimensions seem enormous in relation to the small size of the town, it is nevertheless not nearly large enough to accommodate all the people who come for the major pilgrimages, and many of the congregation have to stand in the churchyard and listen to loudspeaker relays of the Masses.

The church's whitewashed exterior is plain, save for the façade with its twin towers, central pediment and slim Doric pilasters. Its interior is colourfully painted to resemble marble and stucco. The high altar, round which pilgrims hobble piously on their knees, adopts the form of a triumphal arch with sculptured figures of Christ on the Cross, the Virgin and St John the Evangelist. There is a reliquary with a fragment of the cross in addition to the miraculous picture, whose background is studded with gold and silver stars. The altar to the left contains a copy of the Turin Shroud, which was presented by the Bishop of Turin in 2004; on the pillar facing it is a painting of St Casimir, Lithuania's patron saint. Other pillars of the nave have portraits of prominent Samogitian bishops, while the walls of the aisles are lined with pictures of the Stations of the Cross; these differ from those in the circuit of chapels by including one extra scene and varying some of the others. The right aisle also features a statue of the Man of Sorrows dressed in clothes brought by pilgrims. On the left side of the entrance is an intriguing holy water basin which is much older than the church, and possibly pagan in origin.

The chapels In contrast to their counterparts in some other Eastern European Calvaries, the 19 chapels along the 4.5km pilgrim circuit are not imaginary re-creations of the holy places of Jerusalem. Instead, they are simple structures of wood or fieldstones containing a painted and/or carved representation of the scene to which they are dedicated. During the times of the pilgrimages, they are kept open all day long, and can be located with ease by following one of the processions. At other times, they are only occasionally open.

The route starts at the back of the church and goes left uphill to Chapel 1 (*The Last Supper*), then downhill and along the lower ground to Chapel 2 (*Christ Takes Leave of His Mother*). From there, St John's Hill can be seen ahead on the opposite side of the River Varduva. Once the site of Gardai Castle, its summit is now crowned with the octagonal steeple of Chapel 3 (*The Agony in the Garden of Gethsemane*). A little lower down is Chapel 4 (*The Kiss of Judas*). Downhill, the route continues slightly to the right then over another bridge to Chapel 5 (*Christ Bound with Ropes*). It continues onwards, left over another bridge then left uphill to Chapel 6 (*Christ Before the High Priest Ananas*), which stands beside an old fire station constructed out of planks of wood with a look-out post on top. Completing the circle back to Chapel 1, the route continues straight ahead along the same road, before branching uphill to the left and Chapel 7 (*The Arrest and Trial of Christ*). Returning back down the hill, it goes straight on up through the cemetery to Chapel 8 (*Pilate's Judgement*), then descends to the left then up the little slope to Chapel 9 (*St Peter's Denial of Christ*).

From there it doubles back, albeit on the opposite side of the cemetery, to the large Chapel 10 (*The Scourging and Mocking of Christ*). One of the main stops for the processions, this features a statue of Christ at the Column and an open-air pulpit below its gable. The route continues down to the foot of the hill by the path to the right to Chapel 11 (*Christ Taking up the Cross*). A few paces beyond are Chapel 12 (*The Meeting with St Veronica*) and Chapel 13 (*Christ Carrying the Cross*); the latter has doors at both ends, allowing the processions to pass straight through. Directly ahead is Chapel 14 (*Simon of Cyrene Carrying the Cross*). The dirt road ahead leads on past a pond then goes uphill to Chapel 15 (*Jesus Falls for the Third Time*). Doubling back downhill, the route goes over the road then up the slope to Chapel 16 (*The Disrobing of Christ*). At the top of the same hill is another major stop, Chapel 17 (*The Crucifixion*), which is in the form of a miniature cruciform church with a pentagonal apse. The latter's interior is filled by a 15m by 5m mural centred on a carved depiction of the main scene. Painted in the early years of the 20th century by the renowned folk artist Kazys Varnelis, it is full of lively detail, and its sheer scale is unparalleled in Lithuania. Back at the foot of the hill is the stone-built Chapel 18 (*The Entombment*), which features a quirky triple-gabled façade. Back across the road, the route goes up to the right to Chapel 19 (*St Helena's Discovery of the True Cross*), then returns back to the church.

✗ **Where to eat** The only place where hot food can be obtained is the nameless daytime café in the cultural centre directly facing the church; it serves a few Lithuanian staples as well as drinks and home-made cakes.

WESTERN SAMOGITIA

The westernmost part of Samogitia is now part of the county of Klaipėda, the rest of which – the coastal area which was mostly under German domination from the Middle Ages right up until World War I – forms the subject of the following chapter.

KRETINGA Kretinga is pleasantly set on the River Akmena, 40km west of Plungė along the rail line to Klaipėda and the road to Palanga. First documented in 1253, it was a Lithuanian stronghold throughout the medieval period, and one of the very few Samogitian towns which was never at any time captured by the Teutonic Knights. In 1572 it passed into the possession of Jonas Karolis Katkevičius (Jan Karol Chodkiewicz in its Polish form), the Grand Hetman of Lithuania, and was later successively controlled by other prominent dynasties, including the Sapieha, Massalski and Tiškevičius (Tyszkiewicz) families.

Getting there and around
🚌 **Bus station** Šventosios 1; ✆ 445 51333. Situated west of the town centre, on the left bank of the river. Services include 6 buses daily to Telšiai via Plungė, 4 to Mosėdis via Salantai & 3 to Plateliai. Although there are buses to both Klaipėda & Palanga every hour or so, there is a far more frequent service (every 10 or 15 mins in high summer) by the microbuses which leave from the western side of Rotušės aikštė.

🚃 **Railway station** Stoties 1; ✆ 445 51197. Immediately alongside the bus station. There are 4 trains daily to Klaipėda & 4 to Šiauliai, 2 of which continue to Vilnius.

Tourist information
ℹ **Tourist office** Vilniaus 18; ✆ 445 77612; e tickretinga@takas.lt; www.kretinga.lt. Located in Kretinga Palace; ⏰ 08.00–17.00 Mon–Thu, 08.00–16.00 Fri, 10.00–14.00 Sat.

Where to stay

🏠 **Gelmė** Žemaičių 3; 📞 445 76931; **f** 445 76930. A hotel with a café just off the southeast corner of Rotušės aikštė. $

🏠 **Pajūrio Egzotika** (also known as HBH) Žibininkai; 📞/**f** 448 444223/44678; **e** info@hbhjuozas.lt; www.hbhjuozas.lt. This holiday complex 8km northwest of Kretinga is best known for its microbrewery, which produces the award-winning light & dark Juozo beers (the latter available only in winter). These can be sampled in the public bar, which also serves tasty local dishes. Horseriding, angling & boating are among the activities on offer; members of the host family speak some English & German. $$

🏠 **Smagratis** Daujoto 6; 📞 448 76256; **f** 448 77267; **e** smagratis@takas.lt; www.smagratis.lt. A motel with a café-restaurant by the main road at the extreme eastern edge of town. $

🏠 **Vienkiemis** Padvariai; 📞 448 78425, **f** 448 77597; **e** sodybavienkiemis@takas.lt; www.vienkiemis.lt. A holiday & leisure complex situated by a reservoir on the River Akmena, 3km north of Kretinga. Boats, water cycles, bicycles & horses can be hired, & there is a wooden bath-house which can be used for Finnish saunas or Russian steam baths. Typical Lithuanian fare is served in the restaurant. The rooms, especially the 2-tier apts, are very luxurious. $$

Where to eat

✗ **Pas Grafą** Vilniaus 20. The restaurant in the Winter Garden is undoubtedly one of the pleasantest places for a meal anywhere in Lithuania. There are plenty of appropriately exotic & expensive items on the fish-dominated menu, though

there are many reasonably priced options as well. Closed Mon.

✗ **Pas Sigitą** Basanavičiaus 61. A homely café-restaurant located on the opposite side of the river from the town centre.

What to see and do At the heart of town, set well above the right bank of the Akmena, is an open square, Rotušės aikštė, whose vast proportions seem very exaggerated for a town whose population is only just over 20,000. By its southeastern corner is the **Lutheran Church**, a small brick building erected in the 1890s. It still has an active and enthusiastic congregation, and is open on Sunday mornings for services.

Immediately north of the square is the **Bernardine Friary**, founded in 1602 by Jonas Karolis Katkevičius. This was closed down by the Soviets in 1945, and between 1977 and 1992 served as the home of the local museum. In 1993 the complex was returned to the Franciscans, who immediately resumed its monastic tradition. There are currently more than 40 members of the community, making it the main centre of Franciscanism in the Baltic region, though at any one time around half the friars are undertaking missionary work elsewhere.

The friary's **Church of the Annunciation** was built between 1610 and 1617. Architecturally, it is a curious hybrid, mixing elements of the Renaissance style then current with many of what were by then wholly archaic Gothic features. It was extended in 1672 and again in 1905, when the aisles were added. The tall, slender tower, which dominates Kretinga's skyline, had to be rebuilt following damage in World War II. Above its doorway is a highly theatrical statue of the Stigmatisation of St Francis. Inside, the massive high altar features a juxtaposition of Old and New Testament figures in an intricate Renaissance frame. The left side altar is dedicated to the Holy Family, the right to SS Francis and Bernardino; beside the latter are portraits of the founder and his wife. A grandiose Neo-Baroque pulpit in the nave is evidence of the Franciscan emphasis on preaching.

The church is set in an enclosed garden which also contains an octagonal baptistery, which is no longer in use, and a complete circuit of shrines dedicated to the Stations of the Cross. Down in the valley immediately to the north is a **Lourdes Grotto**, where large crowds congregate after the main Sunday Masses.

Further north, almost at the edge of town, the late 19th-century **Palace** of the Tiškevičius family stands at the western edge of its own landscaped park. The

Motiejus Valančius graduated from Vilnius Seminary in 1828, then served as a priest in Belarus, Vilnius and St Petersburg, prior to his appointment in 1850 as Bishop of Samogitia, an office he held until his death. He founded numerous parish schools and libraries, and worked tirelessly to keep the Lithuanian language and culture alive at a time when it was under severe threat from the Tsarist authorities. This situation became acute after the failed rebellion of 1863–64, when the use of the Cyrillic alphabet was made compulsory. Valančius circumvented this by arranging for the publication of Lithuanian texts printed in the Latin alphabet in neighbouring East Prussia, which were then smuggled over the border.

He was himself a prolific writer in a wide range of fields. His publications about Samogitia include a two-volume history of the diocese and a collection of local proverbs. In the devotional field, he wrote about the lives of the saints and the Psalms of David, and published a collection of religious songs. He also wrote didactic tales for both children and adults, as well as *Palangos Juzė*, a story incorporating much information about the everyday life and customs of the Samogitians, the hero being a tailor who personifies all their best qualities.

Valančius was also a high-profile temperance campaigner, declaring that 'hearts of teetotallers are pleasant to God'. He achieved a quite extraordinary success with this. Temperance brotherhoods were established all over Samogitia, with membership as high as 90% in some villages. This inevitably led to a huge decrease in revenue from alcohol taxes, to the further displeasure of the authorities. Valančius died in Kaunas, where he had moved in 1864 as a result of the enforced transference of the bishopric from Varniai, and is buried in the cathedral.

main block is now home to the **Kretinga Museum** (*www.kretingosmuziejus.lt;* ⊕ *10.00–18.00 Wed–Sun*), which contains a good collection of Samogitian folk art, plus archaeological finds and local history displays. There are also a few paintings, the most notable being *The Four Evangelists* attributed to the short-lived 17th-century French master Valentin de Boulogne.

Entered directly from the museum is Kretinga's great pride and joy, the **Winter Garden** (⊕ *Jun–Aug 10.00–18.00 Mon, 10.00–20.30 Tue–Sun; Sep–May 10.00–18.00 Tue–Fri & Sun, 10.00–19.00 Sat*), which is the only one of its type in Lithuania. Its curvaceous glass and iron exterior looks all the more startling for being sandwiched between the sober stonework of the main palace block and one of the wings. The interior, which is on three separate levels, features grottoes, a pool and elaborate stairwells and balconies, as well as a host of exotic plants and trees brought from around the world. It is a true oasis of fragrant tranquillity, even if the central floor, now a café-restaurant, can be busy on occasions. Originally opened in 1875, the garden was destroyed in World War II but painstakingly re-created by the staff of the Kretinga Agricultural College based in the old estate buildings.

NASRĖNAI The little street village of Nasrėnai, 22km northeast of Kretinga, was the birthplace of one of the great figures of Lithuania's 19th-century nationalist movement, Bishop Motiejus Valančius (see box above). His original house has burnt down, but has been replaced by a reproduction, which now contains the **Valančius Museum** (*officially* ⊕ *09.00–17.00 Wed–Sun, though the custodian, who* *lives on the premises, will admit visitors at any reasonable time*). This features documentary material on the bishop, including a few personal belongings and old editions of many of his writings. The well outside the house and the five-roomed granary to the rear are authentic survivals from the time of Valančius's childhood, and the latter is a fine example of the rural architecture of the region. Standing under a shelter in front of the museum is a polychromed statue of Juzė Viskanta (Palangos Juzė), his best-known fictional creation.

KALNALIS A couple of kilometres along the same road is another tiny village, Kalnalis, which is dominated by the wooden **Church of St Lawrence**. This serves as the parish church for the whole of the surrounding area and was therefore the place where Valančius was baptised, and where he worshipped as a boy. It is absolutely typical of rural Lithuania, set in an enclosure on a hillock, with a detached belfry by the entrance, the whole ensemble painted green to match the lush countryside in which it stands.

The church was constructed in 1777 under the patronage of the Oginskis family, and rebuilt in 1882 following a fire. Under the organ gallery is a processional painting of the Virgin in an elaborate carved frame, while beside the altar is a sculptural group depicting the Burial of Christ which serves as a focal point of the Holy Week services. A number of curious wooden tombstones can be seen in the cemetery.

SALANTAI Some 6km further on, at the junction with a road from Plungė, is Salantai, which had a sizeable Jewish population prior to World War II. The tall twin spires of the redbrick **Church of the Assumption**, which stands at the highest point of town, can be seen from afar, and indeed are already clearly visible from just outside Kalnalis. It was built in Neo-Gothic style between 1906 and 1911, on a scale which was far grander than was necessary for local needs. Inside, the pulpit and the three main altars are fine examples of carving from the same period as that of the church's construction. The left altar features an unconventional representation of *The Dormition of the Virgin*, and incorporates a venerated icon of *The Virgin and Child* studded with ex-votos which came from the previous church on the site.

Just over 2km southeast of Salantai, signposted along a dirt track from the Plungė road, is one of Samogitia's strangest and most popular attractions, the **Orvydas Garden** (⊕*09.00/10.00–19.00 Tue–Sun, reduced hours out of season*), which has alternately been dubbed the 'Museum of the Absurd' and the 'Museum of the History of the Nation'. It was created on his family's farm, a distinctively triangular-shaped area of land known as Gargždelė, by Vilius Orvydas (1952–92), a sculptor and mystic who became a fully-fledged member of the Franciscan Order shortly before his sudden death from a heart attack a few days before his 40th birthday. Orvydas learned his craft from his father Kazys, who had been both ploughman and stonemason, specialising in the carving of tombstones for local cemeteries. When the Soviets began their programme of destroying Christian symbols and other facets of traditional rural life, he began saving objects from all over Lithuania, incorporating them into the huge sculptures he made for the garden. Many were confiscated by the authorities, but this did not deter him from his aims, and he continued to pursue his policy of conservation in the independence period, saving Soviet-era artefacts from the destruction that would otherwise have befallen them.

The garden is a somewhat surreal sight. Hundreds of sculptures in both stone and wood are displayed, at times prominently, in other cases half-hidden among the rocks and the trees. Some display the influence of the Italian Renaissance, others recall the art of Polynesia or Easter Island (though Orvydas claimed never even to have seen photographs of these), still others are defiantly avant-garde. There are grottoes and tombstones (including that of the sculptor himself), multitudes of crosses, statues of characters from Lithuanian mythology, and rooms hollowed out of trees. The ancient, half-dead oaks themselves, whose withered branches resemble hands held up in prayer, form a key element in the spiritual emphasis of the garden. While many of the sculptures are directly Christian in their iconography – one of the focal points is a vast open-air altar where Orvydas conducted Masses – others reveal his interest in secular cosmology.

In this setting, the Soviet-era objects stand out as intruders. Particularly prominent are the rocket guarding the entrance to the unfinished amphitheatre and the tank sunk in a ditch by the entrance. The latter formerly stood on the now-empty plinth of the war memorial which can still be seen in Salantai. Its Russian driver died in World War II and was subsequently made a Hero of the Soviet Union, though the story goes that, far from doing anything heroic, he had killed himself in a crash while escaping from the conflict to pay a visit to his Lithuanian girlfriend.

Hidden away in the heart of the garden is the original farm, where members of the Orvydas family continue to live. They have refused to accept public funds for the maintenance of the garden, instead abandoning the tradition of free and unrestricted access in favour of set opening times and admission fees, with extra charges for the use of cameras and video recorders. Despite this, the garden has been allowed to become ever more unkempt; there are no effective measures against thieves, who are steadily plundering the sculptures, while others have been vandalised or allowed to fall into decay; and there is no strategy for preservation or development. As a result, many admirers of Orvydas's work are fearful for the garden's future.

MOSĖDIS Mosėdis, 12km north of Salantai, is home to another bizarre individual creation, the **Museum of Rare Stones** (⊕*May–Oct 08.00–18.00 Mon–Fri, 10.00–18.00 Sat–Sun; Nov–Apr 08.00–12.00 & 13.00–17.00 daily*). In many ways, this was developed as a direct rival to the Orvydas Garden, though there are important differences. For one, it occupies a very visible position right in the heart of the little town; for another, it now has the status of a national museum, even although its founder and driving force, the local doctor Vaclovas Intas, continues to serve as its director. Moreover, its primary purposes are the scientific ones of preserving unusual stones from the Baltic region and raising public awareness of them; such artistic features as it possesses are of incidental importance.

Since 1957 Intas has amassed and documented a collection of 150,000 stones from Lithuania, Latvia, Estonia, Finland and Sweden. These range from tiny examples weighing a few grammes to huge boulders of up to 50 tonnes and are now displayed in various locations in the centre of Mosėdis. The restored 18th-century watermill beside the bridge contains many of the smaller pieces, plus documentary material on the history of the museum. In the park to the rear (to which there is free access all year round), the larger boulders are laid out in the form of a nature trail. Others, including one with an inscription in the Samogitian dialect in praise of local worthies, are prominently displayed on the communal green immediately to the north. On the street immediately beyond is the most obviously attractive section, the garden of Intas's own house. This contains some of the star pieces, including the very first stone he collected, set among a fine arrangement of trees, flowers, shrubs and sculptures.

Mosėdis's other main landmark, set in an enclosure entered via an unusually splendid gateway, is the **Church of St Michael the Archangel**, a classically inspired Baroque building erected in 1783 on the site of its wooden predecessor. The most impressive part of the exterior is the façade, which features a handsome pediment between the two slender towers. Among the furnishings are a carved crucifix adorned with ex-votos and a memorial to the writer Vaižgantas (otherwise known as Juozas Tumas), who served as the parish priest from 1895–99.

In the vicinity of Mosėdis, a number of large boulders deposited by glaciers can still be found in their original locations. The nearest are in the **Šaukliai Reservation** 3km to the south, just off the Salantai road.

✻ Where to eat

✗ **Melnika kamara** Salantų 2. The café-restaurant in the lower rear part of the watermill serves good & inexpensive Lithuanian dishes. There is the opportunity for al fresco dining in good weather. Open summer only.

Roe deer

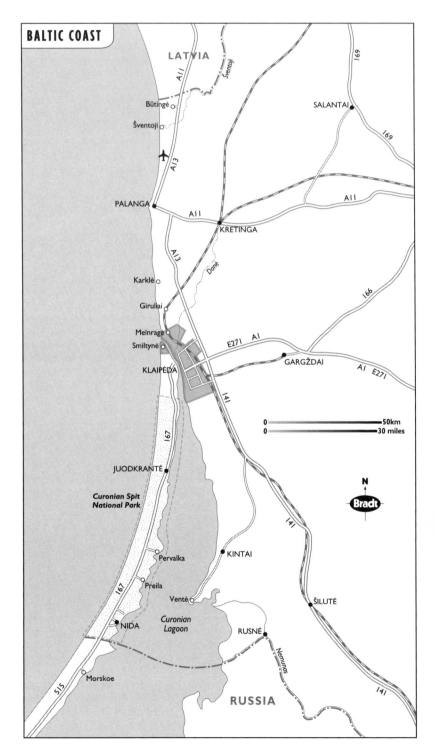

BALTIC COAST

LATVIA

A11

Šventoji

Būtingé

Šventoji

A13

SALANTAI

169

169

PALANGA

A11

KRETINGA

A11

A13

Dane

Karklé

166

Girullai

Melnragé

Smiltynè

KLAIPÈDA

E271 A1

GARGŽDAI

A1 E271

141

0 50km
0 30 miles

167

N

Bradt

JUODKRANTÈ

Curonian Spit
National Park

141

Pervalka

KINTAI

167

Preila

Ventè

ŠILUTÈ

NIDA

Curonian
Lagoon

RUSNÈ

Nemunas

141

515

Morskoe

RUSSIA

11

The Baltic Coast

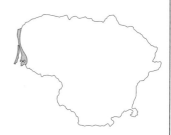

Lithuania's Baltic coastline stretches for a mere 99km. Short as this seems, it is ten times longer than it was in the country's halcyon period as a major European state stretching to the Black Sea. Then, Lithuania had to be content with a tiny strip of land around Palanga which was none the less of huge significance, giving the country a northern outlet to the sea and at the same time preventing the Teutonic Knights from linking up their Prussian and Livonian territories – which, had they been successful, would inevitably have meant German dominance over the whole Baltic region.

In the Dark Ages this coastline, together with that of Latvia to the north, was settled by a tribe of Balts known as the Curonians (or Kurs). They never established themselves as a separate nation, though their name lives on in the Latvian province of Kurzeme (the successor to the former Duchy of Courland), and in the Curonian Spit and Curonian Lagoon, which are both divided between Lithuania and the Russian *oblast* of Kaliningrad. The spit is one of the great natural wonders of Europe, and while it is unfortunate that there are major bureaucratic and logistical hurdles to overcome if planning a visit to the Russian sector, the Lithuanian part, the undoubted scenic highlight of the country, is very well-geared to tourism. Much the same can be said of the other main destinations in the region, the great port of Klaipėda and the seaside town of Palanga, which are just 30km apart.

A fine sandy beach backed by dunes runs all the way along the Lithuanian coastline, and in order to ensure the conservation of this landscape, no seafront promenades or hotels have ever been built. In practice, it is possible to traverse the entire length of the beach on foot, with the proviso that in summer certain sections are marked for the use of women (*moterų*) or men (*vyrų*) only. Nude bathing is permitted on these stretches, but not elsewhere.

PALANGA

Palanga is Lithuania's premier beach and health resort. Its popularity during its short summer season, which lasts from the beginning of June until the middle of September, has to be seen to be believed. The permanent population of 20,000 is often increased five-fold or more, particularly at weekends when there is a relentless stream of sun-seekers from all over the country and beyond, who come to swim in the sea, sunbathe and play games on the long sandy beach, and eat, drink and be merry in the restaurants, bars, cafés, discos, funfairs and other raucous places of entertainment which throng the town centre, maintaining a party atmosphere virtually round the clock.

It was not until the Treaty of Melno in 1422 that the Teutonic Knights agreed to give up their attempts to control the entire southern Baltic coast, leaving Lithuania in undisputed possession of a few kilometres around the mouths of the

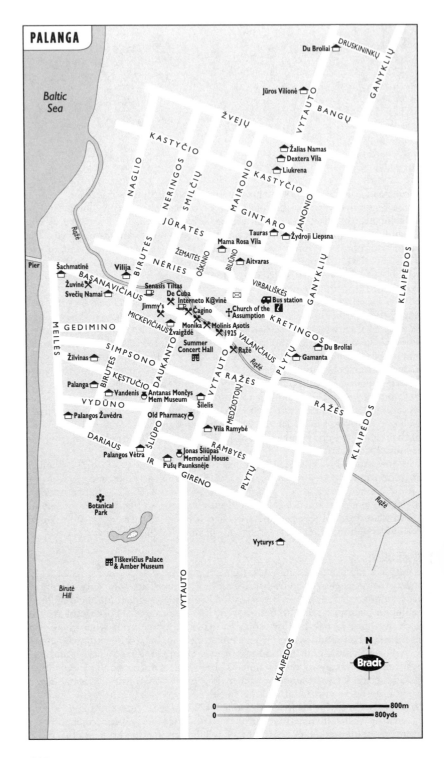

PALANGA

Baltic Sea

Du Broliai

DRUSKININKŲ

GANYKLIŲ

Jūros Vilionė

VYTAUTO BANGŲ

ŽVEJŲ

KASTYČIO

NAGLIO

NERINGOS

SMILČIŲ

Žalias Namas
Dextera Vila
Liukrena

KASTYČIO

O

MAIRONIO

GINTARO

JANONIO

JŪRATĖS

ŽEMAITĖS

Tauras
Žydroji Liepsna

Mama Rosa Vila

BIRUTĖS

OŠKINIO

BILIŪNO

NĖRIES

Aitvaras

Pier

Šachmatinė
Žuvinė
Svečių Namai

Vilija

BASANAVIČIAUS

VIRBALIŠKĖS

Senasis Tiltas
De Cuba

Interneto K@vinė

Bus station

GANYKLIŲ

KLAIPĖDOS

Jimmy's

Cagino

Church of the
Assumption

KRETINGOS

MICKEVIČIAUS

Monika
Žvaigždė

Molinis Asotis
1925

MEILĖS

GEDIMINO

Summer
Concert Hall

VALANČIAUS

Ražė

PLYTŲ

Du Broliai

Žilvinas

SIMPSONO

BIRUTĖS

DAUKANTO

VYTAUTO

RAŽĖS

Gamanta

RAŽĖS

KĘSTUČIO

Palanga
Vandenis

Antanas Mončys
Mem Museum

Šilelis

MEDŽIOTOJŲ

KLAIPĖDOS

VYDŪNO

Palangos Žuvėdra

Old Pharmacy

Vila Ramybė

DARIAUS

ŠLIŪPO

RAMBYĖS

Palangos Vėtra

IR

Jonas Šliūpas
Memorial House
Pušų Paunksnėje

PLYTŲ

GIRĖNO

Ražė

Botanical
Park

Tiškevičius Palace
& Amber Museum

Vyturys

VYTAUTO

Birutė Hill

N

Bradt

KLAIPĖDOS

0   800m
0   800yds

Ražė and Šventoji rivers. For Grand Duke Vytautas the Great this was a matter of some sentimental interest, as Palanga, which lay by the mouth of the Ražė, was the birthplace of his mother Birutė. More importantly, Palanga and its sister village of Šventoji to the north (which now forms part of its municipality) gave the huge Grand Duchy a window on the Baltic, and for its entire history this short stretch was as much as it ever had for a northern coastline.

The development of Palanga and Šventoji as ports was hampered by the fact that their respective rivers were both shallow and sandy, which meant that only small ships could sail in. Jan Sobieski, King of Poland and Grand Duke of Lithuania, attempted to remedy the situation in the late 17th century by encouraging English merchants to develop a harbour, but this was destroyed by the Swedes in 1701 and never revived. Palanga was thereafter no more than a small fishing village until the second half of the 19th century, when seaside holidays first started to become fashionable. When the Baltic states proclaimed their independence after World War I, Palanga was first given to Latvia, on the grounds that it had originally been part of Courland, but was returned to Lithuania in 1921 as a result of a territorial swap.

GETTING THERE AND AROUND

✈ **Airport** Liepos 1; \/f 460 52020; www.palanga-airport.lt. Sited 6km north of town, & served by the regular buses & minibuses (there are usually at least 2 per hr) to Šventoji. In addition to charter services, Lithuanian Airlines flies 6 times weekly to Amsterdam, 5 times weekly to Tallinn, & weekly to Frankfurt, Hamburg & Hannover, while SAS flies daily to Copenhagen.

🚌 **Bus station** Kretingos 1; \ 460 53333. Situated at the eastern end of the town centre. The frequency of services depends on the season, but in high summer there are several minibuses per hr to both Kretinga (which has the nearest railway station) & Klaipėda. There are also at least 10 daily non-stop express buses to Kaunas (taking around 3hrs) & Vilnius (just over 4hrs), plus many more which stop along the way. International services include 1 daily to Minsk, 1 daily to Moscow, 2 daily to Kaliningrad, & 4 daily to Liepa-ja (2 of which continue on to Rīga).

TOURIST INFORMATION

ℹ **Municipal Tourist Office** Kretingos 1; \ 460 48811; f 460 48822, e palangaturinfo@is.lt or info@palangatic.lt; www.palangatic.lt. Located within the bus station. ⏰ Jun–Aug 09.00–18.00 Mon–Fri, 10.00–18.00 Sat–Sun; Sep–May 09.00–18.00 Mon–Fri.

COMMUNICATIONS

✉ **Post office** Vytauto 53. ⏰ 09.00–18.30 Mon–Fri, 09.00–16.00 Sat.

WHERE TO STAY Palanga has the largest provision of rooms for rent of any Lithuanian town, not excluding Vilnius. There is something to suit every taste and pocket, from small family-run houses, via bleak institutionalised holiday homes stuck in a Soviet era time-warp, to ultra-modern hotels with fully equipped apartment suites which offer the last word in luxury. Note that, more than anywhere else in the country, prices are subject to dramatic fluctuations. The codes given here are for summer, but rates are likely to be reduced by up to 50% out of season, or if demand becomes slack because of a long period of poor weather. On the other hand, during particularly hot spells, when the resort becomes even busier than usual, normal high season tariffs may be jacked up.

Hotels The list below offers no more than a sample of what is on offer in Palanga, though it does include virtually all the most enticing choices. Advance reservations are recommended if arriving at the weekend, though there should seldom be difficulty in finding accommodation, particularly at the top end of the market, where the receptionists normally – though not invariably – speak at least basic English. Unusually for Lithuania, room rates, particularly in the cheaper establishments, do not always include breakfast.

Luxury

🏠 **Auska** Vytauto 11; 📞 460 49083; bookings via Baltija, Gankly 30; 📞 460 49184; f 460 49226; e info@baltijahotel.lt; www.baltijahotel.lt. This hotel was where members of the Soviet elite, Brezhnev included, used to take their seaside holidays. Some of the secret atmosphere is still preserved: the 23-hectare grounds, immediately south of the Botanical Park, remain fenced off & closed to non-residents. Facilities include a sauna, a swimming pool with heated sea water, massage & a sports hall. Apts $$$$$

🏠 **Palanga** Birutės 60; 📞 460 41414; f 460 41415; e info@palangahotel.lt; www.palangahotel.lt. New luxury hotel in a leafy setting in the far south of the town centre. Its restaurant specialises in flambé dishes. $$$$, suites & apts $$$$$

🏠 **Pušų paunksnėje** Dariaus ir Girėno 25; 📞 460 49080; f 460 49081; e pusupaunksneje@ palanga.omnitel.net; www.pusupaunksneje.lt. Co-owned by basketball star Arvydas Sabonis, this is arguably the most luxurious hotel in town. Each of its 14 apts – which are grouped around a court which can be used for either basketball or tennis – has a terrace, satellite TV, minibar & AC. The restaurant presents an innovative international menu. Other facilities include a swimming pool, sauna, steam baths & fitness room. Apts $$$$$

🏠 **Mama Rosa Vila** Jūratės 28a; 📞 460 48581; f 460 48580; e vila@mamarosa.lt; www.mamarosa.lt. An immaculately appointed 8-bedroom hotel in a modern villa. All rooms have satellite TV, AC, minibar & ironing press; other facilities are a café, a lounge with hearth, a sauna, a bath with underwater massage & a billiards room. $$$, suites $$$$$

🏠 **Šachmatinė** Basanavičiaus 45; 📞/f 460 51655; e sachmatine@chili.eu; www.sachmatine.lt. One of Palanga's most exclusive addresses, not least because of its location on the famous main street, just a stone's throw away from the beach. There are just 6 dbl rooms & 3 apts, all well appointed with bathrooms, satellite TV & telephone; a sauna & swimming pool are also on offer. The downstairs restaurant is a branch of Čili, the well-regarded Vilnius pizzeria, & understandably gets a huge amount of passing trade. $$$, suite $$$$$

🏠 **Žalias Namas** Vytauto 97; 📞/f 460 51231; e info@zaliasnamas.lt; www.zaliasnamas.lt. A very

attractive & well-run hotel directly adjoining Dextera Vila. The bedrooms & bathrooms are wonderfully spacious & nicely decorated in pale colours. Facilities include a sauna, swimming pool, billiards room, hairdresser & summertime café. $$$, apts $$$$

🏠 **Palangos Vėtra** Daukanto 35; 📞 460 53032; f 460 57231; e hotel@palangosvetra.lt; www.vetra.lt. A plush Scandinavian-style designer hotel located close to the beach in the southern part of town. The bedrooms are tastefully furnished & have satellite TV, minibar, AC & heated bathroom floors. $$$, suites $$$$, apts $$$$$

🏠 **Perliukas** Vanagupės 13; 📞 460 52922; f 460 51533; e musuperliukas@takas.lt; www.perliukashotel.ru. This hotel consists of just 8 spacious apts which are excellent value at the price asked. The 4 standard suites ($$$) are in open-plan style, with a partition separating the bedroom & living room; the 2 middle-range options ($$$$) have massive baths, designer furniture & fittings, bar & kitchen; the luxury apts ($$$$) are full-size flats with 2 bathrooms equipped with a plethora of different kinds of bathing facilities.

🏠 **Gamanta** Plytų 7; 📞 460 48885; f 460 48889; e info@gamanta.lt; www.gamanta.lt. A very professionally run modern business-class hotel in the relatively quiet eastern part of the centre. All rooms have private facilities, satellite TV, telephone & minibar, while the luxury suite at the top of the tower commands fine views through its picture windows. Unusually for Palanga, fluent English is spoken. A wide selection of imaginative fish & other dishes is on offer in the restaurant. $$$, suites $$$$

🏠 **Dextera Vila** Vytauto 97; 📞/f 460 53411; e klaipeda@dextera.lt; www.dextera.lt/vila. A small modern hotel whose bedrooms & bathrooms are admirably large & furnished in a traditional style, though they also have satellite TV & telephone. The largest apt is equipped with a kitchen. Guests have free use of the swimming pool; a sauna & massage are also on offer, while a restaurant & clothes store are also on the premises. $$$

🏠 **Du Broliai** Kretingos 36; 📞 460 48108; f 460 54028; & Vytauto 160; 📞 460 40049; f 460 52889. Appropriately enough, the 'Two Brothers' consists of

2 separately run small hotels, the first in the eastern part of town, the second in the northern centre. Although modern in every way, they are full of traditional touches, & the rooms are equipped with private facilities (some have jacuzzis), satellite TV & telephone. The hotel on Kretingos also has a fine upmarket restaurant, that on Vytauto a piano bar & clothes store. $$$

Mid-range
⌂ **Vandenis** Birutės 47; ℡ 460 53530; f 460 53584; e info@vandenis.lt; www.vandenis.lt. A pleasant hotel in a huge old house in the quiet southern part of town. It has a bar-restaurant, sauna, swimming pool & massage. $$$

⌂ **Palangos Žuvėdra** Dariaus ir Girėno 1; ℡ 460 53253/54082; f 460 53852; e info@palangos-zuvedra.lt; www.palangos-zuvedra.lt. This renovated rest home occupies 3 adjacent buildings. Not the least of its attractions is its tower-restaurant, the only one in Palanga to offer a panoramic sea view. $$, suites $$$

⌂ **Liukrena** Vytauto 93a; ℡ 460 525521; f 460 48954; e hotelliukrena@gmail.com. This reasonably priced modern hotel comes complete with fitness centre, sauna, small swimming pool, billiards room & restaurant. $$, apts $$$

⌂ **Tauras** Vytauto 116; ℡/f 460 49111; e feliksas@feliksas.lt; www.feliksas.lt. All bedrooms at this friendly, recently renovated hotel have balconies, bath or shower, satellite TV, minibar & telephone. Facilities include the Feliksas restaurant, which is decked out in the manner of a luxury yacht, & a sauna, while bikes can be rented. $$, suites $$$

⌂ **Vila Ramybė** Vytauto 54; ℡/f 460 54124; e palanga@vilaramybe.lt; www.vilaramybe.lt. This fine old wooden villa in the southern part of town has 6

Budget
⌂ **Palangos Linas** Vytauto 155; ℡/f 460 52950; e reservacija@palangoslinas.com; www.palangoslinas.com. Dominating a concrete wilderness in the north of town, this resembles a suburban tower block in Šiauliai or Panevėžys, albeit with the compensation of sea views from the west-facing upper storeys. Despite its reminders of the Soviet-style institutionalised holiday experience, it has adapted itself to a more demanding clientele. $$, suites $$$

⌂ **Aitvaras** Biliuno 8; ℡ 460 51560; e info@aitvaras-palanga.com; www.aitvaras-palanga.com. All rooms have balconies, showers & toilets in this basic budget hotel situated on a quiet town-centre street. $$

⌂ **Žilvinas** Kęstučio 26; ℡ 460 49146; bookings via Baltija, Ganyklų 30; ℡ 460 48332; f 460 49226; e info@baltijahotel.lt; www.baltijahotel.lt. There is a choice between the apts in the modern main building in the peaceful southern part of the town centre, & those in the wooden cottages on nearby Gedimino. All guests can make use of the sauna, swimming pool & tennis courts. Apts $$$

rooms for rent plus a good café-restaurant where live jazz is often played in the evenings. $$, suites $$$

⌂ **Žydroji Liepsna** Gintaro 36; ℡ 460 52441; f 460 48250; e zydroji_liepsna@is.lt; www.zydrojiliepsna.lt. A striking designer-style hotel just off the eastern side of Vytauto. All rooms have showers, satellite TV, telephone & refrigerator; 4 have balconies. Facilities include a sauna, swimming pool, bowling alley, bar & restaurant. $$, apts $$$

⌂ **Jūros Vilionė** Vytauto 107b; ℡ 460 51659; e jurosvilione@yahoo.com. A small & very pleasant family hotel, with accommodation ranging from singles with bathrooms shared with the neighbouring room to large suites capable of sleeping 4 people. Among the facilities are a sauna, massage, laundry, billiards room & café-restaurant. $$

⌂ **Šilelis** Kęstučio 2a; ℡/f 460 54592; e vilijagr@one.lt. This fine old villa in the quietest part of Palanga was formerly a sanatorium, but has undergone a full renovation. All rooms have private facilities, satellite TV & telephone; the suites also have a small kitchen. $$

⌂ **Žvaigždė** Daukanto 6; ℡/f 460 54198. Located just off Basanavičiaus, yet far enough away from the noise, this is primarily a restaurant, serving a tasty menu of traditional Ukrainian dishes, though it also has 4 rooms for rent. $$

⌂ **Svečių Namai** Basanavičiaus 35; ℡ 460 52005; f 460 48601. A small guesthouse in a wooden building on Palanga's most famous street – an undoubtedly prestigious location, albeit a noisy one at night. $$

⌂ **Vilija** Birutės 24; ℡/f 460 40038. This curvaceous low-rise concrete block scores for its wonderful location just off Basanavičiaus & the provision of a children's playroom. All rooms have private facilities & satellite TV; the suites also have a refrigerator & small kitchen. $, suites $$

⌂ **Vyturys** Dariaus ir Girėno 20; ℡ 460 49147; bookings via Baltija, Ganyklų 30; ℡ 460 48332; f 460 49226; e info@baltijahotel.lt; www.baltijahotel.lt. This is the bargain-price member of the small Baltija chain, but it has plenty of curative facilities, including sauna, swimming pool, massage & other therapeutic treatments, as well as a hairdresser, billiards room & sports ground. All rooms have a balcony, bathroom & refrigerator. $, suites $$

Bed and breakfast

Accommodation in private houses in Palanga can be arranged via the tourist office or through Litinterp in Klaipėda. Additionally, a group of landladies touting for business can almost always be found in the bus station, with several congregating around every incoming long-distance bus. Others wait in cars all along the entry to town by the Klaipėda road.

Camping

Å Palangos Vytauto 8; ☏ 460 53533. Located in the far south of town, by the main road to Klaipėda, this offers chalets for rent. $

✕ WHERE TO EAT

Most of Palanga's best restaurants are to be found in the upmarket hotels (see above), though there are plenty of alternatives. Basanavičiaus in particular has many eateries of all kinds, as well as stalls selling tasty smoked fish from the Baltic.

✕ 1925 Basanavičiaus 4. A family-friendly restaurant with a well-equipped children's playground.

✕ Čagino Basanavičiaus 14a. An offshoot of the eponymous Russian speciality restaurant in Vilnius, housed in a striking new 2-storey building with front courtyard.

✕ De Cuba Basanavičiaus 28. As the name suggests, this aims at a Latin feel. On fine summer evenings, an open-air grill is in operation.

⎕ Interneto K@vinė Basanavičiaus 16. Café-bar whose dark interior includes a small room packed with computer terminals for surfing the internet.

✕ Jimmy's Basanavičiaus 19. A Wild West theme bar & restaurant.

✕ Molinis Ąsotis Basanavičiaus 8. Housed in an attractive wooden cabin with outdoor seating overlooking the Ąžė, this offers a large menu of tasty Lithuanian dishes at very reasonable prices.

✕ Monika Basanavičiaus 12. Another very pleasant restaurant on the main street, with pizzas as well as local fare.

✕ Ąžė Vytauto 84. A pleasant riverside restaurant serving good-quality traditional Lithuanian cuisine.

⎕ Senasis Tiltas Basanavičiaus 38. A pleasant café in a green wooden house; it serves a wide range of pancakes & is a good b/fast choice.

✕ Zuvinė Basanavičiaus 37a. Plush fish speciality restaurant in a new 2-storey wood & glass pavilion.

ENTERTAINMENT

♫ Summer Concert Hall Vytauto 43; ☏ 460 52210. The main venue for indoor musical events of all kinds. There are also plenty of outdoor performances during the season, notably in the Botanical Park.

WHAT TO SEE

Palanga has an admirably spacious feel. The built-up part of town is laid out in the rough form of a grid, albeit a very irregular one. One long street, Klaipėdos, runs all the way down its eastern perimeter; another, Vytauto, branches off its northern end and neatly bisects the town right down the middle. However, in many ways the real main street is **Basanavičiaus**, the hub of the town's entertainment and nightlife; it runs roughly parallel to the southern bank of the River Ąžė, westwards from Vytauto towards the Baltic. In 2004, it was given a major makeover, being transformed into a sort of inland promenade, with stylish new lamposts to illuminate it at night. As is the case all along the Lithuanian coast, the beach is separated from the built-up area by sand dunes backed by pine woods. Meilės, which runs south along the edge of the woods from the west end of Basanavičiaus, is the nearest the Lithuanian coast comes to having the sort of seaside promenade commonly found in other countries. The northern counterpart of this, Nagilio, cuts through the woods some way back from the sands.

Baltic amber has been prized since the days of classical antiquity; it was mentioned by the Roman writers Pliny the Elder and Tacitus in the earliest extant literary references to the region and was a staple export along the established trade routes to the Mediterranean lands. According to local legend, it came into being as a result of the ill-fated love affair between the goddess Jūratė, who lived in a palace at the bottom of the sea, and Kastytis, a Baltic fisherman. By spurning her original intended, the god Patrimpas, Jūratė so infuriated the mighty Perkūnas, the god of thunder, that he threw down a bolt of lightning which killed her and shattered her palace into tiny fragments, which subsequently became washed up as pieces of amber.

The geological explanation of the origin of amber is that it was formed during the Eocene period, between 40 and 55 million years ago, in the pine forests of a part of the Scandinavian land mass which was later swallowed up by the Baltic Sea. Due to a warming of the earth's atmosphere and other disasters, there was an over-production of resin in the trees. The resin, which filled crevices both inside the trunk and between the bark and the stem, went through a series of chemical changes – polymerisation, oxidisation, isomerisation and fermentation – to form amber.

The freshly excreted sticky resin attracted insects (particularly flies and mosquitoes, but also ants, spiders and beetles, among others) and, more rarely, butterflies, mammals and reptiles. Being unable to escape, these creatures were gradually covered by new excretions, a process which continued repeatedly until they became fossilised within an amber tomb. Various types of flora were also entrapped in the same way, but these are not as common as might be expected, because the times when leaves were shed and new excretions of resin were formed did not coincide. Only 8% of the bigger pieces of amber have fossil inclusions, so these are particularly valued.

Most deposits of Baltic amber are found on the Baltic Sea's southern coast, having been washed there from their original location. There are some 250 colour varieties, ranging from light yellow to dark brown. Amber can be almost white, or have blue, green or violet tints. It can be transparent or cloudy, or anything in between – even in a single specimen.

Traditionally, Baltic amber was gathered from the shore, where it was washed up with flotsam, or else scooped up from the sea floor with the aid of nets attached to long poles. Later, it was collected by divers clad in special gear, and eventually by mechanical dredgers. As it is easy to cut and polish, it has long been a favourite material for making jewellery. Amber necklaces, brooches, bracelets and earrings, which can be bought from countless souvenir sellers as well as highly reputable specialist outlets, remain the most popular souvenirs of the region to this day.

Palanga's L-shaped wooden **Pier** runs 400m into the Baltic from the section of beach at the end of Basanavičiaus. The first such pier was built in 1892, but the present structure dates from 1997, being a direct replacement for its predecessor, which was destroyed by autumnal storms four years previously. Itself badly damaged in 1999 but now repaired, it is a particularly popular rendezvous-point in the evening, when crowds gather to watch the often spectacular Baltic sunsets.

The Baltic Coast PALANGA

11

The main landmark of the town centre, its tall spire visible from afar, is the brick **Church of the Assumption**, which was built in Neo-Gothic style in 1907. However, it is not at all typical of the town. Far more characteristic are the many examples of painted wooden resort architecture from the 19th century and early 20th century which can be seen on Basanavičiaus, the quiet streets to the south, and the southern part of Vytauto. One of the town's finest wooden buildings is the still-functioning **Old Pharmacy** at Vytauto 33. At Vytauto 23 is the **Jonas Šliūpas Memorial House** (⊕*May–Sep 12.00–19.00 daily; Oct–Apr 11.00–17.00 Wed–Sun*). This serves both as the local history museum and, as its name suggests, as a memorial to its former occupant, a distinguished Lithuanian literary scholar and one-time American resident who returned to his native country and served as mayor of Palanga from 1933–39. A short distance to the west, at Daukanto 16, the **Antanas Mončys Museum** (⊕*Jun–Aug 15.00–21.00 Tue–Sun; Oct–May 12.00–17.00 Tue–Sun*) contains works by the eponymous sculptor, who spent most of his life in exile, having fled Lithuania in 1944. According to the terms of his will, the exhibits can be touched.

Botanical Park Immediately south of the built-up area is the 100-hectare Botanical Park, the former estate of the aristocratic Tiškevičius (Tyszkiewicz) family, who ruled Palanga from 1824 until their properties were appropriated in 1940. The park was laid out in the last years of the 19th century to designs by the French landscape gardener Edouard André, who spent three summers supervising the work, and has formal elements as well as features of the naturalistic 'English' style. There are around 500 different types of tree and shrub, many brought from exotic foreign locations. Among the garden sculptures which have been made for the park in recent decades are a monument inspired by Čiurlionis's *Sagittarius* triptych and a statue of *Eglė, Queen of the Serpents*, a popular figure in Lithuanian mythology; both are to be found near the northern entrance.

The centre-piece of the park is the Neo-Renaissance **Tiškevičius Palace**, which was completed in 1897 to designs by a German architect, Franz Schwechten. It is fronted by a terrace approached by a double stairway, at the top of which are ornamental stone vases. Below, floral beds are arranged around a long elongated pool with a fountain, and at the far end is a statue of *Christ Blessing* by the Danish Neo-Classical sculptor Berthel Thorwaldsen. To the rear of the palace is an oval-shaped rose garden.

In 1963 the palace's interior became home to the world's first **Amber Museum** (*www.pgm.lt;* ⊕*Jun–Aug Tue–Sat 10.00–20.00, Sun 10.00–19.00; Sep–May Tue–Sat 11.00–17.00, Sun 11.00–16.00*), which is a model of its kind, with plenty of information translated into English and exhibits displayed behind magnifying glasses when appropriate. The upper floor, where the visiting circuit begins, is dedicated to the geology of amber. Two of the rooms contain amber pieces with inclusions; mostly these are of insects, but there is also a very rare example of a reptile. Examples of other types of fossilised resin from around the world are shown by way of comparison. On the ground floor, the art of amber is illustrated by beads and other jewellery from the times of the early Baltic tribes via religious and decorative artefacts of the Baroque period and later, to the elaborate creations of contemporary Lithuanian craftsmen. The octagonal chapel adjoining the western end of the palace is regularly used for concerts, and also contains a permanent exhibition on the publications of Jonas Kazimieras Vilčinskis (1806–85), notably *The Vilnius Album*, a sumptuous book of coloured prints of the art and architecture of the Lithuanian capital.

Just to the west of the palace is **Birutė Hill**, which at 20.9m is the highest point in Palanga, though the dense woods around mean that it does not command much of a view. It is named in honour of Vytautas the Great's mother who, according to (a possibly true) tradition, was a virgin priestess at the pagan temple which formerly stood at the top of the hill, prior to being abducted by Duke Kęstutis, who took her back to Trakai as his bride. Nowadays, a small brick chapel, built in 1869 by the German architect Karl Mayer, occupies the temple site. Below the hill are a Lourdes grotto and a statue of Birutė.

AROUND PALANGA

ŠVENTOJI AND BŪTINGĖ Šventoji, which lies 8km north of central Palanga, on the opposite side of the airport and at the mouth of the eponymous river, still preserves the feel of a separate village. It is hard to imagine that the present down-at-heel resort, which is favoured mainly by Lithuanian families who find Palanga itself too expensive or too noisy, was once important enough to have attracted the interest of English merchants. The main draw is the relative quiet; the beach is far less protected and hence more windswept than Palanga's and is also very silted, while the pier is a forlorn ruin.

In 1998 work began on the construction of the now operational oil terminal at **Būtingė**, which lies immediately north of Šventoji, just over 1km from the Latvian frontier. The event drew widespread protests from Latvia, which was concerned about the possible dangers and environmental pollution on its doorstep. Not the least of its grievances was the fact that Lithuania's controversial Ignalina nuclear power plant is likewise very close to the Latvian border.

KLAIPĖDA

Klaipėda is Lithuania's third city, with a population of around 185,000, as well as its only commercial port. It occupies a site of huge strategic importance, by the narrow outlet which is the only link between the Curonian Lagoon and the Baltic Sea. Despite its significance to the country, it first became part of Lithuania as recently as 1923, and then only as a result of a rather improbable and impudent land grab by the inter-war republic. Before that, it had spent almost all of its long history as a German city called Memel, and had latterly been the easternmost outpost of the Second Reich.

Since its change of name, it has also changed out of recognition, with only a few heavily restored streets in the compact Old Town as a reminder of its former self. Its population is now more than three times larger than it ever was in German times, even though the German residents have long ago departed, almost to a man. In addition to influxes of Lithuanians (who had long been a significant minority community in the city), Russians were settled there after World War II, and remain a sizeable presence. While primarily an industrial and commercial city and not at all an obvious tourist destination, despite becoming an increasingly popular port of call with cruise liners, Klaipėda is in many ways a strangely compelling place which amply repays an unhurried visit.

HISTORY The official date of the city's foundation is 1252, this being the year that the Livonian branch of the Teutonic Knights built a wooden fortress which they named Memelburg (Memel Castle). Memel is the German name for the River Nemunas, which discharges itself into the Curonian Lagoon 50km to the south, and can thus be said to have its mouth at the point where the lagoon joins the Baltic. It may be that the name Klaipėda is even older, as

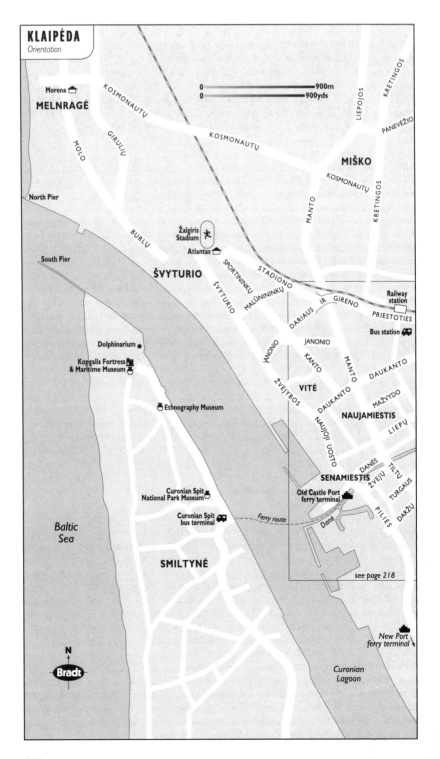

KLAIPĖDA
Orientation

0 ———————————— 900m
0 ———————————— 900yds

Morena
MELNRAGĖ

KOSMONAUTŲ

GIRULIŲ

MOLO

KOSMONAUTŲ

LIEPOJOS

KRETINGOS

PANEVĖŽIO

MIŠKO

KOSMONAUTŲ

KRETINGOS

MANTO

North Pier

BURLŲ

Žalgiris
Stadium

Atlantas

South Pier

ŠVYTURIO

ŠVYTURIO

SPORTININKŲ

MALŪNININKŲ

STADIONO

DARIAUS IR GIRENO

Railway
station

PRIESTOTIES

Bus station

Dolphinarium

Kopgalis Fortress
& Maritime Museum

JANONIO

JANONIO

KANTO

MANTO

DAUKANTO

Ethnography Museum

ŽVEJYBOS

DAUKANTO

VITĖ

MAŽVYDO

NAUJAMIESTIS

LIEPŲ

NAUJOJI UOSTO

DANĖS

TILTŲ

ŽVEJŲ

TURGAUS

Baltic
Sea

Curonian Spit
National Park Museum

Curonian Spit
bus terminal

Ferry route

SENAMIESTIS

Old Castle Port
ferry terminal

Danė

PILIES

DARŽŲ

see page 218

SMILTYNĖ

New Port
ferry terminal

N

Bradt

Curonian
Lagoon

it derives from two words in the language of the Curonian tribe which first settled the site: *klaip* ('bread') and *ėda* ('eat'), though the exact significance of the combination is a mystery.

A town quickly grew up around the more permanent stone castle the Knights built two years after their arrival, and in 1258 this was given municipal rights. Although the Lithuanians sacked Memel on several occasions, they never managed to gain permanent control of the town, which instead became one of the most secure border posts on the European map. It remained in the Knights' hands even after their landmark defeat at the Battle of Žalgiris in 1410, and served as the northeastern frontier town of Prussia from the time of the original duchy's foundation in 1525 until the abolition of the vast kingdom it later became in 1918. Only on two relatively brief occasions did it fall into foreign hands – the Swedes controlled it from 1628–35, the Russians in 1757–62.

Memel had a chequered history. It was burned to the ground in 1540, badly damaged by fire once more in 1678, and devastated by famine and plague between 1709 and 1711, when around 3,000 inhabitants perished. However, it also prospered as a shipbuilding, fishing and trading centre, exporting grain, flax, hemp, linseed and timber, with the last-named spawning a flourishing sawmill industry. Trade with Britain was particularly important. A group of Scottish merchants settled in the city in the early 17th century, to be followed later by a much larger English community. Memel's glory period was in 1807–08, when King Friedrich Wilhelm III decamped there in the wake of the occupation of Berlin by Napoleon's forces, and it thereby became the temporary capital of Prussia.

Following defeat in World War I, Memel and the surrounding territory were confiscated from Germany as part of the punishment for having been deemed guilty of initiating the hostilities. The region was placed under international jurisdiction, and control was handed over to the French. Although much coveted by the fledgling Lithuanian Republic, the intention was to establish it as a quasi-independent territory on the model of the free city of Danzig, which had likewise been detached from Germany, yet denied to Poland, which was equally keen to acquire a major port. As the international authorities procrastinated, the Lithuanians took advantage of the opportunity afforded by French apathy by seizing the territory in 1923. Despite German protests, the annexation was soon accepted as a *fait accompli* by the international community, which saw this as a ready-made compensation for Lithuania's loss of Vilnius to Poland in controversial circumstances three years earlier.

With the advent of a Nazi government in Germany in 1933, Klaipėda's large German population became ever more vociferous in their grievances about Lithuanian rule. On 23 March 1939 the German army captured the city in what was to be Hitler's last territorial annexation before the outbreak of World War II. The dictator himself arrived in the port on the pocket battleship *Deutschland* on the same day, and made one of his most infamous speeches from the theatre balcony.

Nazi rule came to an end in January 1945, when the city fell to the Red Army, by which time most of the German citizens had already fled westwards. Over the next decade the port was rebuilt and developed, gaining three oil terminals and a mechanised loading and unloading process featuring 55 giant cranes spread along 17 quays with a total length of 32km. As the Soviet Union's only ice-free Baltic harbour, Klaipėda was important for foreign trade, and rose to become its fourth largest port in terms of freight turnover. Latterly, it was developed as an international ferry terminal, the inaugural route being that to Neu Mukran on the East German island of Rügen, which was established in 1986. The following year, Klaipėda became accessible to Westerners again, having been a closed city throughout the Soviet period on account of the large number of troops stationed there.

11

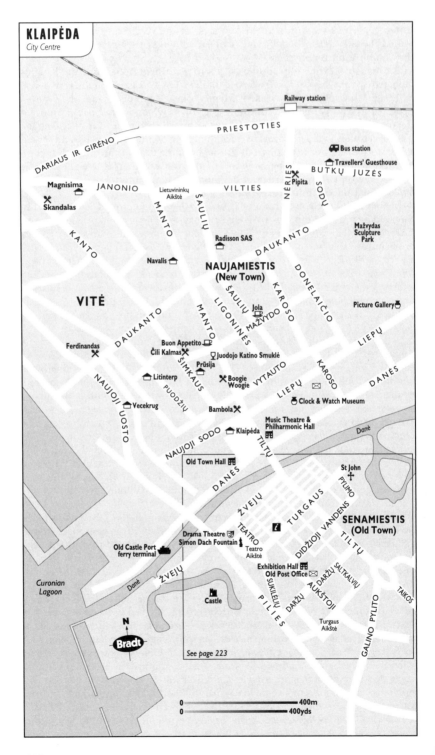

KLAIPĖDA
City Centre

Railway station

PRIESTOTIES

DARIAUS IR GIRĖNO

🚌 Bus station

🏠 Travellers' Guesthouse

BUTKŲ JUZĖS

JANONIO

Lietuvininkų Aikštė

VILTIES

✕ Pipita

NERIES

SODŲ

✕ Magnisima

✕ Skandalas

KANTO

ŠAULIŲ

MANTO

Radisson SAS

DAUKANTO

Mažvydas Sculpture Park

Navalis

NAUJAMIESTIS (New Town)

KAROSO

DONELAIČIO

VITĖ

ŠAULIŲ

LIGONINĖS

Jola

MAŽVYDO

Picture Gallery

LIEPŲ

DAUKANTO

MANTO

Buon Appetito ☕

Čili Kalmas ✕

♫ Juodojo Katino Smuklė

KAROSO

Ferdinandas ✕

ŠIMKAUS

Prūsija

VYTAUTO

LIEPŲ

DANES

Litinterp

PUODŽIŲ

✕ Boogie Woogie

🕐 Clock & Watch Museum

NAUJOJI UOSTO

Vecekrug

Bambola ✕

Klaipėda

Music Theatre & Philharmonic Hall

Danė

NAUJOJI SODO

TILTŲ

Old Town Hall

Danė

St John ✝

DANES

PYLIMO

ŽVEJŲ

TURGAUS

SENAMIESTIS (Old Town)

TEATRO

ℹ

DIDŽIOJI VANDENS

TILTŲ

Drama Theatre 🎭
Simon Dach Fountain

Teatro Aikštė

SUKILĖLIŲ

VANDENS

DARŽŲ

ŠALTKALVIŲ

Old Castle Port ferry terminal 🛳

Exhibition Hall
Old Post Office ✉

AUKŠTOJI

DARŽŲ

Curonian Lagoon

Danė

ŽVEJŲ

P I L I E S

Castle

Turgaus Aikštė

GALINO PYLITO

TAIKOS

N

Bradt

See page 223

0 ——— 400m
0 ——— 400yds

218

GETTING THERE AND AROUND The most useful buses, for which tickets (1Lt) can be bought in advance from kiosks or at a small supplement from the driver, are 1 and 8, whose routes run from the train station through the heart of the city to the market; 4 to Giruliai via Melnragė; and 6 to Melnragė beach. Quicker, more frequent and only slightly more expensive at 1.50Lt (which is paid directly to the driver), are the minibuses of the same numbers, which can be flagged down anywhere.

By car

🚗 **Hertz** Daukanto 4; ↘ 46 310737; f 46 492811; e klaipeda@hertz.lt; www.hertz.lt.

🚗 **Litinterp** Puodžių 17; ↘ 46 410644; f 46 411815; e klaipeda@litinterp.com; www.litinterp.com

By bus

🚌 **Bus station** Butkų Juzės 9; ↘ 46 411547. Located in the northeastern part of the city centre. There are up to 15 buses daily to Vilnius. Other daily services include 12 to Kaunas, 6 to Telšiai, 5 to Šiauliai, 4 to Liepāja (2 of which continue on to Rīga), 3 to Kaliningrad & 2 to Minsk. In summer minibuses run very regularly (at approximately 15-min intervals) from the stands in front of the bus station to both Palanga & Kretinga.

By train

🚂 **Railway station** Priestoties 1; ↘ 46 313676. This German-era brick building with its tall clocktower is immediately north of the bus station.

There are now just 4 arrivals & departures each day. All services go to Radviliškis via Kretinga, Plungė, Telšiai & Šiauliai; 2 continue to Vilnius via Kėdainiai.

By ferry (to the Curonian Spit)

⛴ **Old Castle Port** Žvejų 8; ↘ 46 31425; www.keltas.lt. From the southern bank of the river, a ferry crosses to the terminal of the buses & minibuses going down the Curonian Spit; it is also the one to take if visiting the Maritime Museum. There is an approximately half-hourly service in summer & hourly the rest of the year between 06.00 & 23.30. Tickets cost 1.50Lt for foot passengers, 2Lt for bikes, 18Lt for motorbikes. Theoretically these are return tickets, but in practice are sold only for the journey to Smiltynė;

the trip in the opposite direction is free. In summer Jukunda ↘ 46 300700; www.jukunda.lt runs cruises on Fri, Sat & Sun from the north south of the rivermouth to Nida via Juodkrantė. This costs 80Lt for the day-long round trip, or 25Lt for each stage.

⛴ **New Port** Nemuno 8; ↘ 46 345780; www.keltas.lt. Located in the south of the city, this is the crossing for anyone taking a car down the Curonian Spit, but is of little interest to pedestrians. Prices, which are governed by vehicle size, start at 110Lt.

By international ferry

⛴ **International ferry terminal** Perkėlos 10; ↘ 46 395050; f 46 395052. Located in the south of the city. Lisco (www.lisco.lt) has 6 weekly sailings to both Karlshann (Sweden) & Kiel (Germany), 3 weekly to Sassnitz (Germany) & 1 weekly to Baltiysk in the Kaliningrad oblast. Scandlines (www.scandlines.lt) has 2 weekly sailings to Aabenraa (Denmark).

INFORMATION AND MAPS The most useful publication, which is available in many newsagents, is *Klaipėda In Your Pocket*, produced annually by the *Vilnius In Your Pocket* team. In addition to city listings, it also covers Nida and Palanga; the free *Explore Klaipėda* does likewise. The best cartographic production is published by Briedis: one side is devoted to a map covering most of the urban area, together with A–Z street listings; the other has maps of the city centre and Palanga plus some practical information.

ℹ️ **Tourist office** Turgaus 5; ↘ 46 412186; f 46 412185; e tic@one.lt; www.klaipeda.lt. ⏰09.00–19.00 Mon–Fri, 10.00–14.00 Sat–Sun; reduced hours out of season. 2 internet terminals are available.

WHERE TO STAY

Klaipėda has a reasonable choice of accommodation at all price levels, and there is unlikely to be any problem in finding a room. Some English and/or German is spoken at all the hotels.

Hotels

Navalis Manto 23; ☎ 46 404200; f 46 404202; e info@navalis.lt; www.navalis.lt. This modern business class hotel has been established in a fine 19th-century brick building. The rooms all have bathrooms, satellite TV, internet connections & minibar. There is a fine restaurant, which offers bargain set lunches Mon–Fri. $$$$, suites & apts $$$$$

Radisson SAS Šaulių 28; ☎ 46 490800; f 46 490815; e info.klaipeda@radissonsas.com. Luxury Scandanavian-style chain hotel with restaurant, located on a quiet New Town street. The room price includes a substantial b/fast buffet. $$$$, apts $$$$$

Europa Royale Žvejų 21; ☎ 46 404444, f 46 404445; e klaipeda@europaroyale.com; www.europaroyale.com. This plush new establishment occupies an Old Town building which housed one of the city's top hotels a century ago. It has a fine Italian speciality restaurant, San Marco. $$$$

Euterpe Daržų 9; ☎/f 46 474703; e hotel@euterpe.lt; www.euterpe.lt. New venture with a quiet location in the heart of the Old Town. It features a restaurant, massage & sports facilities. $$$$

Klaipėda Naujoji Sodo 1; ☎ 46 404372; f 46 404373; e hotel@klaipedahotel.lt; www.klaipedahotel.lt. This intrusive 200-room tower-block hotel was a typical product of the last years of the Soviet Intourist organisation. However, a comprehensive renovation programme carried out in 2002–04 has transformed everything except the exterior. The facilities include a gym, swimming pool, solarium, the nightclub Honolulu & a panorama bar-restaurant with open kitchen. $$$, suites $$$$$, apts $$$$$

Atlantas Sportininkų 46; ☎ 46 410077; f 46 410066; e reservacja@atlantas.lt; www.atlantas.lt.. A small modern hotel overlooking the stadium in the north of the city, reached from the centre by minibus 2. All rooms have balconies, private facilities, satellite TV, telephone & minibar. The facilities include a restaurant serving Italian cuisine, plus a sauna & sports room with table tennis & weights. $$$, suites $$$$

Astra Pilies 2; ☎ 46 313849; f 46 216420; e hotelastra@takas.lt. A characterful little hotel with an excellent location across from the terminal of the Smiltynė ferry. The rooms are well appointed with bathroom, satellite TV, telephone & hairdryer. There is also a good café. $$$

Lūgnė Galinio Pylimo 16; ☎/f 46 411884; e lugne@pajuris.lt; www.lugne.com. Situated right beside the market, this hotel is geared primarily to business visitors. Rooms have satellite TV, telephone & refrigerator. There is also a good if relatively pricey restaurant. $$$

Vecekrug Jūros 23; ☎ 46 301002; f 46 312262; e info@vecekrug.lt; www.vecekrug.lt. Shiny new hotel whose facilities include a restaurant, swimming pool & roof terrace, which – like the west-facing bedrooms – commands fine views of the city & coast. $$$

Morena Audros 8a, Melnragė; ☎ 46 351314; f 46 401905; e admin@morenahotel.lt; www.morenahotel.lt. A nicely renovated hotel in the nearer of the seaside suburbs, located beside the bus terminus, 300m from the beach. A sauna, bar & restaurant are among the facilities, while all rooms have private facilities & TV. $$, suites & apts $$$

Pajūris Slaito 18a, Giruliai; ☎ 46 490154; f 46 490142; e info@pajurishotel.lt; www.pajurishotel.lt. An upmarket resort hotel in the more distant of the seaside suburbs. All rooms have balcony, satellite TV, telephone & refrigerator. Facilities include a restaurant, café-bar, swimming pool, sauna, Russian steam bath, solarium, massage & various curative treatments. As is normal at the Lithuanian seaside, rates are lower out of high season. $$, apts $$$

Prūsija Šimkaus 6; ☎ 46 412081; f 46 412078; e prusija@prusijahotel.lt; www.prusijahotel.lt. A small Armenian-run family hotel in a quiet city-centre street. The adjoining restaurant serves dishes from a range of Caucasian countries. $$, suites $$$

Magnisima Janonio 11; ☎/f 46 310901; e info@magnisima.lt; www.magnisima.lt. A small, reasonably priced hotel in a fine old building in a side street in the north of the commercial district. All rooms have private facilities, satellite TV, telephone, minibar & safe. There is also a swish café-bistro. $$

Hostel

Travellers' Guesthouse Butkų Juzės 7-4; ☎ 46 211879; e guestplace@yahoo.com; www.lithuanianhostels.org. This youth hostel occupies a house facing the bus station. It also rents out bikes. $

Bed and breakfast

⌂ **Litinterp** Puodžių 17; ☎ 46 410644; f 46
411815; e klaipeda@litinterp.com; www.litinterp.com.
⏰ 08.30–17.30 Mon–Fri, 09.00–15.30 Sat. As well as
having its own on-site guesthouse, this arranges
private accommodation in Klaipėda, Palanga & the
Curonian Spit, as well as bike & car hire, interpreting
& translating services. Also has offices in Vilnius &
Kaunas. $$, self-contained apts $$$

✗ **WHERE TO EAT** Klaipėda has a good cross-section of restaurants, plenty of
cafés, and the largest choice of beer bars in Lithuania.

Restaurants

✗ **Anikės Kuršiai** Sukilėlių 10. Many of the standard
dishes of Lithuanian cuisine are on offer in this Old
Town restaurant.

✗ **Bambola** Manto 1. Popular pizzeria offering a
wide choice of toppings, some of them decidedly
offbeat; a few Tex-Mex dishes are also available.

✗ **Boogie Woogie** Manto 5. This steakhouse-cum-
bar is the successor to a Soviet-era fast-service
restaurant which gained cult status on account of its
startling décor. Although the interior has been
revamped, the large glass windows overlooking
Klaipėda's busiest street, which gained it the nickname
'The Aquarium', still remain.

✗ **Čili Kaimas** Manto 11. Essentially a theme
restaurant of the Curonian Spit, decked out with all
sorts of fishing paraphenalia, an aquarium & sand & light
installations below the glass floor. There is a special fish
menu, but plenty of other options as well, including the
pizzas for which the Čili chain is best known.

✗ **Ferdinandas** Naujoji Uosto 10. A well-regarded
Russian speciality restaurant in the untouristed western
part of the New Town. Many of the dishes are based
on recipes written down by members of the Old
Believers sect & by the Tsarist statesman Piotr Stolypin.

✗ **Friedricho** Tiltų 26a. Smart restaurant serving
Mediterranean fare, in the recently renovated
passageway alongside the market.

✗ **Hámmerli** Didžioji vandens 13/10. An absolutely
genuine Swiss restaurant, specializing in fondues.

✗ **Kinų** Sukilėlių 6. Klaipėda's first Chinese
restaurant, located in the heart of the Old Town.

✗ **Petit Marseille** Žvejų 4a. A French restaurant
cum wine bar has recently been established in a
renovated warehouse by the waterfront. Unusually for
Lithuania, it offers bargain set lunches.

✗ **Pipita** Nėries 10. Pizzeria which is much
patronised by local students.

✗ **Senoji Hansa** Kurpių 1. Smart new restaurant
serving Lithuanian fare.

✗ **Skandalas** Kanto 44. This American theme bar-
restaurant, whose extravagant décor includes a phone
booth installed in an old car, is deservedly one of the
country's best-known eateries. The huge & succulent
Chicago-style flame grilled steaks are the house
speciality, though there's a wide choice of other
dishes, as well as of wines & liqueurs.

✗ **Stora Antis** Tiltų 6. Basement restaurant
offering dishes drawn from a range of different Slavic
cuisines.

✗ **Trys Mylinos** Taikos 23. It is well worth the
10min walk south from the Old Town to sample the
extensive menu of traditional local dishes, many of
which now rarely feature on restaurant menus. There
is sometimes live folk music in the evenings.

Cafés

🍴 **Buon Appetito** Manto 11a. Italian-style café
which also serves pizza & pasta.

🍴 **Fotogalerija** Tomo 7. A trendy café attached
to a photography gallery; it's primarily a place for a
drink, though snacks are available. ⏰ 11.00–18.00
Tue–Sat.

🍴 **Galerija Pėda** Turgaus 10. Another arty café,
this time offering full meals. There is live piano music
on w/end evenings.

🍴 **Jola** Mažvydo 9. Basement café with outside
terrace.

🍴 **Pas Mario** Turgaus 20. Tiny intimate café in an
Old Town cellar.

Bars

♀ **Juodojo Katino Smuklė** Mažvydo 1 & Žvejų 21.
The original of these pubs is in the New Town; its
younger & much larger sister establishment is just
over the other side of the river. They both serve a full
menu, including excellent steaks.

♀ **Kurpiai** Kurpių 1a. A live music bar, particularly
noted for jazz; also serves full meals.

♀ **Memelis** Žvejų 4. A home brew pub has been
established in this former warehouse on the
waterfront. It makes the light Šviesusis Memelis & the

dark Juodasis Memelis; there is an extensive menu & seating on 2 floors.

♀ Patriko Kurpių 8. The inevitable Irish pub has been established in this Old Town cellar.

♀ Švyturis Kūlių Vartų 7. The oldest brewery on Lithuanian soil, founded in 1784 as the Memel-Aktien-Brauerei, has an on-site tap where its wide range of products can be sampled.

COMMUNICATIONS
✉ **Central Post Office** Liepų 16. ◷08.00–19.00 Mon–Fri, 09.00–16.00 Sat.

SHOPPING
Bookshop
Vaga Manto 9. English-language paperbacks feature among the stock.

Shopping mall
Akropolis Taikos 61. This showpiece development in the south of the city has more than 200 shops, numerous restaurants, a multiplex cinema, an ice rink & a bowling alley.

Souvenirs
Dailė Turgaus 2. Sells amber, jewellery, carvings, ceramics, linen & leather goods.

Marginiai Sukilėlių 4. Klaipėda's biggest souvenir shop has a wide range of artworks for sale, including paintings, carvings, amber & linen.

ENTERTAINMENT AND NIGHTLIFE
Theatre
🎭 **Drama Theatre** Teatro 2; ☎ 46 314453; www.kidteatras.lt. This theatre is heir to a distinguished tradition, though nowadays performances are almost always in Lithuanian only.

🎭 **Music Theatre** Danės 19; ☎ 46 397404; www.muzikinis-teatras.lt. Features opera, operetta, ballet & musicals, plus concerts of all kinds, including those of the Symphony Orchestra of Lithuania Minor.

Festivals The highlight of the calendar is the Festival of the Sea (*www.juros.lt*) on the last weekend of July. It features maritime events, markets, a funfair and live music, and is often held in conjunction with international nautical events, such as Baltic Sail.

WHAT TO SEE AND DO Klaipėda's modest Old Town (Senamiestis) is on the south side of the River Danė, just before it flows into the Curonian Lagoon. The much larger New Town (Naujamiestis) from the 19th and early 20th centuries is on the north side of the river. There are modern suburbs to the south of the Old Town and north of the New Town, while the municipality also embraces the resorts of Melnragė and Giruliai and the northern part of the Curonian Spit, including the village of Smiltynė.

New Town Nowadays the bustling commercial heart of the city, the New Town is bisected from north to south by a single long street, Manto. The district has two other important thoroughfares: Daukanto, which bisects Manto, and Liepų, which parallels Daukanto's course, albeit on the eastern side of Manto only.

Towards its northern end, Manto opens to the east on a large and spacious square, Lietuvininkų aikštė, which is named in honour of the Lithuanian inhabitants of the so-called Lithuania Minor. In Soviet times, the square was home to a monument honouring the Red Army, but this was removed when independence was achieved, to be replaced by the **Memorial to Martynas Mažvydas**, which was carved by Regimantas Midvikis and erected in 1997 to

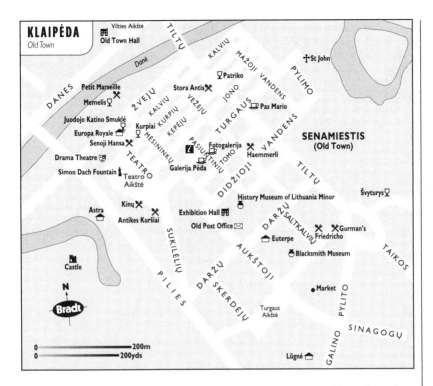

KLAIPĖDA
Old Town

Vilties Aikštė
Old Town Hall

Danė

DANĖS

TILTŲ

KALVIŲ

MAŽOJI VANDENS

PYLIMO

† St John

Patriko

Petit Marseille
Memelis

Stora Antis

JONO

Pas Mario

Juodojo Katino Smuklė
Europa Royale
Senoji Hansa

ŽVEJŲ

KALVIŲ

KURPIŲ

VEŽĖJŲ

MĖSININKŲ

KEPĖJŲ

TURGAUS

Kurpiai

VANDENS

SENAMIESTIS
(Old Town)

Drama Theatre
Simon Dach Fountain

TEATRO

PASIUNTINIŲ

TOMO

Fotogalerija

Haemmerli

Galerija Pėda

DIDŽIOJI

TILTŲ

Teatro
Aikštė

Kinų

Astra

Antikes Kuršiai

SUKILĖLIŲ

Exhibition Hall

Old Post Office

History Museum of Lithuania Minor

DARŽŲ

SALTKALVIŲ

Euterpe

Gurman's
Friedricho

AUKŠTOJI

Blacksmith Museum

Švyturys

TAIKOS

Castle

N

Bradt

PILIES

DARŽŲ

SKERDĖJŲ

Market

PYLITO

Turgaus
Aikštė

GALINO

SINAGOGŲ

0   200m
0   200yds

Lūgnė

commemorate the 450th anniversary of the author's most celebrated work, a Protestant Catechism published in Königsberg which is the first-ever book written in the Lithuanian language. Further south, just a few paces west along Daukanto, is another monument from the same year, the **Memorial to the Victims of the Siberian Deportations** by Juozas Genevičius, featuring a statue of a victim and tombstones commemorating those who died in involuntary exile.

At the southern end of Manto is another large and rather bleak open space which is dominated by the massive bulk of the Hotel Klaipėda. Immediately to its west is the **Old Town Hall**, now the administration building of the university. Although much altered, it was the place where King Friedrich Wilhlem III temporarily established his court in 1807. The central area of the square has a rather empty look, as nothing has been put in the place of the statue of Lenin which formerly stood there.

Liepų is by far the most impressive street in the New Town, with several excellent examples of *Jugendstil* (German Art Nouveau) architecture. Particularly fine is the mansion at Liepų 7, nowadays the **Administration Headquarters of the Museum of Lithuania Minor**, whose façade features humorous updated versions of classical caryatids.

Across the road at Liepų 12 is a somewhat older mansion which was once the residence of an English doctor and is now home to the **Clock and Watch Museum** (⏰ *12.00–18.00 Tue–Sat, 12.00–17.00 Sun*). The ground floor is devoted to technical aspects of the subject (the labelling is in Lithuanian and Russian only), and features water clocks, sundials, sand glasses, clocks powered by fire, pendulum clocks, electronic clocks, electromagnetic clocks and pocket watches. Upstairs is a display of historical timepieces from England, France, Germany, Switzerland and Russia. A huge modern sundial adorns the garden to the rear.

Next door to the museum is the **Central Post Office**, an engaging example of Neo-Gothic brickwork from 1893. It is practically unchanged both inside and out, save for the 42m tower, which was remodelled after World War II and equipped in 1987 with a carillon of 48 bells cast in East Germany. Concerts are given at 12.00 on Saturdays and Sundays, and more regularly during a festival each July.

A bit further along and on the opposite side of the street is a small park with a **statue of Kristijonas Donelaitis**, the 18th-century Lutheran pastor who wrote *The Seasons*, the first and greatest epic poem in the Lithuanian language. On the next block to the east, at Liepų 33, is the **Picture Gallery** (⊕ *12.00–18.00 Tue–Sat, 12.00–17.00 Sun*), which contains work by 20th-century Lithuanian artists, predominantly from Lithuania Minor, and also has an open-air courtyard where sculptures and mosaics are displayed.

Towards the end of the street is the **Mažvydas Sculpture Park**, which was the city's main cemetery until 1977. Before it was levelled by the Soviets, many of the beautiful iron crosses were spirited away by heritage-conscious locals, and are now on display in the Blacksmith Museum (see opposite). There has been talk of restoring the cemetery, though the present park, with its whimsical modern sculptures, is attractive in its own right. The former cemetery chapel, dating from 1938, is now the **Russian Orthodox Church**.

Old Town Klaipėda's Old Town is unusual, principally because it lacks churches. Prior to World War II, it had three, but all were damaged in the conflict (albeit far from grievously), and subsequently razed by the Soviets. Nor is there a single secular building from earlier than the 17th century, with the exception of the **Castle** (⊕ *Jun–Aug 10.00–18.00 Wed–Sun; Sep–May 10.00–18.00 Tue–Sat*), which guarded its western side, and was protected by a moat linked by a channel to the River Danė. For long marooned among industrial buildings, the site, whose entrance is at Pilies 4, was opened up to the public in 2002 in celebration of the 750th anniversary of its foundation. The northwestern part of the fortress has been excavated, though there are only scanty remains above ground level. However, some 16th- to 18th-century underground chambers within the bastions survive intact. These have been fitted out as a museum, displaying artefacts found on site, as well as a scale model of the city as it was in the second half of the 17th century.

Its lack of setpieces notwithstanding, the Old Town has a pleasant aspect, clearly preserving its original grid-plan of narrow, straight streets. There are also plenty of half-timbered town mansions and warehouses – the Klaipėda region is the only part of Lithuania where this archetypally German building style can be seen – as well as several grandiose bank headquarters from the 19th and early 20th centuries. The latter's presence means that the Old Town maintains an important role in the city's commercial life, despite the now long-established primacy of the New Town in this field. Otherwise, the economy of the quarter is now closely tied to the tourist trade, with souvenir shops, restaurants, cafés and bars being much in evidence.

The **Drama Theatre** on Teatro aikštė is the nearest the Old Town now comes to having a focal point. It was built in 1893 on the foundations of its fire-destroyed predecessor, which had numbered Wagner among its guest conductors. Hitler's speech announcing the re-incorporation of the city into Germany was made from the theatre's exterior balcony.

Immediately in front is the **Simon Dach Fountain**, which is topped by the **statue of Ännchen von Tharau**. A native of Memel, Simon Dach (1605–69) was a member of the artistic circle at the Prussian court in Königsberg. According to tradition, he attended the wedding at Königsberg Cathedral of the teenage Anna Neander, who came from the village of Thorau, and was so captivated by the bride that he wrote a dialect poem in her honour. This was set to a folksy tune composed by Johann Albrecht, the cathedral organist, and soon became famous throughout Germany, featuring in numerous songbooks. The original monument was inaugurated in 1912, but the statue disappeared during World War II. It is sometimes claimed that Ännchen was removed by the Nazis as a punishment for having stood with her back to Hitler while he made his speech, but it is far likelier that the Soviets were responsible for her disappearance. Thanks to a joint German-Lithuanian initiative, a replica of the monument, based on old photographs, was made in 1989.

The **History Museum of Lithuania Minor** (*www.mlimuziejus.lt; ⊕ 10.00–18.00 Tue–Sat*) occupies an 18th-century brick house in the heart of the Old Town at Didžioji vandens 6. It contains archaeological finds from Neolithic times onwards; old maps and currency; local folk costume and furniture; a model of Memel, complete with churches, as it was in the early 20th century; and historic photographs, including some of momentous events such as the 1923 crisis and Hitler's 1939 visit.

Aukštoji, which runs perpendicular to the west side of Didžioji vandens, is lined by several picturesque old buildings. These include, at Aukštoji 3, a half-timbered former fish warehouse which has been converted to serve as an **Exhibition Hall** (*www.parodurumai.lt; ⊕ 11.00–18.00 Mon–Fri, 11.00–16.00 Sat*) of contemporary art, and, at Aukštoji 13, the delightfully rustic and still functioning **Old Post Office** (*⊕ 09.00–13.00 & 14.00–17.30 Mon–Fri*). Just around the corner from the latter, at Daržu 10, is one of Klaipėda's finest examples of half-timbering, the so-called **Elephant House**.

Round another corner, at Saltkalviu 2, the **Blacksmith Museum** (*⊕ 10.00–18.00 Tue–Sat*) occupies a still-operational smithy which originally belonged to Gustav Katzke, an accomplished metalwork artist of the early 20th century. On display in both the interior and exterior sections of the museum are many highly elaborate locally made iron grilles and crosses. Some of the latter were saved from the municipal cemetery (whose original appearance is evoked by the photographs on display) on the eve of its destruction by the Soviet authorities.

Immediately south of the museum is the **Market**, one of the largest and best in Lithuania. Trading takes place daily in the market hall, in the covered arcades to its rear, and outdoors in the western part of the elongated market square, Turgaus aikštė. Prior to the Nazi pogrom, the streets beyond were the **Jewish quarter**. Although the synagogue was razed, some original buildings remain, including a hospital and a meeting-house, while a few tombstones can still be seen on the walls of the former cemetery, now a public park.

To replace the Gothic Church of St John, which was once the pride of the city's monumental heritage, its Lutheran congregation adapted the **Parish Centre** at Pylimo 2 at the northeastern edge of the Old Town to serve for worship. Klaipėda's Catholic community built the brand new **Church of Mary, Queen of Peace** on Rumpiškės to the southeast of the Old Town; this was confiscated on its completion in 1962 and used as a concert hall, only being returned in 1988. The church is modelled on the early Christian basilicas of Italy, and features huge Biblical murals, including an unusual one of St Michael the Archangel accompanied by a pack of snarling dogs.

Smiltynė The easiest way of reaching Smiltynė (formerly Sandkrug), the northernmost village on the Curonian Spit, is via the ferry from Old Castle Port,

11

a seven-minute sail which offers the bonus of views of the commercial docks. All the tourist attractions lie north of the jetty, along a road running beside the eastern shore of the spit which is banned to private cars, but plied in summer by horse-drawn buggies for those who do not wish to walk.

First up is the **Curonian Spit National Park Museum** (*May & Sep 11.00–18.00 Wed–Sun; Jun–Aug 11.00–18.00 Tue–Sun*), which occupies four wooden or half-timbered summer villas. One of these houses the administration; of the others, the first is devoted to the history and geography of the spit, the second to its plants, butterflies and insects, while the third contains stuffed animals and birds.

A little further on is the open-air **Ethnography Museum** (unrestricted access at all times), which is in two sections, one of old fishing boats which formerly trawled the waters of the Baltic and the Curonian Lagoon, the other of redundant traditional wooden buildings of the region. Sadly, the large house which forms the centre-piece of the latter display was set alight by vandals and has had to be restored with wood which contrasts jarringly with the darkened original timbers.

Towards the tip of the spit, about 1.5km from the jetty, is the **Kopgalis Fortress**, built by the Prussians between 1865 and 1871 according to the most up-to-date theories of military architecture, in order to protect the port from possible naval attack. It was restored in the 1970s to serve as the home of the **Maritime Museum and Aquarium** (*www.muziejus.lt*; ⊕*May & Sep 10.30–17.30 Wed–Sun; Jun–Aug 10.30–18.30 Tue–Sun; Oct–Apr 10.30–16.30 Sat–Sun*). In the underground chambers of the outer fortifications are displays on the history of Lithuanian navigation. The circular central fort has been adapted to house the aquarium, which features fish from the Baltic Sea and the Curonian Lagoon plus tropical species from around the world and a small colony of penguins. On the upper floor is a colourful display of shells and corals. Several grey seals live in the moat of the fortress. Also within the grounds is the wreck of the boat in which the Klaipėda fisherman Gintaras Paulionis (1945–94) became the first Lithuanian to row across the Baltic. He was drowned on the return journey, caught in the same storm which sank the *Estonia* ferry, with the loss of more than 800 lives. A **Dolphinarium** (*same opening times*) was opened alongside the fortress in 1994. Shows, featuring a sea lion as well as dolphins, are held there at 12.00, 14.00 and 16.00 from June to August, at 12.00 and 15.00 the rest of the year.

At the end of the spit, the 1km-long **South Pier**, which originally dates back to the 18th century, guards the narrow channel linking the Curonian Lagoon to the Baltic. The beach along the western side of the spit is the most attractive near Klaipėda, thanks in large part to being backed by scented pine woods with luxuriant vegetation. However, it can get extremely crowded, particularly on hot summer weekends; the busiest stretch is that which can be reached most directly by the footpath from the ferry landing.

Melnragė and Giruliai

There are two other seaside resorts within Klaipėda's city boundaries. The old fishing village of **Melnragė** is 4km from the centre, immediately beyond the **North Pier**, which is guarded by the so-called **Red Lighthouse**, whose bright paintwork is one of the few significant modifications made to it since its construction in 1796. As Melnragė's beach can be reached from most parts of the city far more quickly than Smiltynė, it is prone to become uncomfortably busy at times.

Giruliai, a further 4km to the north, is rather more sedate and also much pleasanter, with dense woods separating the beach from the village. There are many fine wooden villas, some of which served as trade union holiday homes and sanatoria in the Soviet period, but have since, as a result of the collapse of the subsidised holiday system, fallen into disrepair.

CURONIAN SPIT NATIONAL PARK

The Curonian Spit (which is known as *Kuršių nerija* in Lithuanian, *Kurische Nehrung* in German) is not only Lithuania's most beguiling landscape, but also its youngest, having been formed in what are geologically very recent times. It was only some 5,000–6,000 years ago that this narrow sandbar came into existence, and it has altered a great deal in the course of its history, only assuming its present appearance – which is itself changing, albeit very slowly – about a century ago. In total, the spit is 98km long; at its widest point, it measures about 3.7km across, at its narrowest, just 350m. The spit was originally settled by Balts – Curonians in the north, Prussians in the south – but was conquered by the Teutonic Knights and remained German territory until 1918, when the northern half was confiscated along with Memel and made an international protectorate, before falling into Lithuanian hands in 1923. Until 1939, when the Germans re-established total control, and again since 1990, when the Soviet Union started to break up, there has therefore been an international frontier (which is nowadays between Lithuania and Russia) running through what is virtually the exact centre of the spit.

In 1991 all but the northernmost 7km of the Lithuanian sector, together with the adjacent coastal waters of the Baltic Sea and Curonian Lagoon, was designated the Curonian Spit National Park. Within its boundaries are four lagoon-side villages – Juodkrantė, Pervalka, Preila and Nida – which since 1961 have formed a single municipality known as **Neringa** in honour of the legendary creator of the spit. The story goes that Neringa, the giantess daughter of the goddess Laima, gathered up sand in her apron and deposited it on the spot in order to provide a strong enough bulwark to protect the local fishermen from the storms which continually ravaged the Baltic coast.

In reality, the spit was formed by sand drifts originating in the Samland peninsula (now part of the Kaliningrad *oblast*) following the retreat of the last glacier. Initially, they formed a chain of islands which were eventually bound together by the wind into a desert of shifting dunes. As grasses and trees took root, and as the wind scattered their seeds, the dunes stabilised. Not until the Middle Ages were the trees felled for their timber, the early inhabitants of the spit having been fishermen whose pagan religion regarded woods as sacred places. With the trees removed, the spit was destabilised and the dunes moved again, burying villages in their wake. Following the almost total deforestation which occurred during the Seven Years' War of 1756–63, the spit's situation became critical, and was the subject of an international conference held at Danzig in 1768. Little was done at first, but throughout the 19th century a programme of planting trees, shrubs and grasses was implemented, radically changing the appearance of the landscape. Some moving dunes were preserved and exist today, but are gradually becoming lower; experts think they will disappear in two or three hundred years.

INFORMATION AND MAPS There are National Park information centres in Smiltynė and Nida, as well as tourist offices in Juodkrantė and Nida. For most purposes, the best map is that by Briedis, which is available in bookshops throughout the country. It has a scale of 1:50,000, is printed on both sides, and contains information on all the main sights and landscape features in both Lithuanian and German. The glossier version published by Atkula is also worth having, though more as a supplement than an alternative. It has a scale of 1:65,000 and is printed on one side only, with photographs on the reverse. While not as clear as its rival, nor so detailed in most respects, it is particularly useful for motorists as it marks all the parking places. Another plus is the provision of information in English in addition to the other two languages.

Park administration centre

Curonian Spit National Park Smiltynės 18; �‾ 46 391179; f 46 391113; e knnp@is.lt; www.nerija.lt.

See page 226 for details of the museums run by the administration centre.

Tourist information

🛈 **Curonian Spit National Park** Smiltynės 11; �‾ 46 402257; e info@nerija.lt; www.nerija.lt. ⏲May–Sep 10.00–18.00 Tue–Sun.

TOURISM AND TRANSPORT Nowadays tourism is the cornerstone of the economy of the Curonian Spit. Indeed it is already so well developed that fears have been voiced about permanent damage to the very fragile local ecosystem. There is a plentiful supply of rooms in hotels, rest homes and private houses in all four villages within the National Park, especially Nida, which is Lithuania's classiest seaside resort, as well as the most popular after Palanga. Most guests come purely for a relaxing holiday on the beach; some come to pick mushrooms and berries in the woods, but it seems that only a small minority of visitors are drawn by the unique natural environment of the spit. Because of the large volume of 'nostalgia' tourists from Germany, a sizeable sector of the market aims to deliver Western standards of service. As in Palanga, room rates vary greatly throughout the year, and substantial discounts should be available out of season.

Access to the National Park By far the most atmospheric approach to the National Park was the hydrofoil from Kaunas to Nida, a memorable voyage along the Nemunas and across the Curonian Lagoon. This has not operated since 2000, and the only cruise to have been introduced since then is that from Klaipėda operated by Jukunda (see page 219). Otherwise, the only means of access from within Lithuania is via Smiltynė, the Klaipėda suburb at the northern end of the spit, which can be reached from the main part of the city via the ferries from either Old Castle Port or New Port (see page 219). From the parking lot beside the Smiltynė jetty of the former ferry, there are currently 14 scheduled microbus services down the spit to Nida. This is a far lower total than was the case until recently, though taxis help to fill the gap; these can be shared and are therefore not necessarily an unduly expensive alternative. All microbuses travel via Juodkrantė to their terminus in Nida, but only some make the detours from the main road to Pervalka and Preila. The others drop passengers for these villages off at the crossroads.

From June to August one bus per day in each direction links Nida with Vilnius, another with Kaunas. These go via Klaipėda bus station, and are the only way of avoiding making the ferry crossing independently. Additionally, there are three buses daily which run from Klaipėda to Kaliningrad. Tourists will need to obtain a visa to cross the border into Russia before leaving home; visas may not be obtained in Nida or Klaipėda.

Car drivers reach the National Park via the New Port ferry, and it is not usually necessary to wait long for a place on board. From the Smiltynė terminal, a branch road links up with the main route down the spit. A short distance south of the crossroads is the National Park entrance post.

Getting there and around The main road down the spit initially cuts inland from Smiltynė, but a couple of kilometres past the National Park entrance point it rejoins the shore of the lagoon, following it until just beyond Juodkrantė, from where it deviates inland again and continues all the way to the Russian border alongside the woods backing the Baltic. There are only a few short branch roads leading off it which are open to motor traffic: one to the southern ferry terminal, two to the Baltic beach at Juodkrantė, one each to Pervalka and Preila, and three to various parts of Nida. Other paved roads do exist (for example a direct route from Nida to Preila and Pervalka), but barriers prevent vehicular access.

Quite apart from environmental considerations, this means that a private car offers almost no practical advantages over the local minibuses, which can be flagged down anywhere. Moreover, there is a specially low speed limit (which varies from 40km to 70km) per hour within the National Park, and police routinely hide in wait by the roadside, ready to levy an on-the-spot fine on those caught exceeding it, or committing any other moving traffic offence on a road which, for all its many long straight stretches, has several accident black-spots. The only petrol station in the park is by the main road at the southern turn-off to Nida, but this is not always open.

A bike is a better means of getting around, as it can be taken on the roads banned to cars, but is of no more use for seeing the best of the scenery, which is only accessible on foot. Surprisingly, there are relatively few walking trails, and those which do exist are unmarked and prone to peter out all of a sudden. However, it is almost impossible to get lost, particularly if armed with a map, as the spit is so narrow and the main road never very far away. The lagoon shoreline all the way between Juodkrantė and the Russian border is especially rewarding for walks, presenting as it does a wide variety of often stunning scenery.

GEOGRAPHY The total area of the National Park is 26,474 hectares, of which 9,774 hectares is land, while 12,500 is water in the Baltic Sea, and 4,200 water in the Curonian Lagoon. A fraction over 70% of the land area is forested, with coniferous trees now having an overwhelming predominance over the original deciduous species. All the inland dunes are now covered with trees, masking their original character. Littoral dunes account for almost exactly a quarter of the land area. Of the four main concentrations of dunes which still remain on the lagoon side of the spit, one is solely within Lithuania, while another straddles the border. The former, the Dead Dunes, run for 10km south of Juodkrantė, and are up to 2km wide in places. Their luxuriant vegetation makes them look very different from the more famous High Dunes immediately south of Nida, which still move. In contrast to the dramatic indented lagoon shoreline, which features sheltered bays between the dunes, the almost straight western side of the spit has, like the rest of Lithuania's maritime coastline, a sandy beach along its entire length. There are no lakes or rivers on the spit.

FLORA AND FAUNA Over half the trees in the park are pines of one variety or another, with mountain and dwarf pines, which were imported from Sweden, being particularly prevalent. Firs, spruces, alders, oaks, birches, lindens and willows are also found, as are maples, poplars, ashes, elms, beeches, hornbeams and acacias. Among the shrubs are honeysuckle, berberis, guelder roses and elder. Many varieties of grass grow in the sand, and there are also large areas of sedge along the lagoon shore.

Among the 37 different mammals which live in the park are elk, red deer, roe deer, wild boar, hares, pine martens, foxes, badgers, squirrels, beavers and mink. The most typical of the 100 or so species of bird which nest and breed in the park are cormorants and grey heron, both of which have established colonies. Black-headed and herring gulls, hooded crows, jays and swans are also commonly seen. The list of fish found in the coastal waters of the Baltic includes eel, cod, flounder, herring, salmon, trout, turbot, plaice, ling, sprats and (very rarely) sturgeon; eel, pike, perch, pike-perch, catfish and burbot are among those which inhabit the lagoon.

ETHNOGRAPHY The spit has never been able to support more than a very small number of people, and the total population of the four villages which make up the municipality of Neringa is a mere 2,670. In previous centuries, the villages were much smaller, but also more numerous – no fewer than 15 have been buried by the shifting dunes, and no trace of them remains today. Outside the busy tourist season, fishing is still the mainstay of the local economy. Nowadays, modern boats are used instead of the traditional flat-bottomed wooden *kurėnai* which trawled the lagoon for many centuries.

The most characteristic feature of the villages is the presence of numerous traditional fishermen's houses, which are built of wood and brightly painted, often in blue or reddish brown. Many of these are actually two separate dwellings, each with its own door and either two or four rooms inside, a practice which enabled grown-up offspring to establish their own household yet still live alongside their parents. The houses, which invariably face the lagoon, have modest yet distinctive decoration, almost always including the initials of the original occupant and the date of construction. There is normally a gable at each end, with intersecting carvings of stylised horses or birds, which were believed to offer protection against evil spirits. The weather vanes, which are another recurrent feature, had a more practical function, one which was particularly important to seafaring families. Usually there is an immaculately tended flower garden, which is in full bloom in summer. In the yard, there is a drying area for nets, and sometimes a smoke-house for curing the fish according to a centuries-old formula.

Smoked fish is the undoubted culinary speciality of the spit, and also ranks among the gastronomic highlights of Lithuania. Stalls selling a wide range of fish smoked in the traditional manner (which vary enormously in price, according to the rarity or otherwise of the different species) can be found in the villages of Neringa. They are particularly ubiquitous in Juodkrantė, where every other house seems to have fish for sale.

JUODKRANTĖ Juodkrantė (formerly Schwarzort), a straggling village stretching for some 3.5km, begins 9km south of the National Park entry post. The northernmost of the Neringa communities, it is also the only one directly on the main road. First documented in 1429, it originally lay 2.5km to the north, on the Baltic coast, moving to its present, more sheltered, location in 1429. From the 1840s, it developed as a holiday resort, a role it maintains to this day.

An even bigger transformation occurred between 1860 and 1900, when the erstwhile fishing village of 160 souls became a boom town dubbed the 'Prussian California' as a result of the activities of the Stantien & Becker company, which dredged the lagoon for amber. The only major industrial enterprise the spit has ever had, it employed 600 staff and a fleet of 230 vessels, including 22 dredgers, when at its peak in the 1880s. In the course of its operations, it collected 2.5 million tonnes of raw amber, plus a host of Mesolithic and Neolithic artefacts, some of which are now lost, while others can be seen in the Geological Museum of the University of Göttingen in Germany.

The **Amber Harbour** in the far north of the village was the base for Stantien & Becker's operations, and it is still an evocative spot, even if it is no more than a shadow of the thriving port and township which formerly occupied the site. From there, a path leads westwards through the woods to **Lapnugaris** (53.2m), the highest dune in the vicinity of Juodkrantė, albeit one covered with trees. The lighthouse on top was once a popular tourist attraction with a glass-covered observation platform commanding sweeping views over the spit, but unfortunately it has long been inaccessible to the public. From there, the path continues down to the beach, which can also be reached by two roads and by several other trails from elsewhere in the village.

About 1km south of the Amber Harbour is the start of the main built-up area. Along the northern stretch of the main street, Rėzos, and on Miško and Kalno, which lead off it, are many late 19th-century villas which rank as the most splendid houses on the spit. Prominent among them, at the corner of Rėzos and Kalno, is the **Vila Flora**, which was built for Moritz Becker, one of the founding partners of the amber-digging company. It is now a hotel (see opposite).

Just beyond this part of the village is the so-called **Witches' Hill**, the back of a dune which, prior to being planted with trees, was known as 'Blond Eva' because of its golden sands. Between 1979 and 1981 the hill was adorned with carvings illustrating figures and scenes from Lithuanian fairy tales and mythology, executed by sculptors influenced by traditional folk art. Ever since, it has ranked as one of the spit's most popular tourist attractions. Several of the sculptures – notably *The Birth of Neringa* near the entrance, *The Flying Dragon* further uphill, and *The Witches' Gate* at the summit – adopt the grand manner; most others are more modest, but invariably show a lively sense of humour. Particularly successful in this respect are those at the end of the circuit, which together form a children's playground. They include a 'flying' hobby-horse and a slide in the form of a witch's tongue.

The southernmost part of Juodkrantė is the fishermen's quarter of **Karvaičiai** (formerly Karwaiten), which is named after a now-buried village further south and features a number of pretty old wooden houses with gardens. Since 1989, when it was returned to the Lutheran congregation which rightfully owned it, the Neo-Gothic **Parish Church** of 1885 has, in true ecumenical spirit, been shared by Protestants and Catholics, and holds regular services in both Lithuanian and German, as well as hosting occasional concerts. Outside stands a crucifix executed in a manner akin to that of the secular sculptures on Witches' Hill.

From the far end of Karvaičiai is the southernmost of the paths leading to the beach. About halfway along, there is a junction of three trails, one of which leads south to a wooden dune known as **Heron Hill**. The herons which once nested there have, however, moved further south, to be replaced by a cormorant colony which has left its distinctive imprint on the landscape by denuding the trees. About 1km further south, reached by a marked path from a car park on the main road, is a belvedere which commands a marvellous southerly panorama over the spit, embracing both the sea and the lagoon.

† Where to stay In addition to the hotels listed below, Juodkrantė has more than a dozen rest homes, most of which are pretty basic and geared to holiday-makers staying a week or more. There are also rooms for let in many private houses, which can be booked via agencies in Klaipėda or Nida, or by asking around in the village.

⌂ **Ažuolynas** Rėzos 54; ☎ 469 53310; 🖷 469 53316; e hotelazuolynas@takas.lt; www.hotelazuolynas.lt. A huge modern hotel complex situated just north of the parish church. In addition to the village's most upmarket restaurant, it offers a café, 3 bars, concert hall, commercial art gallery, hairdresser & sauna. There is also a **tourist information** point open to the general public. All rooms have a shower & toilet; apts have a refrigerator & TV. $$$, apts $$$$. A buffet b/fast & supper can be included for a supplement of 50Lt per person.

11

Eglių Slėnis Ievos kalno 28; ☏ 469 53170; f 469 53364; e reception@egliuslenis.lt; www.egliuslenis.lt. Located in the central part of Juodkrantė, well back from the lagoon, this is the nicest place to stay in the village. All rooms, though sparsely furnished, have kitchens, & the spacious 3-roomed apts are very good value for families or small groups. $$$, apts $$$$

Kurėnas Rėzos 10; ☏/f 469 53101; e kurenas@gmail.com. A small modern hotel with a restaurant overlooking the lagoon. $$$

Vila Flora Kalno 7a; ☏ 469 53024; f 469 53421; e vilaflora@takas.lt. The aforementioned historic villa has been converted into a hotel with a café. $$$

Santauta Kalno 36; ☏ 469 53167; f 469 53349. Another enormous holiday complex, very obviously from the Soviet era, & definitely on the expensive side given that the bedrooms are small & rather spartan. It does, however, have plenty of facilities: sauna, swimming pool, tennis courts, bowling alley, billiards room & hairdresser. $$, suites $$$

✗ Where to eat

✗ **Dilė** Rėzos 6a. A small café with a garden, in the north of the village, offering the usual local dishes.

✗ **Pamario Takas** Rėzos 42. A pleasant café-restaurant, in a green wooden house with summer garden, in the southern part of village, serving typical Lithuanian fare.

✗ **Žvejonė** Rėzos 30. Yet another wooden house with garden, with a similar menu to its competitors.

Bookshop

Knygos Rėzos 13. Offers a wide-ranging selection of maps & books (in German as well as Lithuanian) on the Curonian Spit, plus a variety of other souvenirs.

FROM JUODKRANTĖ TO NIDA The walk along the lagoon shoreline from Juodkrantė to the Russian frontier just beyond Nida is by far the finest long-distance hike Lithuania has to offer. It is considerably more demanding and time-consuming than would appear to be the case from looking at a map, as there is often no clear path, and the terrain is on occasions inimical to speedy progress. Although the route can be tackled as a single continuous journey, most people need considerably more than a day to accomplish it, and in any case it is just as satisfying if made in stages over several days from a single base.

The northernmost part of the route, over the 10km-long **Dead Dunes** south of Juodkrantė, is the one which makes the biggest demands on time, as the going up and down the undulating sand formations can be very heavy indeed. However, it is well worth making the effort, as an astonishing range of coastal views can be enjoyed by staying close to the shore, while a marvellous selection of desert-like landscapes can be seen inland. A wondrous sense of peace is also imparted, as these dunes see very few visitors in comparison with their counterparts outside Nida. Even in summer, it is possible to walk the whole stretch and hardly see a soul.

From Juodkrantė, the Dead Dunes are approached by taking an unmarked path leading off the main road south of the village towards the lagoon. For those wanting to do no more than sample the landscape, there are four parking places along the eastern side of the main road, at any of which the local minibuses will stop on request, leaving a short walk over the dunes to the lagoon shore. The most useful is the second after Juodkrantė. This is the nearest to the fourth and final site of the buried village of **Neegeln** (known as Agilos in Lithuanian), which was formerly set beside a particularly beautiful bay.

Beyond the Dead Dunes, there is a narrow stretch of beach stretching southeastwards to a peninsula known as the **Horse Hook** because it is thought to have been a place where the Teutonic Knights once grazed their horses. Immediately offshore is a lighthouse, the only one on the spit which is not on dry land.

A little further south is **Pervalka** (formerly Perwalk), the smallest and youngest of the Neringa villages, founded in 1844 by refugees from Neegeln. Nowadays it lives almost entirely from tourism, being full of cheap rest houses and holiday homes. Many of these occupy converted fishermen's houses, while others are in half-timbered buildings with overhanging roofs which look traditional in style but are in fact modern and uncharacteristic of the architecture of the spit.

For the next part of the journey southwards, the shoreline is at times marshy and inaccessible, and it is therefore advisable to take the direct route via the old road, which is now closed to motor vehicles. A plaque marks the site of the original village of **Karwaiten**, the birthplace of Liudvikas Rėza (Ludwig Rhesa), a distinguished linguist who transcribed Donelaitis's *The Seasons*, supervised the first complete version of the Bible in Lithuanian and compiled books of folk songs.

Preila (formerly Preil), which is 5km south of Pervalka, is one year older than its neighbour, but has preserved its character far better. Only the northern part of the village is dominated by large holiday complexes; the rest consists for the most part of cottages built in the 1920s or earlier. Despite having been subject to sometimes inaccurate restorations, all are under architectural preservation orders, and many are still inhabited by fisherfolk.

Once again, the old road offers much the quickest means of continuing southwards, particularly as thick woods often stretch right up to the lagoon shore, making a coastal walk impractical. About 1.5km south of Preila, there is a fine view, with a meadow in the foreground, of **Vecekrugo**, which at 67.4km is the highest wooded dune on the Curonian Spit.

NIDA Nida (formerly Nidden) has a beautiful setting, stretching northwards for some 3km from the edge of the most impressive of the spit's dune wildernesses, with the rare benefit of a continuous promenade all the way along the lagoon shore. First documented in 1385, it originally lay somewhat to the south, but moved several times as a result of sand shifts, before adopting its present location in 1732. Despite the proximity of the Russian border, which is only 4km from the centre of the village, Nida shows no traces of post-Soviet blight. On the contrary, it has a surprisingly spick-and-span appearance and has already reclaimed its former role as a fashionable year-round resort with a strong cultural tradition. It is particularly popular with German holiday-makers, who are following in the footsteps of such distinguished guests as the novelist Thomas Mann and a host of celebrated artists, including the Impressionist Lovis Corinth and the members of the Expressionist group *Die Brücke*.

Getting there and around

Bus station Naglių 18e; 469 52472. See Access to the National Park on page 228 for details of bus services.

Ferry terminal Naglių 14; 469 51101. See page 219 for information about Jukunda's scheduled services to Klaipėda. Additionally, several operators offer cruises in a variety of vessels, including a replica kurėnas (traditional fishing boat). These range from local trips lasting 60–90mins to 5- or 6hr excursions across the lagoon to the Nemunas delta, or up the shoreline to the Dead Dunes & Klaipėda. Departures are governed by demand as well as weather conditions. Although most frequent in high summer, the limited capacity of the boats often means that advance booking is necessary.

Tourist information

Curonian Spit National Park Information Centre Naglių 8; 469 51256; e infonida@nerija.lt; www.nerija.lt. 09.00–12.00 & 13.00–17.00 Mon–Thu, 09.00–12.00 & 13.00–18.00 Fri/Sat, 09.00–12.00 & 13.00–16.00 Sun.

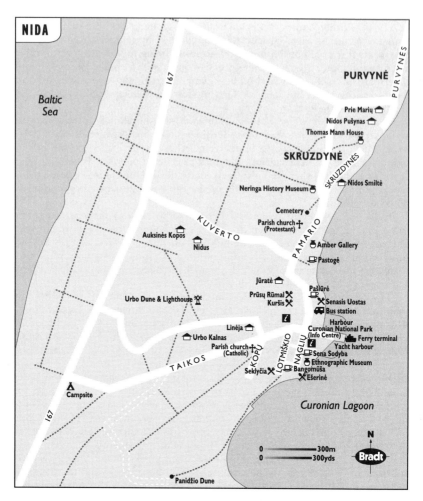

NIDA

Baltic
Sea

PURVYNĖ

Prie Mariu
Nidos Pušynas
Thomas Mann House

SKRUZDYNĖ

Nidos Smiltė

Neringa History Museum

Cemetery
Parish church
(Protestant)

Auksinės Kopos
Nidus

Amber Gallery
Pastogė

Jūratė
Prūsų Rūmai
Kuršis

Pašiūrė
Senasis Uostas
Bus station

Urbo Dune & Lighthouse

Harbour
Curonian National Park
(Info Centre)
Ferry terminal
Yacht harbour

Linėja

Urbo Kalnas
Parish church
(Catholic)
Seklyčia

Sena Sodyba
Ethnographic Museum
Bangomūša
Ešerinė

Campsite

Curonian Lagoon

0 ———— 300m
0 ———— 300yds

N

Bradt

Panidžio Dune

Tourist office Taikos 4; ℡/f 469 52345;
e agilainfo@is.lt; www.neringainfo.lt. Located on the
main square. Offers an accommodation booking
service, including plenty of rooms in private houses at

30–80Lt per head. Some English & German spoken.
⊕ Jun–Aug 09.00–20.00 Mon–Fri, 10.00–18.00 Sat,
10.00–15.00 Sun; Sep–May 09.00–13.00 &
14.00–18.00 Mon–Fri, 10.00–15.00 Sat.

Where to stay Private rooms can be booked via the tourist office or Litinterp in
Klaipėda. In addition to the hotels listed below, there are many rest houses, most of
which are very basic and inexpensive, though they are now easy enough to find as
many owners hang out signs advertising vacancies. These are usually in German
(*Zimmer frei* indicates a free room), but sometimes in other languages as well.

Hotels

Urbo Kalnas Taikos 32; ℡ 469 52428; f 469
52953; e info@urbokalnas.lt; www.urbokalnas.lt. The
main attraction is the secluded hillside setting. There
is a fine view over the High Dunes from the rooftop
café. Although the rooms are recognisably from the

Soviet era, they all have private facilities. $$$, apts
$$$$

Jūratė Pamario 3; ℡ 469 52300/52618; f 469
51118; e jurate-nida@takas.lt. This large wooden
building is one of Nida's most prominent landmarks,

234

located in the very centre of town. The rooms, including the large suites in the rear annexe, are dated but not unattractively so. A café, sauna, massage, fitness room & hairdresser can all be found on the premises. Most rooms are less than half-price out of season. $$$

⌂ **Linėja** Taikos 18; ☏ 469 52390; f 469 52718; e info@lineja-hotel.lt; www.lineja-hotel.lt. This medium-sized hotel on a quiet back street is the most modern in Nida. All rooms have a balcony, toilet with shower, telephone, satellite TV & refrigerator. Other facilities are a restaurant, café, sauna, bowling alley, billiards room & hairdresser. $$$

⌂ **Nidos Pušynas** Purvynės 3; ☏ 469 51131/52221; f 469 52762; e info@smilte.lt; www.smilte.lt. This hotel occupies a trio of fishermen's cottages located by the lagoon shore in the northern district of Purvynė. $$$

⌂ **Nidos Smiltė** Skruzdynės 2; ☏ 469 52219/52221; f 469 52762; e info@smilte;lt; www.smilte.lt. Located close to the lagoon in Skruzdynė, this is the successor to Herman Blode's once-famous inn. An imaginative programme of daily

excursions, some to places not otherwise easily accessible, is offered to guests. It is run by the same management as Nidos Pušynas. $$$

⌂ **Nidus** Kuverto 15; ☏ 469 52001; f 469 50016; e info@nidus.lt; www.nidus.lt. Nida's biggest hotel complex incorporates Rūta, which was once the holiday home of the Communist Party élite, & is appropriately well equipped with restaurant, 3 bars, sauna, solarium, swimming pool, weight training room, billiards room, tennis & basketball courts & roller blade rink. $$$

⌂ **Auksinės Kopos** Kuverto 17; ☏ 469 52387; f 469 52947; e info@auksineskopos.com; www.auksineskopos.com. A holiday complex midway between the centre of the village & the beach. Facilities include a shop selling local handicrafts, a restaurant, café, indoor & outdoor swimming pools, Turkish baths, sauna, massage, billiards & table tennis rooms. $$, suites $$$

⌂ **Prie marių** Purvynės 9-1; ☏/f 469 52489; e sveciunamai@hotmail.com.. This pension in the northernmost part of Nida offers rooms in 3 picturesque wooden houses overlooking the lagoon. $$

Camping

⛺ **Campsite** Taikos 45a; ☏ 469 52045; e infoa@kempingas.lt; www.kempingas.lt. Located by the Baltic shore, this occupies what was intended

as a holiday complex for the Soviet elite. It offers rooms & apts ($$$) as well as spaces for tents & caravans. $

✕ Where to eat Many of the best places to eat are in the hotels; in addition, there are several smoked fish stalls clustered around the harbour, and a variety of other options, some of which are only open in season.

🍴 **Bangomūša** Naglių 5. This café in a wooden house with a garden serves a full menu – try the pancakes.

✕ **Ešerinė** Naglių 2. Directly overlooking the lagoon, this is one of Nida's most eye-catching buildings, a glass-covered version of a South Sea Islands hut, & has an undeniably attractive ambience.

✕ **Kuršis** Naglių 29. New venture with a good range of dishes, including fish.

🍴 **Pašiūrė** Naglių 20. A good choice of local dishes is available at this café overlooking the lagoon just to the north of the centre.

🍴 **Pastogė** Kuverto 2. This handsome old wooden house has found a new lease of life as a café, having previously been the home of the predecessor of the Neringa History Museum.

✕ **Prūsų Rūmai** Naglių 29a. An often raucous restaurant on the main square. It specialises in poultry & fish dishes & its decoration features blown-up black-and-white photographs of old-time life on the Spit.

✕ **Seklyčia** Lotmiškio 1. This wooden hut with a spacious summertime garden is the nearest Nida comes to an upmarket restaurant. It has a good menu of both fresh and smoked fish dishes.

🍴 **Sena Sodyba** Naglių 6. A delightful old cottage with a garden which is particularly recommendable for its wide variety of pancakes.

✕ **Senasis Uostas** Naglių 18. Small harbourside restaurant whose menu, appropriately enough, is strong on fish.

What to see and do Nida has swallowed up two formerly separate communities, **Purvynė** (formerly Purwin) and **Skruzdynė** (formerly Skrusdin), which now form its two northernmost districts. The former preserves a few fishermen's houses, while the latter is distinguished by several handsome villas.

11

Prominent among these is the **Thomas Mann House** (⏱ *Jun–Aug 10.00–18.00 Tue–Sun; Sep–May 11.00–17.00 Tue–Sat*) at Skruzdynės 17. The writer was so captivated by the Curonian Spit when he visited it in 1929 that he decided to build himself a holiday home there. He paid for it with the proceeds of the Nobel Prize for Literature he won that year (thereby imitating his fellow-countryman Gerhart Hauptmann, who had funded his house on the Baltic island of Hiddensee in the same way) and it was ready in time for the following summer. In his 1931 essay *My Summer House*, he described it as follows:

> It is a wooden house with a thatched roof and two crossed horses' heads on the gable. Downstairs is an open verandah, behind which lies the dining room. All other rooms are bedrooms except for one on the first floor, which is fitted out as my workroom. From here I have a wide view over the water to the East Prussian coast, which however one can see only rarely.

Mann spent three summers in the house, working on the Biblical epic *Joseph and his Brothers*, but was unable to return after he went into exile following the Nazi accession to power in 1933. None the less, it has survived in good shape, and now serves both as a museum of the novelist's life and work and as a cultural centre, one of the main venues of the **Thomas Mann Festival**, which is held annually in July.

At 53 on Pamario, the village's main north–south axis, is the new custom-built home of the **Neringa History Museum** (⏱ *1 Jun–15 Sep 10.00–18.00 daily; 16 Sep–31 May 10.00–17.00 Tue–Sat*). This contains both photos and equipment documenting traditional life on the spit, in particular activities such as fishing (which was carried out even when the lagoon was iced over), hunting for amber and catching crows (which were killed by a bite on the neck). There are also views of the Nida during its heyday as a German holiday destination, and a few archaeological finds.

Just to the south, on top of a dune at the edge of the original village of Nida, is the brick **Protestant Parish Church**, built in 1887–88 in Neo-Gothic style. A typical example of rustic German architecture of its period, it has been the subject of an immaculate interior restoration, and the organ is regularly used for recitals and for accompanying choral performances. As the Protestant congregation had fallen to single figures, the local Catholic population was permitted to use the church for many years. This arrangement came to an end in 2003, with the consecration of the new **Roman Catholic Parish Church** on Taikos in the centre of the village.

The surrounding **Cemetery**, which is under a protection order, is also of note. Its most prominent tombstone is the hollowed-out oak stump marking the grave of Herman Blode, a celebrated local hotelier who catered to the German artistic colony. At the northwestern edge of the graveyard is a group of traditional wooden tombstones known as *krikštai*. Shaped like horses' heads, birds or plants, these are peculiar to Lithuania Minor and have an obvious pagan source. Those kept outside are modern replicas of the weather-beaten originals, made by Eduard Jonušas, a local carver who is also responsible for some of the sculptures on Witches' Hill in Juodkrantė.

On the opposite side of the road, at Pamario 20, is the privately run **Amber Gallery** (*www.ambergallery.lt*; ⏱ *daily May–Sep 09.00–21.00; Oct–Apr 10.00–19.00*), a sister establishment to the one in Vilnius. It serves both as a museum of the geology and art of amber and as a shop where certifiably genuine articles can be purchased.

The **Harbour**, which is always a hive of activity, is the heart of Nida. It is divided into two distinct sections separated by the wharf with ferry terminal. The northern part is for fishing and other commercial craft, its southern counterpart for yachts and pleasure boats. Unfortunately, the main square immediately to the west is the least appealing part of town, disfigured by ugly Soviet-era buildings which look wholly out of place. However, the southernmost part of Nagliu (which continues on from Pamario as Nida's main north–south axis) and the parallel Lotmiškio, are both lined with colourful old fishermen's cottages. That at Nagliu 4 is now the **Ethnographic Museum** (⊕ *1 Jun–15 Sep 10.00–18.00 daily; 16 Sep–31 May 10.00–17.00 Tue–Sat*) and is furnished in a manner which would have been familiar to its original occupants.

NIDA ENVIRONS Both Kuverto, which leads off Pamario, and Taikos, which branches off the southwestern corner of the main square, travel westwards in the direction of the beach. From either, the wooded **Urbo Dune**, which is crowned by the local lighthouse, can be reached by footpath.

One of the best views of the dramatic **High Dunes** behind Nida, which stretch 7km southwards into the Kaliningrad *oblast*, is from the yacht harbour pier, where their northern slopes can be seen rising steeply from the lagoon. The path at the south end of Lotmiškio leads through woods and a meadow to the double wooden staircase which enables visitors to climb to the top without damaging the slopes, which are among the most fragile parts of the local ecosystem. *En route* there is a fine view back over Nida.

At the top of the **Parnidžio Dune** there is a large modern sundial; a little lower down is a belvedere. From the latter there is a fantastic panorama – undoubtedly among the most memorable the country has to offer – over the expanses of what is known as 'The Valley of Silence' or 'The Lithuanian Sahara'. As it has been estimated that the High Dunes are decreasing in height by about 30cm per year, environmental purists believe that it is wrong to walk on them at all, and visitors are encouraged to stick to the 1.8km-long route which has been set up along wooden walkways. However, apart from a few signs barring access to the slopes, the only official restrictions on access are about 1km south of the sundial, where rather more prominent signposts in several languages bar entry to what is officially a nature reserve but is in reality a border zone controlled by uniformed guards who ensure that no-one inadvertently strays into Russian territory.

11

Appendix I

ALPHABET The Lithuanian alphabet is as follows (with letters in the order shown):

a ą b c č d e ę ė f g h ch i į y j k l m n o p r s š t u ų ū v z ž

If using a Lithuanian dictionary or directory, beware that these are all considered separate letters in their own right. This means, for example, that a word beginning Ša will appear after one beginning Su, and that ch and y are in a different position from in English.

PRONUNCIATION Vowel sounds can be either short or long: the accented letters have the general effect of lengthening the sound of the comparable unaccented letter.

a	as in amount
ą	as in father
e	as in met
ę	as in amber
ė	as in pair
i	as in sit
į or y	as in feet
o	as in boat
u	as in put
ū or ų	as in sue

Common diphthongs are:

ai	as in aisle
au	as in out
ei	as in may
ie	as in yet
ui	as in phooey
uo	as in the Italian buono

The consonants b, d, f, g, h, k, l, m, n, p, s, t, v and z are pronounced approximately the same way as in English, but the following have a different sound:

c	as ts, as in ants
č	as ch, as in chop
ch	as in the Scottish loch
dž	as the letter j, as in jam
j	as the letter y, as in yes
r	is always trilled or rolled
š	as sh, as in ship
ž	as the letter s, as in measure

GREETINGS AND CIVILITIES

Hello	*Laba diena*	Excuse me, sorry	*Atsiprašau*
Hi	*Labas, Sveikas*	How are you?	*Kaip sekasi?*
Good morning	*Labas rytas*	OK	*Gerai*
Good evening	*Labas vakaras*	Cheers	*Į Sveikatą*
Goodnight	*Labanakt*	Do you speak	*Ar kalbate*
Goodbye	*Viso gero*	English?	*angliškai?*
See you soon	*Iki pasimatymo*	I don't speak	*Aš nekalbu*
Please	*Prašau*	Lithuanian	*lietuviškai*
Thank you	*Ačiū*	I don't understand	*Aš nesuprantu*

BASIC WORDS

yes	*taip*	ticket	*bilietas*
no	*ne*	ticket office	*kasa*
open	*atidaryta*	now	*dabar*
closed	*uždaryta*	today	*šiandien*
entrance	*įėjimas*	yesterday	*vakar*
exit	*išėjimas*	tomorrow	*rytoj*
arrival	*atvyksta,*	daily	*kasdien*
	atvykimo laikas	big	*didelis*
departure	*išvyksta,*	small	*mažas*
	išvykimo laikas		

BASIC QUESTIONS AND REQUESTS

When?	*Kada?*	May I have the bill?	*Prašyčiau sąskaitą?*
Where?	*Kur?*	I would like …	*Norėčiau …*
Who?	*Kas?*	to order	*užsisakyti*
Why?	*Kodėl?*	a single room	*vienvietį kambarį*
How much does	*Kiek tai kainuoja?*	a double room	*dvivietį kambarį*
it cost?		to go to …	*nueiti į …*

DIRECTIONS

left	kairė	north	šiaurė
right	dešinė	south	pietūs
back	atgal	east	rytai
straight ahead	tiesiai	west	vakarai

LOCATIONS

airport	*aerouostas*	hospital	*ligoninė*
beach	*pliažas*	hotel	*viešbutis*
bookshop	*knygynas*	lake	*ežeras*
bridge	*tiltas*	market	*turgus*
bus station	*autobusų stotis*	museum	*muziejus*
café	*kavinė*	pharmacy	*vaistinė*
castle	*pilis*	post office	*paštas*
cathedral	*katedra*	railway station	*geležinkelio stotis*
cemetery	*kapinės*	restaurant	*restoranas*
church	*bažnyčia*	river	*upė*
currency exchange	*valiutos keitykla*	road	*kelias*
forest	*miškas*	square	*aikštė*
harbour	*uostas*	street	*gatvė*
hill	*kalnas*	theatre	*teatras*

AI

FOOD AND DRINK A selection of words for the commoner Lithuanian varieties is given in the text on pages 61–2.

DAYS OF THE WEEK

Monday	*pirmadienis*	Friday	*penktadienis*
Tuesday	*antradienis*	Saturday	*šeštadienis*
Wednesday	*trečiadienis*	Sunday	*sekmadienis*
Thursday	*ketvirtadienis*		

MONTHS

January	*sausis*	July	*liepa*
February	*vasaris*	August	*rugpjūtis*
March	*kovas*	September	*rugsėjis*
April	*balandis*	October	*spalis*
May	*gegužė, gegužis*	November	*lapkritis*
June	*birželis*	December	*gruodis*

NUMBERS

0	*nulis*	16	*šešiolika*
1	*vienas*	17	*septyniolika*
2	*du*	18	*aštuoniolika*
3	*trys*	19	*devyniolika*
4	*keturi*	20	*dvidešimt*
5	*penki*	25	*dvidešimt penki*
6	*šeši*	30	*trisdešimt*
7	*septyni*	40	*keturiasdešimt*
8	*aštuoni*	50	*penkiasdešimt*
9	*devyni*	60	*šešiasdešimt*
10	*dešimt*	70	*septyniasdešimt*
11	*vienuolika*	80	*aštuoniasdešimt*
12	*dvylika*	90	*devyniasdešimt*
13	*trylika*	100	*šimtas*
14	*keturiolika*	500	*penki šimtai*
15	*penkiolika*	1,000	*tūkstantis*

Appendix 2

BOOKS The number of books in English about Lithuania has increased markedly in recent years, thanks in large part to the output of Lithuanian publishers, who now produce a steady stream of titles in translation, notably coffee-table albums and monographs with an academic origin. Most bookstores in Vilnius and other major cities stock at least a selection of those listed below, but they are hard to track down outside the country.

Guidebooks

Joseph Everatt *A Guide to Vilnius* (Garnelis, Vilnius). A very useful and generally reliable guide to the city by a British national who is resident there, though it is noticeable that he smooths over the controversial aspects of its history, presenting it from a strictly Lithuanian nationalist viewpoint.

Government of Lithuania *Lithuania: An Outline* (Akreta, Vilnius). A far more attractive publication than might be expected of an official handbook by a large team of contributors, thanks in no small part to its imaginative choice of illustrations.

Giedrė Jankevičiūtė *Lithuania* (R Paknio leidykla, Vilnius). This adapts the formula of Tomas Venclova's earlier book on Vilnius by the same publisher (see below) to the whole of the country, making a handsome souvenir publication.

Albinas Kuncevičius (ed) *Defensive Fortifications in Lithuania* (Vaga, Vilnius). An illustrated guide to all the main castles and other fortification systems in the country.

Tojana Račiūnaitė *Baroque in Lithuania* (baltos lankos, Vilnius). A richly illustrated new edition of a guidebook, published in association with the Council of Europe, covering nearly all the main Baroque monuments of Lithuania.

Nijolė Strakauskaitė *Klaipėda, Curonian Spit, Königsberg* (T Paknio leidykla, Vilnius). The range of coverage suggests that this book was written primarily with German visitors in mind, but the English-language version is a useful addition to what is effectively a mini-series.

Tomas Venclova *Vilnius* (R Paknio leidykla, Vilnius). This guidebook by a Soviet-era dissident poet turned American academic is lavishly illustrated with new and archive photographs, plus ground-plans and line drawings. Largely as a result of its far superior production standards, it quickly overshadowed the competing book by Everatt, which was published just a few months before.

Neil Taylor *Baltic Cities* (Bradt, 2008)

Travel

Anne Applebaum *Between East and West: Across the Borderlands of Europe* (Pantheon or Papermac). A deeply insightful account of a journey from Kaliningrad to Odessa in the immediate wake of the collapse of the Soviet Union. The Lithuanian section includes chapters on Vilnius, the improbable 'republic' of Perloja, and the ever-controversial issue of Adam Mickiewicz's true nationality.

Alfred Döblin *Journey to Poland* (IB Tauris). The vivid Expressionist prose of Döblin's famous novel *Berlin Alexanderplatz* is foreshadowed in this account of his 1924 journey to seek out

Appendix 2 FURTHER INFORMATION

his Jewish roots. One chapter is devoted to Vilnius, then a city with a large Jewish population and as such hardly recognisable as the place it is today.

Howard Jacobson *Roots Schmoots* (Penguin). Another voyage in search of Jewish roots, this time by a contemporary English novelist, ranges over a much wider geographical area than Döblin's, but likewise includes Vilnius.

Clare Thomson *The Singing Revolution* (Michael Joseph). A chronicle of the travels of a British journalist of Estonian descent in the three Baltic states during the period which saw the break-up of the Soviet Union.

History and politics

Aldona Bieliūnienė et al *Lithuania on the Map* (Lithuanian National Museum, Vilnius). Published to coincide with an exhibition of historic maps at the museum in 2004, this provides copious examples of how the widely differing size and shape of Lithuania has been depicted by cartographers down the centuries.

Arūnas Bubnys *Nazi Resistance Movement in Lithuania 1941–44* (Vaga, Vilnius). One of a series of brief monographs on aspects of recent Lithuanian history, this presents a rejoinder to those who tar Lithuania with the brush of having been a nation of collaborators.

Eric Christiansen *The Northern Crusades* (Penguin). The most lucid and comprehensive single-volume history of the German crusades in the Baltic lands paints a vivid portrait of the Teutonic Knights and their state, and includes full coverage of the campaigns against Lithuania.

Alfonsas Eidintas *Jews, Lithuanians and the Holocaust* (Versus Aureus, Vilnius). This ambitious attempt to present both sides of the argument about the most contentious episode in Lithuanian history is the work of a high-profile diplomat who was formerly Lithuania's ambassdor to the US, and is currently the ambassador to Israel.

Alfonsas Eidintas and Vytautas Žalys *Lithuania in European Politics 1918–40* (Vaga, Vilnius). A short, specialised study of the foreign policy of the inter-war republic.

Alfonsas Eidintas et al *Lithuania in European Politics: The Years of the First Republic 1918–40* (Macmillan). A series of essays on the inter-war republic.

Genocide and Resistance Research Centre of Lithuania *With an Arrow in my Heart* (Garnelis, Vilnius); *Whoever Saves One Life* (Garnelis, Vilnius). The first of these oral history anthologies contains memoirs of survivors of the ghettoes and concentration camps; the second is a tribute to the unsung heroes who risked their own lives by protecting Jews during World War II.

John Hiden and Patrick Salmon *The Baltic States and Europe* (Longman). A study of the diplomatic history of the Baltics. The first edition took the story up to the time of the independence movements and a revised and updated edition has since been published.

Zigmantas Kiaupa, Jūratė Kiaupienė and Albinas Kuncevičius *The History of Lithuania Before 1795* (Lithuanian Institute of History, Vilnius). A virtually definitive account of the entire history of the Grand Duchy, together with an introductory chapter on its antecedents. Despite its scholarly provenance, it was written with a general readership in mind.

Thomas Lane *Lithuania: Stepping Westwards* (Routledge). The most up-to-date book on Lithuania's recent history, beginning in 1914, but with the main focus on the years 1985–99.

Anatol Lieven *The Baltic Revolution* (Yale University Press). The author, who is partly of Latvian descent, reported on the rise and triumph of the independence movements in the three Baltic states for The Times (of London), and this book (since updated) is by far the best eye-witness account of the events, even if some of the historical judgements are questionable.

Jerzy Tadeusz Lukowski *Liberty's Folly: The Polish-Lithuanian Commonwealth in the Eighteenth Century* (Routledge). An analysis of the decline and fall of one of Europe's great empires, which was in large part precipitated by the excessive liberalism of its own constitution.

Romualdas Misiūnas and Rein Taagepera *The Baltic States: The Years of Dependence 1940–80* (Hurst). A study of the first four decades of communist rule in the three Baltic states, written at a time when this still seemed unshakeable.

Bob Mullan *Voices of Pain* (Aidai, Vilnius). An oral history of Lithuania's transition from Soviet occupation and a command economy, and the trouble it brought, focusing on the specific experience of inhabitants of the city of Kaunas.

Grigorijus Potašenko (ed) *The Peoples of the Grand Duchy of Lithuania* (Aidai, Vilnius). As well as a general essay and a case study of Kėdainiai, this little book has separate chapters on some of the prominent minorities which gave the Grand Duchy its multi-ethnic character: the Ruthenians, Jews, Tatars, Karaims, Roma and Russian Old Believers.

Georg von Rauch *The Baltic States: The Years of Independence 1917–40* (Hurst). Translation of a standard German text about the Baltic states from their conception during World War I until their annexation by the Soviet Union.

S C Rowell *Lithuania Ascending: A Pagan Empire Within East-Central Europe 1295–1345* (Cambridge University Press). An in-depth academic study of the consolidation and expansion of the early medieval Lithuanian state.

Linas Saldukas *Lithuanian Diaspora* (Vaga, Vilnius). A brief history of Lithuanian emigration and Lithuanian communities abroad.

Stasys Samalavičius *An Outline of Lithuanian History* (Diemedis leidykla, Vilnius). A useful short survey covering the whole course of Lithuania's history from the prehistoric tribes until the 1990 declaration of independence.

Alfred Erich Senn *The Great Powers, Lithuania and the Vilna Question* (EJ Brill); *Lithuania Awakening* (University of California Press); *Gorbachev's Failure in Lithuania* (Macmillan). The first of these offers a detailed analysis of the post-World War I Polish–Lithuania dispute over Vilnius, and the attempts at international mediation; the second is a study of the rebirth of Lithuanian nationalism; while the third describes the final collapse of Soviet attempts to maintain control of its most reluctant republic.

Desmond Seward *The Monks of War* (Penguin). A broadly sympathetic account of the military religious orders, setting the Teutonic Knights and their Baltic Crusade in a historical context of truly epic dimensions.

William Urban *The Teutonic Knights* (Greenhill Books or Stackpole Books). A scholarly but eminently readable new study of the German military order, with full descriptions of the wars against Lithuania which dominated so much of its history.

V Stanley Vardys and Judith B Sedaitis *Lithuania: The Rebel Nation* (Westview Press). One of a series of books about the former Soviet republics, focusing on the present day but also containing a brief historical survey.

Zigmas Zinkevičius *The History of the Lithuanian Language* (Mokslo ir enciklopedijų leidybos institutas, Vilnius). An absolutely definitive study of the development of a language which has undergone fewer changes than any other Indo-European tongue.

Poetry and fiction

Antanas Baranauskas *The Forest of Anykščiai* (Isleido Baranausko ir Žukausko-Vienuolio memorialnis muziejus, Anykščiai). A translation of this classic of Lithuanian literature, which previously appeared in the literary magazine Vilnius, has been published in booklet format by the local museum.

Stephan Collishaw *The Last Girl* (HarperCollins); *Amber* (HarperCollins). The first of these, an assured debut novel focusing on the guilty conscience of a Lithuanian writer, is notable for some highly evocative writing about Vilnius in the 1990s and also for its presentation of the vexed issue of Lithuanian-Jewish relations in World War II from a variety of perspectives. The Lithuanian theme is continued in the second novel, which unfortunately is not nearly so powerful or convincing. Here the main theme is the way brutality becomes cyclical, with the action shifting between Vilnius and Soviet-occupied Afghanistan.

Kristijonas Donelaitis *The Seasons* (Lithuanian Days). Lithuania's national epic is a vivid evocation of 18th-century peasant life in a Lithuanian-speaking village in Prussia. A marvellously entertaining translation, the only complete one in English, was made in 1968 to coincide with the 150th anniversary of its original publication.

Sigitas Geda *Biopsy of Winter* (Vaga, Vilnius). A powerful collection by one of the major Lithuanian poets of the present day.

Tadeusz Konwicki *Bohin Manor* (Farrar, Straus & Giroux or Faber & Faber). This novel, by one of Poland's leading contemporary writers, has a significance well beyond its ostensible subject of manor life in 19th-century Lithuania. The characters include prototypes of Lenin, Stalin, Piłsudski and Hitler, all of whom would make a profound impact on the history of the region.

Mošė Kulbakas (also known as Moshe Kulbak) *Vilnius* (Vaga, Vilnius). A short poem rich in imagery by an early 20th-century Jewish writer, published in a seven-language version with black-and-white prints and drawings of old Vilnius.

Maironis (also known as Jonas Mačiulis) *Jūratė and Kastytis* (Alka, Vilnius). The most famous ballad in Lithuanian literature (which is included in the Pažūsis anthology listed below) is here presented in a colourful illustrated edition.

Adam Mickiewicz *Pan Tadeusz* (Hippocrene); *Konrad Wallenrod* and *Grażyna* (University Press of America). The Polish national epic *Pan Tadeusz* is set among the gentry of Lithuania at the time of the Napoleonic invasion. In contrast to its characters' self-deluding attitude towards independence, *Konrad Wallenrod* – which, like Grażyna, has as its setting the wars between medieval Lithuania and the Teutonic Knights – shows how that aim can be achieved by stealth.

Czesław Miłosz *The Issa Valley* (Farrar, Straus & Giroux). The Nobel Prize-winning poet's own boyhood in the Lithuanian countryside is evoked in this lyrical prose idyll, the second of his two novels.

Lionginas Pažūsis (ed) *Voices of Lithuanian Poetry* (Tyto Alba, Vilnius). An anthology of Lithuanian poetry, with parallel English translations, ranging from Maironis via Mykolaitis-Putinas to contemporary poets.

Kornelijus Platelis *Snare for the Wind* (Vaga, Vilnius). A wide-ranging selection drawn from the output of another of Lithuania's leading contemporary poets.

Laima Sruoginis *The Earth Remains* (Tyto Alba, Vilnius). One more poetry anthology, in this case drawn exclusively from the work of living writers.

Leo Tolstoy *War and Peace* (Penguin or Oxford University Press). The visits to Vilnius of Tsar Alexander I and Napoleon in 1812 are described at the beginning of Book Three of this great masterpiece of Russian literature.

Tomas Venclova *Winter Dialogue* (Northwestern University Press). This contains a selection of poems by the best-known living writer in the Lithuanian language, plus a dialogue with Czesław Miłosz about Vilnius's mixed Lithuanian-Polish pedigree.

Memoirs and biography

Alfonsas Eidintas *President of Lithuania: Prisoner Gulag* (Genocide and Resistance Research Centre of Lithuania, Vilnius). A biography of Aleksandras Stulginskas, whose chequered career included a four-year spell as President of Lithuania and 13 years as a prisoner of the Soviets.

Dan Jacobson *Heshel's Kingdom* (Penguin). This is part autobiography, part biography, of the South-African-born author's Lithuanian Jewish rabbi grandfather, and part travelogue of a journey through Lithuania shortly after the fall of communism. It is both moving and deeply candid, though the central travel section is marred by factual errors and an almost total indifference towards ethnic Lithuanian culture.

Vytautas Landsbergis *Lithuania Independent Again* (University of Wales Press or University of Washington Press). Published in 2000, this is the first autobiography in English to be published by any of the leading figures in the Baltic states' independence movements.

Hillel Levine *In Search of Sugihara* (Free Press). This scholarly biography of the Japanese diplomat and spy who saved thousands of Jewish lives is broadly sympathetic, but not afraid to dwell on the less attractive aspects of its subject's character. It is generally agreed to be far more reliable than the somewhat self-serving memoir *Visas for Life* by Sugihara's own wife Yukiko.

Czesław Miłosz *The Captive Mind* (Penguin); *Native Realm* (Penguin); *Beginning with My Streets* (I B Taurus or Farrar, Straus & Giroux). The first-named offers an analysis of the reasons so many intellectuals sold out to totalitarian regimes, and concludes with a chapter on the Soviet occupation of the Baltics. The second, Miłosz's autobiography of his first 40 years, is particularly illuminating on the vexed issue of Polish-Lithuanian relations, while the third is a collection of essays and reflections on the Baltics, which starts off with a series of portraits of Vilnius's streets and the dialogue about Vilnius also found in the Tomas Venclova anthology listed above.

Alfred Erich Senn *Jonas Basanavičius: The Patriarch of the Lithuanian National Renaissance* (Oriental Research Partners). A short biography of the man who did so much to rekindle the idea of a Lithuanian national identity in the later stages of the Tsarist period.

Balys Sruoga *Forest of the Gods* (Vaga, Vilnius). The concentration-camp memoirs of the Lithuanian poet and playwright, who was incarcerated with a group of his fellow-countrymen at Stutthof in 1943–45, are now available in a translation made by his American granddaughter.

Avraham Tory *Surviving the Holocaust: The Kovno Ghetto Diary* (Harvard University Press). The diary of one of the relatively small number of survivors of Kaunas's three years of Nazi terror.

Folklore

Galina Bogdel *Legends and Fairytales of Trakai* (Barbora, Trakai). Modern re-tellings of the rich store of myths and stories about Trakai and its lakes.

'Skomantas' *The Captive; The Fen-Wolf, The Blue Raven, Blood Wedding, The Flaming Tower* (Twermė, Vilnius). A series of tales based on the early history of the Baltic tribes.

Norbertas Vėlius (ed) *Lithuanian Mythological Tales* (Vaga, Vilnius). A compilation from oral sources of over 300 tales, nearly all well under a page long, of gods, devils, fairies, witches, wizards, werewolves and enchanted treasures.

Photography

Algimantas Aleksandravičius *Portraits* (Leidykla Varlo, Vilnius). A gallery of photographic portraits of prominent contemporary Lithuanians.

Jan Bułhak *Vilnius Baroque* (Karpavičiaus leidykla, Vilnius). Essentially a photography album rather than the art book its title implies, this has superb black-and-white images of the city's most famous Baroque monuments taken in the early decades of the 20th century by a leading Polish photographer and Vilnius resident.

Balys Buračas *Photography* (baltos lankos, Vilnius). A wide-ranging collection of photographs of life in inter-war Lithuania. *Sacred Arts in Lithuania* (Valstybės Žinios, Vilnius). A well-nigh exhaustive photographic record of the crosses and other religious folk art to be found throughout the country.

Stanisław Filibert Fleury *Photographs* (Lithuanian National Museum, Vilnius). A doorstopper volume of images of late 19th- and early 20th-century Lithuania, with a strong emphasis on Vilnius.

Aleksandras Macijauskas *My Lithuania* (Thames and Hudson). An album of black and white photographs of village markets, Palanga beach, a veterinary clinic and various parades by one of the first photographers in the Soviet Union to show life as it really was, rather than the way the Communist Party wanted it portrayed.

Margarita Matalytė *Photography in Vilnius* 1858–1915 (Lithuanian Art Museum, Vilnius). A handsome collection of images of Vilnius as it was in the last decades of Tsarist rule.

Romualdas Požerkis *Atlaidai: Lithuanian Pilgrimages* (Loyola University Press). A photographic record of pilgrimages to Žemaičių Kalvarija and elsewhere during the communist era, providing clear proof of the hold the Church continued to exert throughout that period.

Kęstutis Stoškus *Vilnius* (Lithuanian National Museum, Vilnius). These black-and-white views of Vilnius are by a contemporary photographer, but their effect is deliberately archaic, omitting all references to contemporary society.

Antanas Sutkus *Photographs* (baltos lankos, Vilnius). Images of Lithuania from the period 1959–99.

Culture

Rasutė Andriušytė-Žukienė *Mikolajus Konstantinas Čiurlionis* (Šviesa, Vilnius). This is the most recent of several de-luxe productions illustrating the work of Lithuania's great painter-composer.

Zygintas Būčys *Seraya Szapszalis Karaim Collection* (Lithuanian National Museum, Vilnius). A richly illustrated album of all the main Karaite objects owned by Lithuanian museums, including those displayed in the Ethnographic Exhibition in Trakai.

Romualdas Budrys and Vydas Dolinskas *Vilnius Cathedral Treasury* (Lithuanian Art Museum, Vilnius). This de-luxe volume has superb colour illustrations of all the artefacts in the treasury, together with notes and a history in both Lithuanian and English.

Stasys Goštautas *Čiurlionis: Painter and Composer* (Vaga, Vilnius). A large collection of essays about all aspects of Čiurlionis's output and its influence.

Birutė Imbrasienė *Lithuanian Traditional Foods* (baltos lankos, Vilnius). Offers a complete guide to the Lithuanian kitchen, complete with recipes for all the most popular dishes.

Raminta Jurėnaitė *100 Contemporary Lithuanian Artists* (R Paknio leidykla, Vilnius). As its title suggests, this provides a comprehensive overview of the modern art scene in Lithuania.

Dovid Katz *Lithuanian Jewish Culture* (baltos lankos, Vilnius). This authoritative study, richly illustrated with archive photos and maps, is among the most ambitious (and expensive) products of recent Lithuanian publishing. Although aimed at a general readership, it is based on years of research by an American-born Jewish scholar who formerly taught at Oxford University and is currently based in Vilnius.

Regina Koženiauskienė (ed) *Martynas Mažvydas and Old Lithuania* (Vilnius pradai, Vilnius). A book of essays published to commemorate the 450th anniversary of the first Lithuanian book, *Mažvydas's Cathechism*.

Vytautas Kubilius et al *Lithuanian Literature* (Vaga, Vilnius). Presents a complete history of the subject, though its interest for the general reader is limited by the fact that very few of the books discussed have been translated into English.

Juozas Kudirka *The Lithuanians* (Lithuanian Folk Culture Centre, Vilnius). Sub-titled *An Ethnic Portrait*, this is a good basic introduction to all aspects of Lithuanian folk culture.

Vytautas Landsbergis *MK Čiurlionis: Time and Content* (Lituanus, Vilnius). Lithuania's independence leader is a leading authority on Čiurlionis, many of whose piano works he has recorded, and this book offers a good academic overview of both the music and paintings.

Marcelijus Martinaitis *The Old Lithuanian Sculpture* (R Paknio Leidykla, Vilnius). A large-format album lavishly illustrated with photographs of the country's most distinctive folk art tradition, with an explanatory text as accompaniment.

Jonas Minkevičius et al *The Art of Lithuanian Churches* (R Paknio Leidykla, Vilnius). A beautiful coffee-table book containing spectacular large-format photographs, accompanied by short descriptions, of the exteriors and interiors of the country's finest churches.

Napoleonas Orda *Views of Ancient Lithuania* (Vilnius pradai). This reproduces selections from a once hugely popular collection of lithographs made in the 1870s of beauty spots in the former Grand Duchy of Lithuania.

Mindaugas Paknys *Pažaislis: Art and History* (E Karpavičiaus leidykla, Vilnius). A handsomely illustrated volume on the celebrated Kaunas monastery.

Andrius Surgailis *Wooden Vilnius* (Versus Aureus, Vilnius). This documents a neglected but distinctive aspect of the Lithuanian capital's architectural heritage.

Dalia Tarandaitė *Sacred Art of Lithuania* (Lithuanian Art Museum, Vilnius). This two-volume set presents a comprehensive history of the subject, embracing both fine art and folk art. Together with the companion volume on the Vilnius Cathedral Treasury, it provides a lasting memento of the extraordinary millennium exhibition *Christianity in Lithuanian Art* held in Vilnius's Museum of Applied Arts from 1999 to 2003.

Birutė Verkelytė-Fedaravičienė (ed) *Mikalojus Konstantinas Čiurlionis: Paintings, Sketches, Thoughts* (Fodio, Vilnius). This luxuriously produced album has several essays to accompany stunning colour reproductions of most of Čiurlionis's major paintings.

Vaidotas Žukas *Vilius Orvydas* (baltos lankos, Vilnius). This is a fine illustrated record of the life of the sculptor and mystic, and in particular the 'museum' he created on his family's farm near Salatai. Unfortunately, the text is in Lithuanian only, though three-page summaries in English and other languages are appended.

WEBSITES Websites of specific interest are detailed at the appropriate point in the text. The following are worth consulting for more general information in English:

www.culture.lt A website covering all aspects of the arts in Lithuania.
www.en.lt.leisureguide.info The English-language version of www.anonsas.lt, a national what's on website which also has plenty of useful practical travel information.
www.explore.eu Features the texts of the free guides to Lithuanian cities.
www.inyourpocket.com Current online editions of the *In Your Pocket Guides*, plus links to other Baltic-related sites.
www.kaunas.lt The official website of the city of Kaunas.
www.ldm.lt The website of all branches of the Lithuanian Art Museum.
www.lithuanianhotels.com Lists lots of Lithuania's hotels and offers an online booking service.
www.litrail.lt Railway network website, with timetables and route-planning information.
www.lnm.lt The website of all branches of the Lithuanian National Museum.
www.maps.lt A website offering comprehensive cartographic coverage of Lithuania.
www.meniu.lt A guide to a large percentage of Lithuania's restaurants.
www.muziejai.lt Comprehensive information about every museum in Lithuania can be found on this website.
www.online.lt An umbrella website for a host of information on Lithuania.
www.stat.gov.lt Has all sorts of official statistics about Lithuania.
www.tourism.lt The Lithuanian State Department of Tourism's official website.
www.travel.lt Another site geared towards tourists, with plenty of useful links.
www.travel-lithuania.com Yet another travel website, this time of a commercial bent.
www.urm.lt The website of the Ministry of Foreign Affairs gives up-to-date information on customs regulations, Lithuanian embassies abroad and foreign embassies dealing with Lithuania.
www.vilnius.lt The official website of the city of Vilnius.
www.yp.lt The online version of Lithuania's Yellow Pages.

A2

Index

Page numbers in **bold** indicate major entries; those in *italic* indicate maps